SUCCESSFUL INCLUSION
FOR
EDUCATIONAL LEADERS

Larry D. Bartlett
The University of Iowa

Greg R. Weisenstein
Montana State University

Susan Etscheidt
University of Northern Iowa

Merrill
Prentice Hall

Upper Saddle River, New Jersey
Columbus, Ohio

Library of Congress Cataloging in Publication Data

Bartlett, Larry Dean.
   Successful inclusion for educational leaders / Larry D. Bartlett, Greg R.
Weisenstein, Susan Etscheidt.
      p. cm.
   Includes bibliographical references and index.
   ISBN 0-13-040488-8
      1. Inclusive education—United States. 2. Handicapped children—Education—United
States. 3. United States. Individuals with Disabilities Education Act. I. Weisenstein,
Greg R. II. Etscheidt, Susan Larson. III. Title.

LC1201 .B35 2002
371.9´046—dc21

2001030859

Vice President and Publisher: Jeffery W. Johnston
Executive Editor: Ann Castel Davis
Editorial Assistant: Keli Gemrich
Production Editor: Sheryl Glicker Langner
Production Coordination: Clarinda Publication Services
Design Coordinator: Diane C. Lorenzo
Photo Coordinator: Valerie Schultz
Cover Designer: Andrew Lundberg
Cover Photo: Super Stock
Production Manager: Laura Messerly
Director of Marketing: Kevin Flanagan
Marketing Manager: Amy June
Marketing Coordinator: Barbara Koontz

This book was set in Shannon, Helvetica, and Garamond by The Clarinda Company. It was printed and bound by Maple Press. The cover was printed by The Lehigh Press, Inc.

Photo Credits:
3, 75, 101, 229, 277, 287, 299, 325, 341: Anne Vega/Merrill; 23, 59, 181: Scott Cunningham/Merrill; 45, 213, 315, 331: Tom Watson/Merrill; 133, Barbara Schwartz/Merrill; 151, KS Studios/Merrill; 253, Anthony Magnacca/Merrill; 307, Todd Yarrington/Merrill.

Pearson Education Ltd., *London*
Pearson Education Australia Pty, Limited, *Sydney*
Pearson Education Singapore, Pte. Ltd
Pearson Education North Asia Ltd., *Hong Kong*
Pearson Education Canada, Ltd., *Toronto*
Pearson Educación de Mexico, S.A. de C.V.
Pearson Education—Japan, *Tokyo*
Pearson Education Malaysia, Pte. Ltd
Pearson Education, *Upper Saddle River, New Jersey*

Merrill
Prentice Hall

10 9 8 7 6 5 4 3 2 1
ISBN: 0-13-040488-8

This book is dedicated to the many educators,
only a few of whom we know by name,
who have led the way in providing a quality education to all children.

PREFACE

Nearly 25 years ago, the Congress and president of the United States declared the public policy of this nation to be one of access to public education for *all* children. Only when the educational needs of a child with disabilities cannot be appropriately met with peers in a public school educational setting may the child be educated in alternative settings. Even segregated settings must provide for meaningful interaction with typical peers.

This enunciation of public policy has resulted in a degree of tension between some educators who would exclude those students who present challenges to their traditional teaching methods and those educators, who in the absence of a justifiable educational reason, disavow the exclusion of children from an educational setting with their peers. This tension is most easily identified in the outworn and legally questionable concept of "mainstreaming." Although the laws of the nation and most states require that students with disabilities be educated in regular education settings "to the maximum extent appropriate," a contrary practice was established. It recognized a "two box" model of regular education and special education, in which both seldom occurred in the same place at the same time. Instead, under the mainstreaming concept, it was expected that children with disabilities would be educated with peers without disabilities only when they could exhibit the proper conduct and could acquire an academic level commensurate with their peers. In the minds of many educators, students with disabilities were expected to "earn" their way into a regular class setting.

In the late 1980s and early 1990s, after 15 years under the national legislation, court interpretations suddenly collided with educators' complacent thinking. The courts ruled that no matter what the concept was called, the process had to be revised. Instead of a child with disabilities having to earn the right to be in a classroom with peers, all considerations of child placement were to begin with the child being placed in the regular class or activity setting. Only when the regular school setting was deemed not appropriate, for an educationally justifiable reason, could an education for the child even be considered in a special setting.

No court interpretation or administrative agency interpretation of special education law has ever found that "full inclusion" (all children with disabilities educated in the regular education classroom they would attend if not disabled) is required. Although the authors of this book salute those who attempt full inclusion, they do not endorse it in its strictest sense as an educationally viable concept. There are some students with disabilities whose needs are such that their presence in a regular class or activity setting is not educationally justifiable or appropriate.

The current approach of presuming regular education placement as the first choice has caught many educators, in both special and regular education, unprepared. This was not the paradigm in which most educators had been trained. This was not the system in which many had spent their professional life. That was not what many were ready to implement. Thus, a large part of new interpretations and understandings of education for children with disabilities has been either rejected or ignored by many practioners, in both regular and special education.

We sincerely believe that much of the reluctance of educators to embrace and practice what has been legally mandated—but largely ignored for 25 years—is not based in laziness, uncaring attitude, or evil intent. Rather it is based in inexperience and the inertia of organizational structures. The purpose of *Successful Inclusion for Educational Leaders* is to provide background information on legal mandates, with the current status of law stated as clearly as possible, and to point toward successful solutions based in research and best practices literature. We provide the broad picture of the current common understanding of the law (what is supposed to be done) and an understanding of currently available research and best practices results (how to do it), so that educational leaders will have the knowledge and information about necessary skills to act from a position of understanding and strength. When educators reject change it is seldom because they are afraid or otherwise burdened by a change. Often, it is done out of lack of experience, knowledge, and support. When aimed in the right direction and provided the proper support, change has been proven to be rewarding and beneficial to all educators.

We have worked diligently to set forth the legal requirements of special education with clarity where possible. There are suggestions in every chapter on how the law may be carried out in ways that help ensure success. Also included are many references and suggested readings in a broad variety of topics to encourage growth in the reader's understanding and skills. At the conclusion of the book, there is a quick but detailed reference guide to the various disabilities students present and how the needs of these students are commonly served by educators.

This book was designed and organized to provide education leaders a clear understanding of student disabilities, relevant legal mandates, and research-based and best practice solution suggestions so that greater success may be had in the management of educational resources to meet the needs of children.

The children of America deserve no less.

Acknowledgments

We would like to thank the reviewers of this text: Andrew Brulle, Wheaton College; Dan Fennerty, Central Washington University; David E. Gullatt, Louisiana Technical University; Michael Kallam, Pittsburgh State University; and Mark P. Mostert, Old Dominion University.

L. B.
G. W.
S. E.

The Prentice Hall Companion Website: A Virtual Learning Environment

Technology is a constantly growing and changing aspect of our field that is creating a need for content and resources. To address this emerging need, Prentice Hall has developed an online learning environment for students and professors alike—Companion Websites—to support our textbooks.

In creating a Companion Website, our goal is to build on and enhance what the textbook already offers. For this reason, the content for each user-friendly website is organized by topic and provides the professor and student with a variety of meaningful resources. Common features of a Companion Website include:

For the Professor—

Every Companion Website integrates **Syllabus Manager™,** an online syllabus creation and management utility.

- **Syllabus Manager™** provides you, the instructor, with an easy, step-by-step process to create and revise syllabi, with direct links into Companion Website and other online content without having to learn HTML.
- Students may logon to your syllabus during any study session. All they need to know is the web address for the Companion Website and the password you've assigned to your syllabus.
- After you have created a syllabus using **Syllabus Manager™,** students may enter the syllabus for their course section from any point in the Companion Website.
- Clicking on a date, the student is shown the list of activities for the assignment. The activities for each assignment are linked directly to actual content, saving time for students.
- Adding assignments consists of clicking on the desired due date, then filling in the details of the assignment—name of the assignment, instructions, and whether or not it is a one-time or repeating assignment.
- In addition, links to other activities can be created easily. If the activity is online, a URL can be entered in the space provided, and it will be linked automatically in the final syllabus.

- Your completed syllabus is hosted on our servers, allowing convenient updates from any computer on the Internet. Changes you make to your syllabus are immediately available to your students at their next logon.

For the Student—

- **Topic Overviews**—outline key concepts in topic areas
- **Characteristics**—general information about each topic/disability covered on this website
- **Read About It**—a list of links to pertinent articles found on the Internet that cover each topic
- **Teaching Ideas**—links to articles that offer suggestions, ideas, and strategies for teaching students with disabilities
- **Electronic Bluebook**—send homework or essays directly to your instructor's email with this paperless form
- **Message Board**—serves as a virtual bulletin board to post—or respond to—questions or comments to/from a national audience
- **Web Links**—a wide range of websites that provide useful and current information related to each topic area
- **Resources**—a wide array of different resources for many of the pertinent topics and issues surrounding special education
- **Chat**—real-time chat with anyone who is using the text anywhere in the country—ideal for discussion and study groups, class projects, etc.

To take advantage of these and other resources, please visit the *Successful Inclusion for Educational Leaders* Companion Website at

www.prenhall.com/bartlett

ABOUT THE AUTHORS

Larry D. Bartlett is a professor and departmental executive officer in the Division of Educational Policy and Leadership Studies at The University of Iowa. He is an administrative law judge for special education hearings in Iowa and for the Bureau of Indian Affairs, United States Department of Interior. Previously, he was the legal consultant to the Iowa Department of Public Instruction and a high school social studies department chair. He currently teaches courses on education law and the administration of special education programs.

Greg R. Weisenstein is dean of the College of Education, Health and Human Development at Montana State University. Previously, he has served as dean of the School of Education at the University of Colorado, Colorado Springs; associate dean for research and professor of education at Clemson University; coordinator of Vocational and Secondary Special Education Programs at the University of Washington; a member of the President's Committee on Employment of the People with Disabilities; and international president of the Council for Exceptional Children's Division on Career Development.

Susan Etscheidt is an associate professor of special education at the University of Northern Iowa and the coordinator of Programs for Children with Behavioral Disorders K–6. She teaches courses in the area of behavioral disorders, behavior management, and special education law and policy. In addition to her involvement in the teacher preparation program at UNI, Dr. Etscheidt is an administrative law judge for special education hearings in Iowa.

Contents

PART I

LEGAL AND POLICY ISSUES

CHAPTER 1

INCLUSION BASICS

Focus

In little more than twenty-five years, major federal laws have revolutionized treatment of persons with disabilities in America, with far-reaching effects on public schools. The new requirements for education of students with disabilities, especially within the regular education environment, place demands on school principals and staff members for which such staff often have not received adequate professional training.

Legal Issues

The three most important laws that directly govern the education of children with disabilities are: the Individuals with Disabilities Education Act (IDEA) (originally passed as P.L. 94-142, the Education for All Handicapped Children Act), enacted in 1975 and implemented in 1977; Section 504 of the Rehabilitation Act of 1973; and the Americans with Disabilities Act (ADA), enacted in 1990.

The IDEA legislation established education as an entitlement for those children with disabilities who are in need of special education and related services in those states accepting federal funds for that purpose. The latter two statutes guarantee basic civil rights by prohibiting discrimination against persons, including children, with disabilities. Section 504 applies to those entities which receive federal funds, whereas the ADA is broader in scope. Both Section 504 and the ADA are somewhat broader in scope than the IDEA in that they affect access to programs, higher education, and employment opportunities, as well as education, and include persons who are not actually disabled but who are regarded as such (e.g., discriminated against because of abnormal, although not disabling, appearance).

From the beginning, enforcement of the ADA in education has been nearly identical to Section 504 interpretations. Although all three laws contain many similar general provisions regarding educational programs, only the IDEA provides funding for education programs. It also goes considerably further in detailing the following basic requirements for special education:

- All children over age 3 who are identified with potential disabilities are entitled to a full, nondiscriminatory assessment of their educational needs and a determination of eligibility;
- Based on data assessed by a team of professionals and the child's parents, an individualized education program (IEP) is prepared, which establishes the structure for the provision of an appropriate educational program and related services;

- An educational placement is chosen in which to carry out the IEP, and it must be the least restrictive instructional environment feasible which meets the child's educational needs. Schools must have a continuum of placements available to meet the needs of children with disabilities; and
- Parents are entitled to an extensive system of procedural safeguards, including confidentiality of education records.

Specific interpretations and understandings of the laws continue to change based on judicial decisions, state laws, congressional acts, changes in government administrations, and other factors. Educational leaders must attempt to keep abreast of the changes.

A major component of all three federal statutes related to the education of children with disabilities is the requirement that children with disabilities must be educated, to the maximum extent appropriate, with children who do not have disabilities. This concept is known as the least restrictive environment. Only in the last decade has it become recognized that for most children with disabilities, the least restrictive environment is the regular classroom and regular student activities. Only when regular placements are not appropriate due to disruption of the environment or lack of educational benefit to the child, may the child with disabilities be placed in special education settings. Educators must consider the use of supplementary aids and services, and accommodations and modifications in establishing a placement environment where the child will benefit and will not be disruptive.

Approaches

There are four basic areas in which supplementary aids and services, modifications, accommodations, and other support in regular school programs—both academic and nonacademic—may have to be provided for individual students with disabilities.

1. Social-behavioral (e.g., behavior plans and interventions, social strategies, special training for staff)
2. Collaborative (e.g., time for staff planning and communication, consultation, and special staff training)
3. Instructional content (e.g., emphasis on daily living rather than advanced academics for some students), strategies (increased repetition, substitution of materials, emphasis on visual communication), and grading and evaluation (oral testing, appropriate test construction, contracting for work, group grades), including methods of regular reporting of progress to parents

4. Physical environment (e.g., nonglare lighting for the visually impaired,
   wheelchair accessibility, assigned seat location, teacher proximity)

The key in each situation is to arrive at modifications, accommodations, and supplementary aids and services that are appropriate to the student's individual needs.

Principals and other educational leaders are essential to the success of inclusion and can greatly contribute through their leadership and by modeling acceptance of special education students and programs, such as setting a positive tone and assigning equally desirable space, schedules, and school duties to both regular and special education staff. Leadership involves facilitating cooperation and collaboration among staff, acceptance among students, and good relations within the community.

BASIC SPECIAL EDUCATION AND INCLUSION CONSIDERATIONS

It is fair to say that every abrupt change catches a certain percentage of the population unaware, or at least insufficiently prepared. That certainly is true of the sweeping changes in the education of children with disabilities that were enacted into law in the United States in the mid 1970s. While parents of children with disabilities had been aware of problems with the public educational system and had struggled toward solutions for agonizing years—sometimes decades—the majority of those in the education system were unaffected by these struggles.

Most educators—principals and classroom teachers—were not trained to work with students with disabilities and did not expect to. Then, in 1977, the situation changed dramatically with the implementation of the Education for All Handicapped Children Act (P.L. 94-142) and the mandate to teach those children in the least restrictive environment (LRE). Regular class teachers found children with disabilities assigned to their classrooms; special educators had to give up ownership of "their" students and routines; new systems had to be set up; parents' doubts had to be quelled; a myriad of smaller changes had to be made; and principals, it often seemed, were given the responsibility to make it all happen.

As with other changes in education, this one has not been, and will not be, accomplished overnight. Passage of the law in many ways marked the beginning, not the end, of the process of change. Much has been learned since the late 1970s, and it is clear that more changes are forthcoming.

The term "inclusion" is not found anywhere in the law and is used inconsistently in the education literature. Although Chapter 6 discusses the term in greater detail, it is important that the reader understand from the beginning the meaning of the term "inclusion" as it appears in this book. Inclusion does not mean that all children with disabilities will be educated in the regular classroom or regular activity environment. Instead, it refers to that aspect of the "least restrictive environment" legal requirement which mandates that all considerations of the educational placement of a child with disabilities begin with placement in the regular classroom and in regular student activities. Inclusion settings in regular classes represent the least restrictive environment setting on the required "continuum" of alternative settings which must be available for the educational placement of children with disabilities needing special education and related services. Other instructional settings, in approximate continuum order, would be resource rooms (in some states this is a related service), separate classes (i.e., self-contained), special schools, home instruction, and hospitals. There is a legal presumption that a child with disabilities will be educated with children without disabilities. It is only when that presumption is overcome by data and the opinions of the placement team members that the child may be placed in special education programs. When the team determines that the child will not receive benefit from the regular education placement, or that the child is significantly disruptive, even with the provision of supplementary aids and services, the child may be placed in special education for programs and services. A full array of supplementary aids and services must be available and considered by the IEP team. Only when the cost of such services is excessive may the team decide to not provide them in the regular class setting.

The information provided here is extremely brief. A more detailed discussion of legal topics is given in later chapters (in Part I, especially); examples of helpful strategies, procedures and processes are covered (in Part II, especially); and the particular needs and suggested modifications for specific disabilities are presented (in Part III).

Early History

Throughout much of human history, the treatment of individuals with disabilities has been defined by superstitions and fear. Infanticide, shunning, attributions of witchcraft or divine punishment, and even awed respect all have been socially sanctioned. Then, with the rise of scientific understanding and democratic values in the late 1700s (the age of enlightenment), attitudes began to change. Disabled persons began to be seen as capable of learning, and the earliest special schools were founded for the deaf and blind. In institutions for the mentally ill and retarded (then grouped together indiscriminately), people were literally freed from their chains and conditions became somewhat more humane.

During the nineteenth century, reformers campaigned for new and more humane institutions, which generally were based on earlier European residential models, each one accommodating a different categorical population (e.g., blind, deaf, retarded). Some were state operated, some private—some obviously better than others. Their overall capacity was limited, programs were methodologically experimental, and many children—especially those with severe or multiple disabilities—were not served. Even though much of the United States later experienced the enactment of compulsory attendance laws for most children, those with disabilities, especially those with noticeable disabilities, were often excluded and even expelled from school (Yell, 1998, p. 54).

The early twentieth century saw the beginning of community-based programs and the first university training programs for teachers of the disabled. However, progress was slow. In most cases, the public attitude was "at best . . . bare tolerance of exceptional children" (Reynolds & Birch, 1977, p. 17). Programs still tended to be segregated along categorical lines and separate from regular classes and schools. Some students attended classes for only a minimal number of hours each day, and many others were not served at all. Students with mild disabilities who did not attend the public schools often were held back and forced to repeat grade after grade.

In the decades since World War II, however, there has been growing momentum for profound and rapid change marked by great increases in student enrollments, teacher training programs, and state support for special programs—even before the federal government became fully involved. Spurred in part by the response of wounded war veterans who were unwilling to accept a segregated, unproductive life, a national change in philosophy was underway. Whereas earlier reformers had argued for segregated schools as the most humane and receptive environment for educating students with disabilities, the new trend was toward inte-gration and "normalization" of individuals' lives.

This trend was supported by the fusion of two important social elements in pressuring for change: (1) the civil rights movement of the 1950s and 1960s and (2) the development of or-ganizations of parents and supporters of stu-dents with disabilities. Many other twentieth century developments also contributed to the advancement of special education, including:

- The development of the first standardized in-telligence tests and other types of reliable ed-ucational assessment;
- The development of new professional fields such as psychiatry, speech pathology, and educational psychology;
- Advances in medical understanding and treat-ment of previously mysterious diseases, such as epilepsy and polio;
- Technological developments in such diverse and important areas such as public trans-portation, artificial limbs and braces, and electronic communication aids for the deaf and blind.

By the mid-1970s, these combined forces and developments had resulted in a legalized commitment to educate all the nation's young people with disabilities and to do it in the most typical school setting possible.

To put this in reasonable perspective, it must be understood that public education itself is a relatively recent institution. Not until 1918 did all states in this country have compulsory ed-ucation laws. Child labor, which had involved a large percentage of school-age children, was not effectively banned on a national level until 1938. Federal government involvement with the spe-cial rights and needs of children also began in the twentieth century with the first White House Conference on Children and Youth in 1909.

The concept of universal public education won wide acceptance in this country only after the tremendous influx of immigrants during the late nineteenth and early twentieth centuries prompted concerns that the U.S. population be "Americanized." Even then, it is well-known that large numbers of the children and youth were seriously under served (as in the case of many students with disabilities, racial minori-ties, and other groups) or given no education at all (as many as one million children with disabilities in the early 1970s). Governmental attention to the needs of all children was a necessary prerequisite for the improvement of special education.

Legal Issues

All of the aforementioned twentieth century developments—governmental, theoretical, tech-nological, medical, and organizational—formed the roots of the powerful movement for educa-tional change in the 1960s and 1970s. The orga-nizations pushing for improvements in educa-tion of students with disabilities were in many ways inspired and influenced by the successes of the American civil rights movement. The five court cases consolidated into the landmark *Brown v. Board of Education* (1954), for exam-ple, had been brought on racial grounds. But the Supreme Court ruling against "separate but equal" schooling under the Constitution's Equal Protection Clause and its affirmation of the im-portance of education to all Americans was also viewed as relevant to students with disabilities. Over the next twenty years, advocacy groups led an active, and ultimately successful, cam-paign to win legal guarantees for the education of children with disabilities.

The efforts to raise public awareness re-ceived an important boost from President John F. Kennedy, whose sister was mentally retarded. In 1961, he initiated a Presidential Panel on Mental Retardation and in the ensuing decade, Congress passed several laws that began to ad-dress the issue of education for students with disabilities. The Elementary and Secondary Education Act (ESEA) of 1965 (P.L. 89-10) provided funding to meet the needs of educationally deprived students, and later ESEA amendments provided state agencies with special funds for the evaluation and education of students with disabilities (and later for gifted students as well). The federal Bureau for Education of the Handicapped was created in 1966 and state grant programs were established. The Handicapped Children's Early Education Act of 1968 (P.L. 90-247) provided funds to establish model demonstration programs for children with disabilities.

Just as *Brown* preceded major congressional acts in the civil rights arena, key court cases also helped set the stage for passage of Section 504 (P.L. 93-112) and the Education for All Handicapped Children Act (EAHCA) (P.L. 94-142). The two cases most often cited as influential are *Pennsylvania Association for Retarded Citizens (PARC) v. Pennsylvania* (1971/1972) and *Mills v. Board of Education* (1972).

The rulings in *PARC* and *Mills* included many of the principles that were later incorporated into federal law, including parent procedural safeguards and the right of all children with disabilities to a free, appropriate education. Section 504, the EAHCA (now IDEA), and the ADA are the three most important statutes governing special education in the United States and form the basis for legal discussions in each chapter of this book. Section 504 and the ADA are essentially civil rights statutes, while the EAHCA specifically defined and authorized funding for special educational programs. Over the years, significant amendments have strengthened and clarified aspects of the original special education laws found in the EAHCA. In 1986, the law was amended to include attorney fees for parents who prevail in due process proceedings and litigation and a new voluntary Part H (now Part C) was added to assist states with early intervention services for infants and toddlers (birth through age 2).

It was also in 1986 that the inclusion movement started in earnest in special education. Although a number of educators and researchers had previously argued for integrating students with disabilities into regular classrooms, it was then that Madeline Will, an assistant secretary of education, spoke and wrote about the "shared responsibility" of regular and special education programs toward students with disabilities. Will (1986) envisioned that the educational needs of all students be met through teams of educators and support staff working toward that goal. Initially the movement toward inclusion was often referred to as the regular education initiative (REI). Its goal was to find ways to serve students with mild and moderate disabilities by encouraging a partnership between regular and special education (Stainback & Stainback, 1995). At various times, the concept has taken on slightly different meanings and has been referred to as "integrated education," "mainstreaming," and "normalization." From 1989 through 1994, the inclusion movement gained significant momentum as a result of a series of important unanimous rulings by federal circuit courts interpreting the least restrictive environment concept of the IDEA.

In 1990, Congress amended the name of the EAHCA to the Individuals with Disabilities Education Act (IDEA). Further amendments in 1994 allowed greater coordination between Chapter I remedial programs for children with disabilities and, in response to public demands for greater school safety, authorized greater flexibility for schools in dealing with students bringing firearms to school. In 1997, after a two-year congressional battle, extensive amendments were written into the law that greatly enhanced and clarified understanding on numerous controversial and complex legal issues. With the 1997 Amendments, the congressional focus shifted from implementation of educational programs and services to a greater emphasis on providing quality public education programs and improving and evaluating student performance (House Report 105-95, 1997, pp. 83–84).

Section 504

While Section 504 is a broad civil rights provision protecting persons with disabilities of all ages, educators come into contact with its provisions most frequently when parents of children with disabilities are unable to establish that their children are eligible for special education programs and services. Thus, Section 504 presents concerns primarily for regular education programs and is usually not considered to be part of special education programming.

Section 504 has potentially broader application than IDEA for those children with physical or mental disabilities which substantially "affect one of the major life activities" (walking, seeing, breathing) but does not necessarily significantly impact the child's ability to learn. An example might be a child with severe arthritis or cancer who can attend school and learn as an otherwise typical student would. For such students, an evaluation is conducted and a determination of eligibility for Section 504 services is made. While schools must conduct an evaluation of the student, most Section 504 evaluations are completed only through the gathering and consideration of existing data, including previous medical records and educational testing (Copenhaver, 1998).

Under Section 504, an accommodation plan must be developed by a group of persons knowledgeable about the student. The plan must document adjustments or accommodations to be made by the school and its staff that will allow the child to benefit from the school's education services in both academic and nonacademic activities. The administration of prescribed medications, longer passing time between classes, alternative passing time to eliminate being jostled by other students, and additional time to complete class assignments or tests might be accommodations considered for

some students. The list of potential accommodations is limited only by students' needs and team imagination. The Bureau of Indian Affairs provides its staff members with a listing of "100 effective accommodations/services" to use as examples (Bureau of Indian Affairs, 1998, pp. 67–72). Accommodations must be based on the student's needs and must be reasonable in nature. The accommodation plan is not required to be reduced to writing, but best practice would indicate that a written plan is the ideal safeguard for all concerned. Sometimes, an accommodation plan merely documents a team's consideration of a student's needs and a determination that no accommodations are justified under the circumstances.

Under Section 504 requirements, schools must implement procedural safeguards for students and parents, including a notice of rights, an opportunity to review student records, an opportunity for an impartial due process hearing, and an opportunity for further review of hearing decisions. Schools may use existing grievance procedures (e.g., equity or sexual harassment) when those procedures are in compliance with Section 504 requirements. Local hearings must allow the parents an opportunity to challenge school decisions regarding identification, evaluation, provision of services, and changes in services. Hearings should be conducted by impartial hearing officers at no cost to the parent, and parents may have legal representation if they wish. Schools should have written procedures that incorporate these procedures and comply with other Section 504 requirements.

To better understand how the IDEA, Section 504, and the ADA impact each other in the educational setting, one can use an analogy of three inverted kitchen mixing bowls, each one a little larger than the last. Likewise, each law encompasses the previous smaller one and is somewhat greater in coverage. The smallest mixing bowl represents the IDEA, which requires that special education and related services be provided to children with disabilities who need special education. The legal provisions of the IDEA are interpreted and monitored by the Office of Special Education Programs (OSEP) in the U.S. Department of Education.

The second largest bowl represents Section 504, which makes it illegal for recipients of federal funds, including public schools and some private schools, to discriminate against persons with disabilities. Section 504 regulations incorporate many of the IDEA concepts, and compliance with the IDEA requirements of free appropriate public education (FAPE) usually signifies compliance with Section 504 requirements in the same area. Some areas of potential discrimination exist under Section 504 outside the IDEA. A student with a specific learning disability, for instance, may be receiving a program under the IDEA, but may be obtaining low grades in courses and thus be ineligible to participate in athletics. The question under the IDEA would be whether the provided program was appropriate, an educational question. But under Section 504, the question would be whether ineligibility owing to low grades was a result of the student's disability, which could be prohibited discrimination and thus a question of law (Sullivan, Lantz, & Zirkel, 2000). Also, under Section 504, a school's refusal to administer needed prescribed medication during school hours to a child with disabilities, regardless of whether he or she receives special education, may establish a claim of discrimination because medication administration may be a legally required "reasonable accommodation."

The ADA, in our analogy, is represented by the largest mixing bowl. It prohibits discrimination on the basis of disability in both the public and private sectors and would include those issues covered by Section 504. At this time, questions of discrimination in education under both Section 504 and the ADA are treated identically by the Office of Civil Rights (OCR), the federal agency which enforces both. It is unlikely that students in public schools gained any more rights under the ADA than they already had under the IDEA and Section 504 (Osborne, 1995, p. 496).

General Purposes of the IDEA

In addition to providing partial funding and establishing a system to monitor and evaluate state and local programs, the IDEA contains a number of provisions which are designed to ensure that all eligible students receive the education programs to which they are entitled. As Yell* points out, the IDEA contains the following major principles:

- Zero reject—States must establish a child-find system to ensure that all children eligible to receive special education are identified. All eligible students are entitled to special education programs and services regardless of the severity of their disability;
- Free appropriate public education (FAPE) —States must assure that eligible children receive specially designed instruction and related services meeting state standards, at no cost to the parents and in conformity with an IEP;
- LRE—Students with disabilities must be educated with nondisabled students to the maximum extent appropriate. Students must be provided supplementary aids and services to the extent that such aids and services will make the regular school setting educationally appropriate. Schools must provide a continuum of alternative placements appropriate to meet the needs of all eligible students;
- Identification and evaluation—States must assure the use of nondiscriminatory and accurate evaluation instruments and procedures;
- Confidentiality of information—Parents may inspect all education records regarding their

---

*From *The Law and Special Education*, by Yell, Mitchell L. © 1998. Reprinted by permission of Prentice-Hall, Inc. Upper Saddle River, NJ. Adapted by permission.

child and have an expectation of privacy in protections from unnecessary disclosure;

- Procedural safeguards—Parents are provided an extensive system of notices, processes, and methods of dispute resolution, including the possibility of being awarded attorney fees if they prevail in hearings or litigation;
- Technology-related assistance—Student IEPs should contain provisions for assistive technology devices and services when necessary to provide a student with a FAPE;
- Personnel development—States must assess their supply of trained personnel to provide special education and related services in special and regular education environments, and develop plans for ensuring an adequate supply of appropriately prepared personnel;
- Placements in private schools—The IDEA addresses the continued responsibility of public schools to assure its provisions are carried out when students are placed by public schools in private settings, and a limited responsibility to students placed in private schools by parents so long as the public school is able to provide a FAPE in the event the student returns to the public school.

Important Terms and Phrases

A number of key terms are used and defined in the law:

Children with disabilities are those children who have been evaluated and found to have one of the following disabilities: mental retardation, hearing impairment (including deafness), speech or language impairment, visual impairment (including blindness), emotional disturbance, orthopedic impairment, autism, traumatic brain injury, other health impairment, specific learning disability; deaf-blindness, or multiple disabilities *and who because of that disability need special education and related services* (34 C.F.R. 300.7, 2000); see that section of the

rules for the definition of children with disabilities for children ages three through five years). Thus, eligibility has two requirements, a child must have a disability, as defined by law, and must also need special education and related services as a result of the disability.

Special education is defined in the IDEA as "specially designed instruction, at no cost to parents, to meet the unique needs of a child with a disability, including instruction conducted in the classroom, in the home, in hospitals and institutions, and in other settings; and instruction in physical education" (34 C.F.R. § 300.26, 1999). The phrase also includes speech-language pathology services, any related service if it is considered special education under state law, travel training, and vocational education, if it includes specially designed vocational instruction for the child. Vocational education can include other skills programs involving problem solving skills, work attitudes, employability skills, and other skills necessary for economic independence.

Related services are referred to in the law, guaranteeing free provisions of "special education and related services." Related services are defined as:

> transportation and such developmental corrective, and other supportive services as are required to assist a child with disabilities to benefit from special education; and includes speech-language pathology and audiology services, psychological services, physical and occupational therapy, recreation, including therapeutic recreation, early identification and assessment of disabilities in children, counseling services, including rehabilitation counseling, orientation and mobility services, and medical services for diagnostic or evaluation purposes. The term also includes school health services, social work services in schools, and parent counseling and training. (34 C.F.R. § 00.22 (a), 2000)

Free appropriate public education means special education and related services provided at no cost to the parent, including preschool, elementary, and secondary school, and are provided under a properly devised IEP.

Individualized education program means a written statement of an educational plan and program based on education data for a child with a disability that is developed, reviewed, and revised in accordance with federal law. An IEP must be in effect prior to the provision of special education and related services.

Least restrictive environment requires that children with disabilities must be educated with nondisabled children to the maximum extent appropriate. Special classes or settings may be used only when the nature of the disability is such that "education in the regular classes with the use of supplementary aids and services cannot be achieved satisfactorily" (34 C.F.R. § 300.530, 2000). Schools must ensure that a continuum of alternative placements are available, ranging from instruction in the regular classroom to special classes, to home instruction, to hospitals and to institutions. Provision for education of children with disabilities in the regular classroom is sometimes called "inclusion," but that is an educational term rather than a legal one.

Supplementary aids and services are those aids, services, modifications, and other supports that are provided in the regular class, or regular education-related settings, "to enable the child with disabilities to be educated with nondisabled children to the maximum extent appropriate" (34 C.F.R. § 300.28, 2000). It may include resource room or itinerant instruction. The phrase differs from "related services" in that the latter phrase often refers to services provided in special education environments.

An *assistive technology* is any device, piece of equipment, or product system which is used to increase, maintain, or improve the functional capabilities of a child, and *assistive technology service* is any service that directly assists a child with the selection, acquisition, or use of an assistive technology device, including evaluation, purchasing, customizing, and training.

Overview of the Process of Special Education

Once a child is identified (through individual referral or routine screening procedures) as potentially needing special education and related services, a chain of activities is set in motion, with the three basic steps prescribed by law:

1. *Assessment.* A full, thorough, nondiscriminatory (e.g., race, language, gender) evaluation must assess all areas of possible disability, and an eligibility determination is made by a team of qualified professionals and the parents of the child (see Chapter 4).

2. *An IEP is prepared.* This document is based on the evaluation data and is formulated in a meeting involving the student's parent(s); at least one regular education teacher if the child is, or may be, in regular education; at least one special education teacher; at least one school district representative who is qualified to provide or supervise the provision of special education, is knowledgeable about the school's general curriculum and is knowledgeable about, and can commit, the resources of the school; a team member who can interpret evaluation results; the child, with parent approval; and other individuals with special knowledge or expertise involving the child. The IEP records the pupil's current levels of functioning, including how the disability impacts the child's progress in the general curriculum; annual educational goals, including benchmarks or short-term objectives; a statement of the special education and related services, supplementary aids and services, and program modifications to be provided; an explanation of the extent, if any, to which that child will not participate with children without disabilities in the regular class; the extent to which the child will participate in general school assessments; and a statement of how the child's progress will be measured and

reported to the child's parents. The IEP must be completed prior to the provision of special education programs and services (see Chapter 5).

3. *The educational placement is chosen.* This must be a setting in which the IEP can be carried out and which meets other requirements of the law. The district must have a continuum of placements available (whether provided by the district itself or under contract through outside agencies) in regular and special schools. Placement decisions must be made by a group of persons knowledgeable about the child, including the parents, and placement must be in the least restrictive environment appropriate for the child (see Chapter 6).

All three of the basic steps may be accomplished by the same core group of team members (IEP team), with additional professional and support persons being involved when appropriate. Specific state, district, and school policies can be, and in many cases have been, developed to help each step proceed smoothly. Such policies include preparing for IEP meetings with thorough knowledge of student evaluation data and the education programs actually available in the school district, preplacement preparation of the student (assuring that the student has the prerequisite skills necessary for success in the setting), and postplacement monitoring and communication systems, ensuring periodic communication between regular and special education staff.

Although the IDEA represents an extremely important milestone, the legal status of special education in this country still is subject to change. It continues to be influenced by such factors as court decisions, changes in government administration, new acts of Congress, and changes at the state and local levels. Some examples include the court decisions affecting program setting options discussed in Chapter 6

and school discipline procedures discussed in Chapter 9.

Each chapter in this book contains relevant information on legal requirements and trends at the federal level. However, state laws and school district policies are not covered here, but will have to be consulted because they affect the options available to education leaders. Congress has consistently affirmed that education is primarily a state responsibility, and although the basic requirements of the IDEA are firm, the states still have a variety of options in specific areas as to how these requirements will be met.

The IDEA is essentially a contract between the federal government and each state, whereby the latter agrees to follow certain regulations in exchange for federal funds. To qualify for these funds, each state must submit program plans, including assurances that the basic principles of the federal law will be followed, copies of related state laws and regulations, counts of children with disabilities in the state and where they are served, monitoring and evaluation activities, use of funds and accounting systems, facilities available, and other information.

The state, in turn, makes funds available to intermediate educational agencies or local school districts upon receipt of their applications, which must include descriptions of facilities, personnel, and services available; guarantees that federal guidelines are being followed; plans for parent participation; accounting systems; and agreement to furnish data required by the state for its reports.

Thus, each state is primarily responsible for fulfilling the terms of its agreement and each school district is held accountable by the state department of education, which itself is monitored by the federal government. To ensure contract compliance, program data and planning information must be collected and delivered to the federal government each year. This, in brief, is the legal and financial reality behind many of the paperwork requirements that go along with special education.

Percentages of Children Enrolled in Special Education

According to the U.S. Department of Education's 1999 Annual Report to Congress on the implementation of the IDEA, in the 1997–98 school year, about 11.6% of all children ages 6 to 21 enrolled in public schools were enrolled in special education. In the 1980–81 school year, about 10% of students enrolled were identified as needing special education. According to the National Center for Educational Statistics (1999), the approximate breakdown, by disability, of the 11.6% of children receiving special education, in 1997–98, was as follows:

Specific Learning Disability	51%
Speech or Language Impairment	20%
Mental Disability	11%
Serious Emotional Disturbance	8%
Hearing, Visual, Orthopedic or other Health Impairments	10%

Data contained in reports to Congress have established that even though national figures for student enrollment have increased slowly over recent years (4.8% increase between the 1988–89 and 1994–95 school years), the number of identified students with disabilities has increased at about three times that rate (12.8% for the same time period). The data also establish that since the late 1980s, the number of students with disabilities who are educated in regular classrooms has increased substantially, about 60% between the 1988–89 and 1994–95 school years. During that same time period, the number of students educated in resource rooms and separate schools both declined (16% and 20%, respectively, between the 1988–89 and 1994–95 school years), but the number of students in separate classes increased slightly (5%) (McLeskey, Henry, & Hodges, 1998).

The current trend toward moving students with disabilities to less restrictive settings has involved all disability categories (McLeskey, Henry, & Hodges, 1999). Not surprising, the greatest movement toward inclusion involved students with the mildest disabilities: specific learning disabilities, speech/language impairments, and other health impairments. Categories of students with more challenging behaviors and substantial disabilities (multiple disabilities and mental disabilities) are experiencing less progress. The available data document substantial progress toward inclusion, but the trends vary dramatically between states and among the various disabilities. The following chart at Figure 1-1 shows the percentages of children with selected disabilities in the regular class setting in the 1988–89 and 1994–95 school years. Regular class setting is defined as not being out of the regular class for more than 20% of the school day.

APPROACHES TO COMPLIANCE

As previously noted, two of the chief mandates of federal special education law are individualization of programming and the integration of students with disabilities and their peers without disabilities. Both concepts are admirable and philosphically sound, but the question is, how are they accomplished in the realistic setting of the classroom? How does a regular classroom teacher, who may have no special training in exceptional education, meet the unique needs of two or three students with disabilities in an already demanding class of twenty-five or more students? And how does the principal/administrator deal with all this?

Part of the answer must be: "With help." In the inclusion classroom, teachers need special consideration as surely as do students with disabilities. This book includes information on structuring supportive relationships between regular class teachers and special education professionals (Chapter 6, Placement; Chapter 11, Staff Relationships and Staffing Patterns). Every chapter contains tips on what school leaders can

FIGURE 1-1   *Trend toward inclusion: The percentage of students with disabilities in the regular class setting*

Category	Year	Regular Education Classes (%)
Specific Learning Disability	1988–89	19.6
	1994–95	41.1
Mental Disability	1988–89	6.2
	1994–95	8.2
Serious Emotional Disturbance	1988–89	14.2
	1994–95	22.1
Speech/Language Impairments	1988–89	75.9
	1994–95	87.5
Health Impairments	1988–89	31.0
	1994–95	39.0
Orthopedic Impairments	1988–89	30.4
	1994–95	40.3
Multiple Disabilities	1988–89	7.5
	1994–95	9.6
Visual Impairments	1988–89	40.8
	1994–95	47.3
Hearing Impairments	1988–89	27.7
	1994–95	35.9
Deaf-Blindness	1988–89	13.3
	1994–95	12.1

From "Inclusion: What Progress Is Being Made Across Disability Categories," by J. McLeskey, D. Henry, and D. Hodges, 1999, *Teaching Exceptional Children, 31* (3), p. 61. Copyright 1999 by The Council for Exceptional Children. Adapted with permission.

do to establish a positive, cooperative atmosphere and sound school policy and practice.

Regular Classroom Modifications

Many answers to the question of accommodating students with disabilities in inclusion programs lie in appropriate modifications and accommodations in the regular classroom and the provision of supplementary aids and services as support for the staff or student. The phrase "supplementary aids and services" means "aids, services and other supports that are *provided in regular education classes or other education re-*lated settings to enable children with disabilities to be educated with nondisabled children to the maximum extent appropriate . . ." (emphasis added) (34 C.F.R. § 300.26, 2000). These aids, modifications, and services are provided to enable the child to benefit from his or her instructional program in the regular class or nonacademic setting without becoming a significant disruption. It is highly desirable that IEP teams develop a clear process for determining the specific accommodations, modifications, and supplementary aids and services to be provided to a student. The following division of IEP team consideration into four separate classroom dimensions of physical, instructional, social-behavioral, and collaborative consideration presents but one appropriate organizational approach to that IEP team consideration.*

Physical Environment

Modifications in the physical environment are the most straightforward. Special environmental considerations related to each disability (covered in Part III) include accessibility, adequate lighting, pre-enrollment classroom orientation, and appropriate seating.

Social-Behavioral

This dimension includes factors related to the student's behavior. The 1997 Amendments to the IDEA requires that the IEP team consider a child's behavior when the behavior impedes the student's learning or the learning of others, and to consider appropriate positive behavioral interventions, strategies, and supports to address that behavior. In fact, one of the reasons that regular education teachers are now required to be included on IEP teams is to gain from their experience and knowledge in determining appropriate positive behavioral interventions, supplementary aids and services, program modifications, and needed supports for school personnel. Students experiencing frequent behavior problems may have a behavior plan attached as part of their IEP.

Collaborative

This area pertains to personnel factors, and includes the establishment of periods of time for joint planning and a means of regular communication about the student between regular and special educators, support staff, consultants, and others providing programs and services. It may also include specialized skill development or special training for staff in working with students with special needs.

The regular class teacher may need regular conferencing times with behavior specialists or curriculum modification consultants. The teacher associate may need training in discipline, instructional models, parent communication, or health procedures. Staff members may require staff-development in sign language, autism, or functional behavioral assessment.

Instructional Strategies, Content, and Assessment

In inclusion settings, educators must assure the availability of appropriate modifications in teaching strategies both in the materials used and the means of presenting information. Some of these modifications are obvious. If a blind student is present in the classroom, for example, it will not be possible to rely exclusively on visual communication. Assignments may have to be tape recorded; visual and spatial concepts may have to be explained; and appropriate tools and materials, such as large print books, word processors, or Braille writers, may be needed.

Other, less obvious, modifications will be required with many exceptional students. These may include the use of concrete examples in explaining new concepts, extra opportunities for rehearsal and repetition, consistent daily schedules, cooperative small group structures, special reinforcers, and so on.

NEW CHALLENGES AND THOUGHTS

Past abuses in education of students with disabilities might be summarized as the "failure to individualize." Despite all the legal progress, today's schools are not immune from the impulse

---

* Summarized from "The IDEA Amendments: A Four-Step Approach for Determining Supplementary Aids and Services," by S. K. Etscheidt and L. Bartlett, 1999, *Exceptional Children, 65* (2), pp. 169–72. Copyright 1999 by The Council for Exceptional Children. Adapted by permission.

to act on prejudice or stereotype rather than to provide supportive understanding of individual students' strengths and needs.

To help combat that impulse, educators (principals and teachers alike) should remember that students' performance problems can be the result of many interacting factors, including inappropriate treatment by the schools. A helpful key to keep in mind when analyzing such problems is the SUM formula (Weisenstein, 1980), where

- *S* indicates skill deficits: necessary prerequisite skills not yet attained that prevent students from completing a given task;
- *U* stands for unrealistic expectations: students' placement in programs where course requirements clearly are beyond their abilities;
- *M* signifies motivational deficits: some students with disabilities often require additional motivation to complete a task; the use of appropriate reinforcers may help close the performance gap.

Some interesting positive side effects of the inclusion effort have been observed. Commentators have noted that the state of Vermont, which has led the nation in the percentage of children with disabilities in regular classrooms (83% compared with 36% nationwide), has experienced observable unexpected benefits in the inclusion process.

Thousand and Villa (1995) report, among other things, the following from Vermont's inclusion efforts:

- The number of students identified for special education has decreased;
- Student performance, behavior, and social engagement have not diminished;
- Other education improvement initiatives have linked with inclusion to their mutual strengthening; and
- Both regular and special educators have come to believe, with experience, that inclusion

results in positive changes in job roles for educators.

While some educators call for an approach which would require all children with disabilities to be placed in the regular class setting all the time (full inclusion), others continue to defend the value of separateness for such students (special education). Yet, many of the most experienced educators and notable researchers do not call for an all-or-nothing approach, but see value in the maintenance of the currently required variety of instructional settings (continuum). It is recognized that inclusion in the regular class setting is not appropriate or desirable for *all* children with disabilities (Zigmond et al, 1998). It is important to keep in mind that one solution does not fit all, and that educators and parents need to protect students from a single-mold mentality. Educators have been known to become overzealous with a good idea.

The growing realization that courts would no longer ignore that portion of the LRE concept of consideration requiring regular class placement, as well as greatly increased coverage of the issue in the education literature in the early 1990's, caused confusion among educators regarding their growing professional role and responsibility. Because many individual teachers remained doubtful and uncertain, the National Education Association established an *ad hoc* committee to study the issue and attempt to establish a national policy statement which represented best practice for inclusion in the school setting. Here is the result of that concerted effort, which in 1994 became the "National Education Association Policy Statement on Appropriate Inclusion":

> The National Education Association is committed to equal educational opportunity, the highest quality education, and a safe learning environment for all students. The association supports and encourages appropriate inclusion. *Appropriate inclusion* is characterized

by practices and programs that provide for the following on a sustained basis:

- A full continuum of placement options and services within each option. Placement and services must be determined for each student by a team that includes all stakeholders and must be specified in the individualized education program (IEP).
- *Appropriate* professional development, as part of normal work activity, of all educators and support staff associated with such programs. *Appropriate* training must also be provided for administrators, parents, and other stakeholders.
- Adequate time, as part of the normal school day, to engage in coordinated and collaborative planning on behalf of all students.
- Class sizes that are responsive to student needs.
- Staff and technical assistance that is specifically appropriate to student and teacher needs.

Inclusion practices and programs that lack these fundamental characteristics are inappropriate and must end.*

Notice the importance and emphasis of the adjective "appropriate" in the NEA statement. The statement recognizes throughout that in the creation of inclusive programs, there is a "right way" and a "wrong way." It is the former, not the latter, that this book was envisioned to foment. In many educator discussions and research publications about inclusion, both appropriate and less than appropriate efforts at inclusion are lumped together without distinction.

Often, schools engaged in inclusion implementation efforts are simultaneously engaged in other positive school reform efforts. Commentators have observed that there may be a relationship between school reform and a school's commitment to the inclusion concept. Schools engaged in reform efforts appear to focus on the preparation and education of all children for productive and satisfying lives (First & Curcio, 1993).

CONCLUSION

Effective implementation of the special education process, as outlined in the IDEA, may require new understanding and awareness, new roles, and new flexibility. Building principals and other education leaders are essential to the success of inclusion through their climate setting activities and practices, modeling acceptance, and meeting challenges in a spirit of togetherness. Meeting these challenges requires a sharing of information, cooperation, and commitment—but it is worth it. The experience in thousands of classrooms across the country has shown that the inclusion experience, if done correctly, can be successful and productive, not only for students with disabilities but for all those persons involved (Power-de Fur & Orelove, 1997, pp. 3–6).

REFERENCES

Americans With Disabilities Act of 1990, 42 U.S.C. § 1401 *et seq.*

Assistance to States for the Education of Children with Disabilities (2000), 34 C.F.R. Part 300.

Brown v. Board of Education, 347 U.S. 483 (1954).

Bureau of Indian Affairs (1998). *Section 504/ADA: Guidelines for educators.* Logan, UT, Mountain Plains Regional Resource Center: Utah State University.

Copenhaver, J. (1998). *A parent guide to Section 504 of the Rehabilitation Act of 1973.* Logan, UT, Mountain Plains Regional Resource Center: Utah State University for the Bureau of Indian Affairs Branch of Exceptional Education.

---

*Emphasis added. From "National Education Association Policy Statement on Appropriate Inclusion." Available at: http://www.NEA.org/published/idea/neainclu.html. Reprinted by permission.

Etscheidt, S., & Bartlett, L. (1999). The IDEA amendments: A four-step approach for determining supplementary aids and services. *Exceptional Children, 65* (2), 163–174.

First, P. F., & Curcio, J. L. (1993). *Implementing the Disabilities Acts: Implications for Educators.* Bloomington, IN: Phi Delta Kappa Educational Foundation, Fastback No. 360.

House Report 105-95. (1997) The Committee on Education and Workforce to Accompany Individuals With Disabilities Education Act Amendments of 1997, 2, U.S.C. *Congressional and Administrative News,* 78–146.

Individuals With Disabilities Education Act, 20 U.S.C. §§ 1401–1487.

McLeskey, J., Henry, D., & Hodges, D. (1998). Inclusion: Where is it happening? *Teaching Exceptional Children, 31* (1), 4–10.

McLeskey, J., Henry, D., & Hodges, D. (1999). Inclusion: What progress is being made across disability categories? *Teaching Exceptional Children, 31* (3), 60–64.

Mills v. Board of Education, 348 F. Supp. 866 (D.D.C. 1972).

National Center for Education Statistics (1999). Digest of education statistics 1999: Chapter 2, Elementary and Secondary Education [online]. Available at: http//:nces.ed.gov/pubs2000/digest99/d99to53.html.

Osborne, A. G. (1955). Court interpretations of the Americans With Disabilities Act and their effect on school districts. *Education Law Reporter, 95,* 489–497.

Pennsylvania Association for Retarded Citizens (PARC) v. Pennsylvania, 334 F. Supp. 1257 (E.D. Pa. 1971); 343, F. Supp. 279 (E.D. Pa. 1972).

Power-de Fur, L. A., & Orelove, F. P. (1997). *Inclusive education: Practical implementation of the least restrictive environment.* Gaithersburg, MD, Aspen Publishers, Inc.

Reynolds, M. C., & Birch, J. N. (1977). *Teaching exceptional children in all America's schools.* Reston, VA: Council for Exceptional Children.

Section 504, Rehabilitation Act of 1973, 29 U.S.C. § 794.

Stainback, W., & Stainback, S. (1995). Contemplating inclusive education from a historical perspective. In: R. A. Villa, & J. S. Thousand (Eds.). *Creating an inclusive school,* 16–27. Alexandria, VA: Association for Supervision and Curriculum Development.

Sullivan, K. A., Lantz, P. J., & Zirkel, P. A. (2000). Leveling the playing field or leveling the players? Section 505, the Americans With Disabilities Act and Interscholastic Sports. *The Journal of Special Education, 33* (4), 258–267.

Thousand, J. S., & Villa, R. A. (1995). Inclusion: Alive and well in the green mountain state. *Phi Delta Kappan, 77* (4), 288–291.

Weisenstein, G. R. (August 1980). *Motivating handicapped and disadvantaged students in vocational education classrooms.* Presentation to the National Conference of Cooperative Occupational Education, Phoenix, AZ.

Will, M. C. (1986). Educating children with learning problems: A shared responsibility. *Exceptional Children, 52* (5), 411–415.

Yell, M. L. (1988). *The law and special education.* Upper Saddle River, NJ: Prentice-Hall, Inc.

Zigmond, N., Jenkins, J., Fuchs, D., Deno, S., & Fuchs, L. S. (1998). When students fail to achieve satisfactorily. *Phi Delta Kappan, 77* (4), 303–306.

RECOMMENDED READINGS

Beninghof, A. M., & Singer, A. L. (1995). *Ideas for inclusion: The school administrator's guide.* Longmont, CO: Sopris West. The authors present specific and detailed rationale, recommendations, and methods for inclusion.

Conderman, G., & Katsiyannis, A. (1995). Section 504 Accommodation Plans. *Intervention in School and Clinic, 31* (1), 42–45. This article provides a sample list of common accommodations and a sample form for documenting accommodation plans.

Greer, B. B., & Greer, J. G. (1995). Questions and answers about inclusion: What every teacher should know. *Clearing House, 68* (6), 339–342. This article discusses the educational and legal justification for the inclusion concept.

Giangreco, M. F. (1996). What do I do now? A teacher's guide to including students with disabilities. *Educational Leadership, 53* (5), 56–59. The author presents practical suggestions in the implementation of inclusion programs.

Huefner, D. S., (1998). The Individuals With Disabilities Education Act Amendments of 1997. *Educa-*

tion Law Reporter, 122, 1103–1122. This article, written by one of the foremost authorities in the field, identifies the major 1997 changes in the IDEA.

Kochhar, A., & West L. (1996). *Handbook for successful inclusion.* Gaithersburg, MD: Aspen Publishers, Inc.; 220 pp. The authors present a detailed explanation of the law, philosophy, and strategy of inclusion; a very detailed and well-documented how-to guide.

Lombardi, T. P. (1994). *Responsible inclusion of students with disabilities.* Bloomington, IN: Phi Delta Kappa Educational Foundation, Fastback No. 373. This brief pamphlet outlines the philosophy of inclusion and suggests appropriate ways to implement it.

Mead, J. F. (1998). Expressions of congressional intent: Examining the 1997 Amendments to the IDEA. *Education Law Reporter, 126,* 511–531. This article reviews the 1997 amendments to IDEA and explains the rationale behind them.

Rosenfeld, S. J. (1995). Planning for ADA compliance. *EDLAW Briefing Paper, (6),* 1–15. This paper describes the legal requirements for school compliance with the ADA.

Relevant Federal Regulations

34 C.F.R. Part 104 Nondiscrimination on the basis of disability in programs and activities receiving federal financial assistance.

34 C.F.R. Part 300 Assistance to state for the education of children with disabilities.

300.7	Child with a disability.
300.13	Free appropriate public education.
300.15	Individualized education programs.
300.16	Individualized education program team.
300.24	Related services.
300.26	Special education.
300.28	Supplementary aids and services.
300.550	General LRE requirements.
300.551	Continuum of alternative placements.

CHAPTER **2**

WORKING WITH PARENTS AND PARENT RIGHTS

CHAPTER PREVIEW

Focus

The IDEA requires that schools optimize parents' opportunity for participation in several aspects of their child's education. However, a number of factors may negatively affect the parent-school relationship, including previous unpleasant experiences with schools and other institutions involving the treatment of their child; teacher reluctance, resistance, or lack of training in working with parents; and numerous related stresses affecting the persons involved.

Rationale

Because parents have the greatest overall responsibility, they are automatically involved in and concerned with their child's education. They deserve the right to help make decisions about it. Further, their special knowledge and commitment can make them valuable partners in that education. Many of the problems currently associated with school-parent relationships should improve as community and professional attitudes change, in part under the impetus of the IDEA, toward wider acceptance of persons with disabilities and their families, and thus toward greater possibilities for mutual trust.

Legal Issues

The IDEA guarantees several rights to the parents of children with disabilities, including the following:

- parents' informed written consent is required before initial evaluation, re-evaluation, and initial placement can take place or student records are released;
- parents must be notified in advance (in their native language or mode of communication) each time the school proposes (or refuses) to initiate or change the child's identification, evaluation, program placement, or free appropriate public education;
- parents may contest any school decision they feel inappropriate or not in keeping with the law, and they have the right to request an impartial due process hearing to resolve disputes;
- parents can expect to participate in their child's evaluation and determination of disability, in preparing the child's IEP, and in determining the appropriate educational placement for their child;
- parents can expect that special education and related services spelled out in the IEP will be provided at no cost to the family;

- parents must be provided access to, and the confidentiality of, the education records created and maintained by the school regarding their child; and
- parents can expect that the school district will notify them of these rights.

Approaches

Principals and other educational leaders should make certain that they as well as the teachers and staff in their buildings accept parents as equal partners in the education of the child. Educators should ask parents for information they have that may be helpful, listen nonjudgmentally, ask how the school can be of help to them, and maintain frequent positive communication about school events, the youngster's progress, and other topics of common interest and concern. School staff should avoid waiting until a problem arises to initiate communications, be aware of legal requirements for parental notice and participation, and develop appropriate forms and procedures to ensure that both legal and educational requirements are met.

Special parent services such as discussion groups, workshops, and forums can be beneficial, but here educators must be cautious. Experience has shown that only a relatively small percentage of parents will attend such events, and speakers/leaders should be chosen carefully. Parents will not benefit from advice unless they are ready for it, and too many services can be a burden.

The Role of Parents

Giving birth to and raising a child with disabilities can be an extremely stressful experience replete with grief, guilt, fears, family disruptions, financial strains, and relentless hard work. The families of the disabled, just as surely as the disabled themselves, need help and support, yet it is striking how often they do not receive it.

Almost every family with a child with a disability has its own accumulation of bad experiences: neighbors and even family members who rejected them and their child; a doctor who distorted or evaded the truth in diagnosis; specialists who offered contradictory explanations in language they could not understand; a religious leader who played on their guilt and implied it was their own fault; or a teacher who was insensitive, disapproving, unapproachable, or frighteningly uninformed. One of the authors distinctly remembers a telephone call received nearly twenty years ago from a parent who had just returned home from an initial IEP meeting involving her newly adopted child with severe and multiple disabilities. One of the educators present at the meeting had remarked "Isn't it too bad that children like this don't die at birth." The mother, through tears, wanted to know why teachers are not better trained and more sensitive. The author had no answer; he could only choke back tears of his own.

One study on the overall family perspective of children with behavior problems conducted by Turnball and Ruef (1997) is helpful in understanding the extent of the problem. Researchers found siblings were resentful, frustrated, and embarrassed by the challenge of a brother or sister with a disability. Extended family members did not feel connected to or comfortable around the child with a disability. Over half of the parents expressed frustration and disappointment in attempting to participate in common family pursuits, such as religious activities as a family, as a result of the child with a disability. Over two-thirds of the families of children with problem behavior could not identify any friends of their child.

By the time the parents of children with disabilities have attended their first or second or tenth school conference, they may have good cause to be suspicious or defensive. Thus, there are three factors in particular to which educators should be sensitive:

1. Parents' stresses in raising a child with disabilities;
2. Parents' previous negative experiences with professionals of various kinds; and
3. Parents' fears about school, based either on their own negative experiences or on the expectation that the schools as they knew them will be unable to accommodate their youngster (e.g., fears that the child will be teased and rejected, that the teacher will set unfair expectations and scold the child for not living up to them, or that the child will not be understood and appreciated).

Like the parents, educators deserve understanding and respect for the stressful conditions of their own jobs. However, it cannot be denied that many educational professionals have contributed to the problem. For a variety of understandable reasons, educators may exhibit:

- a lack of commitment to least restrictive environment (especially inclusion);
- a lack of knowledge, training, or experience; and
- a resistance to sharing decision-making responsibility with parents.

Any of these factors can be perceived by parents and can have a negative effect on the family's relations with the school.

The study of families of children with be-havior disabilities (Turnball & Ruef, 1997) sought to learn about family members' opinions regarding teachers and administrators. A major-ity of the families in the study expressed con-cern and frustration over teacher participation because the teachers were considered unable to deal with important student issues. Teachers were considered unwilling to change, too quick to give in to students with disabilities as a way of dealing with behavior problems, defensive at suggestions posed by parents, not forthcoming with concrete answers to parent questions, giv-ing up too early on efforts with students; and intimidated by students with serious behavior problems. Four specific concerns with adminis-trators expressed by those same families were: (1) lack of resources; (2) constant "pushing" for a more restrictive placement; (3) failure to im-plement the IDEA properly; and (4) using the wrong administrative criteria for placement (i.e., how many students are already in the class ver-sus which teacher will most likely succeed in helping the student). Only one family in the study praised the school administration because it had "set the tone" for an accepting school en-vironment. If the findings of this study are gen-erally representative of the feelings and con-cerns of parents of children with disabilities, then it is understandable that parent relations with schools leave a great deal to be desired. Consequently, educators must be more aware of and sensitive to parents' problems, anxieties, and stresses.

In a review of research results from several studies, Epstein (1995) concluded that good school-family programs can be created where they currently do not exist. This is true because nearly all families, students, and teachers be-lieve that such programs are important for help-ing all students. She concluded from research findings, in part, that nearly all:

- families care about their children, want them to succeed, and are eager to obtain better in-formation from schools and communities in order to remain good partners in their chil-dren's education;
- teachers and administrators would like to in-volve families, but many do not know how to build positive and productive programs and consequently are fearful about trying. Thus, educators are stuck in a "rhetoric rut," expressing support for partnerships without taking any action; and
- students at all levels—elementary, middle, and high school—want their families to be more knowledgeable partners about school-ing and are willing to take active roles in as-sisting communications between home and school.

By setting a tone of cooperation, empathy, and respect for parents and by providing com-mitted leadership in meeting the practical and philosophical goals of the IDEA, educational leaders can bring about significant improve-ments in the delivery of education programs and services. This chapter, after covering re-lated legal issues, provides specific suggestions for further improving school-parent relations. These suggestions are designed to build better communications both in conference situations and on a continuing basis. Also provided are guidelines for offering additional services to parents.

LEGAL ISSUES

Parents

As noted throughout this book, parents must be provided the opportunity to be involved in every major phase of the education of a child with a disability. But what happens when the natural or adoptive parents or the legal guardians are not available? The issue of who can act as a parent arises frequently. The IDEA assigns parental responsibilities in such cases as follows:

To Persons Acting as Parents

Persons acting as parents of the child (grandparent, stepparent, or other responsible person with whom the child lives) or a person legally responsible for the child's welfare can carry out the rights and responsibilities given to parents under the IDEA, unless the state or the state's appointed representative is the guardian. When the child is a ward of the state, a surrogate parent must be appointed.

A foster parent may make educational decisions for the child without being appointed surrogate ("acting as a parent") so long as state law does not prohibit foster parents from doing so. This authority is conditioned on the natural parent's authority having been extinguished under state law, the relationship being long-term, the foster parent being willing to participate in educational decisions, and the foster parent having no conflict of interest with the interests of the child.

When the wishes of persons "acting as parents" conflict with those of the natural parents whose rights have not been extinguished under law, the federal regulations are of little help. OSEP's position is that state law should be consulted for the answer.

To Surrogates

A surrogate parent is a person appointed to represent the child in matters related only to the identification, evaluation, and placement of children needing special education and the provision of a free appropriate public education. All other legal rights and duties remain with parents, guardians, or other legal custodians. According to the law, surrogates must be appointed if no parent can be identified, if a "reasonable effort" to discover the whereabouts of the parents or guardians has failed, or if the child is a ward of the state under state laws. (In some states, natural parents may request the ap-

pointment of a surrogate for educational purposes.) A person appointed as a surrogate may not be an employee of the state education agency, the local school district, or any public agency that is involved in the education or care of the child. A surrogate may be an employee of a nonpublic agency that provides only noneducational care for the child if the person meets the other criteria for being a surrogate. The surrogate may not have any interests that conflict with the child's interests and must have adequate knowledge and skills to appropriately represent the child. Foster parents may be trained for and serve in this role, so long as they have no conflict of interest with that of the child. The means of appointing, monitoring, training, and setting the terms of surrogate parent appointments are decided by the state.

Student Records

The confidentiality and accuracy of student information kept by the school is protected by the federal Family Educational Rights and Privacy Act (FERPA) as well as by provisions of the IDEA. FERPA regulations apply to the education records of all students, not just those with disabilities.

Access

Each school must allow parents and their representatives to inspect and review any education record relating to their child. Schools must comply with a parental request for access without unnecessary delay, especially prior to IEP meetings and hearings, but in no instance more than forty-five days after the request has been made. The school must expect to provide explanations and interpretations of records when necessary, and to provide copies (for a reasonable fee when appropriate, and when the charging of a fee does not prevent access) when necessary to allow the parent to have full access to and inspection of the records. Parents are presumed to have the right of access to their child's education records unless the school has received evidence of legal reasons to the contrary.

When a parent believes that information in a record is inaccurate, misleading, or in violation of privacy or other rights of a child, the parent may request that the record be amended. If the school refuses the request, it must advise the parent of the right to a hearing under local school policy as required for all contested education records. If, after the hearing, the school continues to refuse to amend the records, then the parent must be advised of the right to place a written statement in the records giving their reasons for the disagreement. The statement must be kept in the student's records as long as the contested record is kept and must be disclosed to other persons each time the contested record is disclosed.

Confidentiality

Each school must assure the confidentiality of education records and have policies and procedures for doing so, and must provide notice to parents of such policies and procedures. All school staff members collecting or using student records must receive training or instruction regarding record-keeping procedures, and the school must maintain a list, available for public inspection, of the names and positions of employees who may have access to student records. With several exceptions, similar to other education records, the school must be provided with informed written parental consent prior to the release of special education records to others. When personally identifiable student information is no longer needed, the school must notify the parents. Except for information normally kept in permanent school records, the student's records pertaining to special education must be destroyed at the request of the parent.

Each school must keep a record (log) of all persons and agencies having access to the child's records, except access by the parent, a party having written parent consent, and school employees having a legitimate educational interest in the child. School employees accessing a student's record without a legitimate educational interest must make a record of their access and technically must have the parent's written consent. The log must show the name of the party, date, and the purpose of the access to the records. Only the parent and persons responsible for maintaining the record of access may see the log containing the names of persons who have previously reviewed the student's education records.

While parent rights with regard to education records not used for special education are transferred to students upon turning age 18, or on attendance at a post-secondary educational institution, special education records are treated differently. Only if state law provides for the transfer of IDEA Part B, parent rights to the child at the age of majority, may students exercise formerly parental rights over their own special education records.

Statements regarding a child's disciplinary records may be transmitted to the same extent discipline records of nondisabled children are transmitted in the state, especially when they are relevant to the safety of the child or others. If a state requires the transmission of disciplinary records between schools, then the child's records must also include both the current IEP and any statement regarding disciplinary action taken against the child.

Directory Information

Schools may release "directory information" regarding students without the written consent of the parents if two conditions are met. First, the school must advise all parents that it may release directory information regarding students. Second, it must allow parents a reasonable time to object in writing to the release of directory information regarding their child. Directory information includes record data that generally would not be considered harmful if disclosed. It includes, but is not limited to, the following items: name, address, telephone number, date and place of birth, major field of study, participation in officially recognized activities and sports, weight and height of members of athletic teams, dates of attendance, degrees and awards received, and the most recent previous school attended.

If a school does not have a directory information policy, provide notice of it to the parents annually and allow for individual parents to object to release of the information regarding the child, then the school must have the written consent of parents to release such information. Schools need not include all directory items in their local policy if they do not wish to release them. Schools may also add other information not likely to be harmful through release, such as student photographs for yearbooks and student activities promotion.

State law may allow or require the release of education records necessary for the juvenile justice system to effectively service a student under its jurisdiction prior to adjudication. Officials receiving the education record must certify in writing that information will not be disclosed to third parties except as authorized under state law.

Public Notice

Schools must provide parents with a published or announced notice in the media of a description of the children on whom personally identifiable information is maintained in school records, the types of information sought, the methods of gaining information, and the uses to be made of the information. Schools must also provide a summary of school policies and procedures regarding disclosure to third parties, storage, retention, and destruction of personally identifiable student information. Parents must receive a description of all parental rights regarding education records.

PARENTAL RIGHTS—PROCEDURAL SAFEGUARDS

Informed Written Consent

The school must obtain the informed written consent of the parent for its activities prior to conducting an initial evaluation, a re-evaluation, the initial provision of special education and related services (placement), or the release of confidential student education records. Parental consent is not required for administering a test which is administered to all children, or before reviews of existing data. With regard to re-evaluations only, if the parent fails to respond to a school request for consent without actually refusing to give consent, then written consent for the re-evaluation is not necessary if the school can document that it has taken reasonable measures to obtain consent and the parent has failed to respond.

The concept of "informed" written consent denotes a great deal of communicated information when the parent is requested to give consent. The parent must be fully informed, in the parent's native language, if necessary, and understand all information relevant to the proposed activity (initial evaluation, re-evaluation, initial placement, or release of confidential education records). The notice to the parent must contain the seven content requirements found on page 33 as well as an explanation of parent procedural safeguards also found on pages 33–34.

The parent must agree in writing to the school's carrying out of the activity proposed. A mere parent signature without an affirmative statement of agreement consistent with actually giving consent does not imply consent.

The parent should understand that consent may be revoked at any time, but revocation cannot be retroactive. Revocation of consent does not negate an action that has occurred after proper consent was given and before consent was revoked. Revocation of consent, for instance, is not effective for a change in placement already begun, does not require the return of education records previously transferred, or require that evaluations already partially completed be discarded or ignored.

When parents refuse to give schools informed consent for an initial evaluation, initial provision of special education and services, or re-evaluation, the school has three choices: (1) it may accept the parent's refusal; (2) it may continue to work to gain the parent's confidence and consent while attempting modifications and accommodations in the regular classroom; or (3) it may file a request for a mediation or due process hearing in the same manner in which parents begin the mediation or hearing process, so long as it is not prohibited by state law. After an opportunity for a hearing, a hearing officer may override parental objections to initial consent for evaluation or placement, or consent for reevaluation.

Meeting Participation

Parents must be provided a meaningful opportunity to participate in all formal school meetings regarding the identification, evaluation, educational placement of their child, and the provision of FAPE. The meetings to which this applies does not necessarily include school staff preparatory activities or informal, unscheduled conversations involving school personnel on issues such as teaching methodology, lesson plans, and coordination of services when they are not provided for in the IEP. Neither do meetings to which parents must be invited include school staff activities in preparation of school proposals or response to parent proposals that will be discussed with parents at subsequent meetings.

Generally, decisions may be made regarding evaluation, identification, the IEP, and placement (remember, initial evaluation and initial placement require written consent) in the absence of parent participation in meetings when the school can document its reasonable effort to ensure their involvement, including use of tele-

phone conference calls, home visits, or video conferencing, and when the other appropriate team members are present.

Parents must be notified (orally or in writing) of meetings regarding the identification, evaluation, educational placement, and the provision of FAPE early enough to ensure the opportunity to attend. Notice should indicate the purpose of the meeting, the time, the location, and who will be in attendance (at least by title) as well as the potential participation of other persons with knowledge or special expertise regarding the child. IEP meetings must be scheduled at a mutually agreed upon time and place and notice for IEP meetings must include a written explanation of the procedural safeguards found on pages 33–34. In one case, a federal district court reversed a placement decision, at first agreed to by the parents, because the one-day IEP meeting notice did not advise the parents of the specific reason for the meeting or who would be present. The court ruled the lack of notice to the parents that the team would consider a change in the IEP and a resulting subsequent change in placement deprived the parents of meaningful participation in the team decisions (*Amanda S. v. Webster City Community Sch. Dist.*, 1998).

When student transition services involve secondary students, the parents must be advised that the child will be invited and outside agencies providing transition services may be represented at the meeting.

Although written notice of meetings is not required by law, owing to complicated notice details, a desire for documentation, and a desire to help ensure meaningful parent participation, it is advisable to do so.

Federal law now expressly requires educators to do in meetings what professional educators have done consistently over the years: listen to parents. Parent concerns and information provided by parents must be considered during meetings, especially the development and review of their child's IEP.

Generally, the school has the right to determine the extent of use of recording devices at meetings. However, if a parent, for a variety of reasons (i.e., nervousness, disability), is unable to understand what occurs at IEP meetings and an audio or videotape recording is required to ensure that the parent understands the decision-making process and their rights, then the school may not prohibit the use of recording devices.

Proposed Change Prior Notice Requirement

Throughout the initial evaluation, identification, and placement processes, where prior written parent consent is required, parents are for the most part in control of their child's special education status. Once the initial evaluation has been completed and the initial provision of services has begun, except for re-evaluations and the release of student records, parental consent is no longer required for decisions or changes involving the child's educational program. (State law may be different, and should be consulted.) Once a child has been placed in special education, the school exercises greater control over the child's education through its initiation or refusal of changes in programming and services, evaluation, identification, or placement. In those situations where parent prior written consent is not required, federal law requires that the school provide parents with a full, detailed written notice, in understandable language, regarding the proposed action, just as is required for the initial evaluation and initial placement. Instead of requiring prior parental written consent, however, the school may proceed with the proposed change (whether the parents are in full agreement or not) after waiting a reasonable amount of time following notice. This sometimes brief delay in changing programs allows parents the opportunity to consider the proposed change and to provide time for them to formally request a due process hearing involving the proposed action, if desired.

The prior requirement of notice to parents applies each time the school proposes to initiate or change or refuses, after a parent request, to initiate or change the identification, evaluation, or educational placement of the child or the provision of FAPE to the child. Some schools have been caught off-guard by the requirement of parental notice when refusing parent requests in these areas. Parent requests for evaluation, change of disability label, change from a self-contained class to a regular class setting, or changes in IEP goals and objectives require that the school provide this notice both when the school refuses a parent request and when the school agrees with a parent request and "proposes" to make the requested change. Of course, when the school, not the parent, initiates a change, it must also provide the same notice.

For example, consider the situation where a tenth grade student with a specific learning disability in reading is being provided an inclusion program with appropriate supplemental aids and services, but the child continues to struggle to the point of frustration in specific subjects, such as history and literature. At an annual IEP review, the suggestion may arise that the student's placement be changed to a special class for assistance with reading skills, especially as they apply to history and literature classes. Even with unanimous agreement of the IEP team, including the parents, written notice of the proposed change must be provided to the child's parents within a reasonable amount of time prior to the change. The reasonableness of the amount of time would depend on all the circumstances involved (i.e., urgency owing to rapidly changing circumstances). If the parents change their mind and file a request for a due process hearing prior to the initiation of the change, then the current educational placement (i.e., inclusion program including history and literature) must be maintained until the issue is resolved or the parents and school agree to a change. (See "stay put" in Chapter 3.)

When requesting a due process hearing, the parent or the parent's attorney, must provide the following information:

- name and address of the residence of the child;
- name of the school attended;
- description of the problem that is the subject matter of the request for hearing; and
- a proposed resolution of the problem.

The purpose of this notice to the school is to provide an additional opportunity for schools and parents to develop a common frame of reference about the problem that may lead to a satisfactory informal resolution of the issues. A hearing may not be delayed owing to parental failure to file a request for hearing in the required format; however, if an attorney fails to follow this format, available attorney fees may be reduced.

Notice Contents

The content requirements of the written notice to parents are more detailed and lengthy than any other type of notice that schools typically send to parents. This notice must include:

1. A description of the action proposed or refused;
2. An explanation of why the action is proposed or refused;
3. A description of the other options considered and the reasons they were rejected;
4. A description of each evaluation procedure, test, or observation used as a basis for the proposed or refused action;
5. A description of any other factors relevant to the proposal or refusal;
6. A reminder that parents have protections under procedural safeguards and a statement of where a copy of a description of the safeguards may be obtained. If notice is for initial referral for evaluation or initial provision of services, then a copy of the safeguards must be provided; and

7. Sources from which parents may obtain assistance in understanding their rights.

It is possible that a well-designed and well-written IEP may serve as the "written prior notice" when all of the previously mentioned required information is included in the IEP or is included as attachments to the IEP (i.e., meeting reports) and the parents actually receive a copy (Iowa Department of Education, 1998, p. 106).

Procedural Safeguards

At minimum, written notice of procedural safeguards must be provided to parents in a language or manner understood by the parents upon the school's request for consent for the initial evaluation or re-evaluation of the child, upon notification of each IEP meeting, and upon request for a due process hearing. Good educational practice also requires that parents receive procedural safeguards information any time they appear to be unclear about their rights, or when requested by them.

When notice of procedural safeguards to parents is required, it must contain a full explanation of all the following procedural safeguards:

1. Independent educational evaluation (Chapter 4)
2. Prior written notice (this chapter)
3. Parental consent (this chapter)
4. Access to educational records (this chapter)
5. Opportunity to initiate due process hearings (Chapter 3)
6. Child's placement during due process hearings (Chapters 3 and 9)
7. Interim alternative education setting procedures (Chapter 9)
8. Requirements for parent unilateral placement in private schools at public expense (Chapter 6)
9. Mediation (Chapter 3)
10. Due process hearings (Chapter 3)
11. State-level appeals, if applicable (Chapter 3)

12. Civil actions (Chapter 3)
13. Attorney's fees (Chapter 3)
14. State complaint procedures (Chapter 3)

Notice Summary

In summary, schools must provide parents with:

1. A written notice and procedural safeguards and obtain written parental consent for the initial evaluation procedures, re-evaluation procedures, and the initial provision of IEP programs and services (placement).
2. A detailed written notice of proposed subsequent changes in evaluation, identification, placement, or FAPE and school refusal of parent requests in these same areas. If the parent is provided proper notice and does not file a request for due process hearing, then the school may carry out its proposed action after waiting a reasonable amount of time.
3. A written list of parent procedural safeguards each time parents are provided with notice of initial evaluation, notice of re-evaluation, notice of IEP meetings, notice of initial provision of programs and services, and when a due process hearing is requested.

All of the foregoing detailed legal requirements are required because in the past, educators have exhibited differing degrees of knowledge, skill, and empathy when working and communicating with parents. These "legalisms" will become increasingly obsolete when all educators attempt to "walk in the shoes of others," and "treat others as they would like to be treated."

APPROACHES TO IMPROVING COMMUNICATION

The importance of parent participation in the education of children with disabilities cannot be overemphasized. Cooperation between home and school often can be directly related to successful education programs for students. Unfortunately, the opposite is also true. The lack of cooperation frequently results in less than satisfactory results. Parents must be looked to as partners in this entire process. Parents who appear disinterested in their child's educational programming cannot, for the sake of the child, be given up on or pushed aside.

The key to productive school-parent relationships is good two-way communication. As one parent, also a professional in the field, has put it:

> A parent does not measure the school system by the impressive grouping of buildings and lists of degrees of teachers and administrators but by how well the school helps the child with what the parent thinks the child needs. To a large extent, the parent feels that the child's needs are being met if someone at the school listens and responds when the parent wants to talk about the child's needs.*

Parents should never be talked down to or made to feel that they are less than equals in the educational planning for their child. Instead, parents should be consulted regularly about their expectations and goals for the future as well as their child's educational needs.

Methods and Frequency

How often do principals and teachers communicate with parents? What methods are effective? A teacher whose communication goes no further than necessary paperwork and crisis calls to discuss misbehavior should expect parents to build up negative associations with school contact. Such negative associations are

---

*Note From *Home and School Partnerships in Exceptional Education*, p. 38, by Carol T. Michaelis, 1980, Rockville, MD: Aspen Systems Corporation. Copyright 1980 by Aspen Systems Corporation. Reprinted by permission of the author.

not conducive to a good cooperative relationship. Parents of exceptional children need to know that their youngsters are welcome in the school, as is their own involvement. A much better school climate is created if communications with parents occur frequently and if they stress positive, not just troublesome, aspects of the child's school experience. Some examples (especially for elementary school level classes) include:

- a letter of introduction to parents before the school year begins and a handbook of school/class policies sent home the first week or even before school starts;
- contact with parents early in the year to see if they have any skills they would like to share or ways they would like to help (a questionnaire is useful);
- daily or weekly report cards under certain conditions (sociability, behavior, or academics);
- a notebook that the student carries daily or weekly between school and home, in which either teacher or parents can send messages;
- awards or acknowledgments of positive behavior and achievements;
- periodic newsletters for all parents and students (each student must be recognized at some point during the school year);
- telephone calls or conferences to share positive information about the student;
- a stated time when parents are especially welcome;
- invitations to parents to come see new or special projects;
- notifications to local news media about activities of special interest;
- school programs and workshops scheduled at times when all parents could be invited to attend;
- a policy of sending all school communications home with students each Monday; this provides time until Friday for parents to re-

turn necessary papers and offers the school an opportunity to send home positive news each week; and

- workshops on parenting skills, such as how to help with homework.

Educator's Attitudes

To be effective in communicating with parents, educators must be attentive to their own honest attitudes toward the students and their families. Successful cooperation requires attitudes of mutual trust, respect, acceptance, and sharing. Positive school-parent relationships are not reinforced when educators view parents as clients or patients, the cause of the child's disability, adversaries, or intellectual inferiors. Educators who view the parent conferences solely as an opportunity to deliver information—rather than sharing with equals—can expect problems.

In a review of theory and research articles related to parental involvement in their children's education, Hoover-Dempsey and Sandler (1997) concluded that effective school parental involvement programs are positively related to both student achievement and strong parental support for their children's schools. Schools must take parental contributions and involvement seriously before any school practice to increase parental involvement will be successful; half measures will not be enough. Hoover-Dempsey and Sandler recommended a strong commitment to parental involvement exhibited in ways which parents will consider as evidence of school interest and value in parental contributions. Such efforts could include time for parent conferences as part of a teacher's paid duties, installing telephones in classrooms to facilitate communications, and assigning a professional staff member parent-community liaison responsibilities as part of their job description. For parents of secondary school children, researchers also recommend the hiring of someone professionally prepared to facilitate increased communications about teachers' learning goals, activities, and specific suggestions for parental help at school and at home.

Efforts at improving the high-level involvement of parents are most effective when directed at all segments of the community, regardless of socioeconomic level.

How can an individual educator's support, attitude, and information be conveyed effectively? The following is a list of useful techniques and behaviors suggested by researchers studying the relationship of parent involvement in the specific situation of planning for successful inclusion (Bennett, DeLuca, & Bruns, 1997, p. 129):

- Start where the parent is and realize that this may not be the same place as the teacher is in terms of goals for the child.
- Listen for common understandings with the parents.
- Bring up concerns in an honest way in order to problem-solve together.
- Respond to parent concerns by working with the parent to see how these concerns may be approached at home and at school.
- Communicate an attitude of acceptance of the child and a genuine desire and commitment to make inclusion work.
- Focus on the child's strengths.
- Realize that social concerns are very important to parents.
- Access resources needed to make inclusion work.
- Demonstrate the personal qualities of flexibility and open-mindedness.
- Be determined and committed to make inclusion work.

These researchers learned that inclusion planning by teams of parents and educators presents some especially difficult challenges to cooperation. They found that although many parents of children with disabilities had positive attitudes toward inclusion and voiced strong opinions, teachers were found to have signifi-

cantly less positive attitudes toward inclusion, especially those with more years of experience. Teachers tended to express preference for limited parent involvement, where the parents did not question teachers' expertise or become active advocates for their children. Researchers found that as parents became greater advocates for their children, the natural, if not preventable, result was a decline in parent/educator working relationships. This poses the question of how much introspection educators need to employ when efforts to work cooperatively with parents break down and go badly.

Too frequently educators take for granted that parents are in the same place they are in terms of thinking and planning. Then, without taking parent considerations into account in working for specific solutions, educators push on ahead without parent understanding or support. Imagine the disastrous results of using assistive technology devices with children when family attitudes, interests, and values are not taken into account. In such situations, both parents and educators need an exchange of reliable information in order to prevent the waste of scarce educational resources (Hourcade, Parette, & Huer, 1997).

Student homework appears to be a good focus for parent-school collaboration. Parents and teachers can communicate their expectations and individual needs and jointly determine how to monitor successful homework plans (Bos, Nahmias, & Urban, 1999). Regular planned written communication regarding homework assignments, accommodations, responsibilities, and conferences are highly recommended by regular education teachers (Epstein, Munk, Barsuck, Polloway, & Jayanthi, 1999).

Another area of specialized focus for communication concerns might be with parents of especially troublesome youngsters. The developers of a model project for increasing school involvement for families of students with emotional and behavioral disabilities have developed from their experience the following suggestions for improving parent-teacher communication:*

- Maintain a positive and cheery demeanor when working with parents.
- Meet in a comfortable room with furniture that fits adults while recognizing that school may be an uncomfortable setting for parents.
- Provide snacks or food whenever possible. Feed the mind and body.
- Provide everyone an opportunity to speak.
- Facilitate meetings; don't monopolize or preach to one another.
- Don't interpret behavior as attacking; consider behavior of all involved as that of concern for the student.
- Encourage parents to share their expertise with the group. Ask them to bring background material about their child to the group.
- Build on individual strengths and develop plans based on these strengths.
- Try not to dwell on problems. Use problem-solving to generate solutions.
- Use lots of praise and encouragement, and stay optimistic in meetings.
- Listen, listen, listen—and engage parents as equal partners.

Cultural Considerations

Special care and attention must be given to working with parents of culturally and linguistically diverse students. For a variety of reasons, their needs may be different from other parents and a concerted effort may be needed to understand such parents' perceptions of and communication with the school. As a first step, teachers and administrators should work with parents in an effort to better develop commonality in important areas, such as an understanding of and knowledge about the child's disability, alternatives for dealing with the child's disability and the preferred manner in which to do so, and the method and frequency of communication between school and home (Linan-Thompson & Jean, 1997). Educators should also attempt to gain in their knowledge of and sensitivity to cultural diversity and recognize many parents' lack of understanding of American school systems, special education, and written materials (Craig, Hull, Haggart, & Parez-Sellers, 2000; Sileo, Sileo, & Prater, 1996). An understanding of cultural differences often can be used to enhance appropriate family communication and planning. In some cultures it would be desirable to enlist the help and support of a well-respected community leader to serve as liaison and facilitator until trust and understanding are strengthened. When extended family is a cultural characteristic, those persons who often care for the child should be involved with parents in school conferences and planning (Parette & Petch-Hogan, 2000). Recognizing different familiar cultural traits and making appropriate adjustments will lead to better educational programming for the child (Mathews, 2000).

Conferencing Skills

How are an educator's support, attitude, and information conveyed effectively? Through words and actions. Figure 2-1 is a chart of common "barriers" to open and trusting communication in conferences between educators and parents, prepared by a parent-advocacy trainer. It also provides a mirror image of a list of "bridges" that enhance an effective parent/educator cooperative relationship:

PARENT SERVICES

In spite of problems they may have had with the schools, whether as students themselves or as

---

*From "Project Destiny: Engaging Families With Emotional and Behavioral Disabilities," by D. Cheney, B. Manning, & D. Upham (1997), *Teaching Exceptional Children, 30* (1) p. 29. Copyright 1997 by The Council for Exceptional Children. Reprinted by permission.

FIGURE 2-1 *Effective communication*

Barriers	Bridges
Appear to be the authority	Be interested, not impressive; promote the family's confidence in their own authority
Avoid the issue or patronize and pay lip service to the family's concern(s)	Be interested, not impressive; promote the family's concern(s); not getting their message will "come back to haunt you"
Make snap recommendations based on emotions	Get enough information; find out what has been tried before; ask advice of others
Form opinions based on stereotypes, rumors, etc	Wait and form your own opinions; observe behaviors
Make excuses and blame factors you cannot control	Focus discussion on factors you can control
Assume the family's concern is directed at you or your job performance	Keep in mind that the family is usually concerned or upset about an issue that has nothing to do with you personally
Talk too much and control the discussion	Give the family at least two-thirds of the time allotted to the meeting
Ask questions that intimidate the family	Respond with statements and questions
Use educational jargon; be patronizing and condescending	Be sensitive to the language, levels, vocabularies, and background of the family; adjust your language, but be yourself
Be dogmatic; use simplistic statements	Be open to new approaches, then clarify your position, based on past experiences and observations

participants in their children's educational experience, many parents are likely to look to the schools as an important—perhaps the most important—source of help in raising their children. In addition to scheduling conferences to discuss individual needs, many schools offer more intensive services and structured parent activities, including family counseling and referrals, parent advisory committees, parent-to-parent support groups, and parent training programs and workshops (Bailey & Smith, 2000).

Student IEPs may, when desired, expressly provide for "parent counseling and training" as

a related service. That phrase is defined in federal rules in such a way that parents can be empowered in ways which allow them to provide stronger support to school efforts:

7. Parent counseling and training means
   i. Assisting parents in understanding the special needs of the child;
   ii. Providing parents with information about child development; and
   iii. helping parents acquire the necessary skills that will allow them to support the implementation of their child's IEP or IFSP [34C.F.R. 300.24(b) (7), 2000].

Barriers	Bridges
Give too many suggestions	Ask the family in what areas they want suggestions; keep suggestions limited; ask questions that lead the family to develop their own problem-solving skills
Limit accessiblility to families	Let the family know the times it is most convenient to contact you
Take on a tough problem with too little time for discussion	Schedule discussion times, allowing ample time to reach a resolution
Fail to follow through on promises	Pinpoint and follow through on all things promised by the school
Avoid admitting you made a mistake	Admit openly when you are wrong; accept your share of the problem
Encourage the family to take up a problem they are having with another staff member or person directly, not with you; talk about problems with another staff member when the person is not there	Focus on working together to improve outcomes for the student
Suggest counseling before establishing a relationship built on trust	Wait until the family asks for help or until a good relationship is established before suggesting a counselor or support service
Overuse reflective listening	Be natural and relaxed and use good listening and communication skills

From "Establishing Respectful Partnerships: A Parent Advocate's View," by Diedre Hayden, 1993, *EDLAW Briefing Paper III* (5), p. 8. Copyright 1993 by EDLAW, Inc. Reprinted by permission.

Following is a partial list of the benefits that parent counseling and training may have for the student, parent, and school:*

- Knowledge and understanding will replace fear and anger.
- The parent(s) gain an understanding of their child's disability.

- The parent(s) are better informed to be an equal team member.
- The school can use the same information on disabilities to educate general education teachers.
- The parent(s) will have a better understanding of future ramifications for their child.
- The parent(s) will be better equipped to discuss the disability with their child.
- The student will be better informed to advocate for him/herself.
- They can be trained to implement (or support) certain parts of the IEP.

*From "Parent Counseling and Training: A Related Service Under the Individuals With Disabilities Education Act," (p. 17) developed by J. Copenhaver, 1996, Logan, Utah: Mountain Plains Regional Resource Center. Reprinted with permission.

• Parents can help other parents who have children with the same disability.

Sussell, Carr, and Hartman (1996, p. 55) have provided several specific suggestions for parent services for family support:*

• Parent Advisory Committee newsletter
• List of community resources (e.g., human resources, advocacy, and self help)
• Lists of state and national organizations of interest to families with special needs
• Information folders on different disabilities for distribution to, or reference by, parents and staff
• A file containing articles of special interest to parents
• Parent access to instructional materials
• Parent invitation to participate in staff development activities
• Staff development programs regarding the "changing role of parents"
• Establish parent support groups
• Regular education children educated regarding persons with disabilities
• Establish respite care opportunities.

Donley and Williams (1997) have reported on an excellent family education program in a school that in part involves family members observing their children regularly in school, developing data sets on their own child's progress, and then creating a poster presentation for sharing the year's activities and growth with other parents as an end of the year group activity.

For parents of students in culturally or linguistically diverse schools, the schools can provide many programs that have multiple benefits for the school and community. Parent education programs can be established which are designed to teach English as a second language, basic

reading, and mathematics and reasoning skills to improve parents' functional skills and sense of self-worth. Such programs can be developed to ensure that parents and schools become more equal partners in problem-solving discussions about students. Awareness training programs that utilize role playing and simulations can be used to build parent confidence and understanding in their relationship with school personnel. Employment opportunities for parents, such as teacher associates, can help ensure a bond between schools and their culturally and linguistically diverse communities (Craig et al., 2000; Sileo, Sileo, & Prater, 1996).

Programs directed toward parents can be of value to many parents and certainly can help build trust and involvement in the schools. However, a caution is sounded again and again by experienced educators: Parents have different expectations and different needs. Their ability to cope is affected by a myriad of factors, including the temperament of the child, their own attitudes toward the youngster, their social involvement and support system, their ability and willingness to seek and use help, the ages of their other children, the discipline methods, the parents' personality and time-management skills, and the extent of agreement between parents on child-rearing values and strategies (Bailey & Smith, 2000).

Parents must be respected as individuals. Educators cannot expect all parents to want to participate equally or to take advantage of all the services the school has arranged, particularly if such arrangements are made without asking parents what help they feel they need. Until parents perceive a need for advice or assistance, they may not listen; furthermore, too many offers of help can be overwhelming and a burden in themselves.

Meetings of Parents

Meetings of parents may take many forms, including informal sessions planned and run by

*From "Families R Us: Building a Parent/School Partnership," by A. Sussel, S. Carr, & A. Hartman, 1996, *Teaching Exceptional Children, 28* (4), p. 55. Copyright 1996 by the Council for Exceptional Children. Adapted by permission.

parents in their home, school-wide conferences organized by administration to inform parents of policies or solicit their help in developing school policies, Parent-Teacher Association (PTA) events, and special interest groups small enough to encourage parents to speak and share.

The two general topics of most importance to parents are how to help their children progress in school and how to be effective parents. These two topics can be used as a central focus for providing supporting activities to parents.

Some educators suggest regular monthly telephone calls to parents. The goals are to seek out parents' questions and concerns and to give parents a regular opportunity to talk about their child without being encumbered by negative messages from school. Gustafson (1998) has related great personal success with this approach in terms of consistent, positive parent feedback.

Some schools have experimented with telephone voice messaging systems where teachers and principals leave both general and child specific messages for parents. Parents, in turn, can leave questions and comments in teacher and principal voice mail. Researchers have found that the greater use of these systems was by parents of children in special education programs (Morris, Kay, Fitzgerald, & Miller, 1997). Programs using voice mail can be established on a district-wide basis, or tailor-made for improving communication between the school and specific families.

An indirect service to parents might include planned activities with and for the siblings of students with disabilities. Siblings have many questions that deserve answers, needs that should be met, and perspectives that should be understood. A variety of sibling activities and workshops can be undertaken which will result in a stronger school/family partnership (Cramer et al., 1997).

Some schools and intermediate educational agencies feel so strongly about the importance of the school relationship with parents that programs of assistance and cooperation have become formalized and made part of the agency structure. The Parent Education Partnership (PEP) Program at one intermediate educational service agency maintains a local parent support-group list of over thirty-five area parent, parent-educator, and disability-specific support groups and their primary contact persons so that agency staff can assist parents in locating parent peer-support. The PEP Program provides a resource library and a staff of trained parents and educators who are willing to assist other parents and educators in their efforts to communicate and understand each other. Some local school districts that make up the agency also have appointed "Parent Partners" to assist parents and local groups in identifying additional information resources and support (Grant Wood Area Education Agency, 1997).

SCHOOL CHOICE AND ITS IMPLICATIONS

School choice (i.e., charter schools, vouchers) has gained popularity as a school reform issue, especially among politicians, while little solid research has been completed to help verify its validity. When parents exercise choice options, local public schools lose in numerous ways that extend beyond reduction in local school revenues. When children with disabilities transfer, schools lose the opportunity to have strong school support in the community from parents who are often the most concerned for their children and the most loyal to those who understand their children's needs.

A group of researchers at the University of Minnesota have been paying close attention to the "open enrollment" form of school choice and its impact on students with disabilities. They recently completed a study with the primary purpose of gaining a better understanding of parent motivations for transferring their children with disabilities through the Minnesota open enrollment choice program (Lang, Ys-seldyke, & Lehr, 1997). A total of 12% of the 19,000 Minnesota students transferring to an-other school district in the 1995–96 school year were students with disabilities. The resulting data and analysis have a great deal to say about how some local schools are failing to meet the needs of students with disabilities and the ex-pectations of parents. Researchers learned that Minnesota parents who made the difficult choice to open enroll their children with dis-abilities in another school district expressed the following unmet needs of their children as jus-tification for their decision:

• Access to programs in an inclusive setting with appropriate accommodations and adap-tations to prove real access.
• Opportunities for personal and social adjust-ment among role modeling peers where friendships and sense of belonging is fostered.
• A warm, positive, supportive environment that values their child.
• Good two-way, respectful communication between home and school.

The researchers recommend that each school determine the local reasons for parental decisions to transfer and communicate those findings to all personnel. From there, school staff can examine and improve home-school communications and improve the provision of student accommodations and modifications. School leaders should regularly evaluate school climate and attempt to establish a more positive learning environment, determine whether all students are being challenged, and help per-sonnel to be more sensitive to the needs of chil-dren with disabilities and their families.

CONCLUSION

From its inception twenty-five years ago, the IDEA has placed the importance of parent in-volvement front and center in special education programming for children with disabilities. The 1997 Amendments to the IDEA have greatly strengthened that philosophy by providing for in-creased legal requirements for parental participa-tion in the decision-making processes, especially evaluation and placement. But far and above the legal requirements is the knowledge and experi-ence of educators about how the education of children, both with and without disabilities, is a cooperative effort between home, school, and community. When any one of those factors is di-minished, omitted, overlooked, or ignored, edu-cation efforts are much less likely to succeed.

Educators must treat parents and families of children with disabilities as they themselves wish to be treated. Anything less diminishes us all.

REFERENCES

Amanda S. v. Webster City Community School District, 27 IDELR 698 (N.D. Ia. 1998).

Assistance to States for the Education of Children With Disabilities (2000), 34 C.F.R. Part 300.

Bailey, A. B., & Smith, S. W. (2000). Providing effec-tive coping strategies and supports for families with children with disabilities. *Intervention in School and Clinic, 35* (5), 294.

Bennett, T., DeLuca, D., & Bruns, D. (1997). Putting inclusion into practice: Perspectives of teachers and parents. *Exceptional Children, 64* (1), 115–131.

Bos, C. S., Nahmias, M. L., & Urban, M. A. (1999). Targeting home-school collaboration for students with ADHD. *Teaching Exceptional Children, 31* (6), 4–9.

Cheney, D., Manning, B., & Upham, D. (1997). Pro-ject destiny: Engaging families of students with emotional and behavioral disabilities. *Teaching Exceptional Children, 30* (1), 24–29.

Copenhaver, J. (1996). *Parent counseling and train-ing: A related service under the Individuals With Disabilities Education Act.* Logan, UT. Utah State University: Mountain Plains Regional Resource Center.

Craig, S., Hull, K., Haggert, A. G., & Perez-Sellers, M. (2000). Promoting cultural competence through teacher assistance teams. *Teaching Exceptional Children, 32* (3), 6–12.

Cramer, S., Erzkus, A., Mayweather, K., Pope, J., Roeder, J., & Tone, T. (1997). Connecting with siblings. *Teaching Exceptional Children, 30* (1), 46–51.

Donley, C. R., & Williams, G. (1997). Parents exhibit children's progress at a poster session. *Teaching Exceptional Children, 29* (4), 46–51.

Epstein, M. H., Monk, D. D., Bursuck, W. D., Polloway, E. A., & Jayanth, M. (1999). Strategems for improving home-school communication about homework for students with disabilities. *The Journal of Special Education, 33* (3), 166–176.

Epstein, J. L. (1995). School/family/community partnerships: Caring for the children we share. *Phi Delta Kappan, 76* (9), 701–717.

Grant Wood Area Education Agency (1997). *A solution-focused process for addressing student needs.* Cedar Rapids, IA: Author.

Gustafson, C. (1998). Phone home. *Educational Leadership, 56* (2), 31–32.

Hayden, D. (1963). Establishing respectful partnerships: A parent-advocate's view. *EDLAW Briefing Paper, III*(5), Rosenfeld, S. J. (Ed.), Hollywood, FL: EDLAW, Inc.

Hoover-Dempsey, K. V., & Sandler, H. M. (1997). Why do parents become involved in their children's education? *Review of Educational Research, 67* (1), 3–42.

Hourade, J. J., Parette, Jr., H. P., & Huer, M. B. (1997). Family and cultural alert: Considerations in assistive technology assessment. *Teaching Exceptional Children, 30* (1), 40–44.

Iowa Department of Education (1998). *Their future . . . Our guidance: Iowa IEP guidebook.* Des Moines, IA: Author.

Lang, C. M., Ysseldyke, J. E., & Lehr, C. A. (1997). Parents perspectives on school choice. *Teaching Exceptional Children, 30* (1), 14–19.

Linan-Thompson, S., & Jean, R. E. (1997). Completing the parent participation puzzle: Accepting diversity. *Teaching Exceptional Children, 30* (2), 46–50.

Mathews, R. (2000). Cultural patterns of South Asian and Southeast Asian Americans. *Intervention in School and Clinic, 36* (2), 101–104.

Michaelis, C. (1980). *Home and school partnerships in exceptional education.* Rockville, MD: Aspen Publishers.

Morris, J. L., Kay, P. J., Fitzgerald, M. D., & Miller, C. T. (1997). Home/school communication: The use of a computerized voice message system by families of children with disabilities. *Case In Point, 10* (2), 42–53.

Parette, H. P., & Petch-Hogan, B. (2000). Approaching families: Facilitating culturally/linguistically diverse family involvement. *Teaching Exceptional Children, 33* (2), 4–10.

Sileo, T. W., Sileo, A. P., & Prater, M. A. (1996). Parent and professional partnerships in special education: Multicultural, considerations. *Intervention in School and Clinic, 31* (3), 145–153.

Sussell, A., Carr, S., & Hartman, A. (1996). Families R Us: Building a parent/school partnership. *Teaching Exceptional Children, 28* (4), 53–57.

Turnbull, A. P., & Ruef, M. (1997). Family perspectives on inclusive lifestyle issues for people with problem behavior. *Exceptional Children, 63* (2), 211–227.

RECOMMENDED READINGS

Davern, L. (1996). Listening to parents of children with disabilities. *Educational Leadership, 53* (7), 61–63. This article provides ten specific suggestions for improving relationships with parents of included students.

Donley, C. R., & Williams, G. (1997). Parents exhibit children's progress at a poster session. *Teaching Exceptional Children, 29* (4), 46–51. This article discusses a parent/educator program with some interesting unique elements.

Epstein, J. L. (1995). School/family/community partnerships: Caring for the children we share. *Phi Delta Kappan, 76* (9), 701–717. This is a strong article with research based recommendations for improving school family relationships.

Felber, S. A. (1997). Strategies for parent partnerships. *Teaching Exceptional Children, 30* (1), 20–23. The article provides seven straightforward suggestions for developing mutual trust and respect with parents.

Harry, B. (1992). Restructuring the participation of African-American parents in special education. *Exceptional Children, 59* (2), 123–131. This article presents specific suggestions on how to more actively involve parents in assessment, reporting, advocacy, and policy development.

Jayanthi, M., Bursuck, W., Epstein, M. H., & Polloway, E. A. (1997). Strategies for successful homework. *Teaching Exceptional Children, 30* (1), 47. The article provides suggestions on how to improve student homework results through better communication with parents.

Kay, P. J., & Fitzgerald, M. (1997). Parents + teachers + parents = real involvement. *Teaching Exceptional Children, 30* (1), 88–11. The article discusses the benefits of involving parents in classroom research activities.

Linan-Thompson, S., & Jean, R. E. (1997). Completing the parent participation puzzle: Accepting diversity. *Teaching Exceptional Children, 30* (2), 46–50. The article provides an example of how one school set out to improve communication with culturally and linguistically diverse parents.

McDonald, L., Kisela G., Martin, C., & Wheaten, S. (1996). The Hazeldean Project. *Teaching Exceptional Children, 29* (2), 28–32. The article provides helpful hints on improving relationships with parents through regular parent information sessions.

Sussell, A., Carr, S., & Hartman, A. (1996). Families R Us: Building a parent/school partnership. *Teaching Exceptional Children, 28* (4), 53–57. The article provides specific ideas for building and maintaining good home-school relationship programs.

Williams, V. I., & Carthedge, G. (1997). Passing notes to parents. *Teaching Exceptional Children, 30* (1), 30–34. The article describes a daily notebook communication system used with parents and its success.

Relevant Federal Regulations

34 C. F. R. Part 99	Student records (FERPA).
34 C. F. R. §300.19	Parent.
.345	Parent participation.
.403	Placement of children by parents if FAPE is an issue.
.452	Provision of services—basic requirement.
.500	General responsibility of public agencies-definitions.
.501	Opportunity to examine records; parent participation in meetings.
.502	Independent educational evaluation.
.504	Procedural safeguard notice.
.505	Parental consent.
.515	Surrogate parents.
.562	Access rights (records).
.563	Record of access.
.564	Records on more than one child.
.565	List of types and locations of information.
.566	Fees
.567	Amendment of records at parent's request.
.568	Opportunity for a hearing.
.569	Result of hearing.
.570	Hearing procedures.
.571	Consent.
.572	Safeguards.
.573	Destruction of information.
.574	Children's rights.
.575	Enforcement.
.576	Disciplinary information.

CHAPTER 3

DUE PROCESS HEARINGS, MEDIATION, AND COMPLAINTS

CHAPTER PREVIEW

Focus

Parents and, in some limited situations, the schools may request an impartial due process hearing to resolve differences regarding the identification, evaluation, placement, or right of a student with disabilities to a free appropriate education. In practice, these due process hearings usually are requested by parents but decided in favor of the schools, and they are expensive, time-consuming, and emotionally exhausting for both parties. Consequently, such hearings should be viewed as a last resort in resolving disputes. Alternatives to due process hearings exist and are used regularly.

Legal Issues

The IDEA requires that parents receive written notice each time the school proposes (or refuses) to initiate or change a student's identification, or evaluation, or to change educational placement or provision of FAPE. That notice, in addition to describing and explaining the proposed (or refused) action in detail, must remind parents of their rights, including the right to request mediation and a due process hearing. If a due process hearing is requested, both parents and the school are guaranteed the right to:

- be advised and accompanied by a lawyer or experts if they choose;
- present evidence, call and cross-examine witnesses;
- expect an impartial hearing officer;
- prevent the introduction of evidence not disclosed by the opposing side at least five business days before the hearing;
- receive a written decision within forty-five days after the hearing was requested;
- receive a copy of a verbatim record of the hearing; and
- appeal the hearing decision into court.

     When due process hearings are held, the parents may:

- have the hearing conducted at a convenient time and place;
- have the child present;
- open the hearing to the public if they choose;
- have the child remain in the current educational placement until the dispute is resolved; and
- receive compensation for attorney's fees if they prevail.

The law does not require due process hearings in all dispute situations, only those dealing with identification, evaluation, educational placement, or provision of FAPE, nor does the law explicitly define all aspects of the hearing proceedings. Some variations will occur in the process from state to state and among individual hearing officers. In general, due process hearings can be seen as somewhat similar to court proceedings but usually much less formal.

Parents and organizations may file complaints with the state regarding technical violations of the law. Formal complaints must be investigated and a report of findings issued.

Rationale

The Fourteenth Amendment to the U. S. Constitution guarantees that no state shall "deprive any person of life, liberty, or property, without due process of law." Yet in the past, millions of children with disabilities were systematically denied access to public education. Their parents could protest and negotiate but had no clear legal recourse if they were unhappy with the school's decisions. The due process hearing guaranteed by the IDEA, along with an opportunity for mediation and the complaint process, now provides such recourse and together provide assurance that the intent of the IDEA will be carried out.

Approaches

Most disagreements between parents and schools can be settled without going into due process hearings, and it is to both parties' benefit to do so. Preventive school practices include: creating a cooperative environment in the school, providing satisfying and meaningful opportunities for parents to become involved in their child's education, and providing and using other problem-solving procedures such as nonbinding negotiation and informal mediation by a mutually agreed-upon mediator.

THE SHADOW OF DUE PROCESS HEARINGS

The possibility of due process hearings hangs over most inclusion school environments like a mysterious and ever-present threat. Few staff members know exactly what the hearings entail and fewer still have ever been involved in one, but everyone knows such hearings have a bad reputation. "What makes these hearings happen?", "What goes on in them, anyway?", and especially, "How can I avoid them?" are haunting questions in the back of many an educator's mind.

Where has the overwhelmingly negative reputation of due process hearings come from? Not from frequency of occurrence. The number of disputes between parents and schools that actually end up going to hearings is relatively small. The onslaught of hearing requests that many educators have feared over the years has failed to materialize.

Actually, the number of hearings requested does not necessarily equate to hearings held. Sometimes, hearings are requested to get someone's attention, to qualify for mediation, or to use as leverage for seeking settlement. One study showed that of 189 hearing requests filed in one Midwestern state during a three-year period, 118 were settled prior to the actual hearing (McKinney & Schultz, 1996). In a nation-wide study conducted by the National Association of State Directors of Special Education (1999), the data established that in 1998 there were 9827 requests for due process hearing, but that about 6500 (66.2%) were settled by means other than a formal hearing.

Neither does the bad reputation of hearings result from schools' continued failure in hearings. McKinney and Schultz (1996) found that out of 105 major issues presented in the seventy-one cases actually resulting in a hearing, the parents won 58% of the issues decided. However, this result appears to be an anomaly and may result from the study's methodology. Most other studies among the various states have shown a parent rate of victory between 20% and 43% (Newcomer, Zirkel, & Tavola, 1998).

Although parents initiate the vast majority of hearings, it is not surprising that they win a relatively small number. Schools have the money and staff resources, as well as the opportunity, knowledge, and experience to provide appropriate education programs. When necessary, those same school resources can be used to defend the school's actions in a hearing.

The fact is, of course, that schools have time, money, and resources for hearings only at the expense of educational programs, and this is where the stigma may originate. Due process hearings drain time, money, and emotional energy from the system that would otherwise be more positively directed toward improving childrens' education. Hearings are expensive in a number of ways. An average hearing may cost thousands of dollars and court appeals many thousands more. Such hearings require substantial investments in staff time, thus aggravating resentment at the paperwork already demanded by the IDEA. As if this were not enough, hearings are damaging to community attitudes, because the implicit content of every hearing is an accusation of wrongdoing or, at the very least, neglect on the part of the school. The outcry and zealous lobbying of dissatisfied parents is rarely matched or compensated by testimony from the majority of parents who are satisfied. All this tends to lower staff morale and to increase resentment toward special education.

In a study of parent and school official satisfaction with the due process hearing process in Pennsylvania, Goldberg and Kuriloff (1991) found that both parents and school officials concluded that the legal model of dispute resolution evidenced in the hearings was "ill-suited" to resolving educational disputes. Both parents and school officials expressed belief that participation in adversary hearings created unnecessary antagonism between them. Goldberg and Kuriloff concluded that alternative models of dispute resolution, such as negotiation or mediation, should be used for dispute resolution in special education. Such forms of dispute resolution would allow professional educators and parents to work together to avoid disruptive, divisive, and costly due process hearing battles.

Other hidden costs to education are generated not by due process hearings themselves but by fear of them. The avoidance of hearings too often becomes an end in itself; a goal that begins to divert time and attention away from the effort to meet students' needs. That also means that because of the fear of due process hearings, a child may not receive an appropriate education. As early as 1979, Jacobs warned:

> Constant adversarial pressure cannot help but create in some educators an attitude designed to protect the system rather than the child's best interest . . . to make them reluctant to recommend services which they will be forced to justify at some upcoming hearing. This timidity in professional decision making can . . . place self-protection ahead of concern for the best interest of their client. (p. 88)

The key word here is "adversarial." A cooperative attitude toward decision-making—the sense that the parents and the school share the best interests of the child as a common goal—is difficult to maintain once legal adversarial procedures have been interjected between the bargaining parties. The situation is similar to that experienced by many divorcing couples who find a relatively amicable separation transformed into a legal war over children and possessions fueled by their emotions and the lawyers they have hired. It is the unfamiliar and exhausting role of adversaries that participants in due process hearings often find most profoundly distressing. In the quasi-judicial due process setting, educators find themselves suddenly cast in the role of the villains, the accused, and parents are encouraged, by the legal structure and the proceedings, to view them that way. The child involved cannot help but suffer, no matter what the outcome.

Thus, the challenges confronting educators with regard to due process are two-fold. On one hand, it is important to avoid adversarial settings as much as possible. On the other, it is equally important to avoid sacrificing educational quality for institutional safety. The most productive policy is not to focus on the negative aspect (how to avoid becoming embroiled in hearings), but rather on the positive (how to create a relationship of cooperation and trust with parents and staff in the best interest of the child).

LEGAL ISSUES

Hearings result from primarily two types of situations: (1) the parent has refused consent for initial evaluation, re-evaluation, or initial provision of programs and services and the school has requested a hearing, or (2) the parent objects to the school's proposed change or refusal regarding the identification, evaluation, educational placement or provision of FAPE and has filed a request for hearing.

Conduct of a Hearing

If a hearing cannot be avoided, it is important to be well-prepared for it. Part of that preparation must include knowing what to expect.

Following receipt of a parent or school request for due process hearing, the school or state, depending on the state's system of hearings, has forty-five days in which to render a final decision through an impartial hearing officer. If there is a review of the local level (first tier) decision at the state level (second tier), then the state must complete the review of the local decision within thirty days. Continuances (time extensions) may be granted by the hearing officer at the request of any party. The law does not delineate valid reasons for requesting a continuance, but hearing officers will usually grant requests when "good cause" (such as the need for additional evaluation or time for settlement negotiation) is shown. Approximately half of the states use a two-tier hearing and review process (McKinney & Schultz, 1996; Newcomer, Zirkel, & Tarola 1998). Each hearing or state review must be conducted at a time and place that are reasonably convenient to the parents.

The conduct of a due process hearing is less formal than a court proceeding and will vary somewhat from state to state. The specific procedure is under the control of the hearing officer and usually proceeds through the following steps:

1. The hearing officer will make an introductory statement, including introductions of the parties. The hearing officer then describes what due process hearings are, the conduct and procedures to be followed, and states the issue to be resolved in the present hearing. Frequently, hearings will be preceded by informal pre-hearing conferences, either in person or by conference telephone call, in order to discuss evidentiary issues, interpretations of law, and procedural matters.

   Under the direction of the hearing officer, participants resolve any preliminary matters, such as the absence of a witness, objections to a piece of evidence, whether the hearing will be open or closed to the public (parent choice), and whether witnesses will be prohibited from being present other than while testifying (sequester).

2. Each party (usually the party filing the request for hearing goes first) may present a brief oral opening statement. The opening statement explains what that party will attempt to prove through the introduction of evidence and what result is desired.

3. The first party (again, usually the party filing the request for hearing goes first) presents its evidence, with a cross-examination permitted by the other party. Most trial evidentiary rules, such as "hearsay," do not apply to administrative hearings. The hearing officer determines and allows evidence that is reliable, probative, and relevant.

4. The other party presents its evidence in the same manner, with cross-examination permitted by the first party.

5. A party may prohibit, through objection, the introduction of any evidence that has not been disclosed to that party at least five business days prior to the hearing. The primary purpose of this evidentiary rule is to lessen the likelihood of surprise evidence.

6. Parties must disclose all evaluations and accompanying recommendations at least five business days prior to a hearing, or they may be precluded from introducing the information at hearing.

7. Both parties are allowed to present brief rebuttal and closing statements.

8. Some states allow the filing of written arguments.

9. The hearing officer adjourns the hearing (and must produce written findings and decision within the allotted remaining time period).

10. A party may obtain a verbatim record of the hearing; thus, one must be made. Parents may receive a copy at no cost.

Other interesting and potentially important points to know about hearings include:

- The hearing officer need not decide in favor of either party's recommendation but may come up with an alternative solution;
- Grounds for a hearing decision may include more, but not less, than those spelled out in the law and may not interfere with other legally guaranteed parent/student rights;
- Parents may have the child attend, although educators are divided on the issue. The child

may be called as a witness or may meet with the hearing officer and attorneys before the hearing session begins;

- Federal rules do not state whether either party in the hearing has the burden of proof (some state special education rules provide for the burden of proof on one party or the other). Hearing officers most often simply weigh the evidence presented by both sides and decide in favor of the stronger or more convincing position. One exception may be issues of least restrictive environment; a number of courts have ruled that transfer of a student to a more restrictive program must be justified, and the burden of proof lies with the party proposing the more restrictive placement;
- Hearing officers must be impartial and may not be employees of the school or state educational agency, and they may not be persons with professional or other conflicts of interest;
- Hearing officers may have other titles, such as administrative law judge, dependent upon state law; and
- Although the parties in due process hearings are quite often aided by lawyers, one must be cautious in making this choice. Few attorneys—not even all school district attorneys—are adequately and currently prepared on the complexities of special education law.

Appeals

Local hearing decisions in some states must be appealed to a state hearing reviewer or panel (second tier) for review before being appealed to a court. In most situations, this involves only a review of the records of the original hearing. For this reason, it is important that the original hearing be recorded. If a simple tape-recording system is used, the hearing officer must make sure that the equipment is functioning properly, the voices are clearly audible, adequate blank tapes are available, and speakers verbally identify themselves before speaking. Many states

hire licensed court reporters or stenographers for hearings and have professionally prepared transcripts made of hearing testimony. Although the accuracy is better, it is much more expensive. In some states, a review may include the opportunity to present further oral or written argument and additional evidence.

Administrative hearing decisions at the state level involving either one- or two-tier systems may be appealed further through civil suits in the appropriate state or federal courts. If no appeal is made within the time prescribed by law, then the previous hearing decision becomes the final decision in the matter.

Attorney Fees

Courts may award reasonable attorney fees to parents, but not schools, who prevail in due process hearings and litigation. Fees are prorated when parents prevail only in part. Schools may protect themselves from potential payment of parent attorney fees through the offering of a written settlement more than ten days prior to a scheduled hearing. If the offer is not accepted and the hearing officer does not render a decision which is more favorable to the parents than the offer of settlement, then attorney fees will not be awarded for legal services provided after the offer was made. This provision of law encourages schools to offer reasonable settlement terms in advance of hearings in order to encourage dispute resolution without the necessity of a hearing. Surprisingly to some, there is evidence that the hiring of an attorney for representation by at least one of the parties for due process hearings lessens the likelihood that the disagreement will ever go to hearing (McKinney & Schultz, 1996). It is speculated that settlement in appeals becomes more likely because attorneys are accustomed to settling civil cases before they go to trial and they bring that negotiating philosophy and skill to the special education arena. Thus, in some situations, the risk of creating a more hostile adversarial environment is apparently decreased through the use of attorneys. Pre-hearing settlement greatly reduces the time and financial resources committed by all parties and as lessens the likelihood of damaging the parent-school relationship beyond repair.

Stay Put or Status Quo

During the pending proceedings of the administrative due process hearing, unless the school and parent agree otherwise, the child must remain in the "current educational placement." This provision of law is sometimes referred to as the "stay put" or "status quo" provision. When a child is seeking admission to a school for the first time and a dispute arises, the child must be admitted to school pending completion of the proceedings.

When an initial state hearing officer decision or the state review decision agrees with the position of the parents that a change in placement is appropriate, the change will take place immediately, even though additional court proceedings may be imminent. In some situations where students are involved with drugs or weapons at school or at school events, the "stay-put" concept is applied differently so that school officials may have more latitude in dealing with these important issues (see Chapter 9).

ALTERNATIVE APPROACHES TO RESOLVING PROBLEMS

The law does not require that disputes between schools and the parents of children with disabilities be resolved in due process hearings; it provides that format only as a last legal recourse. Various less antagonistic and less expensive means of resolving conflicts have been used successfully. More and more school districts are adopting less formal models as preliminary alternatives for parents in dispute resolution. Some enter into informal negotiation or informal mediation; another is formal mediation. Not all efforts at dispute resolution result

in hostility. It is, after all, a problem-solving process, and working toward the goal of improving educational opportunity for students can open better lines of communication and lead to the building of trust.

Mediation

For many years, some states have provided a formalized type of mediation on a voluntary basis at the state level. In addition to the benefits of less cost and less time spent in relation to the due process hearing, mediation can salvage a working relationship between parents and schools (Osborne, 1996, p. 242). The high success rates of mediation and the generally more favorable maintenance of a working relationship between school and parent have resulted in the 1997 Amendments to IDEA which now require that states make mediation available on a voluntary basis.

Currently, each school must provide the opportunity for mediation, often through state-prescribed processes, for dispute resolution between parents and schools involving the same issues which are subject to a due process hearing. [These issues are the initiation or change (or school refusal of initiation or change) of the identification, evaluation, placement, or provision of FAPE through an IEP for a child.] At minimum, an opportunity for voluntary mediation between the school and parent must be available whenever a hearing is requested.

Mediation procedures must ensure that participation is voluntary on the part of the parties to the dispute, the hearing does not delay a parent's right to a timely due process hearing decision (forty-five days), and the hearing is conducted by an impartial, trained mediator who is knowledgeable in the law regarding special education. The mediation process must be conducted at no cost to the parent and must be held in a location convenient to the parties.

Agreements reached in the mediation process must be reduced to writing. In order to encourage the parties to put forth, discuss, and consider fully the various options available, mediation proposals and discussions must be kept confidential and may not be used as evidence in due process hearings or court actions. The confidentiality provisions are considered so important to the process that some states may require the parties to sign a pledge of confidentiality prior to the commencement of mediation.

Schools and states may require parents who elect not to participate in mediation to meet with a "disinterested" person from a community parent resource center or dispute resolution entity who will explain the benefits of the mediation process and encourage the parents to participate. Parents may not be penalized for refusal to participate.

Mediator qualifications exclude employees of schools, agencies, or state agencies who provide services or programs to the child, and the mediator may not have a personal or professional conflict of interest in the matter. Selection of mediators for specific disputes should be conducted on a random or a mutual agreement selection process basis.

A mediator, unlike a hearing officer or arbitrator, does not make decisions or rulings. Instead, the role of the mediator is to improve communications and facilitate agreement:

> The mediator is a neutral third party acting as a facilitator to assist parents and school personnel in reaching an agreement. Although the mediator is in control of the session, he/she does not make the decision on how to resolve the issue(s). The mediator allows the parties to present their positions and attempts to achieve mutual understanding and a solution to the problem in the best interest of the student. The mediator facilitates the process. He or she summarizes positions and helps the parties consider possible alternatives.

. . . . .

> The purpose of mediation in special education is to provide an alternative to a due process hearing or complaint procedure

investigation as a way to resolve conflicts, clarify issues and stimulate mutual problem solving efforts between parents and school personnel. Even if an agreement is not reached, there is the potential of both parties leaving the session with an enhanced perspective of the issues and with the focus on the student. Most mediations result in better communication between school and parents. This leads to an improved situation for the student.[*]

The experiences of a mediator in Missouri verify the potential benefits of mediation as an alternative dispute resolution process. However, the process is only as good as the intent of the parties involved. When the parties do not come to the table in earnest and do not have a desire to work together in the best interest of the child, a dispute resolution process other than mediation will be required (Mills & Duff-Mallams, 1999).

Some states have had such good experiences with the mediation process that they now provide for mediation opportunities in which the parties meet and attempt to resolve differences prior to formal requests for hearing (pre-appeal mediation). Some experts feel that even the filing of a request for hearing so solidifies the parties' positions and creates an adversarial atmosphere that an opportunity to resolve issues before the process becomes formalized is beneficial to a solution and maintaining good working relationships between schools and parents.

Complaint Process

Filing a complaint with the state is another alternative form of dispute resolution. Each state must adopt procedures for resolving complaints, either at the state level or local school level, with review by the state being available. Complaints must be investigated and a written decision

---

[*] Montana Office of Public Instruction. (1994). *Montana Mediation Process* (pp. 6–8). Logan, UT: Mountain Plains Regional Resource Center. Reprinted by permission.

issued (within sixty days) which addresses each complaint. Complaint decisions must contain findings of facts and conclusions, reasons for the final decision, and procedures for implementation, if needed.

Complaints are limited to technical and legal violations of the IDEA, such as failure to carry out IEP terms, failure to provide parental safeguards, and refusal to consider some types of services. Allegations of a school's failure to implement a due process decision must be resolved by the state. Disputes involving issues of judgment, such as the appropriateness of IEP goals, may be resolved only through due process hearings or mediation, not the complaint process.

Complaints may be filed by either organizations or individuals under state prescribed procedures. The complaint must outline alleged violations of the IDEA and the facts on which the statement is based. The alleged incident may not have occurred more than one year prior to state receipt of the complaint, unless the complainant is requesting compensatory services for incidents occurring not more than three years previously.

State decisions on complaints may award compensatory services as an appropriate remedy for denial of FAPE. If the subject matter of a complaint is also the subject matter of a due process hearing, then the state must defer the complaint subject matter decision until the hearing is completed. If an issue raised in a complaint has been the subject matter of a previous due process hearing, the hearing decision is binding.

In a study involving state educational agency experience with the complaint process, Suchey and Huefner (1998) found that parent and school awareness of the complaint procedure has not yet greatly increased to a high level, the number of complaints filed have been slowly increasing, and the complaint process has reduced the number of due process hearings in some states.

Suchey and Huefner identified several advantages of the use of state complaint procedures over the use of mediation and due process hearings:

- Costs of the complaint procedure and investigation are borne by the state.
- Attorneys are not usually involved.
- Complaints can be used to address system-wide violations of the IDEA.
- Complaint results are enforceable in court if the state does not enforce its own decision.

Some state educational agencies discourage the use of complaints and, instead, encourage use of mediation. It is felt that the complaint process often results in "winners and losers," which generates antagonisms that are not easily overcome.

Figure 3-1 compares some aspects of mediation, hearings, and complaints to help illustrate which is generally the more desirable.

PREPARATION FOR THE HEARING

Although hearings are not a preferred method for resolving disputes, in some situations other alternatives do not exist or have not been successful. When a due process hearing cannot be avoided, it is imperative that parties be prepared.

Ekstrand's summary of how to prepare for a due process hearing continues to be excellent advice:

> There are two parties to the local level due process hearing: the local school system and the parents. There is no question that preparation by both parties is the most important part of the hearing process. If the local school system and the parents are fully prepared, the hearing will flow smoothly and all necessary information will be presented in an orderly fashion, allowing the hearing officer to make a well-informed decision in the best interest of the child.

FIGURE 3-1 *Comparison of alternative dispute resolutions*

Mediation (not arbitration)

Win/win situation—not a compromise

Parties are in control of decision

Cost is time only

Time spent by parties moderate

No lawyers are involved

Hearing

Win/lose situation

Decision made by outsider

Costly $ $ $ $

Time spent by parties great

Lawyer involvement likely

Complaint

Win/lose situation

Decision made by state department of education

Little or no financial cost

Time spent by parties limited

No lawyers are involved

The federal rules provide that either party has the right to be represented by counsel. While legal representation is not necessary, the parties can often be greatly assisted in the preparation and conduct of a hearing by an attorney who is familiar with special education due process procedures. Although the hearing is much less formal than court and judicial procedures, many legal rights are involved. As a result, both parties often are represented by counsel. The local school system is required to inform parents of any available free and low-cost legal and other relevant services when a hearing is initiated or when the parents request this information.

Preparation for the hearing involves gathering and organizing the relevant information so that it can be presented clearly, completely, and concisely. . . . The evidence presented in such a case will usually be in two forms: documents (such as student progress reports) and testimony (statements made by witnesses).

Preparation should start with a review of the child's entire school file. Those records that appear most informative should be selected as evidence to be submitted at the hearing. So that the hearing officer may easily refer to the documents, it is advantageous to put them in chronological order, with a cover summary sheet identifying each one. And if the records are organized properly, a simple reading of them will give the hearing officer a fairly comprehensive chronological history of the child. Further, each document should be marked as an exhibit (for instance, School Exhibit 1, etc.), or Parent Exhibit A, etc., for easy identification during the hearing. . . .

The documents [should] provide the hearing officer with an understanding of the background of the child and educational needs, and finally, a description of the program and services which the party believes will appropriately meet the needs of the child.

Once the documentation is properly organized, it is necessary to determine what witnesses will testify at the hearing. The federal rules state that any party to a hearing has the right to be accompanied and advised by individuals with special knowledge or training with respect to the problems of children with disabilities. Witnesses are not required but are generally necessary to a sufficiently complete presentation of the position of either party. In determining what witnesses will testify, it is recommended, although not necessary and often not possible, that the witnesses have first-hand knowledge of the child.

The child's school history can be described by any appropriate school representative and by the parent. A specialist . . . can then discuss the handicapping conditions and educational needs of the child. Finally, a representative from the proposed school . . . can describe the programs and services available at that school and explain why those meet the child's educational needs. During their testimony, these witnesses should identify any documents or reports substantiating particular aspects of their testimony. . . .

The preparation for the hearing should be completed at least ten days before the hearing date because the federal rules provide that any party to the hearing may prohibit the introduction of any evidence that has not been disclosed to that party at least five days before the hearing. The meaning of the word "disclosed" is not clear, however. Since both school and parents have free access to the child's school file, it could be said that any document in the child's file is automatically disclosed. Yet a better approach to this issue might require parent and school to inform each other, within the time limit, of each document intended for submission at the hearing. This should be done in writing, and if the other party does not have the document, a copy should be provided. The federal rules require, moreover, that "any evidence" must be disclosed. Because testimony is evidence, a strict reading of this provision would seem to mandate the advance disclosure of any statement or testimony of a witness. Practically, this would of course be unreasonable—if not impossible. It would, however, appear that if the parties disclose the names of the witnesses who will testify at the hearing on their behalf and the subject matter of the testimony, the intent and purpose of the provision will be met. It is clear that the purpose of this rule is to avoid a "hearing by surprise," which would be contrary to the very purpose of a full and fair impartial due process hearing.

Proper preparation and disclosure before the hearing will greatly simplify the conduct of the hearing and will provide the complete information necessary for the hearing officer to make a proper decision.*

---

*From "Preparing for the Due Process Hearing: What to Expect and What to Do," by R. E. Ekstrand, 1979, *Amicus, 4* (2), pp. 93–95. Copyright 1979 by the National Center for Law and the Handicapped, Inc. Reprinted by permission.

SCHOOL'S DEFENSE

An important aspect of a successful school defense at a due process hearing is the important role played by the school's attorney. The role is not played out solely within the walls of the hearing room, however. Providing advice, recommendations, and review of school practices long before any particular conflict arises are also important roles for a school's attorney. Education law and special education law are specializations that require great care in the selection of school legal representation. Osborne provided this advice in the selecting of a school attorney:

As an area of law, special education has become a specialized topic due to the tremendous amount of litigation that has occurred since IDEA was passed in 1975. School officials cannot rely on the school board attorney to defend the school district in a special education lawsuit. Although the school board attorney may be well qualified to handle most of the school district's legal affairs, he or she may not have the specialized knowledge required to adequately litigate a special education case.

School districts should retain a separate attorney to handle all their special education litigation. Many school districts use the services of a large law firm that specializes in education law. A large law firm may have one or two attorneys who further specialize in special education law. If this is the case, school officials need look no further for special education counsel.

However, if the school district is not represented by a large firm with a special education division, a separate attorney for special educational litigation must be located and retained. The attorney chosen should be well versed in education law in general as well as special education law and must have experience in administrative hearing procedures since most of the litigation will be at that level. Furthermore, the attorney should be familiar with educational issues and practices such as evaluation methods, teaching techniques, and various placement options. Naturally, an experienced and talented attorney will cost more; however, there simply is no substitute for experience.

To find a qualified attorney to handle a special education lawsuit a school district should solicit referrals from other knowledgeable parties. Since the person representing the school district in a special education lawsuit may need to confer with the school board attorney, that person would be a logical starting point. The school board attorney may have a ready list of qualified special education attorneys.

Special education administrators from other districts would be another source of referrals.

. . . . .

Choosing an attorney is much like choosing a person to fill any open position in the school district. School officials should examine the attorneys' credentials, seek references from other school districts that have used the attorneys being considered, and interview the candidates that appear most qualified. Choosing an attorney is as important as filling any top-level administrative position in the school district. The process should not be taken lightly.*

CONCLUSION

Working with parents to provide students with appropriate educational programming and services is very rewarding, when successful. When not successful, the mandated process can become frustrating, irritating, and tiresome. This does not mean that school leaders can lower their professional diligence when things do not work out. To do so may result in expensive and time-consuming hearings or embarrassing com-

plaint results. Even winning hearing decisions and complaint investigations bring a real threat of losing those things most important in providing education services and programs to students, such as parent and community support and school resources:

> Resources spent on litigation are resources unavailable for education. Relationships between parents and districts that are fractured by the adversarial system bode ill for a successful team approach, over a period of years, to educate a student with disabilities (Newcomer & Zirkel, 1999, p. 479).

There are some issues which will arise due to "honest differences of opinion" and may need to go to hearing or court for resolution. Most issues, however, may be worked out through honest, sincere communication and mutual trust. The decisions regarding which way issues will go are often determined long before the issues themselves actually arise. For education leaders, good parental working relationships and mutual trust are not only situational, they are full-time considerations.

REFERENCES

Ekstrand, R. (1979). Preparing for the due process hearing: What to expect and what to do. *Amicus, 4* (2), 91–96.

Goldberg, S. S., & Kuriloff, P. J. (1991). Evaluating the fairness of special education hearings. *Exceptional Children, 57* (6), 546–555.

Jacobs, L. (1979). Hidden dangers, hidden costs. *Amicus, 4* (2), 86–88.

McKinney, J. R., & Schultz, G. (1996). Hearing officers, case characteristics, and due process hearing. *Education Law Reporter, 111,* 1069–1076.

Mills, G. E., & Duff-Mallams, K. (1999). A mediation strategy for special education disputes. *Intervention in School and Clinic, 35* (2), 87–92.

Mills, G. E., & Duff-Mallams, K. (2000). Special education mediation. *Teaching Exceptional Children, 32* (4), 72–78.

---

* From *Legal Issues in Special Education* (pp. 244–45), by Allan G. Osborne, Jr., 1996. Boston: Allyn and Bacon. Copyright 1996 by Allyn and Bacon. Reprinted by permission.

Montana Office of Public Instruction (1994). *Montana mediation process for dispute resolution under special education*. Logan, UT: Mountain Plains Regional Resource Center, Utah State University.

National Association of Directors of Special Education (1999). *Due process hearings: 1999 update*. Alexandria, VA: Project Forum, Author.

Newcomer, J. R., & Zirkel, P. A. (1999). An analysis of judicial outcomes of special cases. *Exceptional Children, 65* (4), 469–480.

Newcomer, J. R., Zirkel, P. A., & Tarola, R. J. (1998). Characteristics and outcomes of special education hearing and review officer cases. *Education Law Reporter, 123,* 449–457.

Osborne, A. G. (1996). *Legal Issues In Special Education*. Boston: Allyn and Bacon.

Suchey, N., & Huefner, D. S. (1998). The state complaint procedure under the Individuals With disabilities Education Act. *Exceptional Children, 64* (4), 529–542.

RECOMMENDED READINGS

Goldberg, S. S., & Huefner, D. S. (1995). Dispute resolution in special education: An introduction to litigation alternatives. *Education Law Reporter, 99,* 703–711. This article addresses the use of mediation and hearings in special education and concludes that there may be better ways to resolve disputes.

Schrag, J. A. (1996). *Mediation in special education: A resource manual for mediators*. Alexandria, VA: National Association of State Directors of Special Education: This excellent pamphlet explains the concept of mediation, provides recommendations and forms, and provides case studies for discussion.

Relevant Federal Regulations

34 C.F.R. 300.500	General responsibilities of public agencies—due process procedures
.503	Prior notice by public agency; content of notice
.504	Procedural Safeguard notice
.505	Parental consent
.506	Mediation
.507	Impartial due process hearing
.508	Impartial hearing officer
.509	Hearing rights
.510	Finality of decision; appeal; impartial review
.511	Time lines and convenience of hearings on reviews
.512	Civil action
.513	Attorney fees
.514	Child's status during proceedings
.660	Adoption of state complaint procedures
.661	Minimum state complaint procedures
.662	Filing a complaint

CHAPTER 4

IDENTIFICATION AND EVALUATION OF STUDENTS

Chapter Preview

Focus

States must design and maintain systems for identifying children with disabilities of all ages within their jurisdiction. These systems must be both effective at finding all those who need special education and at producing evaluations upon which rational educational programs can be based.

Legal Issues

The law spells out several protections regarding the evaluation of students with disabilities, including:

- materials and procedures used may not be discriminatory on a racial, language, or cultural basis;
- evaluation must be administered in the child's native language by trained and knowledgeable personnel according to testing instructions;
- evaluations must be validated for the specific purpose for which they are being used;
- evaluations must take into account any sensory, physical, or speech impairments and the child's English proficiency, and must provide an accurate picture of the child's abilities;
- a variety of assessment tools must be used to gather data.
- no single procedure may be used as the sole criterion for determining eligibility.

The evaluation and determination of eligibility for special education must be made by a team of qualified professionals and the parents, the child must be assessed in all areas related to the suspected disability, and tests and other materials must be designed to identify and assess specific areas of educational need.

Parents must receive prior notice of the types of identification and evaluation activities proposed by the school and of their rights in the process. They also must give informed written consent before the initial evaluation or any re-evaluation can take place. Should parents refuse consent, the school may request mediation or a due process hearing. If dissatisfied with the evaluation results, parents may obtain their own evaluation, or they may request and attempt to receive an independent evaluation at public expense. All independent evaluation results must be considered in decisions regarding the child's educational program.

Rationale

A child's educational program is most appropriate and productive when it is based on an accurate picture of that child's abilities and the extent of specific constraints on learning. The multiple, nondiscriminatory evaluation approach required by law is designed to prevent the recurrence of alleged past abuses in which large numbers of children, especially minority children, were mislabeled and therefore miseducated.

Approaches

For the severely disabled in particular, early identification may be critical to educational progress. However, several pitfalls must be avoided. The improper labeling of a child or inaccurate recognition of the student's abilities can lead to lifelong stigma and denial of opportunities to learn and grow. Therefore, it is important to avoid over-identification of children with disabilities. Many school districts are working both to improve the effectiveness of their screening and referral systems and to institute assistance team interventions that can identify and resolve many learning problems without the provision of formal special education services.

CHILD FIND

The law under both the IDEA and Section 504 requires that "child find" efforts be conducted. Each state must develop a plan for locating, identifying, and evaluating all children with disabilities in need of special education and related services, including those attending private schools, those who are highly mobile (such as migrant and homeless children), and those who might otherwise be overlooked because they are successfully advancing from grade to grade. Also called "child search," the identification step includes public awareness programs, such as medical outreach, mailings to parents, television advertisements, and coordination with hospitals, clinics, and service agencies, as well as periodic and continuing school screening and referral systems. In addition to the general child find requirements under Part B (special education between the ages of three and twenty-one) of the IDEA, Part C (special services from birth to two years) also makes participating states responsible for identifying, locating, and evaluating infants and toddlers from birth through two years of age who are disabled or who are suspected of being disabled.

Most schools give standardized tests to all students at certain grades, and many have well-developed observation and screening procedures for preschool or kindergarten populations (i.e., kindergarten roundup). Various kinds of automatic school referrals also fall under this heading, including systems based on frequent or prolonged absences, danger of failure at midyear, irregular attendance, or other criteria that trigger the institution's referral process. Because many of these procedures are oriented toward general populations, not individual students, they fall under the identification rather than the evaluation sections of the law, and parental notice and consent requirements do not apply. Generally, the more individualized the evaluation process becomes, the greater the need to comply with special education legal requirements.

EVALUATIONS

The term "evaluation" refers to those procedures used to determine whether a child has a disability and the nature and extent of the special education and related services that the child needs. The term means procedures used selectively with an individual child and does not include general assessments administered to or procedures used with all children in a school, grade, or class.

Evaluations, re-evaluations, and eligibility determinations are to be conducted by teams of persons consistent with those persons on IEP teams (see Chapter 5), including the child's parents, and other qualified professionals with the knowledge and skills necessary to interpret the evaluation data collected.

It is useful to think of evaluation as an integral part of the law's general thrust toward individualizing education for children with disabilities. Results of the evaluation will form both the basis for development of an eligible child's IEP and for educational placement; therefore, the evaluation process should:

- be readily understood by both parents and professionals;
- help pinpoint needed special education and related services;
- suggest appropriate learning goals and short-term objectives; and
- suggest the extent to which the student can participate in regular education and, especially, can be involved in and progress in the general curriculum (see Chapter 5 on IEPs).

As part of any initial evaluation (if appropriate) or reevaluation, the eligibility determination team must review existing evaluation data, including parent- and child-provided information, and current classroom based assessments and observations, if any. The review of existing data may be conducted by team members individually or at a meeting called for that purpose. If a team meeting is held, the parents must be provided notice and the opportunity to participate. Notice to parents must be provided early enough to ensure attendance at meetings and must indicate the purpose, time, and place of the meeting, who will be in attendance, and that other individuals with knowledge or special expertise about the child may be invited. Parent consent is not required for a review of existing data only. The team must determine whether any additional data are needed to establish several things: whether a child is eligible, or in the case of a reevaluation, whether the child continues to be eligible; the present levels of educational performance and the educational needs of the child; and whether modifications or accommodations are needed to allow the child to participate in the general curriculum. If it is determined that additional data are needed to complete the evaluation, then the school will produce, with informed parent written consent, the additional data identified by the team. If no additional data are needed, then the child's parents will be so notified (even though they are team members) and the parents may request additional assessment. If the school declines (refuses) the parent request for additional evaluation, for instance, because parents want additional testing for reasons not relevant to IDEA determinations, then the school must notify the parents, who may challenge the refusal through mediation or a request for a due process hearing. It should be remembered that for the initial evaluation, the school must conduct a "full and individual" evaluation, but the evaluation will actually be different for each individual child depending on the child's needs.

The assessment team's review of existing data to determine the need for new data, rather than conducting a full new evaluation, is an effort to reduce school time and expense associated with evaluations and re-evaluations. In the 1997 Amendments, Congress intended to help the school and the child by eliminating unnecessary tests and assessments, especially for the purpose of re-evaluations. Congress concluded that when a child's disability and educational circumstance had not changed in a three-year time period, the child should not be subjected to, nor the school be required to pay for, unnecessary additional assessments (House Report No. 105-95, 1997, p. 97).

Eligibility Determination

Following completion of initial testing and the gathering of other data, including parent input, the team of "qualified professionals" and the parents must determine whether a child is eligible for special education. A copy of the evaluation report and documentation of the determination of eligibility must be provided to the parents. If a child's educational needs are determined to be because of a lack of instruction in reading or math, or is due to limitations in English proficiency, then the child cannot be determined eligible for special education.

If, after careful review of all available data, a determination is made that a child has a disability and needs special education and related services, then an IEP must be developed for the child. The first IEP team meeting must be held within thirty days of the eligibility determination. In many situations, an eligibility determination meeting may be phased into an IEP team meeting when the appropriate notice has been provided to the parents and when the appropriate persons for an IEP team are present. Placement in special education programs and related services is expected to begin as soon as feasible following completion of the IEP and obtaining informed written parent consent for the initial provision of special education programs and services.

When a child is suspected of having a specific learning disability, several additional legal requirements are found in the eligibility determination process. The eligibility determination team must include "the child's regular teacher" (rather than any regular education teacher), someone qualified to conduct diagnostic evaluations (e.g., a school psychologist), and at least one team member other than the regular teacher must have observed the child's academic performance in the regular classroom setting.

Unlike other evaluation teams, the team for a child with a suspected specific learning disability must submit a detailed written report documenting the team's determination of eligibility. Likewise, each member involved with suspected specific learning disabilities must certify in writing whether the team report reflects his or her professional conclusion. If it does not, the dissenting team member must submit a separate statement presenting his or her differing conclusions. Nothing in federal law indicates the purpose or consequence of these written differing opinions.

Medical Evaluations

For some children with suspected disabilities, it will be desirable or necessary to have medical professionals on the evaluation team, or at least available to conduct medical evaluations. The IDEA definition of "related services" includes "school health services" provided by a school nurse or other qualified person and "medical services for diagnostic or evaluation purposes." This latter phrase specifically refers to services provided by a licensed physician for the purpose of determining a child's medically related disability that may result in his or her need for special education and related services.

Special education and related services must be provided at no cost to parents. Parents of children with disabilities who are covered by public insurance, such as Medicaid, may be asked to use those benefits for medical and other services so long as several conditions are met.

The school may not require the parents to enroll the child in a public insurance program as a condition of receiving FAPE, incur out-of-pocket expenses, (e.g., deductibles, co-payments), or suffer any detriment, such as a decrease in the lifetime benefit or increased premiums.

A school may access parents' private insurance only so long as there is no cost to the parents, including the lowering of lifetime coverage, increased premiums, or deductibles or co-payments. Each time a school proposes to access parents' private insurance, it must obtain informed prior written consent (see Chapter 2) and it must advise the parents that refusal will not jeopardize services to the child. Federal special education funds may be used to pay private insurance co-payments and deductions in order to provide services at no cost to parents.

LEGAL ISSUES

The most common disputes or problem areas related to identification and evaluation involve the legal relationships between schools and parents (discussed in detail in Chapter 2).

Prior Notice and Parental Consent

There are two points in the identification and evaluation process where informed written parental consent is required. The first is prior to the initial, or preplacement evaluation, and the second is for a re-evaluation when existing data are inadequate.

Re-evaluation must be conducted at least once every three years. It may occur more frequently "if conditions warrant," when requested by the child's parent or teacher, and when making a determination that the child with a disability is no longer considered as such under the IDEA. The latter provision does not apply to graduation from high school or exceeding the eligibility age of twenty-one under the IDEA. If parents fail to respond to (but do not refuse) a school request for consent to conduct any assessment as part of re-evaluation, the school may proceed to conduct a re-evaluation without actual consent when it can demonstrate through documentation that the parents had a full opportunity to be involved in the evaluation process and eligibility determination, and that it used reasonable measures to obtain parental consent. Parental refusal of written consent for re-evaluation may be the subject of a school request for mediation or a due process hearing. Parental consent is not required for staff observations, classroom evaluations, or general assessments administered to all students in a class, grade, or school.

Prior detailed written notice to parents is required for most individualized identification and evaluation activities, including school refusals to parent requests regarding identification and evaluation, screening, and re-evaluation. In addition to describing the activities to be performed (or refused) and the reasons for them, this written notice must: identify and describe the other options considered and the reasons they were rejected; include a description of data used in making the decision; include a description of other factors relevant to the decision; and include a statement that the parents have procedural safeguards available to them. (See Chapter 2 for more details.)

No federally mandated time line has been established for completion of the evaluation process, but schools should not be unreasonably long in completing this phase of the special education process. It can be anticipated that for a child identified as needing special education, no more than sixty days will normally lapse between parental consent for evaluation and the actual beginning of special education programming and services.

When Consent Is Not Given

When parents refuse consent for their child's preplacement (initial) evaluation or for re-evaluation, and the educators involved feel strongly that the pupil should be considered for special education and related services or continuation of those services, then the school may initiate mediation or a due process hearing under the IDEA provisions. When mediation is attempted first, but is unsuccessful, it may be followed by a school's request for due process hearing. If, after a hearing, the impartial hearing officer agrees in the written decision that the child should be evaluated, the evaluation may take place without parental consent, although parents have the right to appeal the hearing officer's decision.

Although the federal regulations indicate that schools have the option ("may") to use the mediation and due process hearing procedures to obtain consent for evaluation and initial placement when parents refuse consent, OSEP interpretations have stated that a school must implement its procedures to override parent refusal in those situations where the interest of the child warrants such action. At no time may a school require parental consent as a condition for any benefit, except for the provision of special education programs and services.

The Right to an Independent Educational Evaluation

When parents consent to an evaluation by the school, but are not satisfied (disagree) with its results, they have the right to obtain an independent educational evaluation (IEE), which is conducted by a qualified examiner who is not employed by the school and is not an agent of the school. In such instances, the school must provide information about where an independent evaluation can be obtained. The parents may obtain an independent evaluation at their own expense or they may request an independent evaluation at public expense. In the latter situation, the school must provide parents with its criteria (i.e., qualifications of the examiner) for such examinations and pay the full cost of the evaluation, or otherwise ensure that it is provided at no cost to the parents. Medicaid may be used to pay for all or part of an IEE for students entitled to Medicaid services. Parent insurance, however, may be used to pay for all or part of an IEE only so long as it does not "cost" the parents anything, such as through increased premiums or reduced claim coverage, and the parents voluntarily consent in writing to claims being filed. Schools are required to pay for only one independent evaluation for each school evaluation, and then only when parents actually disagree with an evaluation conducted by the school (*Hudson v. Wilson*, 1987).

However, when a parent requests that the school pay for the independent evaluation, and the school feels strongly that the evaluation it conducted was adequate and appropriate, it may, "without unnecessary delay," contest the parents' request for an independent evaluation at public expense by filing a request for a due process hearing. If the hearing officer decides in favor of the school, then the parents must pay the cost of the independent evaluation.

The results of any independent evaluation—whether paid for by parents or by a public agency—must be considered in planning the child's educational program and may be offered as evidence at a subsequent hearing. When a hearing officer requests an independent evaluation as part of a due process hearing, it must be provided at no cost to the parents.

An example of the unusual IEE situations in which school officials can find themselves is exemplified in *Evans v. District No. 17* (1988). Parents of a child with disabilities transferred their child to a private school program in another state and had her re-evaluated. They then requested that the school district of residence reimburse them for their costs of evaluation. The school refused reimbursement, but did nothing else. The court ruled that, in such situations, the school either had to pay for the evaluation or take the issue of the adequacy of its own previous evaluation to a due process hearing. Because the school had not requested a due process hearing

to resolve the issue after receiving the parents' request, it was required to reimburse the parents for their expense of the re-evaluation.

In the event a student who has been evaluated for special education transfers to another school across state lines before an IEP is completed, the receiving school district must determine whether it will accept the student's most current evaluation and disability determination conducted in the other state. After all, the former evaluation may not meet the receiving state's education standards for evaluations. If the receiving school district accepts the evaluation and determination of disability, it must so notify the child's parents and begin the IEP development process. If the receiving school district refuses to adopt the former school district's evaluation, the receiving district must provide appropriate notice to the parents and then conduct its own evaluation without unnecessary delay. In the latter situation, the child may be placed into an interim IEP placement, unless the receiving school and parents cannot agree on an interim placement, in which case the student should be placed in the regular school program. If the receiving school's evaluation indicates a disability and a need for special education, the school must convene an eligibility determination meeting and IEP meeting within thirty days of the determination (OSEP Memorandum 96-5, 1995).

PROBLEMS OF IDENTIFICATION, EVALUATION, AND BIAS

Identification and evaluation are the first two steps in providing special education programs and related services to children who need them. In many ways, their importance and utility are self-evident: In order to deliver educational services to children, educators first must identify those who need such services and must know what those needs are in order to design programs relevant to the students' individual needs.

The dangers involved are less obvious but still substantial. With identification, there are problems both of over-identifying (children may needlessly suffer debilitating, lifelong stigma, not to mention the possible unnecessary outlay of district resources) and of under-identifying (those who need services may not receive them).

The more subtle concern of over-identification of children with disabilities is related to the stereotypes which persons, including professional educators who should know better, apply as a result of labeling. Labels such as autism, mental retardation, and emotional and behavior disorders envision certain expectations in the observer that often transfer into how we act toward, and what we think about, the person labeled.

There is always the danger of stereotypes becoming self-fulfilling prophecies. This issue is demonstrated in a study conducted by Fox and Stinnett (1996) involving educational professionals and psychology students. The participants were provided a copy of nearly identical vignettes describing an elementary-school-aged boy with various behavior problems. The only difference between the vignettes was that four different educational labels, including "serious emotionally disturbed," were used in describing the boy. From the information provided, participants were to predict certain aspects of the child's future. Among all groups participating, the label of serious emotionally disturbed resulted in more negative judgments regarding the likelihood of future success in interpersonal relations than any of the other labels. Researchers concluded that merely applying a label to the boy had resulted in greater negative expectations that might eventually perpetuate the child's difficulties in the minds of school staff.

Bias—Racial, Cultural, Language

Certainly the most controversial issue surrounding student evaluations has involved alleged racial and cultural bias. A 1975 study conducted by the federal government found that although only 15% of the nation's students were African American, 38% of students identified as mentally disabled were African American (U.S. Department of Education, 1996).

A 1999 study conducted on a nationally representative sample of data compiled in 1992 indicated that the issue had not abated. African-American students were about 2.4 times more likely than their non–African-American peers to be identified as mentally disabled and 1.5 times more likely to be identified as having emotional disabilities (Oswald, Coutinho, Best, & Singh, 1999).

In the 1970s and 1980s, the courts responded to a rash of lawsuits charging that culturally biased tests had led to the misclassification of large numbers of minority students. The resulting assignment of a disproportionate number of minority and non–English-speaking students to special education programs, especially when the decision was made based on a single IQ test score, was not easily defended. The primary focus of the criticisms was that the tests had been developed for the white, middle-class socioeconomic majority of students in America, and the questions on many standardized tests had no validity when asked of minority and non–English-speaking students. The degree of resultant injury to students who were improperly placed in special education can be compounded by tremendous self-esteem problems related to segregation, isolation, and being erroneously told they are in some way deficient. It is little wonder that judicial rulings included orders to dismantle certain programs for mentally disabled students in which minority children were over-represented. Courts also prohibited the future use of IQ tests to place children in some types of ability tracks or in classes for the mentally retarded when the tests had brought about improper racial imbalance in those classes (Turnbull & Turnbull, 1998, p. 105).

The issue of test bias is probably not a purely racial issue; it is much more complex than skin color. It relates to socioeconomic status, community culture, accepted speech styles, transient status, self-concepts, and stereotypes among other things (Obiakor, 1999).

Issues of cultural bias in standardized testing have not been resolved and do not solely affect African-American children. Such issues also present problems for Native American populations as well as recent immigrants from Asia, Latin America, and Eastern Europe. At a meeting of special educators serving Native American children attended by one of the authors, considerable anger was expressed about the unfairness of standardized testing to such students, including assessments required for graduation. A participant from the Boundary Waters area of northern Minnesota complained about one such examination containing questions involving escalators and elevators, which his students had never seen and to which they could not relate.

The issue of cultural bias in testing, with its associated problem of limited English proficiency (LEP), is rapidly increasing, especially in certain parts of the country. The number of LEP students in California increased from 524,000 in 1985 to over 1,300,000 in 1996, and helped fuel a state-wide political debate over bilingual education (Wenkart, 1998).

The IDEA attempts to address the problems of cultural and language bias in assessment in three ways by requiring: (1) that all the testing and evaluation materials and procedures "be selected and administered so as not to be discriminatory on a racial or cultural basis" (although these terms are not further defined); (2) that they be administered in the child's native language or other mode of communication; and (3) that a variety of assessment tools and strategies are used, including information provided by the parents. The concern regarding language proficiency in the IDEA is apparently directed at misidentification only, because the IDEA does not speak to bilingual education or the provision of special education programs in native languages (Wenkart, 1998).

Even where non-minority children are concerned, there have been documented problems related to inaccurate evaluation. The requirement for multiple evaluative measures for all students is geared toward eliminating inaccurate, incomplete, or irrelevant test results. Thus, conclusions about a child cannot be based on one standardized test; in fact, they should never be based on test-format evaluations alone but should include observation, diagnostic teaching, interviews, or other approaches. The law makes it clear that no single procedure may be used as the sole criterion for determining eligibility or appropriateness of programming. Figure 4-1 highlights the current protections in evaluation procedures under the IDEA.

The particular evaluations used in special education will vary, of course, with the individual child and the preference of evaluators. Such evaluations normally will include at least social/family, medical, educational, and psychological assessments; however, there are exceptions. The full evaluation battery may not be necessary for a child with a simple speech impediment. The key is to assess all areas related to the suspected disability and determine what, if any, effects these potential disabilities have on educational progress. The initial evaluation, especially, must involve a full and individualized evaluation of each child, and the provision of special education and related services may not begin prior to completion of the initial evaluation, determination of eligibility, and development of an IEP.

APPROACHES TO RESOLVING PROBLEMS

Intervention Activities

Once a child has been referred for a formal preplacement evaluation, a series of assessment activities are initiated which are required by law and which generally result in substantial investments of time and school resources. With this in

FIGURE 4-1   *IDEA protections in evaluation procedures summary*

- Tests are provided and administered in the child's native language or mode of communication

- Standardized tests must have been validated for the specific purpose for which they are intended.

- Standardized tests are administered by trained personnel in conformity with the publisher's instructions.

- The evaluation will be tailored to assess the child's specific areas of educational need, including information provided by the parent that may assist in determining disability and the content of the IEP.

- Evaluators must use technically sound instruments that assess multiple areas and factors.

- No single procedure is used as the sole criterion for determining the presence of a disability, the student's program, or placement.

- The evaluation team is comprised of a multidisciplinary team or group of persons, at least one of whom has knowledge in the child's suspected area of disability.

- The child is assessed in all areas related to the suspected disability.

From *The Law and Special Education* by Yell, Mitchell L., © 1998. Reprinted by permission of Prentice-Hall Inc. Upper Saddle River, NJ.

mind, more and more school districts are adopting policies and procedures that attempt to solve individual student learning problems before the legal process of IDEA evaluation is set in motion. These services generally involve informal interventions with students or teachers in the regular classroom and have largely been found to be highly successful. Intervention activities are used in a purely regular education sense; thus, before most children are referred for special education evaluation, a concerted effort will be made in regular education to remediate the child's learning needs.

Many schools now have some kind of intervention assistance team that meets regularly for a short time (twenty to thirty minutes) each week. The name of the teams vary from district to district (i.e., Child Study Team, Child Assistance Team, Teacher Assistance Team), as do their composition, specific activities, and structure. Team members often include special and regular education teachers, the school principal, counselor, or nurse, and possibly other specialists as well. An individual child's parents may be involved in meetings involving their child, but at all times parents are informed of school concerns and informal efforts to resolve those concerns. Communication with parents must always be open and must be designed to go both ways.

Although there are many variations among intervention assistance teams, the procedure generally is as follows: Teachers (and sometimes parents) refer students directly to the intervention team, rather than immediately identifying the student as a focus of special education concern and initiating the formal special education identification procedures. Team members then share information on those students gleaned from student files, interviews with the teacher and parents, and observation of the child in the classroom. They discuss (brainstorm) possible modifications in the curriculum, classroom environment, or mode of instruction and make recommendations to the teacher. In some cases, committee members may offer direct assistance to students or classroom teachers. The goal of intervention assistance teams is to help regular teachers meet the needs of as many students as possible in the regular classroom and to limit the number of inappropriate referrals for special education services. Many state educational agencies recognize the effective and efficient nature of this approach and now require the implementation of intervention teams.

A study of intervention teams conducted in three states concluded that teams generally operate in a positive and effective manner, experienced members strongly endorse their use, and members value the team collaboration as an important aspect of the process. A major concern identified by team members was inadequate assessment of the success of strategies used with students. Researchers recommended that specific indicators of student change, such as graphing results, using pre- and post-intervention measures, and using systematic classroom observation, be included in the assessment of the various interventions. They recommend that states develop a policy of establishing intervention teams and providing staff training funds for consistent implementation (Bahr, Whitten, Dieker, Kocarek, & Manson, 1999).

At least one state has established by administrative rule a Systematic Problem Solving Process that is designed to examine educationally related problems for children in determining whether the child will benefit from general education interventions or whether the child will require referral for special education consideration. Under the process, schools first attempt to resolve problems in the general education environment, and in doing so may use special education support and instructional personnel working collaboratively with regular education staff. "Active parent participation" is mandated. The team has the option of proceeding immediately to referral for special education evaluation when deemed appropriate. Intervention teams cannot be used to deny or slow access to evaluation and programs for children who need them.

The Systematic Problem Solving Process, sometimes referred to as a solutions focused approach, contains elements common to many similar approaches:

a. Description of the presenting problem or behavior in objective and measurable terms.
b. Collection of the data on the presenting problem or behavior is conducted in a variety of settings and through a variety of sources.

c. Interventions are designed based on the defined problem and data collected as determined by the combined judgments of the group and a plan is developed for implementing the intervention, progress monitoring, and persons responsible.
d. Systematic Progress Monitoring is conducted through the use of regular and frequent data collection and analysis and interventions are modified as necessary.
e. Evaluations of the intervention effects are analyzed and decisions regarding effectiveness made. (Special Education, 281–41.47, .48, 2000).

A number of authors have identified the importance of intervention assistance teams and have highlighted the important role played by educational leaders. Whitten has identified three separate role categories that principals play in supporting intervention assistance teams:

A. Training Activities:
   1. Provide in-service for team members in effective communication, the collaboration process, and intervention strategies.
   2. Arrange team visitations to schools with intervention teams in order to exchange ideas.
   3. Provide in-service for every building staff member on the intervention team's goals, purpose, and process.
B. Team Development
   1. Include a variety of professionals as team members.
   2. Encourage parent involvement in a collaborative relationship (and notification).
   3. Emphasize equal status of principal and others as team members.
   4. Assign team roles at each meeting to ensure full participation (brainstormer, recorder, facilitator, follow-up).
C. Team Support
   1. Schedule regular weekly meetings.
   2. Schedule time for the collaborative process.

3. Utilize a collaboration log (documentation) of problem, intervention, evaluation, and follow-up.
4. Ensure team follow-up.
5. Support intervention assistance teams district-wide.*

Some schools also use systematic problem-solving intervention teams as Section 504 teams for considering reasonable accommodations for students in the regular education setting. Both represent a regular education approach to resolving student education needs in the regular education environment, which seems to make efficient and effective use of the expertise and collaborative skills of the team members. However, once a child meets Section 504 requirements and acquires an accommodation plan, parents of the child must be helped to recognize that the procedural safeguards afforded parents under the IDEA are not available under Section 504.

In another approach, some schools have created a full-time professional position with intervention assistance responsibilities. This position requires a teacher with special education training and expertise in diagnostic/prescriptive teaching. This staff person: (1) meets with teachers, when requested, to discuss individual student's needs and offer suggestions for modifying the regular classroom to accommodate those needs; (2) mediates and coordinates relationships between regular and special education teachers; and (3) arranges pre-evaluation conferences. A word of caution in the use of the above described procedures: It is recommended to check state funding requirements carefully where special education staff members are not providing direct education services to students who are ineligible for special education.

*From "Intervention Assistive Teams: The Principal's Role Identified," by E. Whitten (1995–96), *Case in Point, IX*(2), p. 25. Published by the Council of Administrators of Special Education, a Division of the Council for Exceptional Children. Reprinted by permission.

Some schools that make use of the diagnostic/prescriptive teacher model or the intervention assistance teams also use a pre-evaluation conference to inform parents of their rights and the formal special education and Section 504 procedures available. At that point, parents can agree to the proposed program of informal interventions or they can request a formal evaluation and subsequent special education procedures. Intervention strategies should never be allowed or used to slow access to evaluation and special education programs for children who appear to need them. When parent agreement for the informal program is received, the school staff can proceed to assist the classroom teacher by providing materials, demonstrating materials and methods in class, providing direct, short-term instruction to the student in class, or observing student behavior and activities in class. In each case, it is essential that all interventions be documented and recorded in student files.

When intervention assistance efforts to meet the student's needs in the regular class setting have not been successful, the next step is to proceed to referral for special education evaluation. When not previously conducted, an important intervention step may be to have a pre-evaluation conference involving parents and educators to share information and perspectives. This intervening step prior to formal referral for special education evaluation can help to open lines of communication and develop trust.

Referral Process Improvements

Because the identification of children's educational needs is the linchpin of the referral process and provision of special education and related services, cooperation of regular class teachers is vital to the educational success or failure of many children. Over the years, surveys of regular education teachers have reported general, but only lukewarm, satisfaction with the existing special education referral process. In addition to the common complaints about too much paperwork involved in referrals, many regular educators in rural areas have reported that the referral process moved too slowly. They have also complained that the opinions of regular educators were not given enough weight in determinations of eligibility (Chalmers, Ortega, & Hoover, 1996).

Chalmers, Ortega, and Hoover (1996) have recommended a number of approaches for increasing regular education teacher involvement and satisfaction with the referral process. They recommend that staff-development programs and coursework should be used to improve regular educator knowledge of the referral process, including the due process steps, so they can better understand the reasons why the process moves slowly. Also, the rationale for attempts at remediation of student's educational needs prior to formal evaluation for special education should be made known to teachers and ingrained in each school's philosophy. Regular education's important role in the referral process should be recognized and supported by special educators and administrators. Both regular and special educators should regularly review the entire referral process with a view toward improving its efficiency and effectiveness.

Cultural awareness needs to be an important factor in intervention team considerations, when appropriate. Expectations related to behavior, student-adult exchanges, responses to adult questions, asking for help when needed and various other school situations common among white, middle-class students may not be commonplace among children and families new to the traditional majority culture. When identifying educational problems and potential solutions involving students not fully integrated into American culture, intervention teams need to be comfortable with their cultural awareness (Craig, Hull, Haggart & Perez-Selles, 2000).

Obviously, there have been difficulties in the implementation of intervention assistance programs, e.g., teachers' resistance to paperwork, use of specialists, and changes in their own classroom and teaching methods. But in schools where the leadership has taken a strong position in encouraging and coordinating these new approaches, intervention teams have been found to be highly successful in saving specialists' time and district resources through the avoidance of unnecessary referrals for formal special education evaluation (Thousand & Villa, 1995). Seemingly, all segments of the school community, especially the students, benefit from the collaborative efforts of the intervention teams and classroom teachers.

CONCLUSION

Clearly, the first step toward the provision of appropriate education programs and services to children with disabilities who need them is identification, which comes through evaluation. However, that first step includes potential peril through both over- and under-identification. Educators must address the issues with professional caution. Intervention assistance programs, the use of multiple assessments and good professional judgment offer a good measure of protection against both over- and under-identification of children who need special education. An additional important measure of assistance can come through the development of respect and appreciation for the role parents play in the education process. Educators, as good listeners, will help make better decisions.

REFERENCES

Assistance to states for the education of children with disabilities (2000), 34 Code of Federal Regulations, Part 300.

Bahr, M. W., Whitten, E., Dieker, L., Kocarek, C. E., & Manson, D. (1999). A comparison of school-based intervention teams: Implications for educational and legal reform. *Exceptional Children, 66* (1), 67–83.

Chalmers, L., Ortega, J. C., & Hoover, J. H. (1996). Attitudes of rural and small-town educators toward special education referral. *Case in Point, 10* (1); 21–28.

Craig, S., Hull, K., Haggart, A. G., & Perez-Selles, M. (2000). Promoting cultural competence through teacher assistance teams. *Teaching Exceptional Children, 32* (3), 6–12.

Evans v. District No. 17, 841 F.2d 824 (8th Cir. 1988).

Fox, J. D., & Stinnett, T. A. (1996). The effects of labeling bias on prognostic outlook for children as a function of diagnostic label and profession. *Psychology in the Schools, 33,* 143–152.

House Report No. 105-95. (1997). U.S.C. *Congressional and Administrative News,* 78–146.

Hudson v. Wilson, 828 F.2d 1059 (4th Cir. 1987).

Individuals With Disabilities Education Act, 20 U.S.C. §§ 1401–1487.

Obiakor, F. E. (1999). Teacher expectations of minority exceptional learners: Impact of "accuracy" of self-concepts. *Exceptional Children, 66* (1), 39–53.

OSEP Memorandum 96-5 (Hehir), 24 I.D.E.L.R. 320 (OSEP, 1995).

Oswald, D. P., Coutinho, M. J., Best, A. M., & Singh, N. N. (1999). Ethnic representation in special education: The influence of school-related economic and demographic variables. *The Journal of Special Education, 32* (4), 194–206.

Special Education, Chapter 281-41 (2000), Iowa Administrative Code, Des Moines, IA.

Thousand, J. S., & Villa, R. A. (1995). Inclusion: Alive and well in the Green Mountain State. *Phi Delta Kappan, 77* (4), 288–291.

Turnbull, H. R., & Turnbull, A. (1998). *Free appropriate public education: The law and children with disabilities.* Denver: Love Publishing.

United States Department of Education (1996). Profile assessment and resolution reviews. Washington DC: Author.

Wenkart, R. D. (1998). Native language instruction and the special education student: Who decides the instructional methodology? *Education Law Reporter, 125,* 581–594.

Whitten, E. (1995–96). Intervention assistance teams: The principal's role identified. *Case in Point, 9* (2), 21–32.

Yell, M. L. (1998). *The Law And Special Education.* Upper Saddle River, NJ: Merrill/Prentice Hall.

RECOMMENDED READINGS

Craig, S., Hull, K., Haggart, A. G., & Perez-Sellers, M. (2000). Promoting cultural competence through teacher assistance teams. *Teaching Exceptional Children, 32* (3), 6–12. This article includes a number of specific helpful ideas to assist intervention teams in developing cultural awareness.

Falk, C. L. (1997). How to PINPOINT and solve day-to-day problems. *Teaching Exceptional Children, 29* (3), 78–81. This article provides a practical step-by-step review of one example of a systematic problem-solving approach.

Relevant Federal Regulations

34 C.F.R.300.125	Child find.
.320	Initial evaluations.
.321	Re-evaluations.
.344	IEP team.
.500	General responsibility of public agencies; definitions (consent).
.502	Independent educational evaluation.
.531	Initial evaluations.
.532	Evaluation procedure.
.533	Determination of needed evaluation data.
.534	Determination of eligibility.
.535	Process for determining eligibility and placement.
.536	Re-evaluation.
.540	Additional team members—specific learning disabilities.
.541	Criteria for determining the existence of a specific learning disability.
.542	Observation—specific learning disability.
.543	Written report—specific learning disability.

CHAPTER 5

INDIVIDUALIZED EDUCATION PROGRAMS (IEPs)

CHAPTER PREVIEW

Focus

The school administrator's role in the area of IEPs includes devising efficient, effective, and appropriate professional implementation systems; improving communication and cooperation among staff members involved and with parents; and meeting student needs through responsible use of school resources.

Legal Issues

The law addresses two aspects: the IEP meetings and the education program itself. The meetings must be:

- initiated by the school within thirty days after determining a child needs special education;
- held at least annually to review and update each student's program;
- attended by the parent(s), a regular education teacher, a special education teacher, a school district representative, the child (if appropriate), and others at the discretion of parents or school (at least one team member must be familiar with student assessment);
- attended by providers of transition services when older children are involved; and
- followed as soon as possible by implementation of the agreed upon program.

    The IEP document itself must include:

- a statement of the child's present levels of educational performance (PLEP), including how the disability impacts participation and progress in the general curriculum;
- a statement of annual goals and benchmarks or short-term objectives, including measurable criteria in order to monitor progress;
- a statement of the specific special education, related services, assistive technology, supplementary aids and services for the child or on behalf of the child, and modifications and supports for school personnel to be provided;
- an explanation of the extent, if any, to which the child will not participate in regular education programs (including physical education and vocational education when such programs differ from that of regular education students) and nonacademic activities;
- projected dates, frequency, location, and duration of services;

- a statement of appropriate evaluation criteria and procedures, and how the student's progress will be communicated to parents;
- a statement of participation in district-wide assessments; and
- transition services for older children.

As for accountability, the law is clear that no one making a good faith effort may be held legally responsible under federal law if a student fails to meet the IEPs goals and objectives. However, the school district is legally bound to provide all programs and services listed in the IEP and to make a good faith effort to assist the child to achieve the IEP's goals and objectives. Parents who are dissatisfied with their child's education program always have the right to request mediation or a due process hearing to involve outside resources in resolving disputes.

Rationale

The requirement of an IEP for each student with a disability is a response to (1) the reality that students with disabilities differ significantly from each other as well as from the typically developing student, and (2) past abuses, in which students with disabilities frequently suffered from inappropriate educational placements based on categorical labels alone. Furthermore, the practices of IEP process individualization, goal-oriented planning, and periodic evaluation embodied in the law have proved educationally sound for all students.

Approaches

The best aid to efficient and successful IEP meetings is advance preparation, good communication, and the development of trust among the participants. Although staff members should not arrive at the meeting with a completed IEP—meaningful participation of parents and others is a necessary element of the program's success—they should be well-prepared. Persons attending the IEP meeting should be familiar with the student, the evaluation data, and the school's programs and services and should be ready to offer realistic proposals to meet the child's educational needs.

Parents, and students when appropriate, should be encouraged to prepare for and participate in IEP meetings. Prior school staff communications with parents can help to build trust and understanding which, in turn, can make it easier for all parties to reach agreement.

When needed, changes can and should be made in the IEP after implementation has begun but there should be an effort to do the best possible planning the first time. Major changes in the IEP (i.e., goals, services) require a subsequent meeting; minor changes, such as classroom methodology, may not.

The IEP: Key to the IDEA

The individualized education program (IEP) is key to the educational philosophy embodied in IDEA. Whereas in the past, educational placements (or denial of education) were most often based on generalized categorical labels such as "mentally retarded," the law now requires that each student with a disability be treated as an individual and educated according to the child's unique needs and capabilities. Students with disabilities are no longer expected to adapt to the services available; schools are expected to adapt and to devise some means of providing the services that students require. The IEP represents a dramatic change in public school orientation from the general to the specific, and from the convenience of the school district to the needs of the child. The success, or lack thereof, of schools in meeting the needs of the children they serve often depends on ensuring that school staff members understand this basic paradigm shift.

Schools have come a long way in recent decades, from rigid homogeneity to much more flexibly arranged and fluid classrooms. The inclusion of students with disabilities in that milieu can be seen as simply one step in an already established direction. Similarly, the process of writing and implementing IEPs can be seen as a training tool for educators in the continuing process of individualization of instruction for all students.

Writing an IEP for each student is time-consuming and scheduling problems may be substantial and disagreements common. However, a well-designed school process that values, respects, and rewards professionalism can alleviate many problems, and an understanding of the educational value of the process builds tolerance. With this understanding in mind, the IEP has five important purposes.

1. It is an extension of procedural protections guaranteed to parents and students.
2. It is a management tool to ensure provision of appropriate special education and related services. Important in this respect are the ongoing evaluation components which measure a child's progress.
3. It is a compliance monitoring device to determine whether a student with disabilities is receiving a free appropriate public education.
4. It is a written commitment of resources.
5. It is a communication vehicle between/among all participants involved in programming for the student with disabilities. As such, it inherently provides an opportunity for resolving differences of opinion.

This chapter describes current official interpretations of legal points involving IEPs that may be confusing or ambiguous. It then presents a variety of information on "best practices," including sample IEP provisions, examples of IEP goals and objectives statements, suggestions for improving cooperation and communication, and other information related to the five IEP purposes listed above.

Legal Issues

When the IEP Is Required

The first IEP meeting must be held within thirty days of the evaluation team determination that the student needs special education, and additional meetings may be held as often as necessary. The completed IEP must be implemented as soon as possible following the meetings, and the IEP must be in place before the start of special education programs and services. There can be no undue delay in providing special education and related services to the child. It is required that programs and services be provided a student within a reasonable time following receipt of initial parent consent to evaluate a child. For most children it can be expected that services offered under an IEP would begin within sixty days of the school's receipt of parental consent for the initial evaluation.

The IDEA requires that IEPs be reviewed by the IEP team periodically, but at least annually, in order to regularly review and, if necessary, to revise the student's educational program or services. New annual goals must be determined, including short-term objectives (or benchmarks) and appropriate changes made when necessary, including changes in related services or the extent of participation in regular education. Thus, the intent of the law is that school districts and parents, based on assessment/evaluation findings and student progress, regularly review all of the IEP components (service delivery and full continuum of placement options) to determine that program, placement, and services remain appropriate. Changes in the IEP that relate to appropriate programming (including goals, objectives, or benchmarks), related services, accommodations, and supplementary aids and services may be made only through the IEP team review process conducted at a team meeting. Acceptable unilateral changes by the school are very limited, i.e., day-to-day adjustments in methodology or materials used to meet an objective.

Each student's IEP must be accessible to each regular and special education teacher and each related service or other service provider responsible for its implementation. Each teacher and service provider must be personally informed of his or her specific responsibilities regarding implementation of the IEP and specific accommodations, modifications, and supports that must be provided for the student. Education leaders are responsible for establishing and maintaining these important communication processes, and there is no excuse for ignorance

on the part of those persons responsible for the provision of a child's FAPE or their temporary substitutes.

Parents and schools may request IEP reviews more frequently than annually, and schools are likely to respond favorably to parent requests. If a school believes a review is unnecessary and refuses the parents' request, it must provide parents the full detailed notice discussed in Chapter 2 and allow the parents an opportunity to request mediation or a due process hearing on the issue. It is expected that whenever a student is not making meaningful progress under an IEP, the school will reconvene the IEP team to review the student's progress and make necessary adjustments.

Appropriate Programming

Every child with a disability who is entitled to special education under the IDEA must be provided FAPE. Although that phrase conveys some specific meaning (e.g., "free" means no additional cost to parents above what other public school children pay), the word "appropriate" has no clear meaning in statute or regulation, which is probably why IEP teams often struggle with their role under the IDEA.

After twenty-five years of implementation, the IDEA itself still does not provide much direction. Naturally, the courts have been called on to fill that void. The first Supreme Court ruling interpreting the IDEA had as the primary legal issue the interpretation of the word "appropriate." The lower federal courts had issued differing interpretations of the meaning of the term. The Court at least partially succeeded in clarifying an understanding of the term. The Court ruled that schools are required to provide access to educational programs for children with disabilities that are individually designed to provide educational benefit to the child. Schools are not required to "maximize" student potential or provide the "best" programs possible (*Board of Education v. Rowley*, 1982).

Subsequent lower court rulings have made it clear that "minimal" or "trivial" educational benefit will not be considered appropriate (e.g., *Polk v. Central Susquehanna Intermediate Unit 16*, 1988; *Drew P. v. Clarke County School District*, 1989). One court ruling has required the application of a "meaningful educational benefit" standard in determining whether a school's IEP met the minimal standard of appropriateness (*Ridgewood Board of Education v. N.E.*, 1999), and another court has ruled that a determination of benefit for an individual student must be flexible enough to take the student's potential into consideration (*T. R. v. Kingwood Township Board of Education*, 2000).

Neither the law contained in statute, regulations, nor court interpretations clearly establish the standard of "appropriate," which is to be applied to educational programming developed by IEP teams. That determination is left to the persons on the IEP teams, those who know the child's educational needs and available resources best. The IEP must be designed, at minimum, to provide an educational benefit for the child that is meaningful in terms of the child's educational progress.

Participants in the IEP Meeting

The School District Representative

The person designated in the school's procedure to represent the district at the IEP meeting must be "qualified to provide or supervise the provision of specially designed instruction," must be knowledgeable about and have the authority to commit school resources, must ensure that IEP services will be delivered, and must be knowledgeable about the "general curriculum" (curriculum content adopted for all children). This person frequently is the school principal, but it also may be a special education administrator or specialist, such as a speech therapist, as long as this person has been delegated the appropriate authority to fill the role. The school may designate another of the school's IEP team members to also serve as the school's representative, so long as all the qualification criteria are met.

Clearly, the person acting in this capacity should have knowledge of the various school district resources and programs (e.g., transportation) in order to meet the intended role of district representative. It should be further understood that services agreed on at the IEP meeting will actually be provided and may not be vetoed or altered at a higher administrative, or even school board, level.

The process of IEP team decision-making is the epitome of the concept of team empowerment, and IEPs may not be unilaterally changed by any one person or group of persons in the school district, except the IEP team. Team decisions, when made in conformance with the law, may be changed only through a subsequent IEP team meeting decision or a due process hearing decision rendered by a hearing officer.

The Special Education Teacher

At least one of the child's special education teachers or special education providers must be present at IEP meetings. Federal regulations suggest that in deciding which special education teacher will participate in meetings on a specific child's IEP, the school may wish to consider the following alternatives:

a. For a child with disabilities who is receiving special education, the "teacher" should be the child's special education teacher; the person responsible for implementing the IEP. If the child's disability is a speech impairment, then the "teacher" could be the speech/language pathologist.
b. If the child's special education teacher is not yet identified, then a teacher qualified to provide special education in the child's area of suspected disability could attend.

The school must ensure that the child's special education teacher receives a copy of the finalized IEP before beginning work with the child.

The Regular Education Teacher

At least one regular education teacher of the child must attend if the child is, or may be, participating in the regular education environment. Due to the IDEA's strong preference for inclusion of students in the regular classroom, the vast majority of IEP teams will include at least one regular education teacher. The school may designate which teacher will participate when the child has more than one regular education teacher, but it is recommended that the participant be a teacher who will be responsible for implementing the IEP. If the participation of more than one regular education teacher is considered to be beneficial to the child's success in the general curriculum, then her attendance would be appropriate. In the case of a child whose behavior impedes the learning of himself or others, a regular education teacher knowledgeable about "positive behavior strategies" and behavior interventions should be encouraged to attend.

The primary purpose of the presence of a regular education teacher on the IEP team is to help facilitate, through her expertise regarding the general curriculum and regular classroom environment, successful placement of the child in the regular classroom (inclusion). Regular education teachers are especially important in assisting in the determination of positive behavioral interventions and strategies, if necessary, as well as supplementary aids and services, program modifications, accommodations, and supports for the school staff working with the child. This presents an opportunity for regular educators to use new leverage in obtaining the supports they need to provide effective programming to special education students (Huefner, 2000). Congress did not expect that regular class teachers would be required to participate in all aspects of the IEP team's work, only that portion of the IEP content that impacts progress in

the general education curriculum and regular education classrooms (House Report No. 105-95, 1997, p. 101). It anticipated that regular class teachers would not need to attend IEP meetings regarding matters which did not concern the regular class placement (i.e., school nurse's role in a health plan, transportation).

Attendance by too many teachers and other staff members can make an IEP meeting unwieldy and sometimes intimidating to parents. It is advisable to solicit opinions from the student's other teachers before a meeting without requiring their attendance. All teachers of a particular child should be informed about the results of the meeting and should have easy access to a copy of the IEP. All persons responsible for the implementation of the IEP must be informed of their responsibilities and the accommodations, modifications, and supports that must be provided the child. This will help ensure that the child's needs are met across special education and regular education environments. Educational leaders have the responsibility of ensuring that relevant IEP content is made known and available to those staff members who must carry out its provisions.

All school staff members should be reminded from time to time about the confidentiality of education records. Without the written consent of parents, information from education records, including IEPs, should not be disclosed to school employees or volunteers who do not have a legitimate educational interest in the child.

The Parents

Educators must make a conscious effort to ensure that parents have the opportunity to participate meaningfully in the IEP process. Generally, parents must be notified of the first IEP meeting soon after a decision is made that the child is eligible for special education, thus allowing them time to prepare. Meetings can be scheduled, as determined by state law, for the dual purpose of both finalizing the eligibility determination and beginning work on the initial IEP, when the appropriate persons are present and the parents have been appropriately notified.

IEP meetings must be scheduled at a "mutually agreed on time and place." Parents must be advised of the purpose of each planned meeting, and the more detail provided, the better. The role of the parents is that of full and equal participant, along with school personnel. Teams must consider parent concerns and the information they provide in both developing and reviewing IEPs. Surprise situations and issues tend to result in less than meaningful parent participation.

Parents provide critical information about the child that cannot be easily obtained elsewhere, such as health history, interests, behavior outside formal school settings, and special abilities. It has been suggested that educators should encourage parents and their child to think about the likely future needs of the child and what the family sees as the child's future. One source strongly recommends that families be assisted in developing a "vision" of the child's future on which the IEP team can focus its attention (Iowa Department of Education, 1998). (See page 363 on the model IEP form in Appendix E.)

Parents must be afforded the opportunity to participate fully in determinations of the IEP contents described below, and they must be regularly informed of their child's progress. IEP meetings must be scheduled at a "mutually agreed on time and place." Information about meeting agendas should be shared with parents sufficiently in advance of meetings so that they can prepare and be able to participate meaningfully in discussions and decisions. The oral or written notice of IEP meetings must inform parents of the time and location of the meeting, who will be present (at least by title), what will be discussed at the meeting (purpose), and of their right to bring other people to the meeting who have knowledge or special expertise re-

garding the child. The school may inquire in advance as to what persons, if any, the parents may plan to bring to the meetings, but there is no requirement that the parents provide that information. The school must provide an interpreter and other necessary accommodations when the parents require them.

All attempts to contact parents about meetings should be documented. If parents cannot or will not attend the meeting, then other methods of obtaining parent participation, such as individual or conference phone calls or home visits should be attempted. If parents remain unwilling or continue to refuse to participate, a meeting can be held and decisions made without their presence, provided the reasonable efforts to arrange a mutually agreed on time and place for a meeting have been documented.

Parents have the right to request an IEP review meeting at any time. The school generally should agree to hold the meeting when conditions warrant. Should the school refuse to convene an IEP meeting requested by parents, it must provide the parents with a detailed written explanation including a notice of the means by which the parent may obtain a description of parental safeguards, which include the right to request mediation or a due process hearing. (See school's legal duties when refusing parent requests in Chapter 2.)

The school may determine whether an IEP meeting can be audio or videotaped, unless taping is necessary to ensure that the parents understand the IEP process and product. Owing to parent anxiety, lack of familiarity with educational jargon, and the complexity of the IEP process, it is likely that many parents can legitimately claim to need to record all or parts of IEP meetings. A copy of the completed IEP must be provided to parents at no cost.

Maintenance of a good parent/school relationship is of great practical importance. Parent support for the education plan in the home will greatly increase the likelihood of successful results at school. Even though parents are not legally required to carry out the terms of IEPs in the home, they will normally do so in an effort to support their child and the school.

Informed written parent consent is required prior to the initial provision of special education programs and services under the first IEP. Parents must be provided with a full, detailed written notice and a request for written consent (see Chapter 2). In the event that following an appropriate evaluation, a child has been identified as needing special education, an IEP has been completed and the parents refuse to provide written consent for the initial placement in special education programs and services, the school should take appropriate action. In most situations, the school may use mediation or administrative due process hearing procedures in an effort to obtain permission from a hearing officer to proceed with the initial placement of the child.

Although not required by law, a parent's signature, along with a clear statement of agreement, on a continuing IEP is generally considered an efficient way to provide documentation of parent participation in subsequent reviews of the IEP.

Signing the IEP and giving consent does not, however, prevent parents from later disagreeing with the student's program or initiating a mediation conference or due process hearing. Even though the child's parents are in complete agreement with changes in an IEP (the changes may even have resulted from a parent request), they must be provided a detailed written notice of any proposed significant changes and a reminder of how to obtain a description of their parental rights under law. Chapter 2 discusses these notice requirements in more detail.

Others

At least one person on the IEP team must be able to interpret the instructional implications of evaluation results. This person may also play another role on the team, i.e., teacher or school representative.

If appropriate, as determined largely by the parents, the child may attend IEP meetings, in whole or in part. Parents should be advised before each IEP meeting that they may invite their child to participate, and the appropriateness of their decision may be discussed by the team beforehand. The primary questions for consideration on child involvement are whether the child will be helpful in developing an IEP, whether the child will benefit from attendance and participation, or both. If part of the purpose of the IEP meeting is transition services, the school must invite the student and the parents must be informed that their child will be invited. If the child does not attend meetings where transition is considered, then the school must attempt to ensure that the student's preferences and interests are known and are considered.

Students should be prepared in advance for fulfilling their role in IEP team meetings. They should have the IEP concept and process explained or modeled in a way which assures understanding. Students should be helped to organize and prepare their thoughts in advance of the meeting and should be debriefed following the meeting as a follow-up to aid in understanding.

At the discretion of the parents or the school, other individuals "who have knowledge or special expertise regarding the child," including related services personnel, may attend as appropriate. Attendance at meetings of related services staff members, such as physical and occupational therapists, can assist in the resolution of many inclusion concerns, from transportation to student peer support (Szabo, 2000). The above quoted language from the statute represents a subtle but important change in law and policy. Now, attendees must have knowledge about, or an interest in, the child. Previously, any persons could attend when invited, whether or not they had knowledge about the child. This new provision will usually exclude representatives of teacher organizations and school board members from attending. In order for others, such as attorneys, to be present, they would need to possess knowledge of, or expertise regarding, the child. The presence of attorneys has long been discouraged when their participation would have the result of creating an adversarial atmosphere not in the best interest of the child (Diehl from Hehir, 1993). More recent developments indicate that there may be a developing trend toward reducing attorney participation in order to remove some of the legalistic atmosphere from some IEP meetings (Rosenfeld, 1999).

Schools will normally not have to pay parents' attorneys' fees for their work related to IEP meetings unless the IEP meeting has been ordered by a hearing officer or judge.

The final federal regulations implementing the 1997 Amendments to the IDEA reduced the statutory requirement of knowledge and special expertise on the part of discretionary invitees of the parent or school. Under the regulations, the determination of whether the invited person has adequate knowledge or expertise to participate is delegated to the parents or school who invite the person to be a member of the IEP team.

Transition Planning— Agency Representatives

At age fourteen, or earlier if appropriate, a student's IEP team must give consideration to planning for academic coursework and programs that will lead the student into transitioning from school to adult living.

At age sixteen, or earlier if appropriate, students with disabilities who need "transition services" to facilitate the student's movement from school to post-school experiences must have those services included in their IEPs. This requires the consideration of inviting additional persons to the IEP meetings who are representatives of community agencies knowledgeable about available community transition services, such as post-secondary vocational training, adult education, independent living, employment training, and programs to assist young adults with disabilities in the post-school development of employment and adult living skills. Chapter 8 provides more detail on transition programming.

IEP Decision-Making

The IEP team decision-making is accomplished through consensus, not by majority vote. Consensus is a type of decision-making that may be unfamiliar to many educators and requires explanation:

> Consensus is a form of group decision-making based upon general agreement, not on voting. There are several advantages in using consensus:
>
> - It is a win-win solution.
> - It provides ownership of ideas by all group members.
>
> Unanimity is not the objective. Consensus is reached when all members of the group are willing to accept an idea or concept as the best choice for the group.
>
> . . . . .
>
> Consensus is a decision each team member can live with and support. It is a decision each person can agree not to sabotage. It does not involve everyone's first choice or a majority vote. A decision reached by consensus does mean that each individual has the opportunity to voice an opinion and a decision is reached when no one feels the need to veto. If any member of the team cannot live with a particular decision, then he/she has an obligation to state an opinion and prevent the idea from being included.*

When School and Parents Disagree on the IEP

The ultimate responsibility to ensure that an appropriate IEP is developed remains at all times

---

* From *A Solution-Focused Process for Addressing Student Needs* (p. 56), by the Grant Wood Area Education Agency, 1997, Cedar Rapids, IA. Reprinted by permission.

with the school. When disagreements over IEP terms arise, the school and parents should attempt first to resolve differences through negotiation. They may jointly agree to short-term or interim IEPs (one to nine weeks), with appropriate assessment, and then meet again to determine formally whether the interim IEP should be continued or modified. Specific conditions and interim IEP terms should be developed in the IEP format, and parents should be fully involved.

When achievement of consensus is not likely, the school staff should proceed to complete the development of the IEP and provide copies to the parents. Written consent of the parents is required only before the initial IEP may be implemented. Subsequent IEPs may be implemented without parent consent so long as parents are provided proper notice, including a reference to where a list of parent rights may be obtained. As a technical matter, this detailed written notice should be given even when there is no parent disagreement with a proposed change in IEP terms or placement. (See Chapter 2 for details of notice requirements.) From a purely legal standpoint, courts do not normally view harshly a mere technical violation of IDEA procedures unless the parents or student were somehow harmed or prejudiced as a result of the procedural violation.

After the parents receive written notice of a proposed change in the IEP, they may initiate mediation or a due process hearing to challenge the appropriateness of the proposed change in program. If, after a reasonable amount of time, no hearing has been initiated by the parents, the school may go ahead and implement the proposed change in IEP programs and services.

Some states provide for a pre-appeal mediation opportunity to resolve disputes informally before the parents and schools become entrenched in their positions as a result of the actual filing of a request for a due process hearing. Some state protection and advocacy organizations (federally funded advocacy programs for persons of all ages with disabilities) have taken the position that their clients must first attempt the pre-appeal mediation process prior to filing for a due process hearing. This is an effort to maintain a cooperative working relationship which is in the best interest of the child.

If a request for mediation or a due process hearing is filed, then the most current IEP program in which the child had been previously placed remains in effect until differences are resolved by mutual agreement or through a due process hearing (see "stay-put" in Chapter 2).

When Educators Disagree on an IEP

The give and take of consensus building will normally achieve agreement among educators, albeit it may not be strong support. Rarely will educators remain strongly divided and resistant to attempt trial programs and approaches for a student. The IDEA does not address the possibility (eventuality) that educators on an IEP team (and evaluation and placement teams) may remain divided. Thus, while some state laws provide for dissenting opinions to team decisions, the school must implement a "team" decision. The dissenting group of educators has no clear status under federal law (Hehir to Anonymous, 1996).

ELEMENTS OF AN IEP

IEP Format

The format and length of the IEP are not prescribed or determined by the law; historically, three to five pages were sufficient. In 1997, Congress publicly prided itself in reducing the paperwork required under the IDEA. However, it is not likely that with all the currently required elements the IEP was at all shortened. As Huefner has stated, "The IEP paperwork implications are daunting" (2000, p. 203).

A model IEP form, which is quite comprehensive and fourteen pages in length, is included in Appendix E. Although shorter IEP forms may be possible to obtain, brevity may result in important IEP considerations or content being overlooked by IEP teams.

IEP Content

Child's Present Level of Educational Performance

The information contained in the PLEP should describe the effects of the child's disability on any relevant educational area—academic, personal-social, living skills, physical education, or vocational. The information should be accurate, stated in measurable terms as much as possible, and explained in language that is easily understood. The PLEP must include a description of how the disability affects the child's participation and progress in the general curriculum.

The general curriculum is the same curriculum available and provided to nondisabled children. For preschool children, as appropriate, the PLEP should identify how the disability affects the child's participation in age-appropriate activities. The PLEP should also reflect the IEP team's considerations of the child's strengths and the results of standardized tests.

Statements in the PLEP should be based on the results of the evaluation of the student and should address all areas in which special education and related services are needed. The importance of the PLEP in the development of IEPs should not be overlooked by the team. It is the foundational basis for the appropriate educational program and services identified in the IEP. There must be a direct identifiable link between the PLEP and the goals, objectives, and services provided in the IEP. The reporting of mere test score results in the PLEP does not provide sufficient data for the rest of the IEP process. (See Appendix A for sample PLEP statements.)

Goals and Objectives

Annual goals written in response to the PLEP statement must be based on assessment results and parent input where it is provided. Annual goal statements should be specific and indicate (1) the direction of change (e.g., increase or decrease) and (2) the desired or expected levels of change in specific skill areas. These goals should be the team's best estimate of what the student will be able to accomplish within one year. Generally, one to three goals should be provided for each affected area identified in the PLEP statement. (See Appendix B for sample goal statements.)

To assure individualization of short-term objectives in meeting the expressed goals, an estimation of each student's progress per grading period should be considered when writing an IEP. The short-term objectives should include a description of the behavior a student is expected to demonstrate as well as the level of performance that would indicate achievement of the objective. The annual goals and short-term objectives should be related to the child's progress in the general curriculum and the meeting of the child's other educational needs resulting from the child's disability. Objectives should be broad enough to allow for flexibility in classroom teaching methods and materials, while also providing a means for monitoring and evaluating student progress. Objectives must be both appropriate for the student and useful to those carrying out the student's program. Thus, the IEP team must also make an individualized determination of which educational needs will not be addressed in the general curriculum and how those needs will be met, such as in a self-contained special education class. For preschool children (ages three to five), short-term objectives should be designed, as appropriate, to allow the child to participate in appropriate activities. (See Appendix C for sample short-term objective statements.)

Short-term objectives (or benchmarks) should be formally reviewed for progress at regular intervals during the school year, but not less frequently than the times of the regular school district grading periods (i.e., six or nine weeks).

IEP goals and objectives should not be determined for a child's progress in the general curriculum if the child's disability does not affect the child's progress in the general curriculum.

Regular or special education teachers may make day-to-day adjustments in instructional methods and approaches, which are not fundamental elements of the student's special education, in order to assist a student to achieve the goals and objectives without obtaining agreement and approval from the entire IEP team. Changes considered in annual goals, short-term objectives or benchmarks, or other components expressly described in the IEP, require IEP team review and decision.

Evaluation Criteria—"Monitoring"

Each short-term objective (or benchmark) should include specific evaluation criteria, such as percentage of correct responses and minimum or maximum number of behaviors in a time span. Such criteria should be realistic and should not exceed the standards expected of regular students. Evaluation procedures might include teacher observation, frequency counts or other types of continuing data collection, graphs or charts of progress, anecdotal records, student self-evaluation, and so on, as well as tests. The criteria need not be listed as a separate section but may be integrated into student objectives (see Appendix C for examples). The purpose of these evaluation criteria is to objectively determine the child's progress toward the stated objectives. They serve as aids in assessing the effectiveness of the IEP so that the IEP may be revised, when desirable, in order to meet the child's instructional needs. (For exam-

ples of how progress monitoring can be incorporated within IEP forms, see Appendix E.)

In some schools, this continuous assessment is known as "systematic progress monitoring." The name implies a great improvement over the "by guess" or "by gosh" approach sometimes used in the past to monitor student progress on IEP objectives. "Systematic progress monitoring" involves the development of a systematic procedure for collecting and displaying a child's performance on objectives over time. (Iowa Department of Education, 2000). Progress may be displayed on charts, graphs, and other pictorial formats, often using classroom technology, such as computers, available for other classroom uses as well. (For an example of how progress on IEP objectives can be charted within an IEP form, see Appendix E, page 369.)

Examples of Integrated PLEP: Goals and Objectives

The interdependent relationship of the PLEP and the goals and objectives in the IEP is very important. When care and attention is given, in turn, to the successive drafting of each, a better integrated educational program is the result.

In their book on IEP development, Bateman and Linden provide excellent advice about IEP formation, content, and development. Following are two brief examples of their perspective of the important integration of the PLEP, goals, short-term objectives, and services:*

1. PLEP: Reads first grade material at 20–30 words per minute with 5–10 errors, guesses at all unknown words.
    Annual Goal: Will read third-grade material at 80–100 words per minute with 0–2 errors.

---

*From *Better IEPs: How to Develop Legally Correct and Educationally Useful Programs* (3rd ed.) (pp. 104–105), by Barbara D. Bateman and Mary Anne Linden, 1998, Longmont, CO: Sopris West. Copyright 1992–1998 by Barbara D. Bateman and Mary Anne Linden. Adapted by permission.

Objective #1: By December 15, will read
second-grade material at 40–60
words per minute with 0–5 errors.

Objective #2: By March 15, will read
third-grade material at 50 words per
minute with 0–4 errors.

Service to be provided: One-to-one tutoring in a highly structured reading
program; five lessons weekly, 45
minutes each, provided in private,
quiet area of resource room.

2. PLEP: Several times (five to ten) daily,
student draws or talks inappropriately
about bodily functions.

Annual goal: No inappropriate talk or
drawings about bodily functions.

Objective #1: By February 1, fewer than
2 such inappropriate drawings or
vocalizations per week.

Objective #2: By April 15 maintain fewer
than 2 such inappropriate drawings
or vocalizations per month.

Services provided: Behavioral contin-
gency plan with student-selected reward and response cost.

Other examples of integrated IEP components can be found in Appendix D.

Special Education, Related Services, and Other Services

All children with disabilities who need special
education and related services are entitled under the IDEA to such services. "Special education" is defined in the IDEA as specially designed instruction to meet the unique needs of
a child with a disability. "Related services" are
those services necessary to help the student
benefit from special education. The IEP must
include a statement of all education services
needed by the student, not just those readily
available in the district. The document must
identify who will provide the services, even if
another agency provides them. Services must be
delivered at no cost to the student's family
above the cost of fees normally charged to the

parents of students without disabilities as part of
the regular education program.

"Specially-designed instruction" means the
adaptation of content, methodology, or delivery
of instruction to address the child's unique
needs which result from the disability, and
which will ensure the child's access to the general curriculum. "General curriculum" means
that curriculum adopted by the school to be applicable for all children and specifically refers to
content rather than to a particular educational
setting. However, the effort at a clear distinction
between special education and general curriculum for many children may be illusory because
all the IEP considerations and support (i.e., accommodations, supplementary aids and services) for achievement in the general curriculum are driven by the IDEA's strong preference
for the inclusion element of LRE. The goal or focus of the IDEA is to assist the child to meet the
educational standards expected to apply to all
children and to ensure that children with disabilities have the opportunity to achieve those
standards.

The legal requirements of IEP statements
regarding the provision of special education
and related services have been expanded by the
1997 Amendments to include a statement about
supplementary aids and services to be provided
to the child or on behalf of the child. This addition was likely added to nudge the IEP team to
think in the direction of the philosophy of inclusion of the child into the regular classroom
setting as much as is appropriate. The IEP must
now also contain a statement of program modifications, accommodations, or school personnel supports that will be provided for the child.
All of this is to be provided with the motive of
advancing the child toward attaining the IEP annual goals, being involved in and progressing in
the general curriculum, and participating in "extracurricular and other nonacademic activities"
along with other children. Support for school
staff might include such items as specific training in behavior strategies, classroom manage-

ment, collaboration skills, and effective integration of children with disabilities into regular school settings. These normally would be targeted in an IEP for the purpose of assisting staff to meet the needs of a specific child.

Once related services, supplementary aids and services, modifications, and accommodations are provided in an IEP, subsequent significant changes, deletions, and amendments require review and approval by the IEP team. No one person, or group of persons, short of the entire IEP team, may unilaterally make significant changes to the IEP.

In line with the legal requirement that all students be educated in the "least restrictive" or most typical educational environment appropriate, the IEP must include a statement of the extent to which the student will not participate in regular programs. Both academic and non-academic activities should be included. Thus, a presumption has been created that the child with disabilities will participate in education programs and activities along with children without disabilities, unless the presumption is rebutted by a written IEP statement explaining why the child will not participate in the regular class or activities. It is likely that Congress intended to make an IEP team's decision to exclude the child from regular classes and activities more difficult by requiring it to justify its decision in writing. This is yet another example of congressional intent to have students with disabilities included.

The areas of physical education and vocational education are given special status in the consideration of IEP development. If the IEP is silent on these points, then it is expected that the child will participate in the same physical and vocational education programs as children without disabilities. If special or adaptive physical education or specially designed vocational education programs are to be provided, then the child's IEP must expressly describe those programs.

The IDEA requires that assistive technology devices and services be made available to students with disabilities, if required, as part of students' special education, related services, or supplementary aids and services. While assistive technology devices and services are defined in the law, their exact meaning in the context of programming for students has not been made clear. Generally, the phrase "assistive technology device" refers to equipment used to aid the functional capabilities of children with disabilities (e.g., calculator in mathematics, word processor for writing), and "assistive technology service" refers to the human services of a technician or trainer required to assist a child with a disability to make use of and benefit from an assistive technology device. It is likely that the requirement of IEP team consideration of assistive technology devices and services in law was not for the purpose of enlarging the scope of educational service and resource offerings of schools. More likely it was a congressional effort to expand the thinking of IEP teams beyond that of the traditional services of personnel and adaptive teaching strategies historically provided students with disabilities.

Assistive technology devices usually do not include personalized devices such as eyeglasses, hearing aids, or braces that children will require regardless of whether they are attending school. However, if an IEP team determines that a personal device is required for a child in order to ensure that the child receives FAPE, then it must be provided at no cost to the child's parents. Assistive technology includes both technology related to a child's individual needs (e.g., electronic notetakers, cassette recorders) as well as general technology devices used by all students. The school must assure that necessary accommodations are provided to allow the child to use technology devices used by all students. The use of assistive technology devices in a child's home is to be determined by the IEP team based on curricular expectations (i.e., homework). Parents cannot be charged for normal use and wear and tear on the devices; however, subject to state law, parents may be responsible for loss, theft, or damage of assistive technology due to negligence or misuse.

Duration of Services

To ensure that the school's resource commitment is clear to parents and other IEP team members, the projected date for the beginning of services as well as modifications and the anticipated frequency, location, and duration of services must be expressly stated in the IEP. Some general standard of time for services (minutes per day or week) must be indicated that is (1) appropriate to the specific service to be provided and (2) clear to all participants.

Transition Services

The IEP must include for students at age fourteen, or younger, if appropriate (i.e., at risk for dropping out), an updated annual statement of transition service needs, under appropriate IEP components, that focus on the student's course of study (i.e., advanced placement, vocational, or specific academic areas). The course of study identifies the direction of the student's course work and aids in identifying the transition needs and services of the student. Following are some examples of course of study statements:*

- As many family and consumer science classes as possible to acquire adult living skills, functional math, and community-based work experience in the health and food service area.
- Functional classes to develop skills for working on a team collaboratively, work experience in a sheltered workshop, and functional life skills.

---

* From *Their Future . . . Our Guidance* (p. 29), by the Iowa Department of Education, 1998, Des Moines, IA. Iowa Department of Education. Adapted by permission.

- Math through algebra II, all industrial arts classes that focus on engineering and technology path with construction fields, job shadowing, and possible community work experience.
- Health occupation path to include courses in science through physics, math through algebra II, college preparation core classes, and work based on learning experiences in medical settings.

For each child with disabilities who is age sixteen (or younger if determined appropriate on an individual basis), the IEP must contain statements regarding needed transition services and identify each participating community agency's responsibility to the youth's progress before the student leaves school. If any community agency fails to provide a planned transition service while the child is still in school, the school must initiate a new IEP meeting as soon as possible to identify alternative agencies and services to meet the transition objectives provided in the child's IEP. For sample language on how to document transition planning, see pages 370–371 of the model IEP form in Appendix E.

District-Wide Assessments

In its consideration of the 1997 Amendments to the IDEA, Congress was very concerned about determining the general academic progress of students with disabilities. In an effort to determine the degree of success of educating such students, especially in the "general curriculum" areas, the law now presumes that children with disabilities will participate in all state or district-wide student achievement assessments. If a child requires individual modifications or accommodations in the administration of a test, then a statement of needed modifications and accommodations must appear in the IEP and must be provided. Accommodations are meant to make the testing experience fair, not to give some students a special advantage. Accommodations do not change the substance of what is tested. Modifications and accommodations in testing could involve time (length, breaks), directions (highlighting, simplifying), presentation of questions (large print, fewer per page), response (oral, word processor), and setting (lighting, noise).

States appear to have made significant advances in accommodating the needs of students with disabilities and in documenting those efforts. However, much is still needed in terms of consistency in data gathering between states, as well as in the standardizing of terms, tests, and reporting procedures before the data will answer Congress' questions regarding evidence of academic progress (Elliott et al, 2000). The issue of requiring students with disabilities to take district-wide and state-wide exams have their most serious implications when the results of those exams are used to make important educational decisions, such as graduation and retention. O'Neill (2001) has identified several lawsuits arising from the alleged failure of states to appropriately take students with disabilities into account when developing, administering and scoring exams with important educational outcomes. He concluded that the new requirement for testing students with disabilities in such examinations, and the various legal issues inherent in such exams, will result in considerable future litigation.

It is estimated that 85% of students with disabilities will be able to participate in district and state-wide assessments with or without accommodations (Elliott et al, 1998). The other 15% must not be forgotten.

When the IEP team determines that a child's participation in the general assessments is not appropriate and the child will not participate in a state or district-wide assessment, in whole or in part, a statement in the IEP must indicate why that assessment is not appropriate for the child. The IEP of each student with disabilities not participating in state and district-wide assessment must contain a description of the individualized means of assessment that will be used

with that student. Most of the children in this category will be in alternative curricular programs and will not be expected to meet general curriculum goals. Alternative assessment has included the use of portfolios in at least two states that have established alternative assessments (Elliott et al, 1998).

Initial work on alternative assessment activities by researchers has established that the focus of the alternative assessments may be on skills and experiences gained in the real world with only integrated academics being of importance to traditional assessment. Testing methodology may well include a variety of tests, portfolio reviews, student record reviews, observations, and interviews gathered from persons, both adults and students, who know the student (Ysseldyke & Olsen, 1999). Some initial teacher reactions to the early alternative assessment effort have raised issues regarding the amount of time required, increased documentation, reduced time for teaching and the reliability of scoring inherent in alternative assessment strategies (Kleinert, Kennedy, & Kearns, 1999). For a sample of appropriate documentation of accommodations and alternative assessments, see page 375 of the model IEP form found in Appendix E.

Report Card

Each child's IEP must contain a statement of how the child's progress toward annual goals will be measured and how the child's parents will be regularly informed, at least as often as parents of children without disabilities are informed (i.e., report cards) of their child's academic progress. The parents must be expressly advised of the extent to which their child's progress is sufficient to enable the child to achieve the IEP goals by the end of the year. This requirement is in addition to the regular school reports to parents of academic progress in curricular areas which many parents of children with disabilities will receive. For an example of how this report of progress can be an integral part of the IEP, see pages 365–369 of the model IEP in Appendix E.

Transfer of Rights

If, under state law, parental rights under the IDEA will transfer to the student on reaching the age of majority, usually age eighteen, then the IEP must, one year before the student reaches that age, include a statement that the student has been informed of his rights that will transfer at the age of majority. For details on the transfer of rights to the student, see Chapter 8.

IEP Development in a Nutshell

Contrary to expressed congressional goals, the IEP development process and paperwork have not become less burdensome and may seem formidable, if not impossible, the first few times through for team members. Be assured, however, that thousands of educators and parents have survived the process, and in reality have gotten better at it each time. In keeping with their user-friendly approach to advice on IEP development, Bateman and Linden summarized the process nicely in a list of IEP "Do's" and "Don'ts":*

Do's: Program Planning

1. *Do* individualize the child's program.
2. *Do* base the IEP on the individual child's needs, not on the present availability of services in the district.
3. *Do* figure out what supports the child might need to participate in the general curriculum. If there is no need for modifications in the regular classroom, there is reason to question a child's eligibility.

4. *Do* consider the child's strengths and parents' concerns for enhancing their education.
5. *Do* specify all necessary special education, related services, supplementary aids and services, program modifications, and supports for school personnel.
6. *Do* include positive behavioral interventions and discipline strategies when there is reason to believe that behavior is an issue.
7. *Do* meticulously observe all procedural requirements for IEP development and content.
8. *Do* ensure meaningful parent participation.

Don'ts: Program Planning

1. *Don't* worry about "opening the floodgates." Providing certain services to one child does not set a precedent for other children. IEPs address the unique needs of individual children, so what one child needs has no implications for what the district must provide to others.
2. *Don't* clutter IEPs with detailed goals and objectives for all the content standards in the general curriculum. Instead, focus on the accommodations and adjustments an individual child needs for appropriate access to, and participation in, the general curriculum.
3. *Don't* include more than two or three objectives or benchmarks for each annual goal. Objectives and benchmarks should describe "how far, by when" the child should progress toward achievement of each annual goal.
4. *Don't* use lack of funds as an excuse for failure to provide a FAPE.
5. *Don't* ever provide services categorically! For example, don't say that only emotionally disturbed students may have behavioral components in their IEPs or that only students with learning disabilities may be allowed extra time on tests. All services must be based upon the individual child's needs without regard to disability category.

---

* From *Better IEPs: How to Develop Legally Correct and Educationally Useful Programs* (3rd ed.), (pp. 12–13), by Barbara D. Bateman and Mary Anne Linden, 1998, Longmont, CO: Sopris West. Copyright 1992–1998 by Barbara D. Bateman and Mary Anne Linden. Reprinted by permission.

Inclusion Inherent in IEP Process

The word "inclusion" is not found anywhere in the IDEA statutes or regulations, but its presence is obvious. Regular education teachers must be included on IEP teams whenever a child may be placed in the regular classroom. Their participation is to assist in the determination of appropriate supplementary aids and services, class modifications, accommodations and supports for school staff for use with the child while in the regular classroom. The IEP must now specify supplementary aids and services, modifications, accommodations, and support for school staff, and school staff responsible for those services must be advised of their required duty.

The IEP content must include in the PLEP how the child's disability affects the child's participation and progress in the general school curriculum. The IEP must specify that special instruction be provided which will ensure the child's success in the general curriculum.

A presumption has been established that the child will be present in the regular classroom and in regular nonacademic activities. That presumption may be overcome only through a written explanation in the IEP explaining why the child will not participate in regular class or activities.

OTHER IEP ISSUES

Cost of FAPE

Because school budgets have declined relative to an expanding public school mission, many school staff members consciously attempt to keep expenditures low. Generally, there is no reason why members of IEP teams cannot attempt to be conscientious about expenses involved in providing special education programs and services, but they should not allow the costs associated with programming to dictate what is, or is not, "appropriate" for a specific child's needs.

Except for general phrases like "at no cost to parents," "at public expense," and "free appropriate public education," no language is found in the IDEA regarding the expense or cost of programming. The legal result is that for IEP team considerations of appropriateness, cost usually is not relevant to the team's deliberations (Bartlett, 1992; Bartlett & Rosenfeld, 1993). (Cost of supplementary aids and services involved in inclusion may be relevant when significant, see Chapter 6).

In its decision in *Clevenger v. Oakridge School Board* (1984), the Court of Appeals for the Sixth Circuit ruled on the issue of whether it was appropriate to consider the $33,000 difference between the annual cost of the school-proposed program ($55,000) and a parent-proposed program ($88,000). The court ruled that any difference in costs between proposed programs may be considered by the IEP team only when both programs are appropriate. When only one program under consideration is appropriate, the cost of providing the appropriate program should not be a team consideration. Because the parents' proposed placement was determined by the court to be the student's only appropriate placement option, the court ruled that the school could not insist on providing its recommended program on the ground it could be provided at less cost. Schools have found that they cannot refuse to place children with disabilities in appropriate programs on the ground of "difficult budget constraints." One federal court has held that financial "constraints do not provide sufficient grounds for refusing to comply with the Hearing Officer's decision" on placement, and ordered the school to immediately comply with the hearing decision (*Grace B. v. Lexington School Committee*, 1991).

In the 1980s, the Oregon state legislature attempted to limit its financial responsibility for the IEPs of children in certain institutional settings by capping its financial responsibility to the state's "availability of funds." When the legislature subsequently appropriated less funds than were needed to carry out the IEPs of the children in the institutional settings, and consequently their educational programs were curtailed, parents brought suit. The federal courts ruled that Oregon had failed to ensure that the children affected would be provided with a FAPE and ordered the state to ensure that the FAPE of children with disabilities in the institutional settings would be sufficiently funded (*Kerr Center Parents Association v. Charles*, 1988).

School efforts to cut costs in special education programs and services for individual students can backfire. If the cost cutting results in a child not receiving an appropriate program, the parents may unilaterally place the child in a private, often more expensive program and seek reimbursement from the public school. (See Private School Placements by Parents in Chapter 6.)

School District Responsibility and Accountability

An IEP must be fully completed for each public school student who is determined eligible for special education, and IEP programs and services must be provided. Schools and teachers must make a good faith effort to enable the child to achieve the goals and objectives of the IEP. However, federal regulations expressly provide that no school, teacher, or staff member may be held legally accountable under federal law when a child does not achieve the growth anticipated in the IEP. The IEP is not expected to serve as a guarantee that the child will progress at the rate specified in the IEP goals and objectives. Accountability of schools, however, may be achieved through parent due process procedures when parents can establish their children are not receiving an appropriate program.

If the student receives services under contract with another district or with a private

agency, then the district in which the child resides remains responsible for initiating and conducting IEP meetings, covering costs, and ensuring that the pupil's program complies with the law. If a child's placement is out-of-state, the state often, through the local resident school district, remains responsible for ensuring the child receives FAPE through the development, support for, and implementation of an IEP. Once a child is placed in a private facility by the public school, the private facility staff, at the discretion of the school district, may initiate meetings to review and revise the IEP. The public agency still must ensure that one of its representatives and the child's parents attend those private facility IEP meetings and approve any program changes.

Health Plans

Some states require that student health plans be made part of the IEPs for those students needing special health services when the services are related to educational goals, placement in an inclusion setting, or are otherwise referenced in the IEP. Health plans should be kept confidential on a need-to-know basis, whether or not they are made part of an IEP.

Transfer Students

If a student is receiving special education and services from one school district and unilaterally transfers to another school district in the same state (i.e., family moves), then the new district of residence is responsible for providing education and services in conformity with an IEP. An IEP must be in effect before programs and services may begin. A meeting to develop a new IEP is unnecessary if the former resident district's IEP is available, the parents are satisfied with it, and the new school determines that it is appropriate and can be implemented. The IEP from the former district of residence is merely adopted and implemented by the IEP team. If the IEP from the former district of residence is not available, or the parent or school district of residence believes it is not appropriate, a meeting must be conducted for the purpose of creating a new IEP within a short time of enrollment (about a week).

In the latter situation, for a longer period, an interim IEP may be used, so long as parents and the new school agree. If parents and the school cannot agree on an interim IEP, then the IEP from the former school should be implemented, to the extent possible, until a new IEP is developed and implemented. All parental procedural safeguards must be observed (see Chapter 2).

When a student being provided IDEA programs and services transfers from one state to another, the receiving school district is not required to adopt the sending school's IEP. When, however, the receiving school district accepts the other state's most current evaluation and determination of disability, unless the parents indicate they are not satisfied with the IEP, the school may elect to implement the most recent IEP without another IEP meeting. If either the receiving school or the parents are not satisfied with the out-of-state IEP, an IEP meeting would have to be held within thirty days of accepting the receiving school's determination of disability or its own completion of evaluation and disability determination. During the receiving school's evaluation and determination of disability process, the parents and school may agree to an interim IEP and placement. If agreement between the parent and the new school cannot be reached, the student will be placed in regular education. If the parents disagree with the receiving school's new IEP, they may file a request for mediation or due process hearing, and the student will remain in the interim placement or regular education (OSEP Memorandum, 96-5, 1995).

APPROACHES TO RESOLVING PROBLEMS

Good planning and clear communication are essential to the IEP development process. The law implies that school staff members should not arrive at the meeting with the IEP already completed. The participation of parents and others in the discussion must be genuine and meaningful. This is not to suggest that planning or communication among team members should not take place before the meeting. On the contrary, it is desirable to review all assessment results and reports and solicit the opinions of any of the student's teachers who will not be in attendance, as well as those of people who might be providing special services. In situations where trust has been developed, drafts of portions of the IEP may be made in advance, but it must be made absolutely clear to all participants that the drafts are subject to discussion and possible change. In some situations, the sharing of partial drafts with parents in advance of the meeting will deter mistrust and provide parents an opportunity to think about their response or a proposal of their own.

A pre-meeting time for brainstorming among some of the educators offers opportunities to build relationships of trust and cooperation among the professionals involved and to develop a series of well-thought-out proposals based on the input of several individuals. Those persons involved should be reminded that no decisions of a final nature can be made in the absence of a full consideration by the entire IEP team. It is equally important to establish communication with parents before the IEP meeting and to encourage them in advance to come to the meeting prepared to participate. The team should attempt to respond appropriately and in a timely manner to parents questions and concerns in advance of the team meeting. Be sure that staff members make inquiries prior to IEP meetings regarding the types of information parents may need about their children, school programs, and services and the types of support services they need to fully participate in the IEP process (Rock, 2000).

Improving Communication

There are no "typical" IEP meetings. Each is unique unto itself, and each has varying degrees of success. Rosenfeld (1998) has outlined a number of excellent suggestions for improving the likelihood of a successful IEP meeting, which are summarized here:*

- Begin Planning Well in Advance—Inadequate planning and preparation results in too much time being taken up to explain common procedures and unfamiliar terms. Informal preliminary informational meetings, especially for first IEPs with parents, can greatly enhance understanding and cooperation and help parents and educators become comfortable working with each other.
- Give or Send Information Well Before Meeting—Parents need to have a fundamental understanding of the IEP process and what is expected of them. They will have great difficulty participating in a meaningful way if they are absorbed in attempting to understand related services, LRE, and recent evaluation results. Give parents a blank IEP in advance of the meeting and explain the content and structure of the form. Provide recent evaluation results and a list of resources that may be of help to their understanding. Provide a listing of some of the "ideas" school staff members are considering so the parents may give them consideration and ask others about them.
- Beware the "Draft" IEP—When "draft" IEPs give parents the impression that all decision-

making has previously been completed or the burden is on them to challenge existing language, is it any wonder that they may become defensive?

- Offer to Answer Questions Before Meetings —Provide the names, professional responsibilities, and telephone numbers of staff members who will be involved in the IEP meeting, and encourage parents to contact staff and ask questions. Help parents to understand the options available.
- Ask About Meeting Preferences—Times and places of IEP meetings must be mutually convenient to both parents and staff. Ask for and attempt to accommodate parent preferences as much as possible. Parent time and participation are also important.
- Be Flexible in Setting Times for Meetings— When parents indicate problems meeting at times available to school staff, offer to meet early or late in the day so that disruption to the parents' schedules can be minimized.
- Allow Adequate Time for IEP Meeting—Parents will quickly recognize and resent school staff who do not give them adequate time to address their child's needs. Meetings should not have hard and fast times for ending, especially those with the next parents waiting to begin. Time estimates may be given parents, but staff should also advise parents that if the time is not adequate, the meeting will be reconvened so that more time will be available. IEP meetings cannot be limited to predetermined, fixed amounts of time.
- Keep Meeting Size Reasonable—Only school staff required by law or the child's needs should attend IEP meetings. The opinions and views of other staff members should be solicited and reported on, preferably in writing, and made available if needed. Everyone's time is equally valuable and should not be wasted. Unnecessary staff member presence may result in the parents being intimi-

---

* These excellent suggestions were adapted from "Ten Ways to Have More Productive IEP Meetings," by S. James Rosenfeld, 1998, *EDLAW Briefing Papers, VIII* (2), pp. 2–7, Copyright 1998 by EDLAW, Inc. Adapted by permission.

dated or frightened, neither of which adds to meaningful parent participation.

- Choose Adequate and Comfortable Facilities—Child-sized seats may be counterproductive for adult meetings. So, too, may cramped quarters or poor lighting and ventilation. It may be desirable to prepare a folder with all materials in advance and something with which to write. Modest refreshments, especially beverages, are appreciated. The room should reflect the importance of the meeting.

- Agree to Disagree—Although agreement is the recognized goal of the IEP meetings, disagreement is not unhealthy or unwanted. Emphasize areas of agreement and attempt to resolve areas of disagreement, but always move forward. In early communication with parents and staff, it may be desirable to remind participants of this important point. It provides everyone with a "license" to take an active part in the decision-making process.

Rosenfeld concluded his recommendations with the following sage advice: "[t]aking the extra steps to have a calm and cordial meeting is a sign of strength, not weakness, and is likely to return benefits far beyond the effort" (p. 7).

CONCLUSION

The importance of the IEP cannot be overestimated. Even when done correctly, there is no guarantee that all will go well with a student's education; but when done incorrectly, a poor IEP will almost guarantee that a student's educational program will not succeed. The IEP is derived from the assessment of the child's educational needs and is the driving force behind the student's educational placement. There are good arguments for the proposition that because the IEP is the student's program, the IEP is the student's placement.

View from the Court Bench

Board of Education of Hendrick Hudson Central School District v. Rowley (1982). The parents of Amy Rowley, a student with a hearing impairment, who had minimal residual hearing and was an excellent lip reader, requested that the school provide their daughter with a sign-language interpreter for academic class settings. This service was requested in addition to an FM hearing aid and special instruction from a tutor for the deaf one hour each day, as well as a speech therapist for three hours each week that the school agreed to provide. When the school determined that Amy did not need a sign-language interpreter and refused to provide one, the parents sought a due process hearing and later a court review. The case was the first involving special education law to be reviewed by the Supreme Court. Two questions of law were considered by the Court: What did the law mean by the phrase "free appropriate public education," and what was the proper role of the courts in reviewing special education issues?

The Court ruled that the requirement of FAPE meant that schools were not required to "maximize" the potential of students with disabilities or to provide the "best" programs possible. Schools were required only to provide access to specialized instruction and related services which are individually designed to provide educational benefit to the child. The Court noted that the law required that a child with disabilities had to be educated with children without disabilities whenever possible, and if the child is being educated in the regular classroom, then the individualized instruction should be "reasonably calculated to enable the child to achieve passing marks and advance from grade to grade. . . ."

The primary responsibility for formulating the educational methodology to be used with the child rests with state and local educational authorities in cooperation with the child's parents. The parents serve the dual purpose of providing important information into the decision-making processes and serving as advocates for the child when they disagree with the decision being made.

The courts, on the other hand, were relegated the primary task of determining the meaning of technical legal terms and whether the laws' due process and procedural safeguards were properly administered. Courts were directed to enter the realm of determining "appropriateness" with great hesitation and reluctance, and most lower courts have followed that directive.

Timothy W. v. Rochester New Hampshire School District, (1989). Timothy W. had multiple disabilities, including severe and profound mental retardation. He experienced complex developmental disabilities, spastic quadriplegia, cerebral palsy, seizure disorder, and cortical blindness. The school district of residence argued that his disabilities were so severe that he could not benefit from education and, therefore, he was not entitled to any special education.

In reviewing the case, the only major court to rule on the issue, the Court of Appeals for the First Circuit found that in enacting what is now the IDEA, Congress directed that special education was to be provided to all children with disabilities "unconditionally and without exception." It made no difference whether the child derived benefit, and children with disabilities who need special education are entitled to special education, regardless of the severity of the disability.

REFERENCES

Assistance for education of all children with disabilities, 34 Code of Federal Regulations, Part 300 (2000).

Bartlett, L. D. (1992). The cost of FAPE: Can LRE make a difference? *Ed Law Briefing Paper, 1* (9). Hollywood, FL: EDLAW Inc.

Bartlett, L., & Rosenfeld, S. J. (1993). Economic cost factors in providing a free appropriate public education: The legal perspective: *The Journal of Law and Education, 22* (1), 27–60.

Bateman, B. D., & Linden, M. A. (1998). *Better IEPs: How to develop legally correct and educationally useful programs* (3rd). Longmont, CO: Sopris West.

Board of Education of Hendrick Hudson Central School District v. Rowley, 458 U.S. 176, 102 S.Ct. 3034 (1982).

Clevenger v. Oak Ridge School Board, 744 F.2d 514 (6th Cir. 1984).

Diehl from Hehir, 22 IDELR 734 (OSEP, 1993).

Drew P. v. Clarke County School District, 887 F.2d 927 (11th Cir. 1989).

Elliott, J., Ysseldyke, J., Thurlow, M., & Erickson, R. (1998). What about assessment and accountability? Practical implications for educators. *Teaching Exceptional Children, 31* (1), 20–27.

Elliott, J. L., Erickson, R. N., Thurlow, M. L., & Shriner, J. G. (2000). State-level accountability for the performance of students with disabilities: Five years of change. *The Journal of Special Education, 34* (1), 39–47.

Grace B. v. Lexington School Committee, 762 F. Supp. 416 (D. Mass. 1991).

Grant Wood Area Education Agency (1997). *A solution-focused process for addressing student needs.* Cedar Rapids, IA: Author.

Hehir to Anonymous, 25 IDELR 529 (OSEP 1996).

House Report No. 105-95. (1997). U.S. Code Congressional and Administrative News, 78–146.

Huefner, D. S. (2000). The risks and opportunities of the IEP requirements under IDEA '97. *The Journal of Special Education, 33* (4), 194–205.

Iowa Department of Education (2000). *Administrative rules of special education. Chapter 281-41.* Des Moines, IA: Author.

Iowa Department of Education (1998). *Their Future . . . our guidance: Iowa IEP guidebook.* Des Moines, IA: Author.

Kerr Center Parents Association v. Charles, 842 F.2d 1052 (9th Cir. 1988).

Kleinert, H. L., Kennedy, S., & Kearns, J. F. (1999). The impact of alternative assessments: A statewide teacher survey. *The Journal of Special Education, 33* (2), 93–102.

O'Neill, P. T. (2001). Special education and high stakes testing for high school graduation: An analysis of current law and policy. *Journal of Law and Education, 30* (2), 185–222.

OSEP Memorandum 96-5, 24 I.D.E.L.R. 320 (OSEP, 1995).

Polk v. Central Susquehanna Intermediate Unit 16, 853 F.2d 171 (3d Cir. 1988).

Ridgewood Board of Education v. N.E., 172 F.3d 238 (3d Cir. 1999).

Rock, M. L. (2000). Parents as equal partners. *Teaching Exceptional Children, 32* (6), 30–37.

Rosenfeld, S. J. (1999). Should attorneys be in IEP meetings? *EDLAW Briefing Paper, 10* (3), 1–7.

Rosenfeld, S. J. (1998). Ten ways to have a more productive IEP meeting. *EDLAW Briefing Paper, VIII* (2), 1–7.

Szabo, J. L. (2000). Maddie's story: Inclusion through physical and occupational therapy. *Teaching Exceptional Children, 33* (2), 12–18.

Timothy W. v. Rochester, New Hampshire, School District, 875 F.2d 954 (1st Cir. 1989).

T. R. v. Kingwood Township Board of Education, 205 F.3d 572 (3rd Cir. 2000).

Ysseldyke, J., & Olsen, K. (1999). Putting alternate assessments into practice: What to measure and possible sources of data. *Exceptional Children, 65* (2), 175–185.

RECOMMENDED READINGS

Bateman, B. D., & Linden, M. A. (1998). *Better IEPs: How to develop legally correct and educationally useful programs (3rd ed.).* Longmont, CO: Sopris West. This practical, easy-to-use book is a "must have" for learning how to develop good IEPs.

Block, M. E., & Burke, K. (1999). Are children with disabilities receiving appropriate physical education? *Teaching Exceptional Children, 31* (3), 18–23. This article explains the IDEA physical education requirements and suggests ideas for compliance.

Cheney, C. O. (2000). Ensuring IEP accountability in inclusive settings. *Intervention in School and Clinic, 35* (3), 185–189. This article provides and discusses a model form to be used in monitoring student progress on IEP objectives in both regular and special education classrooms.

Elliott, J., Ysseldyke, J., Thurlow, M., & Erickson, R. (1998). What about assessment and accountability? Practical implications for educators. *Teaching Exceptional Children, 31* (1), 20–27. This article provides an explanation of the IDEA state and district-wide assessment requirements for children with disabilities.

Erickson, K. A., & Koppenhaver, D. A. (1998). Using the "write technology" with Patrick. *Teaching Exceptional Children, 31* (1), 58–64. This article explains examples of classroom use of assistive technology for children under the IDEA.

Iowa Department of Education (1998). *Their future . . . our guidance: Iowa IEP guidebook.* Des Moines, IA: Author. This 124-page book, plus appendices, is an excellent reference for the development of IEPs.

Kroeger, S. D., Leibold, C. K., & Ryan, B. (1999). Creating a sense of ownership in the IEP process. *Teaching Exceptional Children, 32* (1), 4–9. This excellent article details an open-ended and flexible IEP team process that ensures good results.

O'Neill, P. T. (2001). Special education and high stakes testing for high school graduation: An analysis of current law and policy. *Journal of Law and Education, 30* (2), 185–222. In addition to a discussion of litigation, this article details the various legal issues and policy considerations associated with the use of examinations as graduation requirements for students with disabilities.

Ysseldyke, J., & Olson, K. (1999). Putting alternate assessments into practice: What to measure and possible sources of data. *Exceptional Children, 65* (2), 175–185. This is an excellent article showing examples of what to assess and how to do alternative assessments.

Relevant Federal Regulations

34 CFR §300.13	Free appropriate public education.
.15	Individualized education program.
.16	Individualized education team.
.17	Individualized family service plan.
.340	Definitions (IEPs).

CHAPTER 6

PLACEMENT

Focus

The placement decision is frequently the most important factor affecting the success of the education of a student with disabilities. It is inherently controversial because it must balance the often conflicting demands and desires of a number of individuals and groups. Although the law requires placement in a program appropriate to the student's needs and educational growth, the school's actual ability to do so often is limited by lack of available trained personnel, variety of program options, support service options, and adequate funding.

Legal Issues

Because it is so important, the educational placement decision is protected by a variety of procedural safeguards, including the following:

- Parents must give informed written consent to the initial placement of their child just as they must give consent for the initial evaluation;
- Parents must receive prior written notice of each proposal to place or change the placement of their child;
- Parents may formally challenge proposals to change their child's educational placement through the mediation or due process hearing procedures.

The law requires that educational placement decisions be:

- made by a group that includes the parents and other persons familiar with the child, the evaluation data, and the placement options;
- reviewed at least annually;
- based on the student's IEP;
- made to provide a placement located as close as possible to the child's home;
- provided in the most typical school setting feasible which allows contact as much as reasonably possible with nondisabled peers; and
- based on documented information from a variety of sources.

A child's placement is presumed to be in the regular class setting and in regular student activities. Special education placements may be considered only when the placement team determines that the child will benefit significantly more from a special class placement, compared with a regular class placement, or will be significantly disruptive in the regular class. The team must consider the provision of the whole range of supplementary aids and services in the regular school setting to provide benefit to the student and diminish disruption. The child may be placed in special education programs only when the cost of supplementary aids and services necessary to allow the child to benefit and not be disruptive in the regular class is significant.

The school district is responsible for providing a continuum of alternative placements, including regular classes, special classes, special schools, or instruction in home, hospital, or institution. Whatever program and support services are prescribed in the IEP must be provided, according to the IDEA, "at public expense, under public supervision and direction and without charge," and any placement setting must meet the state's minimal standards and licensure requirements for public education.

Support services for students include those required to assist a child with a disability to benefit from special education (related services), those provided in regular education classes or activities (supplementary aids and services), and modifications and accommodations in curriculum, instructional methodology, and assessment.

In order to receive appropriate education programs, some students with disabilities will be provided extended school year (ESY) programs, which extend portions of their IEPs to the summer months and other traditional school vacation periods.

Private school placement of a child by a public school carries with it continued responsibility of the public school for provision of the student's IEP terms and parent rights under the IDEA. Parent placement of their child in a private school changes the public school responsibility to provision of more general and limited public school services.

Rationale

Given appropriate opportunities and support, all children can learn. Children with disabilities too often have been placed inappropriately or denied public education altogether, and a strong public commitment has become necessary to correct this problem. Furthermore, children with disabilities and those without disabilities benefit from an integrated educational environment.

Approaches

Educational placement decisions account for a significant number of the formal due process hearings requested by parents. It is unlikely that serious disputes in this area can be avoided entirely. The best preventive strategy lies in attending to the procedural requirements of the law and in developing relationships of mutual trust and respect with all involved, including teachers, parents, special education staff, and community members. Three frequently misunderstood facts regarding inclusion may help clarify communication: (1) the law does not require regular class placement for all students in all academic subjects; (2) the courts have ruled that "appropriate" placement does not necessarily mean the best possible placement, but simply one which is designed to provide the student with benefit through reasonable educational progress; and (3) students whose behavior significantly impedes the learning of others in regular class placements are not entitled to remain in regular class placements.

PROBLEMS IN PLACEMENT

The selection of and placement in an educational program is, quite simply, the most controversial point in the process of educating children with disabilities. Even when all parties agree on the goals and services identified in a child's IEP, the means of carrying out a child's IEP (which is essentially what placement means) may generate heated disputes. As early as 1980, a survey of due process hearings in special education showed that fully 89% involved placement disputes (Smith, 1981).

And no wonder. A great deal hinges on the decision. From the student's point of view, placement is often the main factor in determining whether the educational experience will be rewarding or frustrating, enjoyable or humiliating. Educators see the placement decision as key to the child's educational progress, behavioral and social as well as academic. Parents bring to the decision a host of other fears, doubts, and desires. From the point of view of the school district, the chief question unfortunately often becomes how to maximize resources to students without overtaxing an already inadequate budget.

Other voices in the community, particularly the parents of nondisabled children, may well complain that the exorbitant costs of special programs are draining the school's limited finances, just as they fear that inclusion students drain the resources of the regular classroom teacher. Meredith and Underwood (1995) have observed and reported growing friction between regular and special education communities. They conclude that complaints are especially frequent where school district funds are financing apparently nontraditional educational services, such as school nursing services, physical therapy, and residential care. In each case, the fear is that the result will be a lowered quality of education for all students.

Administrators, meanwhile, occupy a precarious position at the center of the controversy with their simultaneous focus on four directions: the consumers, the staff, the budget, and the law. And what about the law? Doesn't it offer guidelines large enough to stand behind? Don't the federal regulations point out clear resolutions to these controversies?

Not really. On the one hand, it is reassuring for school administrators to know that the majority of impartial due process hearings in special education disputes are decided in favor of the schools. On the other, the laws and regulations governing placements are both intentionally and distressingly vague. They tend not to spell out, but only to imply, how educational decisions must be made and evaluated. This vagueness allows the placement team a great deal of creative latitude in considering placement options, but a side effect is that placement can be inherently contentious.

While recognizing that there are no absolute answers, this chapter reviews the law, including relevant court cases, and provides some practical guidelines and approaches to various aspects of placement decision-making.

LEGAL ISSUES

What Is Placement?

Education placement is the last in a series of three formal steps required in planning and carrying out FAPE under the IDEA. Beginning with the initial evaluation and identification, each step influences (but does not strictly determine) the next. Each subsequent step relies on the satisfactory completion of the previous step. Thus, the evaluation process helps to determine IEP content, which in turn forms the basis for the placement decision.

The IEP identifies the student's educational goals and supports, and placement is the means of carrying them out. In addition to goals, objectives, and related services, a student's IEP must include the special education the child is to receive and an explanation of the extent (if any) the student will be placed in special education settings rather than in regular education settings. The IEP effectively aids in and becomes part of the determination of placement. Placement, therefore, is not simply the "location" where the IEP is carried out. The courts have ruled that mere changes of physical location of programs provided students do not constitute changes in placement so long as the provision of IEP terms and services are not changed as a result of the program relocation. There may be several very different educational settings in which an IEP may be appropriately carried out, and the various parties involved may have very different criteria for deciding which is appropriate. For example, parents may insist that the best placement for their hearing-impaired child is an expensive and segregated residential program, whereas school officials argue for placement in a less expensive, district-run day program in the child's community. The law offers leeway: It requires not the best setting, but an appropriate one.

What then does "placement" mean? The law is not entirely specific, and does not offer a closed and concise definition such that one potential placement can be identified as clearly superior in every case. In fact, quite a large number of the court cases involving special education have, in the end, hinged on the judicial interpretation of this term. Certainly, it means a setting in which it is possible to meet the goals and objectives of the IEP and in which the student can learn and make educational progress. It is also a setting that is the LRE, is located as close as possible to the child's home, is based on a broad range of information, and is reviewed at least annually.

What the law does offer is a procedural definition; that is, an educational placement is technically legal if all the required procedures have been carried out. Thus, even though a school may not be able to completely avoid controversy, after the identification and evaluation of the student, the development of an IEP, and the selection of an educational program based on that IEP have all been completed in compliance with the law, it will at least be on solid legal ground.

The key legal and procedural requirements for the placement stage are listed in the chapter preview and in greater detail later in this chapter. Following are details on specific topics that may prove helpful in the understanding of the concept of placement.

Costs and Parent Responsibilities

The IDEA requires that each child with a disability be provided an appropriate education "at public expense, under public supervision and direction and without charge. . . ." (34 C.F.R. § 300.13(a), 2000). Specifically, this includes special education and related services called for in an IEP which meet state standards and are provided in conjunction with regular education programs. However, parents may be responsible for "incidental fees which are normally charged to nondisabled students or their parents as part of the regular education program" (34 C.F.R. § 300.26(b)(1), 2000).

Accessibility

Inherent in the placement of some students is the issue of accessibility for both students and parents. Accessibility issues are directly covered in the nondiscrimination provisions of Section 504 (34 C.F.R. 104.21–23, 2000). In summary, those regulations require:

1. Each program and activity must be "readily accessible" to persons with disabilities;
2. Not all existing school facilities must be made accessible, so long as all programs and activities are accessible to persons with disabilities;

3. Accessibility may be accomplished through reassignment of classes, services or activities to accessible facilities or parts of facilities, the provision of accommodations, alteration of existing facilities and construction of new facilities; or any other method that results in the program or activity being accessible;

4. Structural changes in existing buildings are required only when other efforts are not effective in making programs accessible;

5. Alternative methods of accessibility must give priority consideration to providing programs in the "most integrated setting appropriate";

6. New facility construction, in whole or in part, must be designed so that the new facility is readily accessible to persons with disabilities;

7. When existing facilities are altered, the alteration shall be conducted in such a way as to allow accessibility "to the maximum extent feasible";

8. The above does not apply to agencies employing fewer than fifteen persons when no reasonable method of accessibility can be determined;

9. Schools must ensure that interested persons, including those with impaired vision or hearing, can obtain information regarding accessibility of programs and services.

Related Services

Related services are a part of the placement issue because they are support services required to assist a child with a disability to benefit from special education. The related services identified in the law are: transportation, speech pathology and audiology services, psychological services, physical and occupational therapy, recreation, (including therapeutic recreation), early identification and assessment of disabilities in children, counseling services, rehabilitation counseling, orientation and mobility services, medical services for diagnostic or evaluation purposes, school health services, social work services in schools, and parent counseling and training. This list of related services should not be considered an exhaustive list and may include other supportive services (i.e., music therapy, independent living services) when such services are required to assist a child with a disability to benefit from special education.

Some related services have special considerations involved and each should be carefully reviewed for appropriate application. For instance, transportation includes travel to and from school and between schools, but also includes travel in and around school buildings and specialized equipment, if required, to provide special transportation for a particular child. Most children with disabilities will be assumed to receive transportation on the same basis as nondisabled students, unless the child's IEP provides otherwise. Obviously, integrated transportation is preferred when appropriate.

Related services provisions for parent counseling and training have taken on new importance in the 1997 Amendments to the IDEA. Such services now include assisting parents in understanding their child's special needs, providing parents with information about child development, and helping parents acquire the necessary skills that will allow them to support the implementation of their child's IEP or individual family service plan (IFSP). (See infant and toddler program requirements in Chapter 7.)

Teacher associates are a commonly used related service. They provide a variety of services to students and staff, and the IEP should specify as clearly as possible the exact nature of the service(s) to be provided. Whenever instruction of students is involved, the teacher associate should be under the direct supervision of a licensed teacher.

The provision of "medical services" and "school health services" as related services have resulted in considerable controversy and litigation. The Supreme Court has seen fit to issue interpretations of those phrases in two decisions.

In *Irving Independent School District v. Tatro* (1984), the Court ruled that clean intermittent catheterization services provided by a school nurse or other qualified person was a related service which the school had to provide in order for the child to benefit from special education. The Court drew a distinction between medical and health services provided by a physician and services performed by other health professionals, such as school nurses. Those services which required the attention of a licensed physician were determined to be properly excluded from the list of required related services under the IDEA.

A series of lower court rulings subsequent to *Tatro* were not faithful to the "bright line" physician test, and involved decisions based on issues related to the complexity and expense of the health services needed. As a result, the issue of nonphysician health services, as a related service, became muddied. The Supreme Court agreed again to hear the issue of health services as a related service in the case of *Cedar Rapids Community School District v. Garret F.* (1999). The question presented in *Garret F.* was whether schools may refuse to provide health services to children at school because the services are unduly burdensome owing to excessive cost or medical complexity. In a brief and succinct opinion, a majority of seven justices ruled that the appropriate distinction on required health services as a related service under the IDEA was whether those services required the attention of a trained and licensed physician. School nursing services are required as a related service, regardless of cost or complexity, so that children with health problems may receive an education in the LRE. The *Garret F.* decision will likely have important implications of the future for the delivery of special education programs and services (Bartlett, 2000). Some persons fear that the result will be extensive increases in medical expenses for services provided by schools. Rebore and Zirkel (1999) have concluded, however, that the relatively small number of students requiring such services and the availability of alternative funding sources (e.g., Medicaid) will not result in an enduring financial impact on school district resources.

Third Party Payers

When related services are of a medical nature, schools may attempt to recover the cost of services from Medicaid or the family's private medical insurance. Medicaid is publicly funded and provides insurance type coverage for children and families who meet specific qualification guidelines, primarily income. While schools may seek reimbursement for related services of a medical nature, they may not require the family to make application for Medicaid or withhold educational services conditioned upon Medicaid coverage.

Private parent health insurance may be used as a potential recovery of the expense of related services of a medical nature. The regulations under the IDEA provide that parent insurance may be requested to pay for student medical services if the parents provide informed written consent each time. In order for consent to be informed, parents must be advised that claims filed by the school may result in increased premiums, lowered payment limits or other potential future financial costs, and that parents should check with their private insurance carrier before giving consent. Parents must also be informed that their refusal to provide consent will not alter the school's responsibility to provide the services to the student at no cost to the parent (Warlick to Thompson, 2000).

Even though the federal rules provide that parent's private insurance may be used, with consent, there is an unresolved legal inconsistency. The courts have consistently interpreted IDEA requirements of FAPE to be at no expense to parents above normal student fee expenses charged to families of all students. This definition of "free" is found elsewhere in federal regulations (34 C.F.R. § 300, 15, 2000).

Medication Administration

An important service that schools commonly provide as a related service to children with disabilities is the administration of physician-prescribed medications during school hours. Students who have accommodation plans under Section 504, as well as some students without disabilities, may also require school staff assistance with medications. Some states require local schools to have medication administration policies for children receiving special education services and require that they contain a number of important provisions. Those provisions should apply to policies covering the administration of medications for all students. Each policy must include statements on the training and other requirements necessary for persons administering medication, as well as the following:

- A requirement that the parent provide a signed and dated written statement requesting medication administration at school.
- A statement that medication shall be in the original labeled container, either as dipensed or in the manufacturer's container.
- A written medication administration record shall be on one file at school including:
  1. Date.
  2. Individual's name.
  3. Prescriber or person authorizing administration.
  4. Medication.
  5. Medication dosage.
  6. Administration time.
  7. Administration method.
  8. Signature and title of the person administering medication.
  9. Any unusual circumstances, actions or omissions.
- A statement that medication shall be stored in a secured area unless an alternate provision is documented.
- A requirement for a written statement by the parent or guardian requesting individual student administration of medication, when competency is demonstrated.
- A requirement for emergency protocols for medication-related reactions.
- A statement regarding confidentiality of information. Iowa Department of Education, 2000, 281-41.12 (11).

LEAST RESTRICTIVE ENVIRONMENT

Under the LRE principle, as defined in the regulations implementing the IDEA, each school must ensure that:

1. To the maximum extent appropriate, children with disabilities, including children in public or private institutions or other care facilities, are educated with children without disabilities.
2. Special classes, separate schooling, or other removal of children with disabilities from the regular educational environment occurs only when the nature or severity of the disability is such that education in regular classes with the use of supplementary aids and services cannot be achieved satisfactorily.
3. Each child with a disability participates with nondisabled children in nonacademic and extracurricular services and activities to the maximum extent appropriate to the needs of the child.

Each school must also ensure that a continuum of alternative placements is available to meet the needs of children with disabilities for special education and related services. This continuum must include instruction in regular classes, special classes, special schools, home instruction, and instruction in hospitals and institutions. Figure 6-1 puts the LRE continuum concept in a visual and student need context. From the available continuum of placements, choices must be made, and the role of making those decisions belongs to the placement team. The placement team must consist of

FIGURE 6-1   *Continuum of educational services*

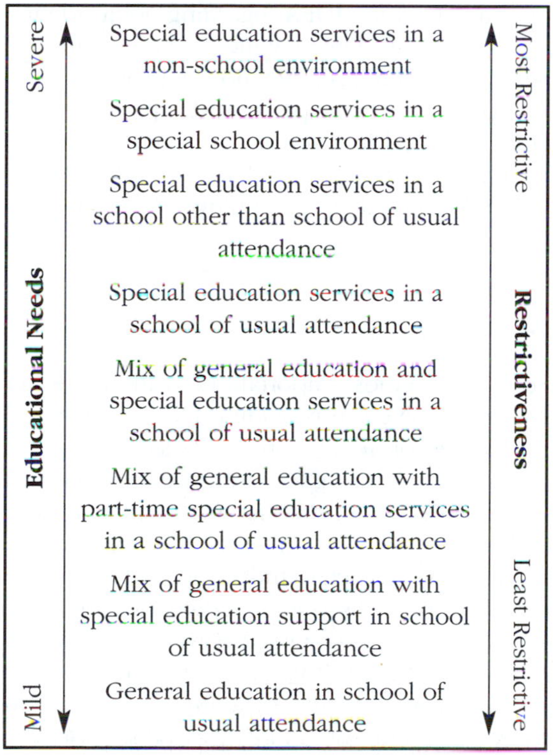

From *The Least Restrictive Environment (LRE) and The Individualized Education Program (IEP): Legal Educational and Practical Guidelines for Educators and Families* (p. 7), Iowa Department of Education, 1996, Des Moines, IA: Mountain Plains Regional Resource Center, Drake University. Reprinted by permission.

a group of persons, including the parents and other persons who are knowledgeable about the child, the evaluation data, and the placement options. Under OSEP interpretations, the IEP team may also serve as the placement team and make the placement determination. In some states, such as South Dakota, the IEP team has served for many years in multiple roles as the placement and evaluation teams.

The placement decision must be made on an individual student basis as opposed to a group or "label" basis, consistent with the LRE concept, based on the IEP, determined at least annually, and provided in an appropriate program as close as possible to the child's home, particularly the school the child would attend if not disabled. Parents may successfully challenge placement in distant schools when it is apparent that an appropriate program exists closer to home. In considering LRE, the placement team must consider the potential harmful effects of the placement on the child or on the quality of services received by the child. This allows school districts some latitude for grouping students with unique needs. For example, visually impaired students in similar grade levels in a district may be assigned to the same regular education attendance center for the purposes of efficiency in providing a mobility training specialist and equipment for producing materials in Braille. Such students may not, of course, be segregated owing to their disability and must be provided programming with peers without disabilities in the LRE.

Some educators have been unnecessarily concerned that LRE requires the placement of disruptive students in regular and special settings. This is not so. For over twenty years, the federal regulations accompanying both Section 504 and the IDEA have clarified LRE and student disruption:

> . . . it should be stressed that where a handicapped [sic] child is so disruptive in a regular classroom that the education of other students is significantly impaired, the needs of the handicapped [sic] child cannot be met in that environment. Therefore, regular placement would not be appropriate to his or her needs. (34. C.F.R. Part 104—Appendix, Paragraph 24; quoted in 34 C.F.R. § 300.552, note 2, 1997)

Under the 1997 Amendments, regular class teachers must be provided necessary assistance when inclusion students present potential problems of class disruption. The IEP team is expressly required to consider positive behavioral interventions, supplementary aids and services, and accommodations and modifications that are designed to reduce or eliminate the likelihood of disruption resulting from a student's placement in the regular class.

Home instruction, sometimes called homebound instruction, should be considered among the last placement options used with disruptive students and should never be chosen when the school staff is seeking respite rather than appropriate placement. Home instruction for school-aged children is considered the most restrictive placement because it does not permit education to take place with other children. Even residential and hospital education settings often have several children present, whereas home instruction does not. Home instruction is usually appropriate on a long-term basis (more than thirty days) for only a small number of children who are medically fragile or who for some other reason are unable to participate with other children in an educational environment (e.g., *Thomas v. Cincinnati Board of Education*, 1990).

Nonacademic LRE Settings

The concept of LRE goes beyond the classroom setting and includes nonacademic settings, such as meals, recess, transportation, health services, and employment, both in and out of school, when arranged by the school. Also included in LRE considerations are such extracurricular activities as athletics, recreational activities, and clubs. The IEP must contain a statement of services and modifications to be "provided to the child, or on behalf of the child" to allow the child to participate in desired nonacademic settings and activities with nondisabled children. If a child does not participate, then an explanation of why the child will not participate in activities with children without disabilities must be placed in the IEP. The restrictiveness of the appropriate placement for a child, including residential settings, should not alter the school's effort to provide opportunities for participation with other children.

Opportunities for interaction, including the bringing of students without disabilities into the segregated environment of children with disabilities, must be found. The above LRE requirements of the IDEA regarding nonacademic settings and student activities are also found in Section 504 nondiscrimination regulations.

The same concepts of LRE apply when a child is placed in a private or public institution by a public school of residence in order to provide educational programming, and each state is expected to make arrangements with private schools for the provision of LRE.

Inclusion

Some of the most important educational terminology involved in providing LRE is not found in statutes or regulations and, as a result, is frequently confusing to parents, educators, and judges alike. "Mainstreaming," "inclusion," and "full inclusion" are such terms. In the vast arena of published articles and court rulings, these terms are often used interchangeably; such use of the three terms is now clearly inappropriate. For the purpose of this book, the authors have adopted and used the meanings as defined in the well-thought-out Phi Delta Kappa *Research Bulletin* entitled "The Inclusion Revolution":*

> *Mainstreaming*: This term has generally been used to refer to the selective placement of special education students in one or more 'regular' education classes. Mainstreaming proponents generally assume that a student must 'earn' his or her opportunity to be mainstreamed through the ability to 'keep up' with the work assigned by the teacher to the other students in the class. This concept is closely linked to traditional forms of special education service delivery.
>
> *Inclusion*: This term is used to refer to the commitment to educate each child, to the maximum extent appropriate, in the school and classroom he or she would otherwise

---

* From "The Inclusion Revolution," by J. Rogers, (1993), *Research Bulletin*, *11*, 4–5. Phi Delta Kappa. Reprinted by permission.

attend. It involves bringing the support services to the child (rather than moving the child to the services) and requires only that the child will benefit from being in the class (rather than having to keep up with the other students). Proponents of inclusion generally favor newer forms of education service delivery . . . , i.e. heterogeneous grouping, peer tutoring, multi-age classes, and cooperative learning.

Full Inclusion: This term is primarily used to refer to the belief that instructional practices and technological supports are presently available to accommodate all students in the schools and classrooms they would otherwise attend if not disabled. Proponents of full inclusion tend to encourage that special education services generally be delivered in the form of training and technical assistance to 'regular' classroom teachers.

The concept of "mainstreaming" that was once prevalent in the provision of special education instructional programs is now clearly inappropriate. A series of court decisions between 1989 and 1994, as well as the 1997 Amendments, have provided a clear understanding that students with disabilities are not required to "earn" the opportunity to be in a regular class placement. Students with disabilities cannot be required to demonstrate achievement of a specific level of performance as a prerequisite for placement into a regular class setting. It is now clear that inherent in the LRE requirement is the presumption (sometimes called a preference) that a child with disabilities will be in a regular class placement. Only when placement in a regular class (or regular nonacademic setting or extracurricular activity) cannot be satisfactorily achieved, even with the use of supplementary aids and services, may the child be placed in a special education class or school.

Although many educators and parents support the attempt to provide "full inclusion" experiences for all children with disabilities, the reality for some children with disabilities is that they would not benefit from the experience,

their needs would overtax the school's resources, or the situation would result in a significant disruption to the learning of other students. The authors applaud voluntary efforts at full inclusion, but the law clearly does not require full inclusion (OSEP Memorandum 95-9, 1994; Davila to Goodling, 1991), and it is not likely to do so in the immediate future.

THE PHILOSOPHY OF INCLUSION

A variety of information and suggestions are offered in later chapters of this book on building better relationships among special and regular education students and staff members. Because these relationships are rooted in a commitment to the concept of LRE and inclusion, it becomes imperative to explore and understand inclusion in a broad philosophical sense. A good understanding of the philosophical underpinnings of inclusion is found in a book entitled *Creating an Inclusive School*, published by the Association for Supervision and Curriculum Development:

Pragmatic Definition of Inclusive Education

So what is inclusion or inclusive education? First, it is an attitude—a value and belief system—not an action or set of actions. Once adopted by a school or school district, it should drive all decisions and actions by those who have adopted it. The word *include* implies being a part of something, being embraced into the whole. *Exclude*, the antonym of *include*, means to keep out, to bar, or to expel. These definitions begin to frame the growing movement of building inclusive schools. The very meaning of the terms *inclusion* and *exclusion* helps us to understand inclusive education.

. . . . .

Inclusive education is about embracing all, making a commitment to do whatever it takes to provide each student in the community—and each citizen in a democracy—an inalienable right to belong, not to be excluded. Inclusion assumes that living and learning together is a better way that benefits everyone, not just children who are labeled as having a difference (e.g., gifted, non-English proficient, or disability).

. . . . .

An inclusive school values interdependence as well as independence. It values its students, staff, faculty, and parents as a community of learners. An inclusive school views each child as gifted. An inclusive school cherishes and honors all kinds of diversity as an opportunity for learning about what makes us human. Inclusion focuses on how to support the special gifts and needs of each and every student in the school community to feel welcomed and secure and to become successful. Another assumption underlying inclusive schooling is that good teaching is good teaching, that each child can learn, given the appropriate environment, encouragement, and meaningful activities. Inclusive schools base curriculum and daily learning activities on everything known about good teaching and learning.

Implications of Inclusive Education

Inclusion is the opposite of segregation and isolation. Segregated specialized education creates a permanent underclass of students, with a strong message to these students that they do not "cut the mustard," and that they do not fit or belong. Segregation assumes that the right to belong is earned rather than an unconditional human right.

. . . . .

The growing diversity of our student population is a topic of great debate and concern. Diversity differences may include language, culture, religion, gender, disability, sexual preference, socioeconomic status, geographic setting, and more. Diversity often is spoken

about as if it were a plight rather than a wonderful opportunity for learning, that is, learning about the rich variety of each others' lives and also learning about what it is to be human—to be included, to be valued and respected for just who we are in a naturally diverse world.

. . . . .

Inclusion is not just for students with disabilities, but rather for all the students, educators, parents, and community members. Experience tells us that as communities and schools embrace the true meaning of inclusion, they will be better equipped to learn about and acquire strategies to change a segregated special education system to an inclusive service delivery system, with meaningful, child-centered learning. In the process, a society and world intolerant and fearful of difference may change to one that embraces and celebrates its natural diversity.

. . . . .

Even after it is operationally defined, inclusion is still an elusive term. Part of the confusion arises from the varying assumptions that people associate with inclusive education— for example, that it is a "program" or that it is a research-devised strategy. The underlying assumption, however, is that inclusion is a way of life, a way of living together, based on a belief that each individual is valued and does belong.*

The philosophy of each student being valued and belonging has pretty much become part of the legal understanding of inclusion as well. One famous court decision on the inclu-

---

sion of students expressed the concept in terms easily understandable by educators and parents:

> The IDEA incorporates a vision of our educational system in which, whenever possible, children with disabilities become fully integrated members of the educational community. The goal of the IDEA is realized when a child with a disability can become included, accepted, and respected as a full member of a regular class, and is no longer seen as an outsider. (*Oberti v. Board of Education*, 1992, p. 1329)

INCLUSION DECISION-MAKING

The primary legal and educational issues involved with inclusion are "who" decides whether regular class placement can be achieved satisfactorily and "how" is it determined. It has long been understood that the placement team (it can be the IEP team), including parents, must make the determination of each child's appropriate placement. The process and the criteria have only recently become clearer.

Even though the law has required, for over twenty-five years, that children with disabilities be educated in the regular classroom unless "the nature and severity of the disability is such that education in the regular classes with the use of supplementary aids and services cannot be achieved satisfactorily," it had been largely ignored by educators. Instead, the concept that a child with disabilities needed to "earn" her way into the regular class environment (mainstreaming) prevailed. A series of important and unanimous court rulings, exemplified in *Greer v. Rome City School District* (1992), have taken much of the guess work out of the placement team's role in planning for the inclusion of a child with a disability (Bartlett, 1992).

Greer and other court decisions issued on inclusion between 1989 and 1994 ruled that the IDEA created a strong preference favoring

inclusion. Thus, a court reviewing a placement team decision regarding LRE must first review the evidence to determine whether the school has taken meaningful steps, generally, to include children with disabilities in the regular classroom. If a school has no history of successful inclusion, then the court need look no further in its review. However, if a school can demonstrate that it has previously taken meaningful steps to include students with disabilities, then court review will turn its attention to the placement team's decision regarding a specific child.

In making its decision, the placement team must first give consideration to the placement of the child with disabilities, in whole or in part, in the regular school environment as appropriate for the individual child, and must consider the provision of supplementary aids and services, or necessary modifications and accommodations, to make the placement situation educationally viable. Only when the child will receive significantly greater benefit, either academically or from role modeling (i.e., language, behavior, social skills) in a special class setting or when the child, through behavior or demands on teacher time and attention, is disruptive so that the learning opportunity of other students is significantly impaired may the child be placed in a special education setting. Meaningful consideration must always be given to the provision of supplementary aids and services that will allow the child to benefit from regular class placement and reduce disruption resulting from the child's presence. As the court in *Greer* said, the IEP team, as part of its process must consider provision of "the whole range of supplemental aids and services" (p. 696) available which will allow the regular class placement to be successful. Only when the extra cost of supplemental aids and services necessary to allow the student with disabilities to benefit from, and not be disruptive in, the regular class is significant may financial cost be a factor in denying regular class

FIGURE 6-2 *Inclusion criteria outline*

Benefit	Disruption
academic	behavior
role modeling	teacher time
Supplementary Aids and Services Cost Excessive?	

placement. Figure 6-2 shows the criteria to be used by placement teams in determining whether children with disabilities should be placed in regular education classes and activities or special education programs.

Figure 6-3 presents a detailed, formalized, step-by-step approach for an IEP team analyzing the question of inclusion for a particular child. This approach is a synthesis of the holdings in major court decisions on the issue of court review of inclusion decisions. As teams become more experienced at applying the concept, their considerations will likely become less formal.

The application of the benefit, disruption, and cost of supplemental aids and services analysis by the IEP team can be quite effective, and will result in legally defensible positions when denying inclusion settings to students who do not meet the criteria. Several courts reviewing placement team decisions have applied the cri-

FIGURE 6-3 *IEP and placement team planning*

Determination of Least Restrictive Environment

Decisions by the IEP/Placement team should be based on data collected throughout the assessment and IEP process. Since there is an educational and legal preference for placement in the regular class setting, that is where consideration must begin. The team members, including the parents, should honestly address a series of questions which will lead them to a proper conclusion.

1. Has the school taken meaningful steps to support and maintain students with disabilities in the regular classroom?

   What supplementary aids and services have been considered? Which have been used? What accommodations and modifications have been considered? Which have been used? What interventions have been considered? Which have been used?

   Note: Only if the answer to question No. 1 is "yes" may the team proceed to questions 2, 3, and 4. If the answer is "no," much more work is to be done.

2. Will the benefits of a special education placement for this student *significantly* outweigh the benefits of placement in regular education even with the provision of supplementary aids and services,?

   Academic benefits?

   Nonacademic benefits (e.g., social, behavior, communication)?

3. Will the education of other students be *significantly* disrupted, even with the provision of supplementary aids and services, as a result of this student's presence in the regular class?

   Due to the student's behavior?

   Due to the inordinate amount of teacher attention diverted from other students?

4. Will the financial cost of supplemental aids and services be *substantial* when compared with the total special education budget?

teria and have found that one or more of the factors weighed against regular class placement for a specific child, e.g., *Clyde K. v. Puyallup School District*, 1994 (secondary student with Tourette syndrome and ADHD); *Hudson v. Bloomfield Hills*, 1995 (seventh grade student with a measured IQ of 42 and other disabilities). Some educators place students in inclusion situations where they know the student will fail under the misguided notion that students need to experience failure in the regular classroom setting before a special education placement can be justified. This is not a good practice from either an educational or a legal perspective [34 C.F.R. Part 300, Appendix A, No. 1, (2000)].

Supplementary Aids and Services

No one should overlook the importance of IEP team considerations of supplementary aids and services for maintaining the regular class placement for a child with disabilities. The courts have repeatedly and unanimously required it since 1989 and the 1997 Amendments to the IDEA have highlighted their importance. Federal law provides the following definition for the phrase:

> . . . , the term *supplementary aids and services* [italics in the original] means aids, services, and other supports that are provided in regular education classes or other

---

Note: Only if the answer to question two *or* three *or* four is "yes," can you go to the next question. If the answer to questions two *and* three *and* four is "no," the student must be placed in the regular class placement. You may not proceed to a special education placement.

5. Has full consideration been given to the previous three questions (Nos. 2, 3, 4) with regard to the student's placement in regular academic settings, at least part-time?
   In which specific academic settings, with provision of supplemental aids and services, will the student benefit and will not be disruptive?

Note: If the answer to question No. 5 is "no," do not proceed. More work is needed.

6. Has full consideration been given to questions Nos. 2, 3, and 4 with regard to placement in nonacademic settings and activities, at least part-time?
   In what nonacademic settings and activities, with appropriate supplementary aids and services will the student benefit from and not be significantly disruptive?

Note: If the answer to question No. 6 is "no," do not proceed. More work is needed.

7. If the student is being educated in a setting other than the regular classroom, is he/she provided the opportunity to interact with nondisabled peers to the maximum extent appropriate?
   In what academic settings is the child integrated with peers without disabilities? In what nonacademic setting is the child integrated with peers without disabilities?

8. What are the reasons that the student cannot be provided all or part of his/her program in a regular school setting? (The answer to this question must now be included in the student's IEP.)

9. What related services are needed to support the student in a special education program? Why can't the child be served in a regular class environment with provision of those related services?

education-related settings to enable children with disabilities to be educated with non-disabled children to the maximum extent appropriate. . . . (34 C.F.R. § 300.26, 2000)

The IDEA now requires supplementary aids and services be considered as part of the IEP development process:

> The IEP for each child must include:
>
> . . . A statement of the special education and related services and supplementary aids and services to be provided to the child, or on behalf of the child and a statement of the program modifications or supports for school personnel that will be provided for the child. (34 C.F.R. § 300.347, 2000)

Figure 6-4 provides examples of but a few of the commonly available supplementary aids and services used in schools.

Due to the importance of supplementary aids and services, Etscheidt and Bartlett (1999) have recommended that IEP teams focus their consideration of supplementary aids and services in four separate dimensions: physical, instructional, social-behavioral, and collaborative. Use of a four-dimensional approach promotes a clearer perspective on specific student, teacher, and staff needs. The physical dimension includes such things as lighting, mobility, room arrangement, and seating; the instructional dimension includes lesson planning, methodology, and evaluation of student achievement; the social-behavioral dimension includes factors associated with student behavior and self-confidence; and the collaborative dimension includes personnel matters such as training, time for planning, and use of teacher associates.

The two most important supplementary aids and services that enhance the likelihood of successful inclusion programs that have been identified by research are specialized training for the staff, including the regular class teacher (i.e., behavior management, communication,

FIGURE 6-4   *Examples of supplementary aid and services*

- Modifications to the classroom curriculum
- Assistive technology
- Peer tutors
- Use of tape recorder
- Read exam orally
- Take-home exams
- Open-book exams
- Use of teacher associates
- Collaboration with special education teacher
- More time allowed to complete assignments or exams
- Shortened assignments
- Cooperative learning
- Carbon copy of class notes
- Teacher presentation of outlines
- Large print materials
- Peer in-service
- Staff in-service
- A highlight marker to identify key vocabulary and concepts

From *Least Restrictive Environment: Supplementary Aids and Services* (p. 12). Developed by the Mountain Plains Regional Resource Center, 1997, Logan, UT: Utah State University. Reprinted by permission.

and collaboration skills), and planned time for staff to collaborate (i.e., plan strategies, communicate, and coordinate activities).

Food for Thought

One of the authors, sitting as a hearing officer, once heard expert witness testimony from a specialist on including children with autism into regular class settings. The witness testified: "Whenever inclusion fails, it is not because the child has in some way failed, it is because the adults have failed." While at first doubtful of the statement, the author has since consciously evaluated the statement against every failed inclusion situation he has observed. Its accuracy has yet to be disproved.

PROCEDURAL SAFEGUARDS

Under federal law, the school must obtain the parents' informed written consent only for the initial placement in special education programs and services. After the initial placement has begun, the school is required only to provide parents with written notice each time it *proposes* to change the educational placement of the child or *refuses* to change the educational placement of the child after a parent request for change.

What confuses many persons is the fact that this detailed notice must be provided to parents any time there is a proposed change in placement (whether the parent agrees or not) or a school refusal of a parent request. Even when a parent initiates a change in placement and has fully participated in a discussion of a proposed change of placement as a member of the IEP and placement teams, the parent must still be provided a formal written notice of the proposed change. Receipt of the notice may trigger a number of parent procedural safeguards, such as requests for mediation, a due process hearing, and an independent educational evaluation. The details of the content of the notice and an explanation of how this notice triggers other procedural safeguard provisions are found in Chapters 2 and 3.

EXTENDED SCHOOL YEAR (ESY) SERVICES

Because some students with disabilities may need school services at times of the year in which schools do not traditionally provide services (i.e., summer months, long holidays, breaks between sessions), schools must be prepared to consider and provide services to students who may need them in order to ensure that the students receive FAPE. Thus, if it is appropriate for an individual child to receive some programs and services at times when nondisabled children do not receive educational services, then arrangements must be made through the IEP and placement processes to see that the child receives an appropriate program. The main difference between ESY programs and other types of summer or vacation school programs is that the former must be expressly provided for in the IEP and the placement decision must be related to at least some of the IEP goals and objectives. ESY must also be provided at no cost to parents.

The courts have provided a much better understanding of the ESY concept and criteria than have federal statutes or regulations. Of course, that may be because the concept was first acknowledged by courts as an extension of an issue of FAPE. Early court decisions made it clear that considerations of ESY were to be individualized to the child and no arbitrary standard criteria could be used. Early court reliance on student regression (education loss) or recoupment (education recovery) as the sole criteria for determining ESY eligibility has given way to additional criteria, such as "emerging skills," "break-through opportunities" (*Reusch v. Fountain*, 1994), potential acceleration of deficiencies, rate of progress, vocational needs, and availability of family and community resources (*Johnson v. Independent School District No. 4*, 1990). The best example of a court-established standard for determining whether an individual child should receive ESY for traditional breaks in educational programming, including the summer months, is an IEP team determination of "whether the benefits accrued to the child during the regular year [under the IEP] will be significantly jeopardized if he is not provided an educational program during the summer months" (*Alamo Heights Independent School District v. State Board*, 1986, p. 1158). IEP teams making decisions on ESY will have no magic formula to assist them. Using their best judgment, professional and parental, teams must review and consider existing empirical and qualitative data, as well as predictive data and reasoned opinions of team members. For some students, it may be determined that only a limited portion of IEP goals, or only one related service, is needed during the summer months.

One of the authors served as a member of an IEP/placement team that considered ESY for a high functioning nine-year-old boy with autistic tendencies. In reviewing the boy's goals and objectives, it was determined by the team that only progress in those goals related to social skills was in serious jeopardy of being diminished over the summer months. As a response, the team determined that the boy should attend a YMCA summer day-camp, accompanied by a teacher associate. The camp staff was advised of the boy's existing behavior plan and social skills needs. It was also determined that the teacher associate and the boy would spend one hour, two days a week, visiting his regular school classroom so that he would remain accustomed to the school environment when the fall term started. All components of the summer program, including transportation and camp fees, were provided under IEP provisions at no cost to the parents. The summer was determined to be very successful by all, except perhaps for the teacher associate, who was exhausted attempting to keep up with the boy's "socialization" goals.

PRIVATE SCHOOL PLACEMENT

Children with disabilities may be placed in private schools by the public school or by their parents. When the public school is responsible for the placement or referral to a private school, the public school must conduct an IEP meeting as for all other eligible children and must ensure that representatives of the private school attend or in some other way participate in the IEP meeting. Reviews of IEPs may be conducted by

the private school, but the parents and a representative of the public school must be involved in IEP decisions and must agree to any changes before they are implemented. The responsibility for compliance with IEP, LRE, parent safeguards, and other provisions of the IDEA remain with the public school and, ultimately, with the state education agency.

When a child's parents unilaterally decide that the child's placement should be in a private school, the public school plays a very different role. The public school is not responsible for the cost of the education at the private school, so long as the public school has a FAPE available and the parents chose the private school placement anyway. Disagreements over the availability of FAPE at the public school are subject to the mediation and hearing process discussed in Chapter 3. If the parents had previously enrolled the child in the public school, and subsequently enrolled the child in the private school, they may recover their education costs if they can establish that the public school did not have FAPE available to the child in a timely manner and their private school placement of the child is appropriate. Recovery of education costs by parents may be reduced when the parents have not informed the public school of their education concerns and their intent to change enrollment no later than the most recent IEP meeting attended by the parents or in a written notice to the public school at least ten days prior to their removal of the child from the public school (so long as the parents have been previously advised of these requirements). The requirement of parent advance notice to the school is for the purpose of giving the school an opportunity to fully consider parent concerns prior to the parent changing the child's placement.

Public school officials must be involved in the education of private school children with disabilities placed by their parents in ways which will at times be confusing. For instance, the public school must spend on parent-placed private school children residing in its jurisdiction an amount of money proportional to what it receives from the federal government under the IDEA. Yet, many public schools do not receive federal funds; they receive state funds, and the state educational agency uses the federal funds in ways other than providing money to local school districts. For some school districts, the amount of federal dollars actually received per student may amount to only a few hundred dollars or less per year.

For parent-placed children with disabilities in private schools, there is no individual student right to special education and related services under federal law. Public school officials are required merely to consult with representatives of private school children and decide what services, if any, will be provided to which categories of children and how the services will be provided. Service plans, rather than IEPs, must be developed for each private school child served and must address only the services the public school has determined it will provide in the private school setting. In those limited situations where some services are available at the private school, the public school is responsible for the service plan development, review, and implementation and must ensure that a private school representative participates. Service plans, to the extent appropriate, must meet the general development, review, and revision requirements of the IEPs. Services may be provided on the private school site, to the extent consistent with law (Osborne, Russo, & DiMaltia, 1999). Some states have enacted laws which require selected special education services be provided to children enrolled in private schools; thus, caution dictates that state law should be consulted.

Some parents who unilaterally place their child in a private school may be willing to dually enroll their child in a public school at the same time in order to take advantage of special education programs and services. Public schools must provide programs and services for dually enrolled children who are entitled to them.

APPROACHES TO RESOLVING PROBLEMS

Controversies surrounding placement can never be entirely prevented. A more realistic goal is to avoid unfavorable hearing and court decisions by following the specifics of the law, minimizing disagreements through the building of a foundation of trust with parents, and increasing the educational options available to students through openness to new opportunities and new ways of doing things.

Some educational leaders mistakenly attempt to use inclusion as a budget stretching device, often to the detriment of the children, both with and without disabilities, and to the staff (Baines, Baines, & Masterson, 1994; Rogers, 1993). While the final word is not yet in on the overall cost of inclusion, it is unlikely, if done correctly, to be much greater than the cost of pull-out programs and services. In response to one school district's argument that inclusion of a particular student was too expensive, a federal district court rejected the school's conclusion, noting that the costs per child between placement in a regular class with support services were comparable to placement in a special class with more support and half as many students (*Board of Education v. Holland*, 1992).

It is a serious professional mistake, with legal implications, to attempt inclusion without proper planning and provision of appropriate support services. With appropriate planning and support, all students in an inclusion environment can benefit from the experience, without academic detriment to anyone (OSEP, Memorandum, 95-9, 1994, research cited; Rogers, 1993; Stevens & Slavin, 1995).

Inclusion Classroom Considerations

Successful inclusion begins in the regular classroom; thus, the regular class teacher must be properly prepared. Many changes occur in the classroom with the introduction of special needs students into the regular class environment. Instructional materials, content, instructional methodology, student assessment, and the reporting of grades must be considered.

Instructional Materials

Familiarity with materials analysis procedures will be helpful during initial selection of the texts to be used in each class and in locating or preparing materials appropriate to specific students. Specialists such as physical therapists, special education consultants, and resource room staff should be able to provide assistance in this process.

Factors to analyze when choosing materials include the following:

- **Reading Level**. This is probably the most critical, because so many disabilities can affect reading skills. Several formulas have been developed to provide quick estimates of the readability of publications.
- **Concept Level**. This is more difficult to assess than basic readability (although in a sense, of course, the two are interrelated). Comparison with standard course goals and objectives, material sampling, student tryout, and the educator's "feel" for the material are several methods used.
- **Graphic Presentation**. Factors such as the following should be checked: Is the print dark and readable? Is it large enough? Are key ideas highlighted through titles, headings, and other graphic means? Are the page layouts too dense and confusing?
- **Skills Development**. Questions in this area include: Does the material offer ample opportunities for practice and repetition? Are skills presented sequentially, so that necessary prerequisites can be mastered before more complex concepts are introduced?
- **Adaptability**. Can the materials be adapted easily to accommodate students' needs? Examples of adaptations are underlining or

highlighting key concepts, preparation of a study guide, location or development of additional practice activities, assigning variable amounts of reading/study to students of different ability levels, recording the text, using high-interest/low vocabulary, preteaching vocabulary, and study cards.

Methodology

Curriculum content modifications are most likely to be required for students with mental disabilities but may also be appropriate for others who for some reason (i.e., lack of prerequisites, poor reading skills) cannot master the normal curriculum. The need for such modifications should never be assumed but rather should be based on individualized assessments that pinpoint each student's specific needs. The following are examples of such approaches:

- **Mastery Teaching/Learning**. The emphasis of this approach is on ensuring that prerequisite steps have been mastered before students progress to more advanced tasks. Teachers may use individually paced curricula, modify time requirements for completing regular class materials, or recycle students through reteaching or new methodology exercises. Task analysis and frequent assessments to see that sequential steps are being mastered are important elements. Coordination is necessary to see that students begin at an appropriate level the following year and have not regressed to an earlier level of mastery.
- **Teaching Only Essentials**. The teacher could either present all content to all students and hold special learners responsible only for the essential key concepts, or allow the special learners extra time with basic skills while the rest of the class completes an enrichment unit.
- **Providing an Alternative Curriculum**. Students who lack necessary prerequisites or whose educational goals are very different from the norm may require a totally different

curriculum. Specialists should be consulted for help in selecting or developing curricula appropriate to the student's special needs as identified in the IEP.

- **Providing a Parallel or Dual Curriculum**. For students with poor reading skills, it should be possible to locate a text that covers the same general content (U.S. history, for example) at a lower reading level and to prepare individualized assignments. It is important to not embarrass the student by assigning material obviously designed for younger children. The students still should be included in group activities and class discussions. For example, in one reported situation where a secondary class had a general goal of "understanding the Civil War," a student who had strong artistic talents but who was unable to read, write, or effectively express herself verbally, participated fully. When most students were given reading assignments, this girl drew poster-sized portraits of the key people studied and worked with other students on a mural displayed in the class. The drawings and mural were used as a stimulus for class discussions, which included the girl in a true share-and-learn situation (Stainback, Stainback, & Stefanich, 1996).

Another example occurred in a language arts class, where the basic goal was to prepare all students to communicate effectively. For many students the lesson was to learn to write letters to friends. For others, a more appropriate approach was to dictate a letter into a tape recorder or increase a picture board vocabulary to allow a child to better communicate with friends (Stainback, Stainback & Stefanich, 1996).

- **Providing Supplements**. These might include separate instruction in study skills, special therapy, or additional opportunities for practicing regular curricular material. Such supplemental services are commonly provided by specialists such as speech therapists or resource room teachers.

- **Altering Expectations**. Individual agreements can be made with students to hold them responsible, for example, for only even-numbered items on assignments; standards for writing can be altered; and so on. However, this method has problems: Some students actually may need more practice, rather than less, and without it, they may never achieve adequate mastery. Extra drill in the resource room may alleviate these difficulties.

Almost all of these modifications, accommodations, and alternative techniques require staff time and planning, which is why they are seldom accomplished by only one teacher working alone. Successful inclusion requires the collaboration of teams of staff members working together to effectuate modifications and adaptations in order to meet the unique needs of individual students, whether or not they are disabled. Chapter 11 discusses staff collaboration in greater detail.

Some special educators emphasize the desirability of maintaining the similarity of curricular activities for all children so that special needs students do not become isolated, even within the regular class environment (Stainback, Stainback, & Stefanich, 1996). Many skills considered desirable for special needs students are also valuable to their peers without disabilities (e.g., shopping, money management, good grooming, attending concerts). The most valuable lesson and asset of special education is, perhaps, the inherent team approach to solving educational issues and providing curricular modification. A problem-solving team which includes students to brainstorm and provide suggestions is valuable. Stainback, Stainback, & Stefanich (1996) emphasize that inclusion of students in the regular classroom presents an important lesson for all the students in the class: "all persons are equally valued members of this society and that it is worthwhile to do whatever it takes to include everyone," rather than the philosophy that "some people are not worth the effort to make the accommodations necessary to keep them included" (p. 19).

The Future of Materials and Methodology

If one believes the adage that "necessity is the mother of invention," then a great deal of talented attention must be turning to issues of presenting general education curriculum to a wider range of diverse learners now enrolled in regular classroom settings. In enacting the 1997 Amendments, Congress made it clear that it wanted a greater emphasis directed toward improving the academic performance of students with disabilities and greater assurance of their receipt of quality public education. This is seen in various new provisions in IEP requirements, including: the PLEP statement of how the child's disability impacts the child's involvement and progress in the regular curriculum; determining measurable goals enabling the child to be involved in and progress in the general curriculum; and the statement of education, services, modifications and accommodations necessary for the child to be involved in and progress in the general curriculum (Annual Report, 1999).

At the same time, Congress recognized that each child with a disability would not be able to learn at the same level, or at the same rate, or through the same methodology or modality. Effectively, Congress anticipated that regular education staff, with the help and support of special education staff, will meet the educational needs of the vast majority of special education students in the regular classroom.

Many teams of local educators have done an excellent job of making more materials and knowledge available to a greater number of children. Unfortunately, most teachers cannot meet all the educational needs of the linguistically, culturally, cognitively, sensorily, and physically diverse student populations sometimes found in a single classroom. Current written materials and

texts and most audiovisual materials are very limited in the flexibility of their use in an inclusion classroom.

That is why many advanced thinkers searching for that flexibility of approaches and accommodations to meet a greater number of individual student learning needs are looking to digital resources for a solution. Computer software already exists through which students can read stories and participate in activities related to the readings, and the text can be enlarged, changed in color, highlighted, or made audible as needed for individual students.

These successes have encouraged a number of professional, corporate, and governmental entities to work together and separately to create and promote a new curricular concept called "universal design curriculum." Universal design curriculum is the concept of diversifying instruction in the general education classroom for nearly every student, regardless of educational need and learning style. It would provide multiple means of presentation style, multiple and flexible means of student engagement and participation, and multiple means of student response (Annual Report, 1999). Disabled, diverse, nondisabled, and gifted students would learn using the same software materials and equipment. Through the use of technology, curriculum can be developed with built-in adaptations and inclusive accommodations to meet students' needs to account for differences in ability to see, hear, speak, move, read, write, understand English, pay attention, organize, interact, and remember. Teachers and other individuals would seldom need to create other new methods and materials to meet diverse individual student needs. Accommodations for wide disparities in student educational needs would be built into the system (Orkwis & McLane, 1998; "Universal Design," 1999).

As this revolution in curriculum occurs, the need for committed educational leaders will be as great as ever. Because this is a regular education and not a special education innovation, all students and all teachers will be involved, not just a few. Teaching staff will need a great deal of professional support, assistance in bringing about the change, professional development opportunities, and innovation in securing needed resources. The community will need to be educated in what for many citizens will be a giant leap ahead of what they personally experienced as students. Business and community leaders must be kept informed and their support solicited for innovations that will have significant impact on the learning of all students.

Grading

Suppose that previously discussed modifications have been made and the regular classroom is accessible. Appropriate texts and materials have been selected and the curriculum altered to match each students' abilities. What happens when grading time comes around? What evaluation system can be fair to both the students with disabilities, who may be putting forth tremendous effort and still not meeting the usual course goals, and those in the nondisabled majority, who may question a grading system they perceive as unequal and unfair?

This is one of the stickiest issues facing educators in an inclusion setting, and it has generated persistent and difficult problems among parents, teachers, and students. For example, teachers have been known to refuse to take exceptional students in their classes because of the awkwardness of developing an evaluation system that is fair to all students, one that reinforces effort but also realistically reports performance. This last point is important both for its present communication value and for its influence on future planning.

It is possible to develop fair, accurate, and justifiable evaluation systems for integrated classes. The paragraphs that follow offer several suggestions. Clearly, it is to the educational leader's advantage to be aware of these strategies and to assist teachers in implementing them

because so many potential problems can be avoided by doing so.

Modifying Assessment

Three aspects of evaluation may have to be modified in an inclusion class setting: test construction, test grading, and the recording of grades.

The same tests that are quite adequate for the majority of students in a class may not yield fair and accurate results for those with special needs. It would obviously be inappropriate, for example, to give an exam to a hearing-impaired student in which all instructions and questions were given orally. The following list suggests a variety of testing modifications that teachers may decide are desirable to meet the needs of individual students. Not all modifications will be appropriate or necessary for all students.

- *Visual Presentation*: Teachers must be sure that the test is clearly printed and easy to read. Small flaws in print may be extremely distracting and frustrating to some students. Teachers should type rather than hand write tests whenever possible, print on only one side of the page, be sure the duplicating or copy machine is working properly, use dark ink on white paper, and avoid presenting too much material on each page.

- *Organization*: Teachers should number all pages, ask questions in sequential order, group questions of the same format (e.g., multiple choice) together, print all instructions on the page and review these instructions orally before testing begins, allow plenty of space for the students' responses and provide lines for them to write on, and group questions (e.g., matching questions) into small sets, rather than long lists.

- *Minimizing Stress*: Teachers must minimize distracting noise and activity levels, place the students in a quiet location, try not to give oral instructions while students are taking the test, and be available to quietly answer individual questions. It is preferable to give several short tests rather than one long one. Timed tests should be avoided, except where speed is an essential element of the skill. Bonus questions or other options for improving grades could be provided for those who perform poorly in exam situations. Bonus points should not be allowed to mask minimum mastery. Point values should be assigned to each part of the test and noted on the page. Teachers should help students prioritize their time in testing situations. Many teachers ease student stress by teaching test-taking skills and providing the opportunity for practice exams.

- *Communication Mode*: Students should be allowed to take a test orally if needed, or the exam should be structured to minimize writing (for example, they could mark an *X* beside the correct response, rather than writing in the entire word). Teachers should give both oral and written instructions, as needed, assign another student to write down responses, tape record the test, or have the student indicate correct answers by pointing to them, as needed.

- *Clarity*: Teachers should provide simple, clear instructions and questions and avoid asking questions with many multi-part answers. They should walk around the room during the tests, checking the students' work to be sure they are all following the directions accurately.

- *Format*: Teachers who discern that a student responds much better to one type of test (e.g., multiple choice) than another should consider preparing tests for that student in the format that assures the most accurate performance. Tests can be offered with a balanced selection of formats and point values (e.g., 25% essay, 25% true-false, 25% matching, etc.). Students may also be allowed to demonstrate knowledge or ability using evaluation techniques other than tests.

- *Extraneous Material*: Material unrelated to student mastery and trivial questions should be eliminated whenever possible.

- *Alternative Assessment*: Many schools are turning to alternative assessment models, such as portfolios, to aid in assessing student progress. As a collection of work samples which serves to integrate academic learning activities, portfolio assessment presents a number of advantages. Portfolios document individual performance and progress, including the documentation of both affective and cognitive skills. Specific skills can be targeted for remedial attention, and progress can be monitored over time. This approach is very helpful in carrying out an IEP. Asking students to evaluate their own work encourages student reflection of their own work and increases student-teacher collaboration in the classroom. Content will vary with subject matter and overall purpose, but creative and flexible approaches will even involve academic areas thought by some to not be suited for portfolios, such as mathematics (Carpenter, Ray, & Bloom, 1995; Prestidge & Glaser, 2000).

Modifications in Grading and Recording of Grades

In grading tests and other class activities, the key issues are fairness and a firm grip on what is being evaluated and what is not. It would be important, for example, that teachers not downgrade a student because of poor handwriting or poor grammar if the test really is designed to assess knowledge of social studies concepts. This is true especially if writing is a skill that is directly affected by the student's disability.

The same may be true of timed tests. Several disabilities may have an adverse affect on students' ability to demonstrate skills and knowledge accurately under time pressure, including physiological impairments that make writing slower and emotional problems that exaggerate stress. If time is not a critical part of the behavior being measured, it would be inappropriate to penalize such students' scores because of it. The goal, after all, is to measure students' acquired skills and achievements, not skills extraneous to content being taught.

An obvious solution to many of these problems is to assign multiple grades for each task or subject. For example, principals could recommend that teachers grade work separately on content and form, individual student effort, and/or amount of time spent; students might receive one grade for individual achievement or improvement and another on their relation to the achievement level of peers. Another possibility is to give a grade that reflects fulfillment of the central intent of the lesson, regardless of specific issues of quality.

Ideally, the concept of multiple grades should be extended to report cards as well, although many computerized systems unfortunately do not offer that potential. The following are alternative means of arriving at reasonable evaluations of student performance.

Contracts. The teacher and student may sit down together and negotiate a specific grade for a specific amount of work at an agreed-upon level of functioning. For example, the agreement might be that over the course of the grading period, the student will earn a B for completing two spelling lists per week with an average of 90% accuracy, and so on. The contracted educational goals must be positive (what the student will do, not won't do), measurable, clearly stated, honest, and reasonable, given the student's current ability levels. Student and teacher must understand and agree on each part of the contract, then each must sign it. Progress toward stated goals should be evaluated periodically.

Differing Requirements. The teacher can allow the student to respond in a different communication mode, require different amounts or kinds of work, or allow a longer period of time for completion of an assignment. For example, a one-page rather than a two-page essay can be required, or one chemical experiment rather than two, and so forth. Care must be exercised in using this option for a variety of reasons. Sometimes students with disabilities need more practice, rather than less, to master a skill. Social factors are important considerations, especially for adolescents who do not want to be perceived as different from their peers. Inappropriately low expectations may hinder chances of reaching true potential.

Small Group Assignments. The teacher can divide the class into small, heterogeneous groups and assign a task to the whole group. Students with disabilities can be assigned specific, appropriate roles in a cooperative learning structure. All group members receive the same grade for work completed, or one group grade and one for individual effort. This structure can generate extra benefits in terms of understanding and acceptance of the classmate with disabilities and sharing of skills.

Staffing Models

Whereas in the past, students with disabilities were viewed as the exclusive responsibility of special educators, inclusion necessarily requires a cooperative effort on the part of a variety of professionals. Such cooperation, in turn, requires new considerations of staffing patterns and administrative structures, including closer involvement of principals. Several such staffing models have been developed and refined over the years since the initial passage of the IDEA. Chapter 11 provides more detail on these models and others in common use.

Resource Room Model

In the resource room model, students with mild to moderate disabilities spend a great part of the day in the regular classroom and part with specially trained staff in a separate special education classroom. The amount of time spent, subjects covered, and type of programming are determined on a highly individualized basis. Varying degrees of collaboration occur depending on the experience and interest of staff. In some states, the resource room is considered a related service, whereas in others it is considered a special education program.

Itinerant Teacher Model

The itinerant teacher, like the regular classroom teacher, works with students in their regular classroom environment, but the itinerant teacher is responsible only for the one or two identified students, not for the entire class. The itinerant teacher may provide a direct service to the student with disabilities or may supplement the instruction of the regular teacher. This model is frequently used with low incidence disabilities, such as students with visual impairments.

Consulting Teacher Model (Collaborative Consultation)

Another common inclusion special education model makes use of a consulting teacher. Consultation requires a strong belief in inclusion, a strong communication system, time for communication, and great mutual trust. These specialists, often special education teachers, differ from those discussed previously in that they normally do not work directly with students but rather with the regular classroom teacher. Consulting teachers accept responsibility for the child and share their knowledge of disabilities, special materials, instructional techniques, independent learning activities, diagnosis and evaluation techniques, class arrangements, and class management. This model is sometimes called the diagnostic-prescriptive teacher model.

Peer Collaboration

Peer collaboration is merely the formalization of the informal collegial brainstorming which fre-

quently occurs in the hallway or teachers' lounge. Two or more regular education teachers are grouped for the purpose of engaging in structured mutually beneficial dialogues about learning problems experienced by each others' students. They serve as sounding boards for each other's ideas and assist in evaluating the success of attempted interventions.

Team Teaching

Team teaching can be orchestrated in a number of ways, but involves special education and regular education teachers in the same classroom. This can work with small groups, tutorial or teaching together at the same time or taking turns. Group communication and using each others' strengths are keys to success. Because much time is devoted to working alongside each other, a similar belief in inclusion and an interest in developing collegiality are important.

Other Inclusion Considerations

Staff Readiness and Understanding

American educators are as good as any found in the entire world. Yet many are not ready, or do not think they are ready, for the opportunity and the challenge of implementing inclusive educational practices. There seems to exist a general feeling of inadequacy and lack of preparation for what lies ahead. In a survey of building principals in Illinois, Barnett and Monda-Amaya (1998) found that there was a common lack of clear understanding, or even a definition, of "inclusion" among school leaders, regardless of their length of administrative service experience.

Experience from research involving classroom teachers establishes a similar pattern, and the perspective of regular education teachers has significant implications for administrative support and assistance in classroom problem-solving. In a review of twenty-eight research studies conducted between 1958 and 1995, Scruggs and Mastropieri (1996) found that regular education teachers felt that they were not provided the sufficient time to successfully provide inclusion services to children with disabilities. The vast majority of general education teachers felt that they had inadequate training for inclusion and that inadequate resources were available. These viewpoints from various research studies were not new and were consistent over several decades. Over the decades, the perceptions of teachers did not change significantly when identifying their needs to help facilitate successful inclusion: time for planning; training and working with consultants and colleagues; personnel resources in the form of teacher associates and regular contact with special education teachers; materials and equipment resources appropriate for the students' needs; and consideration of the severity of the disability—the more severe the disability, the more time and resources must be made available.

In the past, teachers have been justified in feeling alone and unsupported when faced with the challenges of mainstreaming and inclusion. Educational leaders must do a better job of allaying concerns and supporting teachers who are involved with inclusion efforts. Long gone is the day when the principal escorted the student with a disability to the classroom, opened the door, gently nudged the child into the room, closed the door, and left. Both good educational practice and the law dictate that meaningful support and necessary resources accompany that child into the regular classroom.

Community Readiness

The primary goal of this book is to provide educational leaders with the knowledge, the basic skills, and the incentive to enable their staff, through the provision of adequate resources, to provide good and meaningful educational experiences for all the children of America. The trend across all disability categories, but especially the mildest, has been toward moving students to less restrictive placements (McLeskey, Henry, & Hodges, 1999).

However, not all the attention needs to be focused internally. Although there is strong support among families of children with disabilities for inclusion, the general public appears to be lagging in its support for, or knowledge of, the inclusion concept. The annual Phi Delta Kappa/Gallup Poll of public attitudes toward education provides evidence that a great deal of understanding and support for inclusion is lacking among the general public. In 1995 and again in 1998, participants were asked whether children with "learning problems" should be placed in the same classroom with other students, or in special classes of their own. Table 6-1 shows a comparison of responses.

Obviously, little change occurred in responses given in 1995 and in 1998. Other groups included, but not broken out in the table that were most likely to prefer special class placement were adults age sixty-four and older (74%), high school graduates (71%), and laborers (71%).

Charter Schools

When Congress approved the 1997 Amendments it expressly required for the first time that all charter schools that are part of local public school systems comply with the legal requirements of the IDEA. Whereas many definitions of charter schools exist, commonly they are public schools freed from many state and local regulations, such as collective bargaining, which sometimes seems to hamper the delivery of good educational services and programs. The preliminary evidence of the overall academic success of charter schools is mixed (Rosenfeld, 1998). So too, is their record of meeting the needs of children with disabilities. Although many charter schools were established for the express purpose of providing quality education programs to children with disabilities, thus far they have had a mixed record of success regarding serving such children. Some for-profit charter schools

TABLE 6-1 *Whether Children with "Learning Problems" Should Be Put in the Same Classroom with Other Children or in a Special Class*

	National Totals 1998 1995	No Children in School 1998 1995	Public School Parents 1998 1995	Nonpublic School Parents 1998 1995
Yes, same classrooms	26%	26%	29%	10%
	26%	25%	29%	25%
No, special classes	65%	65%	63%	70%
	66%	68%	60%	66%
Don't know	9%	9%	8%	20%
	8%	7%	9%	9%

From "The 30th Annual Phi Delta Kappa/Gallup Poll of the Public's Attitudes Toward the Public Schools," by L. C. Rose and A. M. Gallup, 1998, *Phi Delta Kappan, 80* (1), p. 53. Copyright 1998 by Phi Delta Kappa International, Inc. Adapted by permission.

have been accused of forcing or counseling students with disabilities to attend school elsewhere when the school did not wish to attempt to meet students' individual educational needs (Zollers & Ramanthan, 1998).

CONCLUSION

The proper placement of children with disabilities is a complex and important task for educators and parents. Advance preparation of the school staff, environment, and system will aid greatly in successful placements; so will a trusting relationship with parents. Inclusion, a part of the LRE concept, is most achievable when all of those involved, including parents, have an opportunity to plan, modify, and prepare. Improperly implemented placements have a significant potential for student failure, administrative headaches, staff morale problems, and unwinable legal battles. Although proper implementation of student placements requires a good deal of time, thought, communication, and effort, im-

proper placement implementations have potentially catastrophic consequences for some or all of those involved.

View from the Court Bench

Florence County School District Four v. Carter, 1993

In *Carter*, the parents of a child with specific learning disabilities objected to an IEP that established goals in reading and mathematics of only four months progress for the entire year, and they placed the child in an unapproved private school. The parents then requested reimbursement for their expenses from the public school. The trial court ruled that the school district had not met the IDEA's requirement of providing an appropriate educational program, but that the private school program was appropriate for the child. The girl had experienced three years' academic growth in her three years at the private school. The issue before the Supreme Court was whether parents could recover their expenses for a unilateral placement in a private school that did not meet state approval requirements.

The Court had previously ruled in another decision that parents could recover their educational expenses if the local public school did not provide an appropriate program and the parent placement was an appropriate program. (The IDEA regulations now expressly provide for this two-pronged test.) The Court ruled in favor of the parents. In doing so, it admonished the public school, which had complained about the high tuition rate for the private school and said that it could avoid high tuition rates for private schools by providing children with FAPE itself, or by placing children in appropriate settings of its own choosing.

Irving Independent School District v. Tatro, 1984

A school district refused to provide eight-year-old Amber Tatro with clean intermittent catheterization while at school. The procedure was necessary because Amber was born with spina bifida. The school claimed that the procedure was medical in nature and thus was not a "related service" that it was required to provide under the IDEA. The Supreme Court ruled that health services necessary to allow a child to benefit from special education are a related service under the IDEA so long as they do not require the services of a licensed physician. This view was reaffirmed fifteen years later in *Cedar Rapids Community School District v. Garret F.* (1999).

Greer v. Rome City School District, 1990

Greer is representative of unanimous rulings on the requirement of inclusion in four federal circuit courts of appeal. The issue before all four circuits was the appropriate criteria for determining individual student inclusion programming. Christy Greer was a child with Down syndrome who the school refused to allow to attend regular class programming to meet her

educational needs. Christy's parents insisted that she would benefit from placement in regular classrooms and brought suit. The court recognized a legal "preference" for regular class placement and developed a legal standard for determining whether a child with disabilities could be placed in special education, rather than in a regular education setting.

The court ruled that schools must consider, during the IEP process, the "full range of supplemental aids and services" that may be provided in conjunction with the regular classroom placement. Then, the IEP team, keeping the supplementary aids and services in mind, must consider the educational benefit the child will receive in the regular classroom and the effect of the child's presence in the regular classroom. The child may be placed in special education, in whole or in part, only if the child will benefit academically or through role modeling (i.e., social, behavior, language) significantly less in a regular classroom compared with a special classroom, or if the child's presence in the regular classroom is likely to significantly disrupt the education of the other children owing to the child's misbehavior or need for teacher time and attention.

As a third prong of the test, in addition to benefit and disruption, the IEP team is to determine whether the cost of supplementary aids and services necessary to make the regular classroom placement otherwise viable would significantly impact the education of other children in the district. Only when the cost of supplementary aids and services would significantly impact the education of others would regular classroom placement be inappropriate.

The Court applied the three-pronged test to Christy and concluded that she would benefit academically in the regular classroom, that she would not be disruptive, and that the supplementary aids and services would not be "cost prohibitive." Christy's appropriate placement, at that time, was determined to be in the regular classroom.

REFERENCES

Alamo Heights Independent School District v. State Board, 790 F.2d 1153 (5th Cir. 1986).

Annual Report—21st Annual Report (1999). Office of Special Education and Rehabilitation Services. Available: *http://www.ed.gov/offices/OSERS/OSEP/ OSEP99* Anl. Rpt.1/DOC-Files/CH 1.doc.

Assistance to the states for the education of children with disabilities, 34 C.F.R., Part 300 (2000).

Baines, L., Baines, C., & Masterson, C. (1994). Mainstreaming: One school's reality. *Phi Delta Kappan, 76* (1) 39–40, 57–64.

Barnett, C., & Monda-Amaya, L. E. (1998). Principals' knowledge of and attitudes toward inclusion. *Remedial and Special Education, 19* (3), 181–192.

Bartlett, L. D. (2000). Medical services: The disputed related service. *The Journal of Special Education, 33* (4), 215–223.

Bartlett, L. D. (1992). Mainstreaming: On the road to clarification. *Education Law Reporter, 76* (1), 17–25.

Board of Education v. Holland, 786 F.Supp. 874 (E.D. Cal. 1992).

Carpenter, D. D., Ray, M. S., & Bloom, L. A. (1995). Portfolio assessment: Opportunities and challenges. *Intervention in School and Clinic, 31* (1), 34–41.

Cedar Rapids Community School District v. Garret F., 24 IDELR 648 (N.D. Ia. 1996), *aff'd.,* 106 F.3d 822 (8th Cir. 1997), *aff'd.,* 526 U.S. 66, 119 S.Ct. 992 (1999).

Clyde K. v. Puyallup School District, 35 F.3d. 1396 (9th Cir. 1994).

Davila to Goodling, 18 IDELR 213 (OSEP 1991).

Etscheidt, S., & Bartlett, L. D. (1999). The IDEA Amendments: A four-step approach for determining supplementary aids and services. *Exceptional Children 65* (2), 163–174.

Falvey, M. A., Givner, C. C., & Kimm, C. (1995). What is an inclusive school? In: R. A. Villa, & J. S. Thousand (Eds.), *Creating an inclusive school.* Alexandria, VA: Association for Supervision and Curriculum Development, 1–12.

Florence County School District Four v. Carter, 510 U.S. 7, 114 S.Ct. 361 (1993).

Greer v. Rome City School District, 950 F.2d 688 (11th Cir. 1991), *withdrawn and remanded* 956 F.2d

1025 (11th Cir. 1992), *reinstated* 967 F.2d 470 (11th Cir. 1992).

Hudson v. Bloomfield Hills Public Schools, 23 IDELR 613 (E.D. Mich. 1995); aff'd 25 IDELR 607 (6th Cir. 1997).

Iowa Department of Education (1996). *The least restrictive environment (LRE) and the individualized education program (IEP): Legal educational and practical guidelines for educators and families.* Des Moines, IA: Mountain Plains Regional Resource Center, Drake University.

Iowa Department of Education (2000). *Administrative rules of special education.* Iowa Administrative Code, 281–41.

Irving Independent School District v. Tatro, 468 U.S. 883, 104 S.Ct. 3371 (1984).

Johnson v. Independent School District No. 4, 921 F.2d 1022 (10th Cir. 1990).

McLeskey, J., Henry, D., & Hodges, D. (1999). Inclusion: What progress is being made across disabilities categories? *Teaching Exceptional Children, 31* (3), 60–64.

Meredith, B., & Underwood, J. (1995). Irreconcilable differences? Defining the rising conflict between regular and special education. *Journal of Law and Education, 24* (2), 195–226.

Mountain Plains Regional Resource Center (1997). *Least restrictive environment: Supplementary aids and services.* Logan, UT: Utah State University.

Nondiscrimination on the basis of handicap in programs and activities receiving federal financial assistance. 34 C.F.R. Part 104. (2000).

Oberti v. Board of Education, 789 F. Supp. 1322 (D.N.J., 1992).

Orkwis, R., & McLane, K. (1998). *A curriculum every student can use: Design principals for student access.* ERIC/OSEP Topical Brief, ERIC Clearinghouse No. EC 306760, e-mail: *ericec@ced.sped. org.*

Osborne, Jr. A. G., Russo, C. J., and DiMaltia, P. (1999). IDEA '97: Providing special education services to students voluntarily enrolled in private schools. *The Journal of Special Education, 33* (4), 224–231.

Prestidge, L. K., & Glaser, C. H. W. (2000). Authentic assessment: Employing appropriate tools for evaluating students' work in 21st century classrooms. *Intervention in School and Clinic, 35* (3), 178–182.

OSEP Memo 95-9, 21 IDELR 1152 (OSEP, 1994).

Rebore, D., & Zirkel, P. A. (1999). The Supreme Court's latest special education ruling: A costly decision? *Education Law Reporter,* 135, 331–141.

Reusch v. Fountain, 872 F.Supp. 1421 (D. Md. 1994).

Rogers, J. (1993). The inclusion revolution. *Research Bulletin No. 11,* Phi Delta Kappa, May 1993, pp. 4–9.

Rose, L. C., & Gallup, A. M. (1998). Public's attitudes toward the public schools: The 30th annual Phi Delta Kappa/Gallup Poll. *Phi Delta Kappan,* 80 (1), 41–58.

Rosenfeld, S. J. (1998). Charter schools and special education. *EDLAW Briefing Paper, 8* (7), 1–7.

Scruggs, T. E., & Mastropieri, M. A. (1996). Teacher perceptions of mainstream/inclusion, 1958–1995: A research synthesis. *Exceptional Children, 63* (1), 59074.

Smith, T. C. (1981). Status of due process hearings. *Exceptional Children, 48* (3), 232–236.

Stainback, W., Stainback, S., & Stefanich, G. (1996). Learning together in inclusive classrooms: What about curriculum? *Teaching Exceptional Children* 28 (3), 14–19.

Stevens, R., & Slavin, R. (1995). The cooperative elementary school. *American Educational Research Journal, 32,* 321–351.

Thomas v. Cincinnati Board of Education, 918 F.2d 618 (6th Cir. 1990).

Universal design: Ensuring access to general education curriculum (1996). *Research Connections in Special Education (5);* ERIC Clearinghouse No. EC307411; Available at: http://www.ericec.org.

Warlick to Thompson, 34 IDELR ¶ 29 (OSEP, 2000).

Zollers, N. J., & Ramanthan, A. K. (1998). For profit charter schools and parents with disabilities: The sordid side of the business of schooling. *Phi Delta Kappan, 80* (4), 305–312.

RECOMMENDED READINGS

Carpenter, C. D., Ray, M. S., & Bloom, L. A. (1995). Portfolio assessments: Opportunities and challenges. *Intervention in School and Clinic, 31* (1), 34–41. This article describes portfolio assessment use in special education and provides recommendations for future applications.

Elliott, D., & McKenney M. (1998). Four inclusion models that work. *Teaching exceptional children, 30* (4), 54–58. This article discusses the experience of a special education and regular education teacher with various models of inclusion.

Erickson, R., Yesseldyke, J., Thurlow, M., & Elliot, J. (1998). Inclusive assessment and accountability systems. *Teaching Exceptional Children, 31* (2), 4–9. This article discusses policy associated with assessment and provides specific recommendations on appropriate assessment.

Etscheidt, S. K., & Bartlett, L. (1999). The IDEA Amendments: A four-step approach for determining supplementary aids and services. *Exceptional Children, 65* (2), 163–174. This article explains the legal importance of supplementary aids and services under the IDEA and suggests an approach to more effectively determine appropriate supplementary aids and services for children.

Meese, R. L. (1992). Adapting textbooks for children with learning disabilities in mainstreamed classrooms. *Teaching Exceptional Children, 24* (3), 49–51. This article presents practical ideas on accommodating the reading needs of special students.

Salend, S. J. (2000). Strategies and resources to evaluate the impact of inclusion programs on children. *Intervention in School and Clinic, 35* (5), 264–277. This comprehensive article provides a variety of strategies and resources to be used in assessing the impact of inclusion programs on all students.

Relevant Federal Regulations

34 CFR § 104.21	Discrimination prohibited.
104.22	Existing facilities.
104.23	New construction.
300.5	Assistive technology device.
.6	Assistive technology service.
.24	Related services.
.26	Special education.
.28	Supplementary aids and services.
.241	Treatment of charter schools and their students.

CHAPTER 7

INFANT AND TODDLER AND PRESCHOOL PROGRAMS

Focus

Because federal legislation and some states mandate educational programs for children with disabilities under age five, educational leaders without special training for this age group may frequently become involved in preschool administration or programming. Some aspects of infant and toddler programs (birth to age three) may also be housed in elementary school buildings, thereby adding to administrator responsibilities.

Legal Issues

Several key federal laws and policies relate to the education of children from birth to age five. These include:

- Head Start (1965), amended in 1972 to require that at least 10% of the opportunities for enrollment be available to children with disabilities;
- Handicapped Children's Early Education Act (1968) provided funds for the establishment of demonstration projects designed to test innovative models for early education of children with disabilities;
- Education of All Handicapped Children Act (EAHCA), 1975 (P.L. 94-142), as amended, first gave states the option of providing education for children with disabilities ages three to five, but later preschool became a requirement;
- Part C, added to IDEA in 1986, provides optional state programs for infants and toddlers under age three.

Part C

Part C programming for infants and toddlers uses a comprehensive multi-service agency approach for resolving the needs of the members of the family, not just the child with disabilities. States may also individually choose to serve at-risk children in the under three-year-old age group. Each child served must have an individual family service plan (IFSP), and each plan must have a person designated as coordinator of services. By age three, a smooth plan for transition of the child to education services under an IEP must be completed. Under the IDEA, preschool children between the ages of three and six are legally treated the same as elementary age children.

Rationale

Research suggests that early intervention increases the likelihood of children with disabilities remaining in school, keeping up with nondisabled peers, or maximizing their educational potential.

Approaches

Generally, early childhood programs use a variety of settings to meet the needs of children and preschool programs are school-based or center-based. Early childhood education for children with disabilities encompasses a great variety of programs, including interventions provided in the child's home; classes at schools or centers; parent training; infant stimulation programs; traditional, nondirective preschool programs; highly structured curricula focusing on the development of pre-academic skills as well as other structured but child-directed curricula; programs for homogeneous (e.g., hearing-impaired) and for highly heterogeneous populations (inclusion).

All of these approaches have proved beneficial for young children with disabilities when the programs emphasize:

- collaborative teaming processes;
- strong parent participation;
- well-designed and adaptive learning environments;
- social growth;
- positive disciplinary techniques; and
- age appropriate and individualized learning activities.

Emerging Early Childhood and Preschool Programs

Few children are identified as having disabilities at birth. Mild disabilities in such categories as emotional disturbance, mental disabilities, and specific learning disabilities often do not emerge until the school years, and even rather severe cognitive or sensory impairments may not be correctly identified until the child is two years of age or older. Yet many states begin educational programming for identified children with disabilities from the first days of life. Who, exactly, are the children served by these programs, and what do educators hope to accomplish?

The answers to these questions can be summarized under the headings of prevention and compensation. The latter, compensatory programming, is the oldest approach and the easiest to understand. A child who is blind, deaf, or paraplegic cannot be expected to make normal developmental progress with the same type of informal parental guidance that is adequate for most preschoolers. Such children will need special training in speech, mobility, and other skills. In addition, they will need time, training, and special equipment to help them compensate for their disabilities. The advantages of beginning such training as early as possible include maximizing the children's ability to keep up with peers in later schooling and allowing them and their families more positive experiences in the early years. Research, including longitudinal studies, has demonstrated the general effectiveness of developmentally appropriate early education programs for at-risk children, those with special needs, and those with normal development (Hibbert & Sprinthall, 1995).

The notion of prevention in this context is a relatively new one. It evolved from a complex set of developments during the 1950s and 1960s, including animal research on the effects of early stimulation, the child development theories of Piaget, Erickson, and others, and mounting statistical evidence from actual program evaluations. Emerging themes such as the critical importance of early childhood development and the effect of the child's environment on intelligence were picked up and promoted by contemporary social movements. The result was widespread belief that gaps in educational achievement among different social groups could be mitigated or prevented through early intervention.

The Head Start program, begun in 1965, was one response. Head Start was amended in 1972 to set aside 10% of enrollment opportunities for children with disabilities, establish a number of programs with the goal of preventing or limiting the effects of disabilities at an early age, and provide extra monies for preschool demonstration projects.

In the following decades, as new attitudes toward education of the disabled developed, it was natural that the principle of preventive early intervention should be extended to the young disabled population. Early childhood education was advocated as a means of preventing or limiting the effects of disabilities on children's school experience. This is what some authors have referred to as the "downward escalation of educational services" (Ysseldyke, Algozzine, & Thurlow, 2000, p. 215). Initially, preschool services were extended for the three- to five-year-olds, and then services were expanded to the early childhood years, infants, and toddlers, ages birth to three years. Even pre-birth services to the mother and child are provided in some areas of the country as preventative measures against future potential problems of an at-risk nature. Colorado, for instance, provides extensive medical and counseling services for expectant mothers who receive public assistance.

Efforts to increase the educational opportunities of pre-kindergarten children are not limited to those children with disabilities. There is a national trend to provide greater educational opportunities at an earlier age to more children. Currently, thirty-nine states support preschool programs for parents who need it in an effort to provide what some persons refer to as "universal pre-k." Georgia has spent $217 million per year to support universal pre-k for 61,000 children enrolled in preschool programs, and New York where universal pre-k is a goal for the year 2003, has supported 19,000 children ($62 million) in preschool programs through a lottery system (Morse, 1998).

The relation of preschool intervention for the disabled to earlier movements for social equality involved more than a simple historical precedent. Early research showed that the great majority of children identified as mildly disabled in the early school years were from socially or economically disadvantaged families, including a disproportionate number of racial minorities. As the President's Committee on Mental Retardation (1976) reported:

> In perhaps 85–90 percent of cases, mild retardation not involving identifiable organic or physical causes is associated with conditions arising from the environment, poverty, racial and ethnic discrimination, and family disorders. (p. 80)

From studies and statistics such as these, the concept arose that some infants and young children were "at risk" for developing disabilities. It is important to note that although race and ethnicity were later discarded as independent at-risk factors, when combined with factors such as poverty and single-parent families, they continue to represent a significant source of the acknowledged increase in rates of childhood disability (Fujiura & Yamaki, 2000). Children living in poverty is a growing phenomenon in America. Other at-risk groups have also been identified, including children born prematurely, those of low birth weight or stressful births, those born with the HIV infection that causes AIDS, and those born to mothers exposed to toxic drugs or infections during pregnancy. Unfortunately, little is being done to deal with these new social issues, and the task to ameliorate their impact will likely fall on the public schools (Ysseldyke, Algozine, & Thurlow, 2000, pp. 226–30).

In many cases, "at risk" is a more useful and more accurate term than "disabled" when referring to very young children. Some early-childhood educators prefer it exclusively, fearing that the early application of labels, (e.g., mentally retarded) may negatively affect adults' attitudes and expectations of a child and result in ongoing and permanent damage. In partial recognition of concerns of labeling children at an early age, and the recognition of the difficulty of assessment in the early years, the federal government now allows the use of the phrase "developmental delay" to identify those children ages three through nine who are appropriately diagnosed with special educational needs.

Because early educational opportunities have an important impact on the future needs of children at risk of developing educational problems, their need for early identification and provision of services is obvious. Yet America's record in identifying and serving those in society who are least able to fend for themselves is not stellar.

It is estimated that during the 1991–92 school year approximately 593,000 American children under six years of age were served under IDEA programs. One researcher (Bowe, 1995) has estimated, however, that the number of children eligible for programs was actually 851,000, which means that public schools were reaching only about 70% of the eligible preschool population. That same research further determined that most of the unserved or underserved children were from low socioeconomic or minority families, societal groups that could least afford to be left out of educational opportunities.

Research results focusing on the level of need for special education services among homeless children living in emergency homeless shelters have identified the dual problem for such children: They are at risk for learning problems and they do not have regular and consistent access to special education programs. In one study, nearly one-half (46%) of the homeless children screened positive for at least one disability requiring special education services (Zima et al, 1998). These homeless youngsters present a significant challenge for school officials, who have an obligation to identify children with disabilities and provide appropriate special education services. Child find requirements of Part B in the 1997 Amendments expressly require the identification and evaluation of highly mobile children with disabilities, including migrant and homeless children.

Families with children, mostly single-parent families, are the fastest growing group of homeless persons in America, and attendance at school is especially important for the children of such families. The effects of homelessness present significant health and nutrition issues as well as developmental, psychological, social growth, and academic progress issues without schools adding to the problem (Yamaguchi, Strawser, & Higgins, 1997). Schools may provide the only opportunity for stability for a homeless child in a life otherwise filled with uncertainty. Therefore, schools must make conscious efforts to not make life more difficult for homeless children. Schools can help such children by establishing a stable, safe, and nonthreatening educational environment and by establishing as typical a school experience as possible. Congress has passed and amended the McKinney Homeless Assistance Act, which requires public schools be a help rather than a hindrance in the life of homeless children. Figure 7-1 provides a summary of the terms of the McKinney Act that impact schools.

Does Early Education Work?

Although still a new and rapidly changing field, especially with the birth-to-age three population, early childhood and preschool education have been around long enough to generate some follow-up data. What have been the results? Does early intervention work? The answer, it would seem, depends on the expectations and on the definition of success.

Early education does not seem to be preventive in the sense, say, that the Salk vaccine prevents polio. One or two years of special education—no matter how early—cannot be expected to counteract the effects of most risk factors or disabilities. On the other hand, at-risk children who have experienced early intervention do fare better in measures of educational achievement later in life than those who have not.

The gains can be sustained when students continue to receive special education services during their school years. A number of studies have identified early childhood and preschool education for at-risk students as a cost-effective strategy for future savings in education, welfare, and crime prevention (Turnbull & Turnbull, 1998, p. 98).

Legal History

In 1964, the Economic Opportunity Act provided funding for preschool education programs designed to compensate for the negative effects of poverty. By the following year, 550,000 children were enrolled in preschool programs as part of Head Start. Early research studies indicated that most anticipated academic gains for those children disappeared by the end of second grade. However, more recent controlled studies have identified lasting gains for Head Start students (Udell, Peters, & Templeman, 1998; Ysseldyke, Algozzine, & Thurlow, 2000, p. 214.)

Several efforts through the late 1960s provided funding for model programs, including

FIGURE 7-1   *Provisions of the Stewart B. McKinney Homeless Assistance Act of 1987 and Amendments of 1990 and 1994*

- All homeless children have the same right to a free and appropriate public education as non-homeless children.
- Children who are homeless will receive the same services or be placed in the same programs as their classmates who live in permanent housing.
- States are required to review and revise their requirements to remove barriers to enrollment, including
  - the residency requirement,
  - the guardianship requirement,
  - previous school records, and
  - immunization records.
- Children who are homeless must be placed
  - in the child's original school for the remainder of the school year
  - in the school district where the child currently resides
  - in the school that meets the best interests of the child, and in the school requested by the parents.
- A homeless liaison shall be designated to
  - ensure that children who are homeless receive educational services for which they are eligible and
  - coordinate with social service agencies for appropriate referrals (e.g., health care, dental, mental health services).

From "Children Who Are Homeless: Implications for Educators," by B. J. Yamaguchi, S. Strawser, and K. Higgins, 1997, *Intervention in School and Clinic, 33*, p. 91. Copyright 1997 by PRO-ED, Inc. Reprinted with permission.

children with disabilities in preschool programs, and for early child find efforts. In 1975, the forerunner of the IDEA included funding for preschool programs serving children ages three through five years. In 1986, the special education statutes were amended through the addition of Part H (P.L. 94-457) to provide early intervention services for infants and toddlers with disabilities from birth through age two. Part H (changed to Part C in 1997) was initially written to provide a five-year phase-in period for states; this lead-in time was primarily to allow for possible difficulties in incorporating a number of new approaches to dealing with children with

disabilities and their families, including its requirement of inter-agency cooperation. For most states, this preparation period had to be extended an additional three years, and many states are still finding full compliance difficult.

LEGAL ASPECTS

For the purposes of the IDEA Part B, schools have generally considered their responsibility toward younger preschool-aged children differently than that of children of traditional school age. Under the early versions of the IDEA, public schools were responsible for education services beginning at age five or six, depending on each state's laws regarding school entrance. The law was later amended to require that FAPE be provided all children age three through twenty-one who were entitled to special education, unless such a requirement would be inconsistent with state law.

By 1987, nearly 261,000 children ages three to five were receiving preschool special education services, and two years later the number had increased to 362,443. Unfortunately, this extraordinary growth highlighted many of the difficulties in identifying disabilities in children of such young age, determining appropriate programming, and increasing concerns about early age labeling of children (Ysseldyke, Algozzine, & Thurlow, 2000, pp. 215–16).

For children ages three to five, and for some two-year-olds who will turn three during the school year, states may receive federal grants for preschool programs. Preschool special education grants to states for the 1998 fiscal year were $500,000,000. Provisions of the law for those preschoolers are the same (FAPE, parent safeguards, IEP, discipline, etc.) as they are for school-aged children with disabilities.

Child find provisions (discussed in Chapter 4) now require that states must have procedures in place to ensure that all children with disabilities residing in the state and who are in need of special education (birth through age twenty-one) are identified and evaluated, whether or not the state participates in Part C. All states must have an IEP in place for each identified child by the child's third birthday. Congress reaffirmed its commitment to the infant and toddler program in the 1997 Amendments. The Committee Report from the House of Representatives had the following to say about such programs:

Infants and toddlers with disabilities whose families receive early intervention services often need less intervention services when

they reach school age. The Committee believes that it is in the best interests of the infants and toddlers, their families, schools, and society in general that these services continue to be provided. (House Report No. 105-95, 1997, p. 113)

Under Part C, parents and educators as well as appropriate staff members from health, job services, human services, mental health, and other agencies are to work in a coordinated effort to meet the unique needs of the family of an infant or toddler with disabilities and to fund necessary services. The focal point of these services is the individual family service plan (IFSP), which serves a function similar to an IEP. The main differences are that the IFSP is interagency in approach and deals with the needs of the entire family (i.e., housing, employment, health) in addition to the child's educational needs. The IFSP may not be implemented without the informed written consent of the parents. With parent permission, early intervention services may commence prior to actual completion of evaluations. The IFSP must be evaluated once a year, and the family must be provided a review of the plan at least every six months. Under the IFSP, someone must be designated as a case manager in the organization of service delivery and follow-up and in maintaining important communication networks.

An interesting aspect of the Part C process is that it is based, in part, on the current school reform component that schools work cooperatively with other agencies that serve children in order to bring about a stronger and unified effort to the at-risk child issues. The inherent generalities of Part C also exhibit a greater congressional trust in states' abilities to work through and implement their own solutions to problems involving children (Turnbull & Turnbull, 1998). Owing to the difficulty of diagnosing disabilities in young children, and in recognition of the role environmental and socioeconomic factors play in identifying children with special education needs, states participating in the Part C Program may voluntarily agree to serve children who are "at-risk" in areas other than disabilities. An "at-risk infant or toddler" is defined as a child under three years of age who is at risk for experiencing a "substantial developmental delay" if intervention services are not provided.

The five goals for Part C, as expressly identified by Congress, are preventative in nature and are broader and more comprehensive than those of Part B:

1. To enhance the development of infants and toddlers and minimize their potential for developmental delays;
2. To reduce the costs of special education to schools;
3. To minimize the likelihood of institutionalization of individuals with disabilities and maximize their potential for independent living;
4. To enhance the capabilities of families in meeting the needs of their children;
5. To enhance the capacity of state and local agencies and service providers to identify, evaluate, and meet the needs of historically underrepresented populations. (20 U.S.C. § 1431 (a))

Contents of IFSP

The IFSP must contain (1) a statement of the child's present levels of physical, cognitive, communication, social or emotional, and adaptive development; (2) a statement of the family's resources, priorities, and concerns with regard to the child; (3) a statement of major outcomes expected and the criteria to be used to determine the degree of progress toward the outcomes; (4) a statement of early intervention services; (5) a statement of the natural environments in which services will be provided, including justification for any service not provided in a natural environment; (6) the projected dates and duration of services; (7) the identification of the service coordinator who will be responsible for the

implementation and coordination of the plan; and (8) the necessary steps to support the transition to preschool or other services.

The IFSP process plays an important role in solidifying the family as a resource. Active participation in the problem-solving process rewards individual family members through their sense of sharing, cohesiveness, and mutual support (Turnbull & Turnbull, 1998, p. 144).

The IFSP process is accompanied by procedural safeguards. A process must exist for the timely resolution of parent complaints and when necessary, an appeal into court; confidentiality of information, including the written notice of and written consent to agency exchange of information; outsider access to information; parent right to reject any proposed services; appointment of a surrogate parent; written notice of proposed changes (or refusals to change); and other rights. Although it is not made clear in the law, some persons are convinced that the LRE provisions of Part C are nearly identical to those of Part B, including the legal requirement of inclusion where appropriate (Turnbull & Turnbull, 1990).

If an IFSP is developed in accordance with the provisions and terms of IEP development (i.e., appropriate team, and content), then the IFSP may serve as the IEP when the child transitions from an early intervention program to a preschool program at age three when the school and parents agree. The school must provide the parents with a detailed explanation of the differences between an IFSP and an IEP, and the parents must express their consent in writing. The alternative is to hold a transition meeting no later than age three, and develop an IEP which conforms to the IEP requirements of Part B (see Chapter 5).

The state-wide organizational requirements of Part C are somewhat unique. Because Part C envisions an interagency approach to family needs, not just the child's needs, the governor of each participating state must designate one state agency, usually education or health, as the lead agency for carrying out the administration and supervision of the program. This includes the identification and coordination of all available resources, a resolution process for intra-agency and interagency disputes, and the assignment of agency financial responsibility. The governor must appoint the members of an interagency coordinating council (20% parents, 20% service providers, and at least seven members who meet specific criteria, i.e., state health insurance agency representative) to plan, coordinate, and assist the state's lead agency on infant and toddler service issues.

The federal appropriation for Part C in fiscal year 1998 was $400,000,000. Part C may not apply to any child (ages three to five) receiving preschool program services under Part B of the IDEA.

APPROACHES TO RESOLVING PROBLEMS

Preschool programs involving children with disabilities, ages three to five, take many different forms based on such factors as age, location, disability, state law and funding levels, and educational philosophy and professional competencies of the staff. Many authors, such as Power-de-Fur, and Orelove (1997, pp. 135–142), suggest that the specific preschool curriculum used is not as significant as other program characteristics. For best results, it is recommended that (1) staff use a collaborative team approach, including early childhood special education and specialist staff members; (2) strong parent involvement be encouraged and supported with established regular and open lines of communication; (3) the learning environment be well-designed (learning centers, child-sized furniture), and appropriate individualized adaptations be made; (4) the environment be conducive to social growth with planned social strategies; and that (5) positive discipline techniques be used that stress behav-

ioral change brought about through education. In general, curriculum should emphasize two dimensions: age-appropriate activities and individual child differences (e.g., different learning styles). This allows for individualized curriculum adaptation and teaching strategies which meet the needs of each child. No one program model is appropriate for all communities; and no one curriculum is appropriate for all children.

Curriculum and Instruction

In addition to the variety of locations of early childhood programs and the student population served (including the varying extent of inclusion), there are a number of alternatives exhibited in educational philosophy—each one giving rise to different approaches. Following are descriptions of a few of these alternatives:

- *Child Development Model.* This traditional approach to preschool emphasizes age-appropriate skills and social-emotional development. Many activities are made available for the children to explore as they choose. The teacher's role is a relatively informal one.
- *Montessori Model.* Children are provided with a carefully sequenced and structured series of activities to explore at their own pace. The program emphasizes individual autonomy and the development of sensory, motor, and language skills.
- *Cognitive Development Model.* This approach is based on the theories of Piaget and others who conceive of development as the product of maturation through a sequence of distinctive stages and through interaction with the environment. Emphasis is on integrated cognitive development and children are encouraged to invent, explore, play, question, observe, and experiment.
- *Behavioral Model.* This is the most controlled of the approaches and emphasizes the acquisition of defined, measurable skills. These skills are broken into their component parts (task analysis) and taught sequentially. As each skill

is mastered, the next is introduced. Desired behavior is rewarded and continuous data collection guides the child's program planning.

- *Direct Instruction.* A highly defined and specific method that includes essential behavioral elements, this approach was developed for use with children of low-income families who are at risk for educational failure. It has six distinguishing elements: a movement from simplified to complex contexts, practice, prompting and fading of cues, teacher feedback, a transition from overt to covert problem-solving strategies, and a shift from teacher to learner as a source of information (Carmine, 1979).

- *Combinations.* New curricula are being developed that combine cognitive developmental theories with measurable behavioral objectives and useful techniques from multiple approaches.

Differing approaches have yielded statistically significant improvements in children's tested achievement, and some are more appropriate for certain groups than others. For example, the behavior modification model has been found to be particularly successful with populations with severe disabilities. The greatest and most lasting achievements come from programs that last two to four years and are followed by appropriate special programming in elementary schools.

Location and Population

One major difference among preschool programs is whether they are center-based (the children go to a school or other location), home-based (program staff members go to the children's homes), or a combination of the two. Center-based programming may be difficult or impractical in rural areas, and for programs which are directed toward a single type of disability, such as hearing impairment. Indeed, in many areas limited funds and other restrictions

may generally dictate that preschool programs be designed to accommodate children with a variety of disabilities and individual needs.

At the preschool as well as primary school-age level, there is increasing interest in inclusion settings (Wolery et al, 1993). Inherent in the early childhood inclusion movement is the belief that in such settings children with disabilities will improve their social and communication skills. Not surprising to many educators, this has been verified through research findings. Jenkins, Odom, and Speltz (1989) found that even the mere placement of children with disabilities in the same classroom with typically developing children without special support resulted in positive impacts (albeit minimal) on their fine motor, language, preacademic, and social skills. An effort at planned and organized social interaction between advanced and less competent peers was found to result in significantly greater interactive and social play, improved social competence, and improved language development. When done correctly, inclusion of preschool students with special needs can produce positive gains for all students in a class, and neither their nor the nondisabled childrens' educational interest has to be sacrificed to the benefit of the other group.

Additional studies have found that planned inclusion efforts are needed for the best educational results. One group of researchers found that by using rotating trained (stay-play-talk) peers (buddies) with children with disabilities in a preschool setting, social and communication interactions of children with disabilities were greatly improved (English et al, 1997). Researchers also concluded that results might improve further in relationship development if the trained peers remained consistent and were not regularly rotated, as had been done in their study. Collaborative staff interaction, planning, and ongoing assessment and program revision have been found to be important keys to a successful inclusion preschool program. (English et al, 1996).

Hibbert and Sprinthall (1995) found that even in a classroom where nearly half of the preschool children had special needs, all the children with disabilities made important positive growth gains in social, emotional, and cognitive areas. These gains exceeded the growth experiences of some students with disabilities in the more typical inclusive setting with only one or two children with special needs in a class.

Over the years, a number of studies have determined that students who are placed in segregated settings make fewer developmental gains than children placed in integrated settings. For instance, a Canadian study of preschool-age children showed that children with severe disabilities in a segregated setting made fewer developmental gains over eight months than similar students placed in inclusion settings (Hundert et al, 1998).

A group of researchers working with kindergarten-age children determined that the best way to develop positive student attitudes toward their peers with disabilities was through a planned promotional program of acceptance. The researchers developed and implemented a program which involved the use of children's books depicting persons with disabilities, guided adult discussions with the children, provision of appropriate materials to parents, encouragement of discussion between parents and children regarding disabilities, and structured play between young children with and without disabilities (Favazza & Odom, 1997).

Staffing models for the integrated preschool vary greatly. At one extreme is the "pullout" model, where a student is removed periodically from class for work with a specialist who may or may not coordinate directly with the preschool classroom teacher. At the other extreme are fully cooperative models where all staff members are considered to have joint responsibilities for all the students and there is extensive collegial sharing of skills and expertise.

Inclusion of young children can result in unexpected staffing problems. For example,

many teachers who have general early childhood education background may have little training in disabilities, and problems may arise among professionals from different disciplines regarding coordination, turf protection, and the sharing of skills and responsibilities. These issues, however, should not pose insurmountable problems. Programming at this particular age level allows for a great variation in developmentally appropriate activities and inherently allows for the inclusion of children with disabilities with a minimum of advanced planning or adaptation (Udell, Peters, & Templeman, 1998).

The single most important influence on the successful implementation of inclusion practices in preschool programs is the attitude and support of educational leaders toward the concept of inclusion. Also important is whether the staff has a shared vision which holds the inclusion concept in high regard, and whether state and local practices and policy support inclusion (Lieber et al, 2000).

The more cooperative and integrated early childhood and preschool models require more time for staff members to plan and collaborate with their co-workers. Meaningful and continuing staff development opportunities need to be available to all, but especially to teacher associates who may not have the skills, experiences, or positive beliefs to adequately support inclusive practices (Stoiber, Gettinger, & Goetz, 1998). Teacher associates assigned to early childhood and preschool programs need to exhibit competencies which may be in addition to those exhibited in other educational settings:

• an ability to use developmentally appropriate instructional interventions for curricular activities in the area of cognitive, motor, self-help, social/play, and language development for infants and young children ages 0–5;
• an ability to gather and share information with professional colleagues about the performance of individual children;

- an ability to prepare and use developmentally appropriate materials; and
- an ability to communicate and work effectively with parents and other primary care givers.*

Inclusion settings for preschoolers and early primary school-age children with disabilities are readily available owing to the nature of center-based and school-based programming. For early childhood programs, inclusion opportunities present a greater challenge. The most common approach is through use of community-based early childhood programs and child-care centers. Many private child-care centers make a concerted effort to enroll children with various disabilities, sometimes numbering up to 50% of their clients.

Just as a variety of needs and requirements exist among different communities and individual children, so also will there be differences among the childrens' parents. Providing support to families should be one of the chief goals of early education programs for children with disabilities, and parent participation is perhaps the most important aspect of a successful program.

The needs of the families of young children with disabilities may be especially great. There are tremendous emotional adjustments to be made and feelings of grief, guilt, or fear to be dealt with. There are new parenting skills to be learned and new burdens on family time and finances. Some early childhood program activities are planned to focus primarily on the parents. An example is parenting classes for parents of children with mental disabilities or visual impairments. Program staff members must be sensitive to parental preferences, needs (including the need to sometimes not be involved), culture, and so on. Siblings may need special support. Families should participate in all planning and decision-making, experience occasional opportunities to actually participate in the child's education program, and be assisted with linking into community services and resources (Udell, Peters, & Templeman, 1998).

Transition

Transition is an issue of concern for any significant change in a child's formal learning experience, sometimes even between grade levels or between attendance centers. Certainly, the transition from an infant and toddler program (often provided in the home setting) to a preschool program (often a center-based program) begs for a smooth program change. That is why federal law requires that educators pay special attention to the planning entailed in the transfer of responsibility for a child's learning between Part C and Part B education programming. It must be "smooth and effective," and the IEP, or a comparable IFSP, must be in place no later than the child's third birthday. Education leaders should not expect to place young children in new environments with new expectations without a good deal of advance preparation and planning (one to two years in some situations) and fully informing the family, sending teacher, future teacher, and relevant staff members (Udell, Peters, & Templeman, 1998). It is quite surprising that more problems do not arise for students during this period of transition than currently occur.

Le Ager and Shapiro (1995) found that school staff members who formally anticipate the demands and expectations that the child with disabilities is likely to experience at the next level and teach the child the necessary skills prior to entrance into that next level aid greatly in the child's successful integration into the new setting. O'Shea (1994) has recommended preparing for transition by sharing with the child and family descriptions of the future site, curricula and materials, teaching methodologies,

*From *Guide for Effective Paraeducator Practices in Iowa* (p. 47). Developed by the Iowa Department of Education, 1998, Des Moines, IA. Reprinted by permission.

expected behaviors and responsibilities, assessment methods and rules, and overall expectations. Especially helpful are visitation and conversation opportunities where the child and family can meet and become familiar with the new program staff members and surroundings.

Hadden and Fowler (1997) have emphasized the need for improved communication with the family about the inherent differences between early intervention programs and preschool programs. The former are usually home-based services for infants and toddlers, which allow opportunities for open communication with parents each time the service provider visits the home.

That frequent opportunity for communication is seldom available at the preschool program site. Even when center-based program families are encouraged to participate in family activities and with service providers, the logistics of center-based preschool programs often work against family-school interaction. School-provided transportation schedules and the more hectic atmosphere of children simultaneously arriving and leaving center-based programs are not conducive to quality school-family interaction.

Because so many interruptions to communication are present, Hadden and Fowler recom-

FIGURE 7-2 *Worksheet for sharing information about your child*

1. What types of things does your child enjoy learning?
2. What things are the most difficult for your child to learn?
3. What are your child's favorite toys?
4. How does your child get along with other children?
5. What types of rewards work best for you child (e.g., hugs, praise, stickers)?
6. What types of discipline work best with your child?
7. What kind of support or help, if any, does your child need during routines such as eating, dressing, toileting, and napping?
8. What was your child working on in the last program that you would like to see continued in the new program?
9. What other goals would you like to see for your child in the new program?
10. What other information would you like to share about your child?

From "Preschool: A New Beginning for Children and Parents," by S. Hadden and S.A. Fowler, 1997, *Teaching Exceptional Children, 30* (1), pp. 37–38. Copyright 1997 by the Council for Exceptional Children. Adapted by permission.

FIGURE 7-3 *Items for teacher questionnaire for families of new students*

1. How does your child communicate?
2. What words does your child use?
3. What gestures does your child use?
4. What words does your child understand?
5. What are your child's most and least favorite foods?
6. Are there activities that your child really likes or dislikes?
7. How does your child ask to go to the bathroom?
8. Does your child like to be hugged or touched?
9. Are there certain textures that your child dislikes?
10. What directions does you child follow easily?
11. How does your child indicate displeasure?
12. Does your child need to nap?
13. Does your child take medication?
14. What do you see as your child's strengths?
15. How does your child ask for help?
16. What other information would you like to share?

From "Preschool: A New Beginning for Children and Parents," by S. Hadden and S.A. Fowler, 1997, *Teaching Exceptional Children, 30* (1), pp. 37–38. Copyright 1997 by the Council for Exceptional Children. Adapted by permission.

mend a continuous, concerted school effort to encourage communication between the new program staff and families through the transition phase. In addition to informal exchanges, they specifically recommend the formal exchange of school questionnaires and family responses that may be kept by the school staff for future reference, discussions, and conferences. Figures 7-2, 7-3, and 7-4 provide good examples of ways to secure information needed by school staff which are likely to open and maintain good communication.

Although all three of these sample questionnaires to families present good ideas for opening lines of communication, they should not be abused or used indiscriminately. Not all questions are relevant to all situations, and parents should not be made to wonder why the school would ask irrelevant questions. Also, schools should not file and then forget the information. Parents will rightly presume that if the school took the time to ask the question, and they, the parents, took time to answer the question, then the school will know and remember the answers.

Relations with Public Schools

Frequently, preschool education programs and child-care centers, even those privately owned, are housed in local elementary school buildings. Many of these programs now provide services for children with disabilities. Where such preschool education programs, public and private, are located in public school buildings, it is important that:

- preschool and regular school staff members have an opportunity to meet with each other before the school year begins;
- regular class teachers understand the preschool program and the rationale behind it;
- the building principal maintains a committed leadership role and helps create channels for communication, interaction, and input between the two systems; and
- the principal facilitates maximum inclusion opportunities for preschool program students.

Educational leaders should also be open to expanding the inclusion opportunities of children in early childhood programs as well as

FIGURE 7-4   *Communication schedule*

Child _____		
How will we communicate?	**How often will we communicate?**	**Best times to communicate:**
_____ telephone	_____ daily	_____
_____ notes	_____ weekly	_____
_____ conferences	_____ monthly	_____
_____ notebook	_____ other	_____
_____ pickup		
or		
drop off		
_____ talks		
_____ other		
_____ other		

From "Preschool: A New Beginning for Children and Parents," by S. Hadden and S. A. Fowler, 1997, *Teaching Exceptional Children, 30* (1), pp. 37–38. Copyright 1997 by the Council for Exceptional Children. Adapted by permission.

institutional or home-bound settings. At times it may be appropriate to establish a type of "reverse integration" programming, where typically developing children are encouraged (and assisted) to interact with children with disabilities in home-bound or segregated institutional settings. Many activities, such as play and reading aloud, readily adapt to such situations.

Although preschool special education programs in a public school building are generally the responsibility of the building principal, expressly or implied, clear legal responsibilities may not always be obvious. Various state laws establish the rights of children within a state to regular education programming; however, the right to special education programming may begin at an earlier age than that for regular education. The legal responsibility for the preschool special education programs in a school building may or may not lie with the building principal. The additional consideration of infant and toddler programming, with the involvement of a variety of service agencies, may also result in additional confusion of authority and responsibility. It is very possible, for instance, for state law to provide for general school district responsibility for the education of children with disabilities from birth through twenty-one years of age and yet fail to take into account the ultimate specific responsibility for the birth through two-year-old age group. Hopefully, the interagency coordinating councils under Part C will resolve such inconsistencies regarding the responsibilities of building principals.

CONCLUSION

The value and need for planned quality educational experiences for children with disabilities from birth forward are obvious. Although those needs are being met on a professional and consistent basis in some localities, in many others they are ignored or provided only isolated appropriate programming.

Educational leaders, working with a variety of professionals from other fields, play an important part in ensuring that children with disabilities and their families receive timely needed assistance and support. Future special education programming and parent-school relationships are both likely to be more effective as a result.

REFERENCES

Bowe, F. G. (1995). Population estimates: Birth-to-5 children with disabilities. *The Journal of Special Education, 28* (4), 461–471.

Carmine, D. (1979). Direct instruction: A successful system for educationally high-risk children. *Journal of Curriculum Studies, 11* (1), 29–45.

English, K., Goldstein, H., Shafer, K., & Kaczmarek, L. (1997). Promoting interactions among preschoolers with and without disabilities: Effects of a buddy skills-training program. *Exceptional Children, 63* (2), 229–243.

English, K., Goldstein, H., Kaczmarek, L., & Shafer K. (1996). "Buddy skills" for preschoolers. *Teaching Exceptional Children, 28* (3), 62–66.

Favazza, P. C., & Odom, S. L. (1997). Promoting positive attitudes of kindergarten-age children toward people with disabilities. *Exceptional Children, 63,* 405–418.

Fujiura, G. T., & Yamaki, K. (2000). Trends in demography of childhood poverty and disability. *Exceptional Children, 66* (2), 187–199.

Hadden, S., & Fowler, S. A. (1997). Preschool: A new beginning for children and parents. *Teaching Exceptional Children, 30* (1), 36–39.

Hibbert, M. T., & Sprinthall, N. A. (1995). Promoting social and emotional development of preschoolers: Inclusion and mainstreaming for children with special needs. *Elementary School Guidance and Counseling, 30* (2), 131–142.

House Report No. 105–95. *United States Code Congressional and Administrative News* (1997), 78–146.

Hundert, J., Mahoney, B., Mundy, F., & Vernon, M. L. (1998). A descriptive analysis of developmental and social gains of children with severe disabilities in segregated and inclusive preschools in southern Ontario. *Early Childhood Research Quarterly, 13* (1), 49–65.

Individuals With Disabilities Act, 20 U.S.C. § 1401 et seq. (1999).

Iowa Department of Education (1998). *Guide for effective paraeducator practices in Iowa.* Des Moines, IA: Author.

Jenkins, J. R., Odom, S. L., & Speltz, M. L. (1989). Effects of social integration of preschool children with handicaps. *Exceptional Children, 55* (5), 420–428.

Le Ager, C., & Shapiro, E. S. (1995). Template matching as a strategy for assessment and intervention for preschool students with disabilities. *Topics in Early Childhood Special Education, 15* (2), 187–218.

Lieber, J., Hanson, M. J., Beckman, P. J., Odem, S. L., Sandall, S. R., Schwartz, I. S., Horn, E., & Wolery, R. (2000). Key influences on the initiation and implementation of inclusive preschool programs. *Exceptional Children, 67* (1), 83–98.

Morse, J. (1998). Preschool for everyone. *Time, 15* (19), 98.

O'Shea, D. J. (1994). Modifying daily practices to bridge transitions. *Teaching Exceptional Children, 26* (4), 29–34.

Power-deFur, L. A., & Orelove, F. P. (1997). *Inclusive education: Practical implementation of the least restrictive environment.* Gaithersburg, MD: Aspen.

President's Committee on Mental Retardation (1976). *Mental retardation: The known and the unknown.* Washington, DC: U.S. Government Printing Office.

Stoiber, K. C., Gettinger, M., & Goetz, D. (1998). Exploring factors influencing parents' and early childhood practitioners' beliefs about inclusion. *Early Childhood Research Quarterly, 13,* 107–124.

Turnbull, H. R., & Turnbull, A. P. (1990). The unfulfilled promise of integration: Does Part H ensure different rights and results than Part B of the Education of the Handicapped? *Topics in Early Childhood Special Education, 10,* 18–32.

Turnbull, H. R., & Turnbull, A. P. (1998). *Free appropriate public education.* Denver: Love.

Udell, T., Peters, J., & Templeman, T. P. (1998). From philosophy to practice in inclusive early childhood programs. *Teaching Exceptional Children, 30* (3), 44–49.

Wolery, M., Holcombe, A., Venn, M. L., Brookfield, J., Huffman, K., Schroeder, C., Martin, C. G., & Fleming, L. A. (1993). Mainstreaming in early childhood programs: Current status and relevant issues. *Young Children, 49,* 78–84.

Yamaguchi, B. J., Strawser, S., & Higgins, K. (1997). Children who are homeless: Implications for educators. *Intervention in School and Clinic, 33* (2), 90–97.

Ysseldyke, E., Algozzine, B., & Thurlow, M. L. (2000). *Critical issues in special education* (3rd ed.). Boston: Houghton Mifflin.

Zima, B. T., Farness, S. R., Bussing, R., & Benjamin, B. (1998). Homeless children in emergency shelters: Need for prereferral intervention and potential eligibility for special education. *Behavioral Disorders, 23* (2), 98–110.

RECOMMENDED READINGS

Collins, B. C., Ault, M. J., Hemmeder, M. L., & Doyle, P. M. (1996). Come play: Developing children's social skills in an inclusive preschool. *Teaching Exceptional Children, 29* (1), 16–21. The authors provide a step-by-step approach for developing and implementing a social intervention program in an inclusion preschool program in a rural community.

Jones, H. A., & Rapport, M. J. K. (1997). Research to practice in inclusive early childhood education. *Teaching Exceptional Children, 30* (2), 57–61. The authors review research results which directly impact early childhood inclusion classrooms.

O'Shea, D. J. (1994). Modifying daily practices to bridge transitions. *Teaching Exceptional Children, 26* (4), 29–34. This article presents detailed suggestions for sending and receiving teachers in order to smooth a child's transition between programs.

Visoky, A. M., & Poe, B. D. (2000). Can preschoolers be effective peer models? An action research project. *Teaching Exceptional Children, 33* (2), 68–73.

Yamaguchi, B. J., Strawser, S., & Higgins, K. (1997). Children who are homeless: Implications for educators. *Intervention in the School and Clinic, 33* (2), 90–97. The authors provide an excellent overview of problems faced by children who are homeless and offer examples of appropriate school response.

Relevant Federal Regulations

34 C.F.R. 300.17   Individualized family service plan.

.121   Free appropriate public education (ages three to twenty one).

.122   Exception to FAPE for certain children.

.123   Full educational opportunity goal (FEOG).

.124   FEOG—timetable.

.125   Child find.

.132   Transition of children from Part C to preschool programs.

303   Infant and Toddler Program.

.342   When IEPs must be in effect.

34 C.F.R. 303   Early intervention programs for infants and toddlers with disabilities.

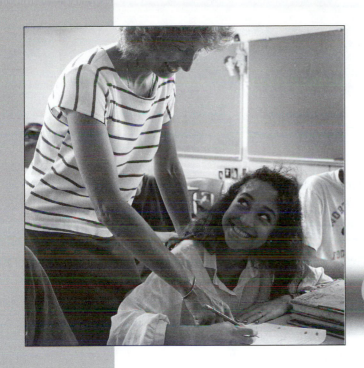

SECONDARY SCHOOL
CONSIDERATIONS

Focus

Special education programming at the secondary level must take into account a variety of factors, including diploma and graduation requirements, the coordination of class schedules, social and behavioral issues associated with adolescence, the cumulative effects of past schooling, vocational training, and preparation for adult life. Yet the great majority of special education models are elementary-age oriented and few regular or special secondary teachers have adequate preparation in secondary special education. Consequently, many secondary students with disabilities, especially those with mild and moderate disabilities, are inadequately served.

Legal Issues

Consideration of graduation requirements for individual special education students must be flexible and must be based on the individual student's educational needs. This allows some students to remain in secondary school through age twenty one and establishes opportunities for additional education and training. Education and training designed largely for preparation for life as adults are planned as part of the IEP development process. This planning for transition to adult life must take into consideration the various future needs of the student, such as decision-making skills, employment skills, continuing education, mobility, leisure, and daily living skills. The goals and needs of each student must be considered as reflecting the vast differences in individualized interests and abilities that will dictate the rest of their lives. Students should be encouraged and assisted in their participation in the development of their own IEPs.

Because of the uniqueness of each student with disabilities, individual issues arise regarding school, activities, grading, graduation, and diplomas. For these reasons, as well as others, inclusion programs are more difficult to implement at the secondary level than at the elementary level. However, participation in inclusion programs, when appropriate, is vitally important to the likelihood of future success of students with disabilities as adults. Inclusion programs also assist students who develop typically to better understand and relate to the diverse society they are about to enter.

Rationale

Appropriate educational programming at the secondary level greatly increases the chances of individuals with disabilities for success in finding and maintaining employment and leading independent adult lives. These benefits extend beyond individuals with disabilities to society as a whole. Effective programs that prepare students for transition to adult lives capture otherwise lost human potential, reduce the costs of social programs, and relieve the fear and anxiety experienced by family members who are concerned about their child's future.

Types of Secondary Programs

Generally, the secondary program of special needs students will fall into one of four categories:

- regular college preparatory programs, with support for student and teachers, such as consultation, deaf interpreter services, physical therapy, assistive technology, and resource room tutoring;
- regular vocational programs with appropriate support services that meet standard graduation requirements;
- special vocational and community living preparation programs that emphasize practical skills, with part-time placement in regular classes as appropriate; and
- special individualized programs for students with severe disabilities.

Approaches

Education leaders should:

- model acceptance and understanding of the students, acknowledge individual differences, and encourage flexibility in accommodations of school schedules and programs to meet individual needs;
- promote cooperation and regular communication among regular, special, and vocational educators, and ensure that teachers are provided with needed information, training, and support;
- guarantee that students with disabilities have equal access to vocational training programs;
- assign a faculty adviser to each student (one individual with responsibility for overall coordination and advocacy for that student), but also give all the student's teachers an opportunity to participate in program planning; and
- make use of community resources for transition services and vocational education.

The overall goal of secondary special education is to maximize all students' potential for independent, productive, and satisfying lives in the adult community. This should be reflected in the IEPs, which in turn should take precedence over standard graduation requirements as the guideline for programming. For many students, the focus of the curriculum in high school will shift from academics to practical skills, including self-help, social skills, and vocational education. Educators should plan ahead to prepare students with the necessary prerequisite skills for each course and for transition from school to the post-school environment.

COPING WITH SECONDARY SCHOOL

Adolescence can be a rough time for almost everyone. The complex and mysterious process of transition from childhood and dependence to adulthood and independence is full of familiar perils, from acne to awkwardness, social and family pressures, and emotions that sometimes seem to race out of control. As every adult who works with adolescents knows, it is a time of testing authority (often of rebelliousness) as well as optimism, as emerging identities are explored and plans for the future begin to be made.

Young people with disabilities experience the same physical changes, the same quest for independence, and the same feelings of hope and doubt, joy, and disappointment that other adolescents must confront. But in addition to the challenges faced by all young people as they mature, these youths have the added challenge of learning to manage a disability. It can make the difficult transitions of adolescence even more stressful when a young person is faced with the problems of:

- coping with a frustrating learning difficulty at a time when there is such a desire to feel competent and in control;
- looking visibly different from one's peers when there is so much emphasis on achieving a common style, on "fitting in"; and
- managing behavior problems in a period of life when peers and personal stresses often encourage acting out.

Some disabilities may not be serious enough to warrant special programming at a younger age (e.g., certain behavior disorders or health impairments), but would identify a student for special education in secondary school. Discrepancies between actual performance and academic or social expectations may also tend to increase as the student moves into the upper grade levels. Although certain learning problems, such as some speech disorders, may be solved effectively through temporary interventions at an early age, many more will require lifetime accommodations.

As the teen years pose special challenges for young people with disabilities, they also bring special problems for educators. The size, diversity, and complexity of the secondary curriculum make individualized instruction difficult to plan and carry out. The stress on Carnegie Units (a year-long course of study of fifty minutes each day, five days per week) and graduation requirements also contribute to the relative inflexibility of secondary, as opposed to elementary, programming. A secondary teacher who sees 130 to 150 students per day cannot be expected to assume the same level of knowledge and responsibility for an individual student's educational program as can the elementary school teacher who has the same twenty-five to thirty students in class throughout the school day. The vision of a regular secondary teacher is one who primarily works individually in a lockstep, grade-by-grade curriculum with an emphasis on competition for grades, students tracked by ability, and learning occurring only within the four walls of the classroom, and who would seldom have contact with, much less responsibility for, special education students. Moreover, secondary teachers' training and orientation is generally more subject-centered than student-centered.

The teachers in junior and senior high schools are not as likely to have received the preservice course work necessary to prepare them for the task of accommodating exceptional learners in the secondary classroom. Indeed, few teacher training institutions in the country offer programs of study in secondary special education and many states lack special licensure for those who work with this population. The entire field of secondary special education remains relatively undeveloped. Most special education instruction is still based on an elementary model, although clearly the approaches, strategies, and materials are sometimes inappropriate for secondary students and are unsuited to the secondary school environment.

These are but some of the inherent difficulties in the implementation of any special education program at the secondary level. Thus, it is not surprising that special education inclusion programs have developed more slowly at the secondary level compared with the elementary level. Cole and McLesky (1997) have identified eight general barriers to inclusion programs at the secondary level that in some ways overlap the issues previously stated regarding special education generally:*

1. Secondary teachers emphasize complex curricular material, whereas elementary teachers focus on basic academic and social skills.
2. Secondary students with disabilities exhibit larger gaps between skill level and classroom demands and expectations.
3. Secondary curricular content is much broader in range than elementary curriculum.
4. Secondary classrooms are teacher-centered in which instruction is usually didactic and infrequently differentiated for varying student needs.
5. Secondary teachers are trained as content specialists, and sometimes are not inclined to make individual adaptations for students with disabilities.
6. Secondary students are going through a complex, frustrating time called adolescence, which impacts them in every conceivable way.

7. Secondary schools are subject to greater pressure from outside agencies, such as businesses, state government, and colleges and universities, to provide students with specific skills and knowledge.
8. Secondary teachers have a significant autonomy in the development and delivery of curriculum.

For many years, the effectiveness of schools meeting the needs of adolescents with disabilities was taken for granted. Then, follow-up studies conducted in the 1980s and 1990s established that following high school many of these students were ill-equipped for adult life. Many were found to be dependent on their families, unemployed, underemployed, and lacking in the ability to become successfully involved in their own community (Smith, 1997). Such studies paint a bleak picture that can be greatly, modified with improved educational opportunities for students with disabilities.

LEGAL ISSUES

All the legal protections of the IDEA for non-discriminatory evaluation, individualized safeguards in programming, LRE, parent procedural safegards, and so on apply to students in secondary level educational programs, whether academic or vocational. For example, youths with disabilities should be placed into regular vocational programs, with appropriate support for the student and teacher when that is the LRE in which to meet the goals of the IEP.

The term "special education" is defined in federal law to include vocational education if it consists of "specially designed instruction." The obvious inference is that a child with disabilities will be in regular vocational programs unless "special" vocational programs and services are required to meet the child's needs. Any special vocational programming must be provided at no cost to the student or the family. Vocational

---

*From "Secondary Inclusion Programs for Students With Mild Disabilities," by C. M. Cole and J. McLesky, 1997, *Focus on Exceptional Children, 29* (6), pp. 1–2. Copyright 1997 by Love Publishing Co. Adapted by permission.

education means those educational programs related to preparation for a career not requiring a college degree.

Opportunities

The IDEA requires most states to provide special education and related services through the end of the school year in which students with disabilities turn twenty-one, if they have not already graduated from high school. This requirement gives students who need more time the extended opportunities for vocational training or additional courses for which they may not previously have had the necessary prerequisites or maturity. It gives schools the opportunity to develop special programs in vocational training, work experience, cooperative placements with business and industry, and life skills. It is not intended as a time to recycle students through academic courses they may have already completed. Planning for these school years, as for others, should be appropriate and individualized.

Programs and services for eighteen- through twenty-one-year-olds need not be provided to all students with disabilities, but only to those whose IEP calls for them. Such an IEP would likely contain goals related to readiness for jobs, postsecondary education programs, or related life-skill objectives. Although students who complete standard graduation requirements are no longer eligible for continued services under the IDEA, it is not legal for schools to award a diploma inappropriately or to force graduation on the student as a means of removing her from the school system. The school's responsibility to provide special education to students with disabilities ends upon graduation, but only if the student is awarded a "regular" high school diploma. If the school awards an alternative document to the student (i.e., certificate of attendance), then the student remains entitled to special education until she is later awarded a regular diploma, or attains the age of twenty-

one, in most states. In consideration of social and family needs, it is common for schools to permit students to participate in graduation ceremonies with their peers without having actually earned or received a diploma until they later complete their planned additional years of study.

Graduation with a regular diploma ends the student's eligibility for FAPE, and for that reason is considered a change in placement. Remember from Chapter 2 that changes in educational placement require a detailed written notice to the student's parents of the proposed change and a reminder about parent safeguards, including the parents' right to challenge the proposed change through a due process hearing. This applies to graduation when the parents believe that appropriate graduation requirements have not been met. Re-evaluations normally required for changes in placement, however, are not required when a student graduates with a regular diploma or exceeds eligibility for special education as determined by state law (usually age twenty-one).

TRANSITION IN THE IEP

In recent years, much attention has been paid to the period of transition from the school to adult work and life activities. The federal Office of Special Education and Rehabilitation Services explained the term in its early usage as follows:

> Transition is a period that includes high school, the point of graduation, additional postsecondary education or adult services, and the initial years of employment. Transition is a bridge between the security and structure offered by the school and the opportunities and risks of adult life. Any bridge requires both a solid span and a secure foundation at either end. The transition from school to work and adult life requires sound

preparation in the secondary school, adequate support at the point of school leaving, and secure opportunities and services, if needed, in adult situations.

Since the services and experiences that lead to employment vary widely across individuals and communities, the traditional view of transition as a special linking service between school and adult opportunities is insufficient. The present definition emphasizes the shared responsibility of all involved parties for transition success, and extends beyond traditional notions of service coordination to address the quality and appropriateness of each service area. (Will, 1984, p. 2)

Transition Planning

Both common sense and contemporary research suggest that planning for the successful transition from school to adult life should be a continuous process, beginning in the very early grades and gaining increased emphasis through the advanced grades. The development of personal, social and self-help skills critical to successful adult living can often be most effectively taught in the early grades. Remediation of inappropriate behaviors becomes increasingly difficult over time when such behaviors are practiced without question or consequence. The most successful transition programs provide for the coordinated development of transition competencies from elementary school through high school.

The significance of formal planning for the important step from school to adult life is obvious, and the law requires that special consideration must be given to this important time in a student's life. The IEP must contain, for students at age fourteen (or earlier, if appropriate) a statement of transition service needs related to courses of study (i.e., advanced placement, technology course work, vocational programming). The focus is to be on the planning of the education program to aid the child in a successful transition to life after school. An example would

include instruction on how to get to a job site using public transportation or how to use public transportation for independent living in the community.

No later than age sixteen (or younger, if appropriate), IEPs must contain a statement of needed transition services designed to promote successful movement from school to post-school activities, as well as a statement of each participating community agency's responsibilities in providing those services. Representatives from the outside agencies providing transition services (e.g., Vocational Rehabilitation, Department of Human Services) must be invited to IEP meetings and are expected to participate (see Chapter 5 on IEP development).

If an agency participating in providing transition services under an IEP fails to provide the agreed upon service, the school must reconvene the IEP team to determine alternative strategies. Those services included in transition plans might include postsecondary education, vocational training, integrated employment (including supported employment), continuing and adult education, adult services, independent living, community participation, and other relevant services. Based on the student's individual needs, transition services may be in the form of instruction, related services, community experiences, functional vocational evaluations, development of employment and other adult living objectives and, if appropriate, the acquisition of daily living skills.

Remember that at any age, the student will be invited to participate in IEP meetings if the purpose of the meetings involves issues of transition services. If the student does not attend, then the school must determine alternative methods to ensure that the student's preferences and interests are made known to the IEP team.

The primary reason the law allows for transition planning earlier than age fourteen and transition services earlier than age sixteen is the great need to increase schools' commitment to potential dropouts. An Arizona study conducted by Malian and Love (1998) found that students who complete high school special education programs were more likely to have favorable post-high school outcomes in terms of maintaining gainful employment, fewer criminal arrests, and fewer drug problems than those who dropped out. Researchers also determined that a greater percentage of young people with disabilities who completed high school had spent large amounts of time in the regular classroom. As a result, they recommended that greater attention be given to regular class support, adaptations, and accommodations for those students with disabilities identified as potential dropouts. The teaching of relationship-building skills, accessing community services and counseling services, and the use of advocacy systems, both in school and the community, were also determined to be of importance in helping students complete school.

Some educators recommend a formalized document of important information about individual students as they work with different transition service providers (Neubert & Moon, 2000). These "transition profiles" contain relevant personal information, such as medical history, personal goals, and strengths and needs, as well as skills, characteristics, and service eligibility status. The profile serves a variety of purposes, including documentation of progress, program eligibility determinations, employment, and reminders of unmet needs, and gives service providers and counselors current and accurate information about the young adult leaving the school system.

The use of a transition case manager or transition coordinator to help students stay in school is a growing practice in many parts of the country. Its growth is based largely in the IDEA emphasis on transitioning and the general historical lack of success of transition programs. In Virginia, where the practice is well-established, a group of transition coordinators have attempted to clarify, and even define, their job descriptions (Asselin, Todd-Allen, & deFur, 1998). The

group was able to identify seventy-one specific job tasks for transition coordinators and organized them into nine general categories:

- Intra-school, intraagency linkages
- Interagency linkages
- Assessment and career counseling
- Transition planning
- Education and community training
- Family support
- Public relations
- Program development
- Program evaluation

Vision Strategy

Miner and Bates (1997) have described a process for transition planning they call "person-centered transition planning," which incorporates elements of self-determination and family involvement. Sometime prior to the scheduled transition planning session, one or two educators meet with the student and family members to explore the needs and resources of the family group. They identify the student's preferences and dislikes, strengths and needs and, especially, what the family and student foresee as a desirable future lifestyle. The educators are especially interested in ascertaining the family's perspectives and use open-ended inquiries in their quest:

> Where will Carla live? What will Carla do during the day? What will Carla do for fun and recreation?

Focusing on the student's strengths, the educators, the student, and the family then develop a vision statement about what the student's daily life will look like in the future. From that perspective they can draw on resources available to aid the student in achieving the vision (see Chapter 5 on IEP development). Oftentimes, changes are made in the service delivery system and planned steps are altered as a result of taking the time involve the student and family from a personalized perspective. Many family members who are involved in the "vision strategy" have expressed strong support for this method of planning.

Sensitivity

Although parents of students without disabilities share similar concerns for their children's future with parents of students with disabilities, it is the latter group who experiences a much greater sense of discomfort and concern about what the future holds. Educators need to be aware of the parent's sense of "helplessness and vulnerability" at this important juncture and be ready to help assist families in preparing for life after schooling (Whitney-Thomas & Hanley-Maxwell, 1996).

IMPORTANCE OF THE IEP IN INCLUSION

Inclusion does not mean that teenagers with mild disabilities should be "dumped" into regular secondary classrooms without special assistance for the students or their teachers. Neither does it mean that they should be directed automatically through a standard curriculum that is not attentive to their special needs. As at every other education level, the placement of a student with disabilities must be determined individually by a placement team, including parents, based on thorough and appropriate evaluations and the contents of the IEP. Generally, a secondary program for students with special needs will fall into one of four categories:

1. Regular college preparatory programs, with support for students and teachers, such as consultation, deaf interpreter services, physical therapy, and resource room tutoring
2. Regular vocational programs that meet standard graduation requirements, with appropriate support services

3. Special vocational and community living preparation programs that emphasize practical skills, with part-time placement in regular classes as appropriate
4. Special individualized programs for students with severe disabilities

The importance of the IEP in individualizing this process cannot be overemphasized. Secondary students, like elementary students, who qualify for special education and related services represent a full range of intelligence, skill levels, and abilities. Some will be able to complete a college preparatory curriculum and go on to postsecondary and even graduate study. For others, the focus on secondary programming will be on mastery of basic social, self-help, and vocational skills. It is as harmful to deprive an able student of the opportunity to achieve as it is to force another student through a standard high school curriculum at the expense of needed training in survival skills. Students who, with appropriate programming, can complete mandated Carnegie Units for graduation along with their peers should be assisted in doing so. For other secondary special-needs students, the IEP goals and objectives (not standard graduation requirements) must be the ultimate guide to educational programming and graduation.

It should also be acknowledged, however, that traditional high school academic programming will not be appropriate for all youths. Some simply will need too much of their limited school time to master practical skills. For many students, the overriding goal of secondary education is to maximize their potential for independent adult functioning and not necessarily to earn a diploma, although this should be attempted if possible. The focus should be on applied skills and related academic course work. For a secondary student of low mental ability, it may be much more critical to learn how to make change for a dollar or how to use the local transportation system, rather than to struggle through algebra. It may be essential to learn how to vote, but it may not be possible—within the time remaining after classes in vocational and daily living skills—to study more abstract social studies concepts such as the Constitution and the structure of American democracy. Ideally, the school will be flexible enough to acknowledge this and to arrange, in some cases, for a student to attend a class, such as civics, only when relevant lessons are being taught.

Inclusion for secondary students is essential for several reasons:

- Continued association with nondisabled peers in a variety of environments provides needed role models and socialization experiences and helps prepare students to function in the world as adults;
- Placement in segregated settings, after successful integration experiences in elementary schools, would be traumatic and harmful to students' self-esteem;
- Typically developing students learn that persons with disabilities have many of the same fears, interests, and hopes about the future that they experience, and both are better prepared for integrated life situations as adults, including in the workplace; and
- Education in the most typical environment possible is required by law.

A study conducted by Jung (1998) involving twelve high schools with successful inclusion programs found several consistent themes. Jung concluded that education leaders are crucial to successful secondary inclusion programs. Each school in the study had a principal who was committed to the concept of inclusion, helped establish a positive school climate through decision-making and practices, helped locate resources, and rewarded participating staff through praise and annual evaluations. As with any educational reform, inclusion is a lengthy process and teachers must be properly supported and rewarded for their courage, persistence, and optimism. Most programs in

the study involved co-teaching between one regular education and one special education teacher, and most experienced a continuous struggle with coordination (i.e., lack of adequate planning time) and classroom management issues. Owing to the stresses of the new teaching style for all teachers, participants were usually limited to volunteers, actual course content was not greatly altered, and teachers focused on learning multiple teaching styles. More class time was used to teach study skills and more accommodations were provided students.

Cole and McLesky (1997) drew similar conclusions regarding the importance of voluntary teacher participation and administrative support in secondary co-teaching efforts. Teachers have a legitimate need to know that necessary support in terms of creating time for communication, collaboration, and planning, and the facilitation of staff development programs as well as emotional support for the "tough" times will be available. Chapter 11 contains more detailed information on co-teaching models and other alternative collaborative teaching methodologies.

ASSIST

A flexible, but complex, collaborative secondary school instructional model is recommended by Gable and colleagues (1997) and involves the use of teams to support regular education teachers. A secondary student instructional support team (ASSIST) is made up of two or more supportive teachers of various subject content areas along with specialists, special education teachers, and service providers. This mixture of staffing for collaboration affords a mix of direct and indirect, and large and small group instruction. A wide range of class arrangements can be devised depending on student needs. While the focus is on a regular individualized supervised work curriculum, student instructional needs can be met through one-on-one, small group, parallel teaching, and large group activities; thus this arrangement is sometimes called a "class-within-a-class." A wide range of student needs and issues can be addressed by the team, i.e., failing grades, absences, and lack of completion of assignments.

ASSIST members work in a variety of configurations, share their knowledge of students, methodologies, and content and plan accordingly. Having several different adults moving in and out of student activities aids in sharing each other's strengths (i.e., student praise and motivation) and lessens the impact of individual staff weaknesses. Teachers who observe and interact with their peers also grow in their skills to the benefit of all students. New instructional arrangements, such as ASSIST, represent a paradigm shift for which many secondary teachers are ill-prepared. It takes a wise and energetic educational leader to plant the seeds, create the climate, and support the growth of such innovations.

IEP Issues

In addition to the above needed considerations, other factors not present at the elementary level affect the processes of assessment, IEP development, and placement of secondary students. One is coordination of the many teachers involved. It usually is not feasible for all of a student's teachers to be present at IEP and placement meetings. However, all teachers should have the opportunity to provide input into the process, and all must be familiar with the contents of the completed IEP. At a minimum, each teacher should contribute essential information about courses taught, including initial student competencies required and the expectations of students, so that a reasonable match between students and classes can be made. Students should not be placed in classes unless they have the skills and special assistance (for both student and teacher, and possibly other students) reasonably necessary for success. Each teacher and service provider must have access to every child's IEP and must be expressly informed of the specific services for which they

are responsible, including accommodations, modifications, and supports which must be provided the child.

Educational leaders must accept the primary responsibility of ensuring that IEPs are available to staff and appropriate IEP information is shared with staff, including support staff, custodial staff, bus drivers, and secretarial staff, on a need-to-know basis.

While elementary educators enter the IEP conference with a focus on basic skills and the current school year, at the secondary level the focus should be more on applied skills and long-term planning. Another important consideration at the secondary level is the student's future as an adult. For many individuals with special needs, high school is the last opportunity for formal education before entering the adult world. The drafters of an adolescent's IEP must ask themselves: "When that transition comes, will the student be ready for it? What skills must this student master before the end of schooling in order to achieve a maximum level of independent adult functioning? Which of these skills—or their prerequisites—should be taught this year to enable the student to meet those long-term goals?"

Over the years, a number of authors have compiled lists of the recommended and necessary competencies that should be mastered by a student for independent functioning in adult life. Those lists have differed in form more than substance. To assist planners in the assessment and transition planning from a holistic perspective a contemporary list of critical areas of student need has been identified by a state educational agency as follows:*

> *Self-Determination*—Competencies needed to understand one's abilities, needs, and rights; to speak for one's self; and to act as

---

*From *Infusing Transition Into Individual Education Programs* (p. 23), by the Iowa Department of Education, 1996, Des Moines, IA: Iowa Department of Education. Reprinted by permission.

one's own advocate. Competencies needed for problem solving and decision-making.

Mobility—Academic and functional competencies to interact and travel within and outside the community.

Health and Physical Care—Academic and functional competencies needed to maintain the full range of physical, emotional, and mental well-being of an individual, such as selecting health care professionals, determining whom to contact in the case of emergency, obtaining assistive devices, and using personal hygiene skills.

Money Management—Academic and functional competencies such as budgeting, balancing a checkbook, and doing insurance planning.

Social Interaction—Competencies needed to participate and interact in a variety of settings in society.

Workplace Readiness—Academic and functional competencies and basic work behaviors, such as staying on task as expected, responding appropriately to instructions, and working under pressure. Knowledge of occupational alternatives and self-awareness of needs, preferences, and abilities related to occupational alternatives.

Occupationally Specific Skills—Academic and functional competencies required in specific occupations or clusters of occupations.

Academic and Lifelong Learning—Academic and functional competencies needed to pursue and benefit from future educational and learning opportunities.

Leisure—Academic and functional competencies, interests, and self-expression of the individual that can lead to enjoyable and constructive use of leisure time.

IEP goals and objectives based on these young adult need areas may seem a mystery to many educators involved in transition planning for the first time. The task is not as difficult as it may seem at first. Examples of transition goals and objectives are found in Appendix F.

Self-Determination

Traditionally, young adults with disabilities have had others (i.e., parents, teachers) make decisions for them. It has become evident to many persons working with secondary school students that skills associated with self-determination can be critical to the success of the transition process. Stated in its simplest terms, "self-determination" is the student acting as a primary choice maker in the decisions which are important to his quality of lifestyle. Researchers have found that students who exhibit higher measures of self-determination at graduation are more likely to prefer to live elsewhere other than with parents or family, maintain a bank account, and be employed one year after leaving high school than those who score low on measures of self-determination (Wehmeyer & Schwartz, 1997). Educators should encourage self-determination (decision-making) activities for students, such as role playing, simulation, modeling, and brainstorming. Students should be encouraged to make choices, express priorities and preferences and, importantly, actually be allowed to experience the outcomes of good and poor choices (Kling, 2000). All of this includes learning how to access resources and information and playing an active role in the planning, implementation, and assessment of their own education program as soon as practicable. Over sixty curricula have been developed to promote self-determination skills, and help is available to assess the appropriate one for specific students (Test et al, 2000).

Kaiser and Abell (1997) have identified the benefits of a "Life Management Curriculum" to aid mildly disabled secondary school students to progress toward successful transition in areas other than academic and vocational skills. Woven throughout is skill development in problem-solving and self-advocacy. The content blends daily living and social skills with career awareness and is functional in the sense that it focuses on developing appropriate adult behaviors. The four main components are:

- Daily Living: basic personal wellness with sections on hygiene, community resources, and finances
- Personal/Social: interpersonal communication and conflict-resolution activities
- Occupational Exploration: job and career guidance information
- Community and Federal Program Awareness: state and federal assistance programs that students may find useful after they leave school (p. 72)

The curriculum advocated by Kaiser and Abell includes a guide for transition planning which helps the IEP team determine the specific progression of skills the student has achieved following assessment and how much more the student has yet to achieve. All skills are divided into a progressive continuum: entry level, intermediate, advanced, and exit. The modified examples from the progressive continuum presented here represent the ease with which this can be applied:*

Job Retention Skills

Entry—Limited awareness of how to lose a job.
Intermediate—Can list three to five reasons people lose jobs.
Advanced—Can list ten qualities employers seek in their employees and can rate herself based on those qualities.
Exit—Demonstrates the ability to maintain employment for a minimum of six months.

Goal Setting Techniques

Entry—Has not set personal goals related to
_____.

---

*From "Learning Life and Management in the Classroom," by D. Kaiser and M. Abell, 1997, *Teaching Exceptional Children 30* (1), p. 74. Copyright 1997 by The Council for Exceptional Children. Adapted by permission.

Intermediate—Has received some formal classroom training in setting goals related to _____.
Advanced—Can give concrete examples of specific long-range and short-range goals regarding _____.
Exit—Has developed three to five short-range goals and one long-term goal regarding _____.

Some authors are critical of waiting until high school to provide specialized living skill courses. Instead, they advocate infusing life skills components into the broad general curriculum offerings and beginning early in children's school experiences (Patton, Cronin, & Jairrels, 1997); students do not have to wait until high school to begin.

Sex Education

Certainly, an important aspect of a young adult's health and physical care are those issues related to sex education. Despite the fact that many adolescents and young adults are sexually active, sex education in most schools remains controversial or ignored. Many teenagers with disabilities need access to sex education, and the issue has largely remained ignored, thus exposing that population to greater risk of abuse, exploitation, and exposure to sexually related health problems. Studies have reported that significantly less than half of the students with disabilities have received sex education. This may be in part owing to the fact that less than half of persons in special education teacher programs have had preservice preparation for teaching sex education.

In replicating a 1980 study, May and Kundert (1996) found that little change had occurred in sex education training in the preparation of special education teachers. Only about 40% of the special education teacher preparation programs they studied offered any sex education course work, and the actual amount of time spent in courses on sex education had decreased since

1980. In some cases, only a few minutes in pre-service programs were spent on sex education coverage. Even though this topic is controversial, IEP teams should give greater consideration to this issue, and for some students it may be considered as a transition planning requirement. Teams need to recognize that some parents may look unfavorably on sex education programs because of family beliefs or unspoken fears related to risks of adult sexuality, i.e. pregnancy or disease.

Post-High School Education

A significant number of students with disabilities will attend college, community college, trade school, or some other form of specialized training school. Gartin, Rumrill, and Serebreni (1996) have provided guidelines in three areas of transition consideration for those students with disabilities who may be considering post-high school education:*

Psychosocial Adjustment

1. Development of self-advocacy skills: personal decision-making, expression of needs.
2. Development of assertiveness skills: transform frustration and aggression into positive outlets.
3. Development of social skills and social strategies.
4. Development of transfer of skills to post-secondary settings: role playing, group learning.
5. Development of student mentor relationships.

Academic Development

1. Provide information about college entrance requirements and examinations: Scholastic Aptitude Test (SAT), American College Test (ACT), personal essay.

2. Provide information on requesting in-class accommodations.
3. Encourage visits to summer camps, museum tours, and sports events to acquaint students with a variety of social and cultural activities.
4. Encourage participation in career day programs, vocational assessments, and occupational informational programs.
5. Regularly assess transcripts for potential academic deficiencies or areas of remediation.
6. Regularly review career choices in relation to student's interests, skills, and proficiencies.
7. Teach study and research skills.
8. Familiarize students with study guides, taped texts, and technology that will be used.
9. Teach about potential services available and how to access them.
10. Make the connection to disability services personnel on-campus.

College and Community Orientation

1. Encourage students to "link" with colleges and trade schools through science fairs, band camps, and other special events.
2. Help facilitate friendships.
3. Help obtain college catalogues and financial aid information.
4. Assist in merging campus tours and facilities familiarity.
5. Assist in attending college orientation program.
6. Assist in developing an interest in campus activities and support groups.
7. Teach students and parents how to access community services.

*From "The Higher Education Transition Model," by B. C. Gartin, P. Rumrill, and R. Serebreni, 1996, *Teaching Exceptional Children, 29* (1), p. 31. Copyright 1996 by The Council for Exceptional Children. Adapted by permission.

CAREER AND VOCATIONAL EDUCATION IN THE IEP

Appropriate career and vocational goals, like all goals written into the IEP, should be based on accurate and appropriate assessments. Voca-

CHAPTER 8: SECONDARY SCHOOL CONSIDERATIONS

tional assessments should address students' academic, perceptual, and social skills, and should include assessments of interests, attitudes, aptitudes, and achievement levels in areas related to work. They may include pencil-and-paper tests, apparatus tests, situational assessments, and job tryouts. Smaller districts that cannot afford work sample tests will find that they can work out an adequate combination of other types of assessments.

Three levels of vocational assessment may be carried out in the schools:

1. Screening, including a limited number of tests, often general ones.
2. Partial vocational assessments, including only tests selected to answer specific questions.
3. Comprehensive vocational assessments, including a full range of tests of interests, aptitudes, and abilities.

Before completing a vocational assessment, an individual vocational evaluation plan should be developed that lists the questions to be answered by the assessment, provides background information on the student, and identifies the tests and situations to be used. It is essential to personalize the vocational evaluation, otherwise it will be too time consuming and expensive and will not yield useful information essential for planning.

At any level, the assessment process will yield a report that must be interpreted and used by the student's teachers. Therefore, the information must be clearly presented and easily understood. It is recommended that the vocational evaluator who prepares the report sit in on the ensuing IEP meeting.

When writing the program plan for a student in vocational education, the IEP team should analyze both the student's abilities and the entry level requirements of the job or vocational course. Weisenstein, Stowitschek, and Affleck (1991) developed and successfully field tested the Vocational Education to Work Model

that serves as a system of communication and support between vocational and special educators. The model is composed of four separate but sequential components:*

1. Active Recruitment—special education students, their parents, and other educational staff who offer guidance to students are informed of vocational education opportunities.
2. Guided Placement—special education students are matched with vocational education courses according to their interests and abilities, and to ensure a communication flow between special education and vocational education. This component includes: (a) development of vocational course profiles which identify entry skills needed by the learner, (b) development of a learner profile which assesses student skill development over the same skills included in the course profile, (c) generation of a report matching the two profiles, and (d) development of a vocational placement plan in which the student's strengths and weaknesses are identified relative to each placement.
3. Continuing Support—Support is provided to vocational education teachers so that special education students can successfully complete vocational education courses. This includes development of a menu of accommodations, development of a specific accommodation plan, modification of placement accommodations as necessary, and tracking of continuing support.
4. Job Placement and Follow-up—the goals of job placement and follow-up is two-fold: first, to increase the number and diversity of community placement opportunities; and second, to provide continuing support to students once they are placed.

*From "Integrating Students Enrolled in Special Education into Vocational Education," by G. R. Weisenstein, J. J. Stowitschek, and J. Q. Affleck, 1991, *Career Development for Exceptional Individuals, 14* (2), pp. 133–136. Copyright 1991 by Division on Career Development of The Council for Exceptional Children. Adapted by permission.

For special needs students in vocational education, four basic types of educational placement are available:

1. Regular vocational program with minor adjustments and/or consultative assistance to the teacher;
2. Regular vocational program with more substantial direct assistance to the student;
3. Remediation first, then vocational program placement; and
4. Specially designed vocational programs.

Although vocational educators' participation in IEP meetings is not required, it can be beneficial. As demonstrated above in the Vocational Education to Work Model, instructors can contribute such important information as expected course entry skills, physical and intellectual requirement of course activities, materials and equipment used and possible adaptations, supplemental materials and instruction required for attainment of vocational objectives, prerequisite courses, job opportunities and postsecondary training opportunities in the vocational area, work study and on-the-job training available, and courses available within each vocational area.

In turn, IEP participation can provide nonspecial education vocational staff with information about:

• the student's learning style and achievement levels (in academic, personal and social, and daily living skills);
• special teaching techniques;
• classroom accommodations;
• assistance available from other staff members;
• the most effective reinforcers for the student;
• special education vocational options; and
• a system for monitoring student progress.

Employment Data

The employment statistics for the nation's citizens with disabilities are poor. Studies have documented the difficulty that graduates of special education programming are having, making the transition into adult life.

One study found a 71% employment rate for males with disabilities one year after school completion, and only 40% for females (Benz, Yovanoff, & Doren, 1997). A much larger longitudinal study of former high school students for up to five years after leaving school showed an improved competitive employment rate for youth with disabilities in the late 1980s over previous years (Blackorby & Wagner, 1996). However, it showed a continued significantly lower young adult employment rate for those with disabilities compared to youth generally, two years (46% compared with 59%) and three to five years (57% compared with 69%) after leaving school. Only 17% of youth with multiple disabilities reported being competitively employed five years after secondary school. Females with disabilities continued to be employed at a lower rate and at lower pay than their male counterparts five years after high school. Attendance in all types of postsecondary education after five years showed a much higher rate for youth in the general population compared with those with disabilities (68% compared with 27%). Independent living became more common the longer youth with disabilities were out of high school but still lagged behind young adults in the general population (37% compared with 60%) (Blackorby & Wagner, 1996).

Improving Vocational Programs

Certainly there are many reasons for this deplorable situation, but it must be acknowledged that one of them is inadequate student preparation and training. The record of public schools in the vocational preparation of students with disabilities definitely can be improved. It has been shown that students with disabilities who gain access to vocational education programs and who are given necessary support systems leading to successful program completion obtain employment at about the same rate as nondisabled students (Rockwell, Weisenstein, & LaRoque, 1986).

A study involving several hundred students, both with and without disabilities, in Oregon and Nevada one year after school completion has helped identify valuable components in good vocational programming (Benz, Yovanoff, & Doren, 1997). The findings support a common need for students with and without disabilities to be involved in combined school-based and work-based programs and continued support following school. To be successful, students must have a work-based learning program which integrates related academic skills, communication skills, and social skills. Work-based learning can include service learning, job shadowing, internships, apprenticeships, school-based enterprises, and paid work experience.

The concept of integrating academic and vocational program components is neither new nor unique. The educational concept of Tech Prep incorporates a curriculum designed as a parallel to college preparatory curricula, which combines mathematics, science, communications, and social sciences in an applied academic mode and competency-based curriculum. The curriculum is based around a career cluster of occupations and is designed to build a strong foundation for later advanced course work. It is generally believed that such integration of academic and "world of work" increases student retention in school and raises overall student academic achievement.

All of this must be well founded in effective career guidance and planning by competent staff. Support services, remedial assistance, and counseling should not end with the traditional conclusion of secondary school. Networking between and among various agencies and support services is the goal of modern transition.

Special educators can provide expertise in the integration of academics through curricular design, instruction techniques, accommodation strategies, the use of technology, and individualization of support services.

Weisenstein and Rockwell (1987) developed a checklist for evaluating a successful vocational program for students with disabilities. The checklist includes thirteen key elements.

____ Individualized instruction for all students with disabilities

____ Flexibility in modifying programs and student schedules

____ Community involvement in vocational education

____ Early experiences that lead youths to high school success

____ Advanced preparation to ensure entry-level skills

____ Materials development and modification to help students succeed

____ Time necessary to teach slow readers

____ Use of resources outside the school building

____ Training teachers to work with special needs students

____ Participation in IEP development by special and vocational teachers

____ Cooperation among regular, special, and vocational education teachers

____ One person solely responsible for coordinating services for each student

____ Special vocational offerings to prepare those students with more severe disabilities

Some contemporary researchers in career development and employment for students with disabilities stress career development in a broad, general sense. They emphasize that few young adults will leave school with realistic career goals and stick with them for life. Instead of teaching skills for a specific job or career, focus should be on lifelong career development. Morningstar (1997) has made several recommendations to educators for such nonspecific career development:

• Consider developing skills and values across an entire lifespan and for career maturity and change;

- Establish an understanding of self, of the world of work, of decision-making, of implementing decisions, and of adapting and advising;
- Provide meaningful community-based work experience;
- Involve the student's family in career development; and
- Support student participation and involvement in career development.

Source of Help with Career and Vocational Needs

Some schools are less prepared than others to meet the career and vocational needs of students with disabilities. Consequently, they must look to outside agencies and providers of these unique services.

Frequent participants on the IEP teams of secondary students are representatives of Vocational Rehabilitation Services. Vocational Rehabilitation is a federally funded program designed to help persons with disabilities of all ages reach their employment goals. Each eligible student (or adult) works with a trained counselor to develop a plan designed to lead to successful employment. Employment goals are individualized depending on abilities, needs, and preferences. Options available include working for wages, sheltered work, supported employment, and self-employment.

In order to be eligible, a person must have a physical, mental, or emotional disability which presents problems preparing for, obtaining, or keeping employment. Vocational Rehabilitation Services must be needed to get and keep a job. Disability is defined similarly to that for Section 504; an ongoing condition that limits any major life activity, including walking, learning, working, or caring for oneself. A disability must be related to a diagnosis by a physician, psychoanalyst, or similar health professional.

Vocational Rehabilitation is very active in assessing the employment needs of persons with disabilities, assessing career interests, training, and counseling persons on employment and job placement. It also helps with supported employment services, such as special training, equipment, or a job coach, as well as independent living training services.

Intergency Cooperation

Many special vocational education programs have involved agreements among various public agencies with sometimes overlapping responsibilities for vocational training. Typically, these involved money-saving arrangements in which specialists from various fields (e.g., special and vocational education) combine their expertise and the resources and facilities of their programs to meet the needs of a varied client population. Blalock (1996) has concluded that the development of community-wide transition teams is critical for the development of meaningful transition programs at the local school level. Aspel et al, (1999) have reported on a successful community-wide transition program in North Carolina, where the consumers, students, parents, and services providers all have indicated a high level of satisfaction with its results.

A variety of resources, from businesses to charitable organizations to state agencies, have figured productively in schools' vocational education programs for exceptional students.

In one rural community, for example, the 4-H Club developed a curriculum for vocational education of the mildly mentally disabled and provided club members as volunteer tutors. In return, the special education teacher supervised the 4-H students, made arrangements with their high school for released time and participation credit, sent written reports to the school to form the basis for grades, and the school paid the costs of the students' transportation from district funds. The results were an adequate curriculum and tutorial assistance where none had previously existed.

Secondary vocational education programs provide especially good examples of educational needs that have drawn together resources from the local school district, community colleges, colleges and universities, state departments of vocational rehabilitation and developmental disabilities, federal programs under the U.S. Department of Labor, charitable organizations, professional organizations, and private businesses. The authors have observed many examples of success and some failures in the effort to link schools with other agencies to provide services for children with disabilities. The greatest successes are found where the needs have been the greatest and the staff members have been determined to overcome obstacles. The following is a brief synthesis of several similar cooperative secondary transition programs observed by the authors as one example of an area of successful interagency cooperation.

As the need for a variety of secondary student transition services, especially vocational and life skills, became evident, many high schools began to look for resources outside their own agencies in meeting the IDEA legal requirements and the needs of their students. For many students with mild and moderate disabilities who had the potential to achieve skill success leading to gainful employment and a good degree of independent living in adulthood, the services available were often inadequate. A common solution attempted in some communities was for school districts to approach community colleges, which have long experience in vocational training, for help. However, community colleges and technical schools had little experience working with students who had a wide variety of skill deficits which required differentiated training and support services.

Given time, effort, planning, and flexibility a number of school districts, area community colleges, and vocational schools were able to work out jointly, through trial and error, the details of many high quality programs to aid in the transition of young adults with disabilities from school to varying degrees of gainful employment and independence in community living.

Commonly, community college staff members would attend transition planning IEP meetings to obtain an individualized picture of the students' strengths and needs. Vocational assessment was often accomplished by staff members from state vocational rehabilitation programs, and vocational rehabilitation funding was sometimes available. The high school staff worked with the individual student in the development of basic skills and a knowledge base and with the parents to prepare them for their child's next step into the future.

In order to assure adequate funding, it was often found desirable to continue the student's enrollment in high school beyond the traditional age of graduation. This allowed the school to continue receiving state aid revenues for support of the young adult's continued education; however, it also meant the student could not officially graduate with receipt of a regular diploma. Graduation would end the student's entitlement to special education under federal law and the laws of most states. Because the IEP documented the student's continued need to learn more vocational and life skills, it was not illegal or unethical to continue the student's enrollment in school, past the traditional graduation age of eighteen or nineteen. In fact, for some students with disabilities it might have been illegal and unethical to end their secondary school experience when they had not met their IEP transition goals and had not yet reached twenty-one years of age.

Many families wanted their child to participate in graduation ceremonies at the traditional age of eighteen or nineteen. Different arrangements were worked out locally so the student could participate in the graduation ceremony but not actually graduate with a regular diploma.

Not having graduated from high school in the official sense, the student could attend a community college transition program under his IEP. The local resident school district continued to receive state, and sometimes federal, funds to pay to the community college in the form of tuition for the continued educational program. The student received vocational training and vocational readiness training as called for in the IEP. Many students needing life skills education (e.g., social skills, hygiene, nutrition, personal purchases, self-determination) lived in supervised dormitories or group homes with nearly continuous opportunities for education provided by trained staff.

A specific example of such programming was the Secondary Transitional Education Program (STEP). Through the cooperation of Southeastern Community College, thirteen public school districts, and an intermediate educational agency in southeast Iowa, students with mild disabilities were referred to the program. The program had six steps or components: assessment of needs, counseling in the establishment of student priorities, vocational training, tutoring in related academics, independent living skills, and gainful employment. The career options provided through the joint effort, as listed here, was much greater than one school district could have possibly provided by itself:*

accounting	emergency medical technology
agriculture business	gunsmithing
agriculture production	heating and air-conditioning
auto body repair	machine shop
auto mechanics	mechanical drafting
computer programs	medical assistant
cosmetology	nurse's aide
criminal justice	office adaptors
electronics technology	welding

Independent living skills offered STEP students, based on individual IEPs included:

budgeting
banking
purchasing habits
health care
home management
job search skills
job related behavior

The philosophy, management, administration, and funding arrangements were provided in a two-page, three-party agreement between the community college, the intermediate educational service agency, and each individual school district (Morgan, 1989). Under the laws of that state, any public entity, through agreements with other entities, was authorized to conduct any activity or provide any service jointly which any one of the parties to the agreement was otherwise legally authorized to do. Such laws are obviously provided to make it easier for agencies to cooperate.

Experience in STEP established that the community college had to be flexible in its programming. If one or more students needed special tutoring in academically related vocational training areas, then it was provided. For the students who lived off campus, a widespread tutorial system was established in order that students had support in the communities where they lived. Adjustments to students' needs were achieved through joint agency problem-solving. When the students finally completed their IEPs, they received their diplomas, sometimes from both the resident school district and the community college.

Schools and community colleges in such programs have proved that together they can

---
*From *A Description of the Development and Implementation of the Secondary Transitional Education Program at Southeastern Community College* (pp. 76 & 88), by Dennis P. Morgan (1989), an unpublished doctoral dissertation. The University of Iowa. Copyright 1989 by Dennis P. Morgan. Reprinted with permission.

be more effective in providing needed community services than either can be individually. Given unlimited resources, either could provide an excellent vocational transition program, but in the reality of limited resources, neither could do an adequate job alone. This is but one example of interagency cooperation where the whole can be greater than the sum of its parts. Many such successful school/community college transition programs remain active today.

THE PRINCIPAL'S ROLE

There are several things that educational leaders can do to improve the enrollment of special education students in career and vocational programs. Vocational education instructors, like other regular education teachers, often lack training and experience in working with students with disabilities and may have specific concerns about safety, behavior management, extra time requirements, ultimate employability of the student, and other similar issues. Such concerns are understandable and deserve serious consideration and response.

To win instructors' support for including students with disabilities in regular and vocational education programs, IEP teams and educational leaders should take the following steps:

1. Assign students appropriately, based on an honest and reasonable assessment of their abilities and of the requirements of the course (with reasonable adaptations and assistance).
2. Provide adequate support to the instructor(s).
3. Involve the regular educator(s) in program planning and establish open lines of communication with special education staff.
4. Inform instructors about requirements of the law.

5. Counter stereotypes and misconceptions with the reality of disabled employees' record of job success.
6. Take advantage of community resources available.
7. Encourage flexibility in scheduling, to accommodate such possibilities as eight-hour job placements one or two days a week, attending regular classes for some units of study and not others, and so on.
8. Acquaint the instructors with the disability and what can reasonably be expected from the student.

There also are many strategies for facilitating students' successful integration into regular secondary and vocational classes. A trial period in which the student is exposed to several class sessions one semester before placement may be helpful. An orientation to the classroom that is sensitive to the student's needs may also be beneficial. For example, a blind student should be introduced to the location of all desks and equipment, and should have an opportunity to get accustomed to the room when no other students are present. A student with mental disabilities may simply need extra orientation to equipment use and safety strategies. Before the course starts, the vocational instructor should meet the student and learn about the disability. In class, it is important that the instructor:

- accept the student as an individual;
- avoid overprotection;
- encourage independence;
- adapt the task and environment as necessary;
- provide ample time for completion;
- work ahead to avoid problems (e.g., introduce vocabulary before the lesson);
- use resource personnel within and outside the school;
- be sensitive to the student's endurance/attention span;
- provide simple, concise instructions; and
- change a strategy that does not work and try another.

THE QUESTION OF DIPLOMAS, TRANSCRIPTS, AND HONOR ROLLS

The inclusion of students with disabilities into the traditional secondary school environment raises some difficult questions. Should a student who completes the IEP but not the required Carnegie Units be included in graduation ceremonies with classmates? Should a diploma be awarded? Should the diploma be the same as that earned by other students or a special certificate instead? How does the nondiscriminatory requirement of Section 504 of the Vocational Rehabilitation Act apply? What about the current push for competency tests for graduating seniors and for so-called excellence in education?

Advocates of competency testing and "excellence" would add more academic courses to those already required for graduation, thereby making it more difficult for even regular vocational students to complete both school diploma requirements and important vocational training. The demand for pregraduation competency testing also would seem to jeopardize the ability of students with disabilities to earn regular diplomas (Benz, Lindstrom, & Yovanoff, 2000). The problem is controversial. On one side is the popular complaint that a high school diploma does not mean anything anymore. If students cannot meet reasonable levels of competency in reading, other basic skills, and general knowledge, then they should not receive a standard diploma—perhaps a certificate of attendance or some other alternative, but that is all. Others argue that exceptional students should not be penalized or stigmatized by receiving an alternative certificate. Some suggest that this would, in fact, be an illegal denial of equal benefits under the law.

The issues are complex and solutions vary from state to state. It is important for school leaders to understand the nature of the dispute and the range of alternatives that are in place around the country. Some states do recommend awarding a standard diploma for completion of the IEP; others issue certificates of attendance instead. Some states administer competency tests but have special guidelines or accommodations for students with disabilities; others simply stress the importance of reviewing a student's transcripts to determine what the diploma really means. In some cases, the policies apply statewide; other states allow district discretion. Federal law does not explicitly address exit policy for high school students, although several statutes seem to apply. Many of the issues of graduation and diplomas for students with disabilities are currently in the process of interpretation (O'Neill, 2001).

The Office of Civil Rights (OCR) issued a ruling interpreting the application of Section 504 and the ADA to graduation and diploma issues (Dunbar to Runkel, 1996). Although Section 504 and the ADA do not require parent procedural safeguards be provided for graduation, the IDEA does (Lanford & Cary, 2000). Under the IDEA, graduation is a change in programming, and a graduated student is no longer entitled to special education services. Students with disabilities may participate in the school's graduation ceremony if the student wishes to do so. If a separate graduation is preferred, then comparable facilities must be used.

The OCR also stated that special education students are entitled to a diploma when they complete a school's criteria for graduation. Diplomas should be similar in all significant respects. Variations in wording should not be based on disability as a category of students. Objective criteria must be used for differing diplomas and all students must have had an opportunity to complete the requirements for and be awarded any diploma on a nondiscriminatory basis. Diplomas may refer to individual transcripts for exact courses completed. Schools, through the IEP team, may modify or adjust local graduation requirements in order to be consistent with the student's IEP (Lanford & Cary, 2000).

Whenever a student receives a graduation document other than a regular diploma, the student remains eligible for IDEA programs and services until age twenty-one. Thus, the awarding of a certificate of completion or attendance before that age, rather than a regular diploma, does not end the school's duty to provide the student with a FAPE.

In some rare instances where the IEP planning has not addressed the issue, a student may complete a school's minimum graduation requirements, but may not have completed all of the goals in the IEP. Until the student has reached age twenty-one, the school is not required to end FAPE for the student.

Transcripts

Student transcripts should be careful to not designate courses as "special education," "resource room," or "home-bound" because by doing so they identify the student as having a disability. Permissible labeling might include "modified curriculum," "basic level," or "practical," so long as such terms are also used with courses for students without disabilities, such as those in remedial and at-risk programs. Identification symbols should not be used to identify only students with disabilities. Asterisks or other symbols on transcripts may be used to designate modified curricula, so long as they are also used for modified curriculum for nondisabled students, such as for accelerated course work or remedial course work. Symbols or asterisks should not be used to identify completion of course work where only accommodations and modifications were provided. Students and parents should be notified regarding transcript content before it is released to third parties.

Grades

Grades may not be modified or determined based on the student's disability status or status as a special education student. Alternate grading systems may be appropriate only if they are also used for nondisabled students. It is desirable to discuss alternative grading systems in the IEP, especially with respect to classes taken in the regular education setting. As a general rule, students in inclusion settings with reasonable accommodations and modifications should not receive altered grades owing to altered teaching or testing methods. Accommodations and modifications are usually changes only in the way things are done and are not changes in a school's expectations or standards for a course. However, whenever a course's content standards or expectations are substantially changed for an individual student, the student may be awarded an alternate grade for that course. Education leaders and teachers must be conscious of the relative purpose of a grade; whether it is to relay the quality of the work, readiness for future learning, level of mastery, or progress and effort. Changes in curricular expectations for a student and the alternative grading should be included in the student's IEP. When a student is placed in a general education course for other than content purposes, i.e., social skills, the IEP should outline the planned criteria for grading. In many situations, it may be appropriate for the regular and special education teachers to collaborate on grades. In some situations, it may be desirable to use a pass/fail grading system, but to eliminate justified claims of discrimination, participation should be voluntary and available to all students.

Honor Rolls

Honor rolls and grade point averages used for scholarships and class ranking present a special problem. Grades received in special education classes or in regular education classes by students with disabilities with support from special education services should never be arbitrarily discounted or excluded. However, an objective weighting system may be established, or an established list of "core courses" open to all students, may be the only course eligible for honors consideration. A weighted grading system should assess actual differences in content or difficulty compared with regular education courses and should never arbitrarily assign lower weights or values to all special education classes. Such a system would prevent all special education students from ever being recognized for their accomplishments.

Eligibility for Activities

Academic eligibility for school activities, including athletics, presents issues of fairness and potential discrimination. When a student's low grades may be the result of a disability, the school should make a conscious determination of whether a relationship exists. If it does, and other reasons (e.g., lack of motivation) are absent, then the academic eligibility criteria may need to be waived or based on other criteria, such as progress on the IEP. IEP teams may also want to revisit the accommodations, modifications, and support services being provided the student and the student's teachers in order to determine whether they are appropriately meeting the student's academic needs.

NONACADEMIC CONSIDERATIONS

Secondary students have a variety of educational needs, not all of which are strictly vocational or academic. School personnel should also be sensitive to students' social needs, an area that has implications for classroom management as well as student growth.

All adolescents are affected by a strong student culture and a need to experience acceptance by their peers. Students with disabilities, particularly those of low mental functioning, may be especially vulnerable to peer pressures that result in negative or socially unacceptable behaviors. When making placement decisions, it is important that school personnel safeguard against negative influences by assigning these students to classes where they will encounter positive, not detrimental, role models.

The conscious development of social skills and self-esteem will contribute to positive in-school behaviors and preparation for adult life. Many excellent social and interpersonal curricula for exceptional students are now available.

Within secondary school settings there are often educational programs that have obvious benefits for typical students, such as the currently popular service learning programs. Service learning is a program, voluntary or required, where students are provided an opportunity to take part in community service projects (e.g., working with the elderly or environmental projects in an effort to make the students more aware of their community and themselves. Sometimes, the benefits of service learning can be as important, or more important, for students with disabilities. One report of a service learning project involving a combined seventh and eighth grade resource room, English as a second language (ESL) class, and students without disabilities, concluded that the students with special needs learned a great deal about themselves and greatly increased their self-esteem through working with and helping younger children and elderly in the community (Yoder, Retish, & Wade (1996). Principals can help such programs through facilitation, support, and even participation.

Another means of promoting social development is through students' participation in extracurricular activities. Frequently, this does not occur without conscious effort from the school staff, including the principal. Exceptional students are sometimes excluded formally or informally from clubs, organizations, and athletics through stereotyped negative attitudes, lack of recruitment efforts, lack of needed support, low social status, and lack of a role to play that matches their abilities and needs. Consequently, these students are deprived of important opportunities to develop self-confidence, mix socially with their peers, and gain a sense of ownership and belonging to the school. This sense of belonging, in turn, can be instrumental in improving students' attitudes toward school and in reducing the likelihood of their dropping out.

In a large three-year study of high school transitioning in Arizona, Malian and Love (1998) observed that extracurricular activities ranked high on both student and parent indicators of quality of life. They also learned that 70% of special education students who dropped out of high school before graduation had not been involved in extracurricular activities. Strategies for increasing exceptional students' participation in extracurricular activities suggested by Malian Love include:

- actively recruiting the students (this can be done by teachers, special educators, club advisers, or other students);
- identifying or designing roles in the club or activity that the students can fulfill;
- considering setting up a buddy system with a respected peer who is involved in that club or activity; and
- providing positive role models (faculty advisers should demonstrate acceptance of the exceptional students and respect for their contributions).

In recognition of the importance of nonacademic activities in the life of a child, the law now requires that individual student IEPs contain a statement of supplementary aids and services to be provided the child, and supports for school personnel, so the child may participate in extra-curricular and other nonacademic activities with other children. If a child with disabilities cannot participate with nondisabled children in activities, then the IEP must provide an explanation.

Competitive Athletics

Special problems may arise in varsity athletics. Some special needs students have the potential to become outstanding athletes but are pre-

vented from participation in varsity sports for a number of reasons:

- The attitude that winning is the only goal often prohibits consideration of athletes with special needs. Some coaches and some schools are simply more open to the importance of other values, such as teaching cooperation and teamwork, developing self-confidence, and rewarding excellence of effort.
- The lack of time can pose problems. Although clearly talented, exceptional students may require much more individual coaching and supervised practice to achieve their athletic potential.
- Some states have health and safety requirements that legally prevent such participation. This should be checked out in every case.

Some possible strategies and solutions for the school to increase participation of athletes include:

- encouraging students to try out and coaches to be open-minded;
- setting up extra coaching assistance provided by aides, adult volunteers, or other students; and
- making minor adaptations as needed; for example, a blind student could compete in varsity wrestling if competitors are required to be in physical contact at the beginning of the match.

Teachers should be aware that alternative sports opportunities exist for students with disabilities outside the school. Those with mental disabilities can participate in Special Olympics, which is relatively noncompetitive and emphasizes self-concept. For those with physical and sensory disabilities, other organizations provide highly competitive athletics such as wheelchair sports and athletics for the blind, including skiing. Students may be encouraged to participate in community leagues and recreational teams. However, these alternatives alone should not be considered sufficient for students who, with a little assistance, really are capable of participating in varsity sports.

One of the authors attended a high school homecoming football celebration where returning athletic letter winners were introduced during the half-time ceremony. The crowd gave a standing ovation to a returning alumni football letter winner with Down syndrome. Another of the authors witnessed a highly talented athlete being denied an opportunity to play varsity football because of a coaching staff's concern that "he might do something to embarrass the team." Given these two scenarios, it is not difficult to choose which one most contemporary school leaders would like to promote among staff.

TRANSFER OF RIGHTS IN SOME STATES—AGES OF MAJORITY

States may provide that a child with disabilities reaching the age of majority under state law (age eighteen in many states) will be granted the procedural safeguard rights previously reserved to the child's parents. If states do transfer parent rights to the child at age of majority, then schools must notify both the parents and the child of the transfer of rights. At least one year beforehand, IEPs must include a statement that the student has been informed of the rights to be transferred under state law at the age of majority. States may develop procedures for appointing someone, including parents, to represent the educational interests of the student when it is determined that the student does not have the ability to provide informed consent and make decisions but has not been the subject of a state legal proceeding to establish incompetency.

Even when rights are transferred to the student after age eighteen, both the parents and the student must be provided any notice (i.e., IEP meetings, change in FAPE) required by the law that formerly had to be given only to parents.

GENERAL CONSIDERATIONS

In addition to these specific topics, successful integration of exceptional students at the secondary school level can be enhanced in several general ways. One is to assign responsibility for each student to one staff member, much as each college student has a faculty adviser. Professionals such as therapists, consultants, special educators, and willing regular class teachers can be assigned a limited number of special needs students for whom they will serve as advocates, advisers, and coordinators of overall educational plans. A significant need of students with disabilities which has been related to successful completion of high school is that of a personal relationship with a trusted adult who will be available to support and encourage them when needed (Benz, Lindstrom, & Yovanoff, 2000).

No matter how the responsibilities are divided, it is always essential in secondary school settings to keep lines of communication open among the various professionals involved in the education of students with disabilities. For example, if a resource room model is being used, the resource teacher might send a weekly or biweekly note to each instructor asking how the student is progressing and whether any particular assistance is needed. Technology, such as use of e-mail and list-serve, may ease the burdens of such regular communication. Correspondence will help build beneficial relations of trust and cooperation. Building principals must accept responsibility for seeing that staff members are regularly and fully informed.

Behavior is often a priority issue for teachers of included secondary students. Chapter 9 offers a variety of concrete suggestions to promote positive behavior within the complex restrictions of special education law. Discipline and good educational environment are not the sole domain of special education. All staff, including support staff, have a role to play in maintaining a school climate of safety, support, acceptance, and cooperation. It is the educational leader's responsibility—through facilitation of training and services, keeping communication channels open, and role modeling—to develop and maintain a proper climate of school discipline.

The slogan "plan ahead" is useful for educators of secondary level students with disabilities. The schooling time at this point in these adolescents' lives is limited, and attention must be paid to making the best possible use of it. This applies to adequately preparing students for course work (so that they get the most out of their formal schooling), as well as for productive employment and adult life.

Secondary educators of students with disabilities have greater challenges, in some respects, than those at the elementary level because of the unique problems of their students and their schools and because of the relative newness of the field. But the role they play is no less important to the students and to society as a whole. The continued evolution of secondary special education—and especially of assistance in the process of transition from school to adult life—will undoubtedly be a focus of educational research and development efforts over the next decade. The principal, as education leader, plays a key role in that continued and progressive evolution.

CONCLUSION

The concept of educational leadership, as opposed to mere school management, finds a significant challenge in the secondary school setting. It is there that traditions and values are most difficult to alter, and some persons may ponder whether a feather or a sledgehammer will achieve the most successful results. Whichever it is, climate change is a necessity in many secondary schools. Too many students, with or without disabilities, are harmed by content-driven curriculum, prevailing lecture methodology, and apprehension of anything smacking of change.

The law and good education require that students with disabilities, to the maximum extent appropriate, must be educated with students without disabilities. An inability to do this successfully would tell us a great deal about our current education system and its leadership. Challenges help us all to grow. The challenges of legally mandated special education and the necessary accompanying inclusion teamwork and collaboration provide us all the opportunity to grow together.

REFERENCES

Aspel, N., Bettis, G., Quinn, P., Test, D. W., & Wood, W. M. (1999). A collaborative process for planning transition services for all students with disabilities. *Career Development for Exceptional Individuals, 22* (1), 21–41.

Asselin, S. B., Todd-Allen, M., & deFur, S. (1998). Transition coordinators. *Teaching Exceptional Children, 30* (3), 11–15.

Benz, M. R., Lindstrom, L., & Yovanoff, P. (2000). Improving graduation and employment outcomes of students with disabilities: Predictive factors and student perspectives. *Exceptional Children, 66* (4), 509–529.

Benz, M. R., Yovanoff, P., & Doren, B. (1997). School-to-work components that predict post-school success for students with and without disabilities. *Exceptional Children, 63* (2), 151–165.

Blackorby, J., & Wagner, M. (1996). Longitudinal post-school outcomes of youth with disabilities: Findings from the National Longitudinal Transition Study. *Exceptional Children, 62* (5), 399–413.

Blalock, G. (1996). Community transition teams as the foundation for transition services for youth with learning disabilities. *Journal of Learning Disabilities, 29* (2), 148–159.

Cole, C. M., & McLesky, J. (1997). Secondary inclusion programs for students with mild disabilities. *Focus on Exceptional Children, 29* (6), 1–15.

Dunbar to Runkel, 25 IDELR 387 (OCR 1996).

Gable, R. A., Manning, M. L., Hendrickson, J. M., & Rogan, J. P. (1997). A secondary student instructional support team (ASSIST): Teachers face the challenge of student diversity. *The High School Journal, 81* (1), 22–27.

Gartin, B., Rumrill, P., & Serebreni, R. (1996). The higher education transition model: Guidelines for facilitating college transition among college-bound students with disabilities. *Teaching Exceptional Children, 29* (1), 30–33.

Iowa Department of Education (1996). *Infusing transition into individualized education programs.* Des Moines, IA: Author.

Jung, B. (1998). Mainstreaming and fixing things: Secondary teachers and inclusion. *The Educational Forum, 62,* 131–135.

Kaiser, D., & Abell, M. (1997). Learning life and management in the classroom. *Teaching Exceptional Children, 30* (1), 70–75.

Kling, B. (2000). ASSERT yourself: Helping students of all ages develop self-advocacy skills. *Teaching Exceptional Children, 32* (3), 66–70.

Lanford, A. D., & Cary, L. G. (2000). Graduation requirements for students with disabilities. *Remedial and Special Education, 21* (3), 152–160.

May, D. C., & Kundert, D. K., (1996). Are special educators prepared to meet the sex education needs of their students? A progress report. *The Journal of Special Education, 29* (4), 433–441.

Malian, I. M., & Love, L. L. (1998). Leaving high school: An ongoing transition study. *Teaching Exceptional Children, 30* (3), 4–10.

Miner, C. A., & Bates, P. A. (1997). Person-centered transition planning. *Teaching Exceptional Children, 30* (1), 66–69.

Morgan, D. P. (1989). *A description of the development and implementation of the secondary transitional education program at Southeastern Community College.* Unpublished doctoral dissertation. The University of Iowa.

Morningstar, M. E. (1997). Critical issues in career development and employment preparation for adolescents with disabilities. *Remedial and Special Education, 18* (5), 307–320.

Neubert, D. A., & Moon, M. S. (2000). How a transition profile helps students prepare for life in the community. *Teaching Exceptional Children, 33* (2), 20–25.

O'Neill, P. T. (2001). Special education and high stakes testing for high school graduation: An analysis of current law and policy. *Journal of Law and Education, 30* (2), 185–222.

Patton, J. R., Cronin, M. E., & Jairrels, V. (1997). Curricular implications of transition: Life skills an integral part of transition education. *Remedial and Special Education, 18* (5), 294–306.

Rockwell, G., Weisenstein, G., & LaRoque, T. (1986). *Cooperative Education: A Transition Option for High School Youth With Disabilities–A Literature Review and Empirical Study of Cooperative Education Programs in Washington State.* Seattle: University of Washington.

Smith, T. E. C. (1997). Adolescence: A continuing challenge for special educators. *Remedial and Special Education, 18* (5), 258–210.

Test, D. W., Karvonen, M., Wood, W. M., Browder, D., & Algozzine, B. (2000). Choosing a self-determination curriculum: Plan for the future. *Teaching Exceptional Children, 33* (2), 48–53.

Wehmeyer, M., & Schwartz, M. (1997). Self-determination and positive adult outcomes: A follow-up study of youth with mental retardation or learning disabilities. *Exceptional Children, 63* (2), 245–255.

Weisenstein, G. R., & Rockwell, G. K. (1987). *A checklist for building a successful vocational program for handicapped high school students.* Seattle: University of Washington.

Weisenstein, G. R., Stowitschek, J. J., & Affleck, J. Q. (1991). Integrating students enrolled in special education into vocational education. *Career Development for Exceptional Individuals, 14* (2), 131–144.

Whitney-Thomas, J., & Hanley-Maxwell, C. (1996). Packing the parachute: Parents' experiences as their children prepare to leave high school. *Exceptional Children, 63* (1), 75–87.

Will, M. (1984). *OSERS programming for the transition of youth with disabilities: Bridges from school to working life.* Washington, DC: Office of Special Education and Rehabilitation Services, pp. 1, 2.

Yoder, D. I., Retish, E., & Wade, R. (1996). Service learning: Meeting student and community needs. *Teaching Exceptional Children, 28* (4), 14–18.

RECOMMENDED READINGS

Asselin, S. B., Todd-Allen, M., & deFur, S. (1998). Transition coordinators. *Teaching Exceptional Children, 30* (3), 11–15. This article identifies the various rules and duties appropriate for transition coordinators.

Battle, D. A., Dickens-Wright, L. L., & Murphy, S. C. (1998). How to empower adolescents: Guidelines for effective self-advocacy. *Teaching Exceptional Children, 30* (3), 28–33. This article identifies and describes a school program designed to increase student participation and skills in self-advocacy.

Field, S., Hoffman, A., & Posch, M. (1997). Self-determination during adolescence: A developmental perspective. *Remedial and Special Education, 18* (5), 285–293. This article highlights the content, structure, and strategies to incorporate into secondary self-determination programs.

Kaiser, D., & Abell, M. (1997). Learning life and management in the classroom. *Teaching Exceptional Children, 30* (1), 70–75. This article presents a detailed perspective on the infusion of life skills into the curriculum.

Lindstrom, L. E., Benz, M. R., & Johnson, M. D. (1996). Developing job clubs. *Teaching Exceptional Children, 29* (2), 18–21. This is a practical article on promoting transition skills in an informal environment.

Miner, C. A., & Bates, P. A. (1997). Person-centered transition planning. *Teaching Exceptional Children, 30* (1), 66–69. This article provides a detailed look at planning for transition from the student's perspective.

O'Neill, P. T. 2001. Special education and high stakes testing for high school graduation: An analysis of current law and policy. *Journal of Law and Education, 30* (2), 185–222. In addition to a discussion of litigation, this article details the various legal and policy considerations associated with the use of examinations as graduation requirements under the IDEA.

Patton, P. L., de la Garza, B., & Harmon, C. (1997). Employability skills + adult agency support + family support + on-the-job support = successful employment. *Teaching Exceptional Children, 29* (3), 4–10. This article presents a practical comprehensive transition program for students with mild disabilities. Contains checklists and suggestion lists.

Sodac, D. G. (1997). Join the AMICUS Club. *Teaching Exceptional Children, 29* (3), 64–67. Discusses the development of a club designed to address the development of student social skills, social acceptance, peer interaction, and self-confidence among both special and regular education students. (Amicus means "friend" in Latin.)

Wall, M. E., & Dattilo, J. (1995). Creating option-rich learning environments: Facilitating self-determination. *Journal of Special Education, 29* (3), 276–294. This article focuses on strategies to enhance self-determination in secondary programming.

Relevant Federal Regulations

34 C.F.R. 300.25	Secondary school.
.29	Transition services.
.122	Exceptions to FAPE for certain ages.
.146	Suspension and expulsion rates.
.306	Nonacademic services.
.344	IEP team.
.347	IEP content.
.348	Agency responsibility for transition services.
.517	Transfer of parental rights at age of majority.
.553	Nonacademic settings.
Appendix A #11	
#12	
#13	

CHAPTER 9

DISCIPLINE

Focus

Schools are prohibited by law, in some situations, from applying the same disciplinary procedures to special education students as have been traditionally used with regular education students. This problem is compounded by the fact that a small percentage of special education students exhibit unusually difficult and disruptive behavior problems.

Legal Issues

The law on disciplining students with disabilities may vary somewhat owing to differing state laws. Moreover, the relevant state and federal laws are complex and are continually being reinterpreted. Specific problems should be reviewed with school legal staff.

The major points are as follows:

- School officials may unilaterally place a student with disabilities in an interim alternative educational setting for up to 45 calendar days when the misconduct involves weapons or drugs;
- School officials may seek a hearing officer's approval for a student's placement in an interim alternative educational setting for up to 45 calendar days when the student is likely to injure someone;
- When school officials unilaterally change a student's placement to an interim alternative educational setting, exclude a student for more than 10 consecutive school days, or suspend a student for an accumulated number of school days in excess of 10 days, whether it results in a change of placement or not, they must conduct a functional behavioral assessment, if not previously completed, and plan and implement (or review) the student's behavior intervention plan;
- When school officials consider placing a student with disabilities in an interim alternative educational setting or expelling or suspending the student in a manner which constitutes a change in placement, the IEP team must conduct a manifestation determination review;
- When a student's misconduct is determined to be related to the student's disability, the student may not be excluded from an education for more than ten days, but the IEP and placement may be revised to take the student's misbehavior into account;

- Parents may challenge decisions regarding manifestation determinations and placement for disciplinary reasons through an expedited due process hearing procedure;
- Student "stay put" requirements differ from the norm for parent appeals regarding placement in interim alternative educational settings;
- A student with a disability who is excluded from school for more than 10 school days in a school year for disciplinary reasons, consecutive or not, remains entitled to FAPE; and
- Students involved in minor disciplinary infractions may be disciplined as other students are disciplined, so long as the discipline does not result in a change in placement, the deprivation of FAPE, and students without disabilities are treated in the same manner.

In general, expulsion of a student with disabilities, suspension for more than 10 consecutive school days, and some accumulated suspensions must be viewed as a change of educational placement and must be preceded by the standard parent safeguard procedures, including parental notice and opportunity for a due process hearing, required for changes in placement. The burden of proof, or justification, for unilateral long-term exclusion from school for disciplinary reasons is on the school.

Some students not previously determined to be eligible for special education, and who are being subjected to school disciplinary procedures, may assert the protections provided students with disabilities if the student can establish that the school had "knowledge" that the student was a child with a disability before the behavior at issue occurred.

Rationale

Denial of an education to students because of their disability-related behavior may violate several aspects of the IDEA and the principles behind it: (1) the right to an appropriate public education; (2) the right to an education in the LRE; and (3) the right to prescribed procedures for changes in placement. It is neither legal nor logical to remove a student from special education programs and services for the same behavioral characteristics and disability which entitled the student to such programs in the first place.

Children with disabilities are more like children without disabilities than they are different. All children need to receive approval and to experience success and self-worth, and all can grow in their mastery of appropriate behavior. Effective disciplinary systems for children with disabilities are based on techniques that benefit all students.

Approaches

To minimize behavior problems and to avoid unnecessary hearings and unfavorable court decisions, school systems should have the following: (1) a clearly stated and consistently followed disciplinary system for all students; (2) a flexible, cooperative, problem-solving approach involving parents and regular and special education staff members; (3) established disciplinary alternatives short of suspension from school, such as time-out rooms, or supervised in-school suspensions; (4) opportunities for all students to achieve a sense of success and belonging in the school; and (5) commitment to the philosophy that every student deserves and can benefit from an education.

Even for the most difficult of student behaviors, the IEP process provides the ultimate tool for resolving school disciplinary concerns experienced by individual students with disabilities and for maintaining an educational environment conducive to learning.

CONCERNS FOR EDUCATIONAL LEADERS

"I was unprepared. It was a real shock," said one assistant principal of his experiences with a behavioral disability (BD) program that was moved into his high school. "Nobody let me know what kind of problems I was going to have to deal with."

In this case, the high school was a relatively tranquil one in an affluent suburb. The BD program—still separate from other classes—had just been placed in a regular school setting for the first time and the "shocking" problems included several seizures of deadly weapons. A number of factors—the type of students, the isolation of the program, the lack of preparation for both students and staff—helped make this situation extreme. But the fact remains that new responsibilities for educating and disciplining students with disabilities often make unfamiliar and stressful demands on school administrators.

The stresses have two sources: (1) uncertainty about, and in many cases resentment of, the demands of the law; and (2) unfamiliarity with the students themselves, with the nature and needs of different disabilities, and with proved methods for solving or preventing their sometimes unique disciplinary problems. At the same time, it is important to emphasize that the majority of students with disabilities do not present discipline problems of a nature different from regular student populations, and disciplining youngsters with disabilities may involve some new knowledge, procedures, and philosophy. But in the end, the process is based on the same principles that apply to other students.

With discipline, as with other aspects of special education, the most fruitful approach for educational leaders generally is an assertive one. They must understand the legal and educational realities involved and plan ahead to minimize problems.

The various disabilities are discussed more fully in Part III. This chapter concentrates on general legal issues of discipline and alternative approaches that apply to all special and regular education students.

LEGAL HISTORY UNDER THE ACT

The original legislation that became the IDEA did not address student discipline. That void in the statutes was partially filled through numerous court decisions which resulted from expensive litigation. Those law suits, beginning at least as early as 1978, cost schools and parents a great deal of time, money, and effort that could have been better spent on successful educational programming. When Congress reviewed the IDEA for possible revisions in 1995, a great debate ensued regarding student discipline. The focus of concern was the perception of many persons that a lack of fairness existed in differing school punishments handed out to students with disabilities and those without disabilities, and that the behavior of a few students with disabilities unfavorably impacted school safety.

As a result, Congress took a long, hard look at school discipline as it related to students with disabilities, and the review and amendment process begun in 1995 was not finally completed until June, 1997. In the 1997 Amendments, Congress attempted to "strike a careful balance" between the school's duty to ensure a safe environment conducive to learning and the school's obligation to ensure that children with disabilities receive a FAPE (House Report No. 105-95, 1997, p. 106). Also of specific interest to Congress was the fostering of greater parity in the handling of the discipline of students with and without disabilities.

In order to bring consistency to what it considered the chaotic state of court and administrative interpretations on discipline of students with disabilities, Congress determined to place nearly all legal guidance on discipline in one location, the IDEA. The result was expected to be a better understanding of the protections available to children with disabilities by educators and parents. Congress also required that states gather, analyze, and report data regarding long-term suspensions and expulsions of children with disabilities. If discrepancies in the disciplinary treatment of children with disabilities occur within a state, the state must ensure that policies and practices are reviewed and necessary changes are implemented.

Whether Congress' treatment of the student discipline issues achieved its goals of school safety and parity in the treatment of students will likely be debated for many years. The statutes do resolve some of the disciplinary legal issues that have had school officials confused. However, they do so in a detailed and complex piece of legislation.

LEGAL REQUIREMENTS

IEP Process Alternative

Various efforts of school officials engaging in the discipline of students with disabilities, especially when exclusion from school is involved, are fraught with difficulty. A sound and more educationally appropriate means of dealing with student behavior is available. The IDEA anticipates that changes in student program and placement, including those resulting from the behavior needs of students, may be necessary and has established procedures to facilitate such changes. Chapters 5 and 6 discuss the process and procedures by which the IEP team, including the parents, can legally identify and carry out necessary programming and placement changes. When the parents are in agreement

with a program change based on behavior, which they will be in the vast majority of instances, the school may make the changes efficiently and effectively, and will be continuing to fulfill its responsibility of providing FAPE under the law. When parents disagree with school proposals, those processes and procedures related to parent rights and hearings found in Chapters 2 and 3 become more relevant, but the IEP process may still remain the best alternative from an educational and financial standpoint. From the school's financial standpoint, any litigation regarding a school's unilateral exclusion of a student will be costly, risky, and often counterproductive. Litigation over exclusion will drive the school and parents further apart and the best interests of both the student and school will suffer. School money and staff time will be best utilized through existing procedures of the IDEA to determine an educational program that meets the needs both of the child and the school. Thinking long-term, not short-term, is the prudent approach.

Educators must remember that any time a student's repetitive behavior or reasonably expected behavior impedes the student's learning or the learning of others it is anticipated that the IEP team, in the development and review of the IEP, will consider appropriate strategies, including positive behavioral interventions and supports, to address student behaviors. The failure to do so is considered by OSEP to constitute a denial of FAPE to the child. During the last decade, the results of significant research efforts establishing the efficacy of positive behavior interventions have been published regularly in the education literature (Turnbull, Wilcox, Stowe, Raper, & Hedges, 2000). Short-term suspensions and denial of some privileges for infraction of school rules could be part of a behavioral intervention plan, so long as they do not result in the student being denied a FAPE. Short-term suspensions of students should not be used as a substitute for appropriately considering and addressing a student's behavior problems.

Short Fixed-Term Suspensions

Congress intended, and the regulations of the U.S. Department of Education provide, that students with disabilities may be unilaterally removed from their current educational placement (i.e., suspension) for up to 10 consecutive school days by school authorities, without IDEA implications, so long as children without disabilities are subject to the same discipline.

School officials are allowed a reasonable degree of flexibility when dealing with violations of school rules by children with disabilities, and a student's loss of educational programming for 10 consecutive school days or less is not considered to impose an unreasonable educational burden on a child with disabilities. This time period can be used as a "cooling down" period for reflection, planning, and time for additional assessment when desirable.

An overriding legal problem is that the language of the statute, for many purposes under the IDEA, does not appear to treat suspensions of 10 days or less differently than other forms of more severe discipline and, as a result, may require additional amendment by Congress (20 U.S.C. § 1415(k) (4) (A); Huefner, 1998; Mead, 1998). The authors have proceeded under the likelihood that the technical legal issue will be resolved as Congress had intended, as the regulations provide, and as previous court rulings have consistently found: short-term suspensions amounting to 10 school days or less do not implicate the IDEA. Readers will have to determine whether subsequent events do not bring this about.

Suspensions of indefinite length can result in special problems. Although it may be desirable in some situations to make a student's return to school following a suspension conditional upon some occurrence (i.e., until parents come to school to visit with the principal, until completion of additional assessment), it remains the duty of the school to see that the legal requirements of the IDEA are met. When a student's indefinite suspension exceeds 10 consecutive school days because a condition for return has not occurred, then the school is legally responsible, not the student or the parents.

Accumulated Suspensions

The IDEA regulations provide that a series of suspensions for separate incidents of student misconduct in the same school year, which are not more than 10 consecutive school days each, is a viable disciplinary technique. However, problems arise if suspensions are not also used with nondisabled students or if, as a result of their length, total amount of time suspended, and proximity to each other, they constitute a "pattern" of exclusion. When accumulated suspensions exceeding 10 school days constitute a "pattern," the result is considered a change in educational placement, and as explained in Chapter 2, the IDEA requires a placement team decision and parental procedural safeguards, including notice to parents, and re-evaluation for changes in placement. This regulatory provision is consistent with OSEP's long-standing administrative interpretations involving accumulated short-term suspensions.

The primary dilemma presented by this situation is that local school officials may determine that a series of accumulated suspensions (i.e., $3 + 3 + 3 + 3 = 12$) does not constitute a "pattern" and that determination may later reversed by a hearing officer or a judge. It is then too late to comply with all the legal requirements involved in a change in placement and the school is in an impossible situation.

The two preventive alternatives to potential legal complications arising from "patterns" of accumulated short-term suspensions are: (1) never exceed 10 days of suspension in a school year for an individual student; or (2) treat each accumulated suspension exceeding 10 days in a school year as if it were a change in placement.

When suspension from school is for only part of a school day, the part day is applied to the 10-day consecutive and cumulative limitations. An in-school suspension is not normally considered a part of the 10-day suspension limitation (either consecutive or accumulated) so long as the student is afforded the opportunity to appropriately progress in the general curriculum, continue to receive services under the IEP, and continue to participate with nondisabled children.

When suspension from school transportation occurs, when transportation is part of the IEP, and when the child is unable to attend school, the suspension from transportation must be treated as a suspension from school. If transportation is not part of an IEP, OSEP does not consider removal from transportation itself to be a "suspension." It is expected that the child's parents will be responsible for transportation on the same basis as parents of nondisabled children. However, some state laws treat transportation as an integral part of special education and should be consulted. Student misbehavior occurring during transportation can be addressed in the IEP and behavioral intervention plan of the child, and should be addressed when misbehavior on the school bus is similar to that experienced in the classroom.

Because exclusions from school will have a significant negative impact on a student's ability to succeed in school, FAPE must be provided for all removals exceeding 10 school days in the same school year, whether or not a change in placement resulted.

Expulsion and Long-Term Suspensions

The IDEA allows for the expulsion, long-term suspension (more than 10 consecutive school days) and accumulated suspensions exceeding 10 school days in a school year which result in a change in placement for students with disabilities only so long as the student's misbehavior is not related to the student's disability and the same disciplinary procedures are applicable to children without disabilities. The process for de-

termining relationship, manifestation determination, is detailed in the law and is explained later in this chapter. When it is determined that no relationship exists between a student's disability and the misconduct, and the parents do not request a due process hearing on the relationship determination or the proposed change in placement resulting from the exclusion from school, the student may be excluded from school in the same manner as students without disabilities.

When parents file a request for a due process hearing regarding either a change in placement resulting from the proposed exclusion exceeding 10 days or a manifestation determination, the school cannot unilaterally change the student's educational placement (except to alternative educational settings [AESs]) until the hearing has concluded and the school has prevailed. (See the "stay-put" discussion in Chapter 3.)

Schools engaged in long-term exclusion of students with disabilities from schools must conduct a manifestation determination, a functional behavioral assessment, develop or review a behavioral intervention plan, and continue to provide FAPE, as discussed later in this chapter.

When the IEP team determines that the student's misbehavior was manifested in the student's disability, the student may not be unilaterally excluded from school in a manner which results in a change in placement for more than 10 days in the school year. The IEP team must instead review the student's IEP and make appropriate adjustments, and the placement team must consider potential changes in the student's educational placement.

In summary, students with disabilities may be excluded from school for more than 10 consecutive school days in a school year, and accumulated suspensions exceeding 10 school days which result in a change in placement may occur only when there is a finding of no relationship between the student's disability and the student's misbehavior; a functional behavioral assessment has been conducted; a behavioral intervention plan has been implemented or reviewed and modified; the parents have been notified in writing of the exclusion as a proposed change-in-placement, and the parents do not file a request for due process hearing (or the hearing decision was in favor of the school); and FAPE is continued. This is as complex and exhausting as it sounds.

Unilateral removal from school for even short periods of time will also require the provision of constitutional procedural due process. (See the discussion of *Goss v. Lopez* (1975) at the end of this chapter.)

Unilateral Authority of School Personnel—AES

In three student disciplinary situations, school personnel (e.g., principals) have limited unilateral authority to remove a child with disabilities from the child's current educational placement and to place the child in an appropriate interim AES for up to 45 days (calendar days, not school days—weekends and school vacations count toward the 45-day limitation). The three situations include when a student:

1. carries a weapon to school or to a school function or possesses a weapon at school or at school activities. Weapon means a "weapon, device, instrument, material, or substance, animate or inanimate, that is used for, or is readily capable of, causing death or serious bodily injury," except a pocket knife with a blade less than 2 1/2 inches in length (18 U.S.C. § 930). Included are guns, acids, and poisons, but questions will arise about many items. For example, a pencil might be a weapon depending on its intended use.
2. possesses or uses illegal drugs, such as cocaine or methamphetamine, while attending school or a school function.
3. sells or solicits the sale of prescription medication, such as Ritalin, while attending school or a school function.

Unilateral placements in an AES may be repeated for separate offenses during the school year so long as other legal requirements (i.e., manifestation determination and functional behavioral assessments) are met. Placements in an AES may also be administered in conjunction with other disciplinary removal. For instance, the school may suspend a child for up to 10 consecutive school days while convening the IEP team to determine an appropriate AES. In such situations, the student should be placed in the AES no later than the end of the 10th day of suspension.

Congress created the AES placement to enable schools to ensure learning environments that are safe and conducive to learning for all, and to give schools the opportunity to determine appropriate future placement for the student. Placement in an AES by school officials is an exception to the "stay-put" requirement and may continue even when the student's behavior is determined to be related to the student's disability, or when the parent requests a due process hearing to challenge the AES placement.

Placements in an AES can be for periods of time shorter than 45 days. Also, AES placements may be shortened by events, such as when the IEP team (including parents) and school officials mutually agree to a change in placement to another educational setting.

Determination of AES

The greatest limitation on the authority of a school official in unilaterally placing a student in AES is presented by the criteria requirements of the placement. These determinations are made by the IEP team, which must include the child's parents, not by the school official placing the student in an AES.

The IEP team must determine that the proposed AES setting meets the following criteria:

- The setting must allow the student to continue to progress in the general curriculum, although in another setting;

- The student must continue to receive services and modifications, including those in the IEP, that will enable the student to meet IEP goals; and
- The student must receive services and modifications designed to address the misbehavior for which the student is being disciplined so that it does not recur.

Violence—AES Placement

If a child engages in misbehavior which poses a threat of harm to himself or to others, but does not involve weapons or drugs, school officials may request that an expedited due process hearing be held, after which a hearing officer may order the child placed in an AES for not more than 45 calendar days. An expedited hearing must result in a decision within 45 calendar days of the request for hearing. Specific procedures for expedited hearings may be determined by states.

Only a hearing officer may make a decision on an AES for students who are alleged to pose a threat to themselves or others. In doing so, following hearing, the hearing officer must:

- Determine that the school has demonstrated "beyond a preponderance of the evidence" that maintaining the current placement is substantially likely to result in injury to the student or others;
- Consider the appropriateness of the current educational placement;
- Consider whether the school has made reasonable efforts to minimize the risk for harm in the current placement, including the use of supplementary aids and services (for example, could staff-development training or the assignment of a teacher associate minimize the risk?); and
- Determine that the AES setting proposed by school personnel, who have consulted with the student's special education teacher, will enable the student to progress in the general curriculum, continue to receive services and modifications (including those in the IEP that

will enable the child to achieve IEP goals), and receive services and modifications to address the behavior in order to prevent the behavior from recurring.

The hearing officer must review the adequacy of the proposed AES setting and direct appropriate modifications if necessary.

When the school has not previously removed the student from school through suspensions of 10 consecutive school days or less in a manner that resulted in a change of placement for the student, the school may remove the student through a short-term suspension so long as a change in placement does not result. During the time of the removal, arrangements may be made for an expedited due process hearing to determine whether an AES is appropriate.

Obviously, there are few appropriate school settings currently available that will meet the AES criteria. How will schools comply? Are alternative schools with appropriately licensed staff an answer?

Home-Bound

Many educators considering AES options will, at least briefly, consider some form of home-bound education program (sometimes called home-study) as a respite for school personnel. Home-study placements are not conducive to appropriate educational programming for the vast majority of students, are among the most segregated of placements, and are not favored by parents or courts. When used as an AES, home-bound instruction must meet all the criteria required of AES settings. As such, attempts to use home-bound as an AES will be difficult to defend (Huefner, 1998), and OSEP has expressed concern regarding the use of home-bound instruction as an AES.

Functional Behavioral Assessment and Behavior Intervention Plans

Either before or not later than 10 business days after commencing a student removal of more than 10 consecutive school days, commencing a unilateral change in placement to an AES for drugs or weapons, or first removing a student for more than ten non-consecutive school days in a school year, if it has not already done so, the school must convene the IEP team and develop a functional behavioral assessment plan. Behavioral assessment plans which require new individualized student assessment and are not merely a review of existing data may require written parent consent for evaluation (see Chapter 4).

As soon as is practicable after an assessment plan is developed and assessments are completed, the IEP team must meet to develop appropriate behavioral interventions and then implement those interventions. The functional behavioral assessment planning and behavioral intervention planning meetings may be held in conjunction with a manifestation determination review (as discussed later in this chapter) when desired. If a behavioral intervention plan already exists for a student, then the team must review the plan and its implementation and make modifications as necessary.

Federal law does not define or explain the phrase "functional behavioral assessment." A perhaps oversimplified understanding of functional behavioral assessment provides that it is an effort to determine the purpose of the student's behavior. Taking the context of the situation into account (What events occurred prior to the event? What misbehavior occurred? What happened to the student?), the educators attempt to determine the reason for the student's behavior. The focus is on the "function" or purpose of the behavior from the perspective of the student. When the function is determined, educators can then develop and teach an appropriate alternative behavior for the student to attain what the student wants without having to resort to improper behavior. Inappropriate behavior will no longer be necessary for the student to use in order to obtain the result wanted, i.e., peer attention, adult attention,

or escape from the situation or environment. For example, if a student hits a neighbor in order to escape the embarrassment of doing long-division problems at the board, being sent to the principal's office would not be appropriate. It would reinforce the student's reason for the misbehavior. An acceptable way for the student to communicate the need to avoid doing division at the board, and thereby escape embarrassment, can be identified and taught (such as express permission to request excusal), and thereby replace the inappropriate behavior.

McConnel, Hilvitz, and Cox (1998) note the functional behavioral assessment process was originally developed to help provide an understanding of behaviors exhibited by students who were limited in verbalizing the function of their behavior. For instance, it has been determined that for some self-injurious behavior in severely disabled students, the behavior serves the child as a function for obtaining attention from adults. As an appropriate alternative, the child might be taught to use an electric switch which activates a colorful light or music to draw adult attention to the student's needs. Thus, the self-injurious behavior is no longer needed by the student in order to obtain attention. Historically, in clinical situations involving children who do not communicate easily, functional behavioral assessment has taken on a scientific approach of making and testing formal hypotheses regarding the student's function. This approach may be too formalized for most classroom use.

McConnel, Hilvitz, and Cox (1998) have developed a 10-step functional behavioral assessment (FBA) and behavior plan process that is appropriate for use by regular and special educators in most school situations:*

---

*From "Functional Assessment: A Systematic Process for Assessment and Intervention in General and Special Education Classrooms," by M. E. McConnel, D. B. Hilvitz, and C. J. Cox, 1988, *Intervention in School and Clinic, 34* (1), pp. 11–16. Copyright 1998 by PRO-ED, Inc. Adapted with permission.

1. *Identify the student's behavior.*
2. *Describe the problem behavior.*
   Use clear, specific, and detailed terms.
3. *Collect behavior baseline data and academic information.*
   Document frequency, duration, and intensity.
4. *Describe the environment and setting of the behaviors—when, where, who, what.*
   (See behavioral observation sample form in Appendix G1.)
5. *Complete functional assessment interview form.*
   The IEP team will attempt to identify the context of the behavior (See functional assessment interview form in Appendix G2.)
6. *Develop a hypothesis.*
   The team will look at the factors surrounding the behavior and develop a theory about the purpose or function of the student's behavior.
7. *Write a behavioral intervention plan (BIP) or review the existing plan.*
   Include a description of the specific interventions to use in the classroom. (See sample behavioral intervention plan form in Appendix G3.)
8. *Implement the behavioral intervention plan or review the existing plan.*
   The classroom teacher will have the primary responsibility.
9. *Collect behavioral data.*
10. *Conduct assessment meeting.*
    The IEP team will review and assess data results. Modifications and adaptations to the plan will be made, if successful. If not successful, a new hypothesis will be developed and a new behavioral plan constructed.

Although all authors may not be in agreement (Smith, 2000), initial research has established that regular classroom teachers are able to perform FBAs with minimal specialized training (Ellingson, Miltenberger, Stricker, Galensky, & Garlinghouse, 2000).

A BIP must be discussed and developed at an IEP meeting. Such plans consist of planned behavioral interventions and strategies to address the student's behavior and normally would include behavior goals and objectives and strategies, as well as positive behavioral interventions to address behavior problems, regardless of the student's disability category (Yell, 1998, p. 347). The plan should identify expected behaviors and inappropriate behaviors, and provide for appropriate consequences and strategies. Intervention techniques should be outlined in the plan, beginning with less intrusive procedures. If behavioral crises are anticipated, procedures for dealing with them should be included. Data regarding the plan's success must be regularly kept and reviewed when the plan is regularly reviewed.

Subsequent disciplinary removals of the student from school will each time result in IEP team member reviews of the plan. A formal team meeting will be required only whenever one or more team members determine that modifications to the existing plan are desirable.

FBAs may be conducted for students not being considered for exclusion from usual educational programming. When IEP teams proactively address a student's behavior in the IEP because the behavior impedes the student's learning or the learning of others, those strategies provided, including positive behavioral interventions and supports, may constitute a BIP. When a student's IEP includes strategies to address a particular behavior, the appropriate school response to student misbehavior would almost always be to use the behavioral strategies in the IEP, rather than the implementation of school punishment, especially removal from school. For this reason, it is imperative that educational leaders be aware of individual student BIPs.

Manifestation Determination

When the traditional approach of expulsion or long-term suspension (more than 10 consecutive school days) is considered for student disciplinary infractions, when a student is considered for placement in an AES, or when a student's accumulated suspensions of over 10 school days result in a change of placement, the school must determine whether the student's misconduct was a manifestation (result) of the student's disability.

Only when the behavior was not a manifestation of the student's disability may the student be disciplined in the same manner as students without disabilities, including possible expulsion. If a determination is made that the student's misbehavior was caused by or related to the student's disability, then the student may not be punished by unilateral long-term exclusion. Instead, when a student's misbehavior is related to the disability, the IEP team must take the disciplinary needs of the student and the needs of the school into account, and identify and implement a revised appropriate education program and, possibly, placement. If the student has been excluded for more than 10 consecutive school days from school and it is determined that a relationship between the disability and the misconduct existed, then the student must be returned to IEP educational programming. If the student has been placed in AES, then the school may return the student to IEP programming, but it is not required to do so until the time assigned to AES has run out (Analysis of Comments and Changes, 1999, p. 12625).

A review of the potential relationship between the student's disability and the student's misbehavior must be conducted no later than 10 school days after the date on which a decision by school officials to take disciplinary action is made, and sooner when possible. There is a legal presumption that a relationship exists between the disability and the misconduct, which must be overcome during the review. If the legal presumption of the existence of a relationship is not overcome during the manifestation determination review, then the child may not be expelled or otherwise unilaterally removed from school for more than 10 days dur-

ing a school year (except accumulated suspensions not resulting in a change in placement). The review is to be conducted by the IEP team, including parents, and other qualified school personnel (which are not specified in the law). The team must consider all relevant information regarding the student's behavior subject to disciplinary action, including evaluation results, parent information, observations, the IEP, and placement. If a determination is challenged, the burden of proof falls on the school to prove that no manifestation existed.

The IEP team must make favorable determinations regarding all of the following statutory "standards," or the presumption of the existence of a manifestation is not overcome (Mead, 1998):

- The child's IEP and placement were appropriate and special education services, supplementary aids and services, and behavior intervention strategies were provided consistent with the IEP and placement;
- The child's disability did not impair his ability to understand the impact and consequences of the behavior for which he is being disciplined; and
- The child's disability did not impair his ability to control the behavior subject to disciplinary action.

When the standards are considered in conjunction with court decisions occurring prior to the 1997 Amendments, it is probable that the second standard refers to direct forms of relationship, such as a severe mental or behavioral disability which may prevent a student from understanding that the behavior was inappropriate. The third standard seems to refer to indirect relationships where the student may have understood that the actions taken were "wrong," but did them anyway because of personal needs resulting from the disability. In such situations, a student with a specific learning disability may have knowingly violated school rules in order to enhance self-esteem or relationships with peers. Turnbull and Turnbull (1998) refer to this as a "behavioral incapacity" defense (p. 65).

If a relationship is found to exist between the misbehavior and disability, or if the school did not provide or properly implement an appropriate program and services through an IEP and placement, then the team must conclude that a manifestation existed and immediate steps must be taken to remedy deficiencies in the existing IEP or placement. (See Appendix G4 for a model disciplinary action form, including documentation of manifestation determination.)

No detailed explanation of the manifestation determination process or application of the standards is provided in law, and IEP teams will be on their own in determining what these standards mean. It is clear from previous court and administrative interpretations that this decision is one of team consensus and may not be made unilaterally by administrators or other school officials. In the final analysis, taking all the data into account, it will be up to sound professional judgment (with parental participation) to determine whether the misconduct was, or was not, a manifestation of the disability: "There is no cookbook criterion" (Osborne, 1997, p. 330).

Only when the IEP team concludes that no manifestation existed between the student's misbehavior and the student's disability may the school consider using its disciplinary penalties, including expulsion, which are applicable to all students. If the school initiates its normal disciplinary procedures regarding a student receiving special education, then all special education and disciplinary records must be provided to and considered by persons making final determinations regarding school disciplinary action.

When, after all this effort, a school remains intent on expulsion as a possible punishment for the students' actions, it must be remembered that expulsion is considered a change in placement. A change in placement triggers the right of parents to receive a detailed written notice of the proposed change, procedural safeguards such as the right to file an appeal, and when an appeal is filed, to have the child's status quo maintained until the dispute is resolved, attorney fees if the parents prevail, an independent educational evaluation, and others (see Chapter 2 for details). In *Honig v. Doe* (1988), the Supreme Court ruled that when parents request a due process hearing, schools must maintain students' educational placement and cannot unilaterally exclude students, even those with violent tendencies. In extreme situations, schools may seek court approval.

When students needing special education are unilaterally disciplined for behavior that is a manifestation of their disability, and that discipline results in a change of placement, the disciplinary action would violate Section 504.

IEP Process Reminder

Attempting to comply with the foregoing disciplinary requirements in many situations will not be easy. Even with the best legal assistance, steps may be overlooked and problems may still arise. This is a good place to again consider whether the IEP process, which can call into play all of the school's resources to provide the child an appropriate program, isn't preferable to the disciplinary legal hurdles and the potential legal traps involved. The time and money it will take to discipline students with disabilities in the traditional manner will be better spent implementing a new appropriate IEP and placement. Instead of spending money on legal fees (including the parents' fees if they prevail) and staff time fighting for the right to exclude the student, the money would be better spent on staff training or student services that are directed toward a long-term solution to the student's disciplinary problem.

When the IEP process is used to deal with problems of discipline, none of the limitations about days of exclusion will come into play, manifestation determinations will not be needed, and the various situations involving the provision of FAPE to excluded students will not have to be defended.

Parent Appeals

No later than the date on which a decision is made to exclude a student from school for more than 10 consecutive school days, to suspend a student for less than 10 school days in a series of suspensions which constitute a pattern of exclusion, to place a child in an AES, or to seek hearing officer approval for an AES placement, school officials must notify parents of that decision and provide them with notice of the general procedural safeguards available to them (see Chapter 2).

A parent may request a hearing regarding any decision regarding disciplinary placement, including those involving a change in placement, a manifestation determination, or placement in an AES. Parent requests for due process hearings regarding school disciplinary decisions are handled differently than those involved in other due process hearings.

When a parent requests a hearing on a decision regarding discipline, the school must arrange for an expedited due process hearing. Expedited hearings must meet the requirements of standard due process hearings (see Chapter 3), except that the decision must be rendered within 45 days of the parent request for hearing without extensions or continuances. Time periods for mandated exchange of evidence are shortened from 5 to 2 business days prior to the hearing, and individual states may establish different procedural rules for expedited hearings. Decisions resulting from expedited hearings may be appealed the same as nonexpedited due process hearing decisions. Mediation remains available as an alternative dispute resolution process.

"Stay-Put" (Status Quo) and AES

Unlike the typical due process hearing requested by parents, a parent request for a hearing regarding disciplinary placements involving AES and related manifestation determinations do not result in the child remaining in the current educational placement ("stay-put"). Instead, the child remains in the AES until the hearing officer renders a decision, or until time of placement in AES expires, whichever occurs first. Of course, the parent and school may mutually agree on a placement alternative to AES.

Normally, following the expiration of the time of placement in AES, the student will be placed back in the previous educational placement. When the school proposes to change the student's educational placement through the IEP change-in-placement process following an AES placement, the parent may challenge the school's proposed change in placement. In these situations, the student will still normally be returned to the previous educational placement.

When, during the pending due process proceeding on the proposed change-in-placement, school personnel consider a return to the student's previous educational placement to be dangerous for the child or others, the school may seek an expedited due process hearing on the issue. In an expedited proceeding, the school may seek a hearing officer's ruling allowing an additional alternative placement by the school for up to 45 days. Subsequent additional expedited hearings may be requested by school officials if deemed necessary.

If the parent due process hearing request is for the purpose of challenging disciplinary decisions other than those regarding placements in AES and related manifestation determinations, such as an expulsion and related manifestation decisions, then the general "stay-put" rule applies (see Chapter 3). Thus, when parents appeal the proposed expulsion of a student or the school's determination that no manifestation existed regarding that situation, the school would be required to maintain the student in his current educational setting until the dispute was resolved. That had been the consensus of court rulings prior to the enactment of the 1997 Amendments.

Noneligible Student Discipline Protections

Any student not currently identified as being eligible for special education, and who is in danger of being disciplined for violation of school rules, may assert protections provided for identified students, when the school had "knowledge that the student was a student with a disability" prior to the behavior that precipitated the disciplinary action. If the school did not have knowledge that the student had a disability and was entitled to special education prior to the misconduct, then the student may be subjected to the same disciplinary procedures as students without disabilities.

Much of the philosophy or policy inherent in the "knowledge" provision is based in the school's duty to continuously carry out its "child find" function. School staff members are expected to refer students for evaluation when their behavior or performance indicates they may have a disability covered by the IDEA, even when they are "advancing from grade to grade" (34 C.F.R. § 300.121 (e), 2000).

A school is considered to have "knowledge" of a student's disability when:

- the parent has expressed concern to school staff that the student is in need of special education and related services;
- the parent has requested an evaluation of the student to determine eligibility for special education services;
- the behavior or performance of the student demonstrates the need for services; or
- the student's teacher, or other school personnel, has expressed concern about the child's behavior or performance to school personnel

responsible for child find or the special education referral system.

A school is deemed to not have "knowledge" when, as a result of the information it had previously received, the school either:

- conducted an evaluation and determined that the child was not eligible; or
- determined that an evaluation was not necessary.

In both of these determinations, the school must provide notice of its determination that is consistent with other parent notification requirements, including provision of parental safeguards information. Parents should have had the opportunity to challenge the school determinations regarding their child's eligibility for special education.

If a parent request for evaluation for a non-identified student is made during the time the student is being disciplined, then an evaluation and determination of eligibility must be expedited. Until the requested evaluation is completed, the student will remain in the educational placement determined by the school. If the child is subsequently determined to be a child with a disability and is eligible for special education, then the school must provide the child special education and related services, including those required under the disciplinary procedures of the IDEA, if appropriate.

FAPE Continues

Because exclusions from school will have a significant negative impact on a student's ability to later succeed in school, FAPE must be provided for all removals exceeding 10 school days in the same school year, whether or not a change in placement resulted. Beginning on the 11th day, the school must ensure that the child is provided FAPE. For students with disabilities suspended for 10 school days or less in the school year, the school is not required by federal regulations to provide special education programs and services, unless students without disabilities are provided educational services.

When several suspensions of 10 school days or less in one school year accumulate to more than 10 school days of suspension but do not constitute a change in placement, for each subsequent removal, school personnel must determine, in consultation with the student's special education teacher, the extent to which maintenance of services to the child are necessary to enable the child to progress in the general curriculum and to appropriately advance toward achieving IEP goals. The school must continue to provide those special services even though the child may be suspended from school. Extensive previous exclusions from classes will likely mean that many of the services contained in the IEP must be provided to allow the student to advance toward meeting IEP goals.

In the situation of a student who has been placed in an AES owing to drugs, weapons, or violence, the criteria for such settings must be reviewed and approved by the IEP team.

When the behavior of a child is determined to not be a manifestation of the child's disabilities and the child is excluded from school for more than 10 consecutive school days owing to expulsion or long-term suspension, or accumulated suspensions exceeding 10 school days resulting in change-in-placement, the child's IEP team must determine the extent of services to be available to the student. The FAPE services required are those necessary to enable the child to appropriately progress in the general curriculum and appropriately advance toward achieving the IEP goals.

Those schools which may consider expulsion or other long-term exclusion of students with disabilities will want to consult state funding laws for a determination of the impact of exclusion of a student on future school revenues. Because schools are required to continue providing services (FAPE) to students after they are excluded, school officials may want some assurance that the school will continue to receive the funds to provide those services.

Referral to Law Enforcement

Schools may report crimes committed by students with disabilities to appropriate authorities, if it would also do so regarding students without disabilities. However, schools may not use this process to circumvent their IDEA responsibilities, such as IEP review and revision and manifestation determinations. Law enforcement and judicial authorities may exercise their regular jurisdiction over children with disabilities who commit crimes.

A school reporting a crime committed by a child with a disability must ensure that copies of special education and disciplinary records of the child are transmitted for consideration by the appropriate authorities to whom it reports the crime, but only to the extent that education record transmission is permitted under the Family Educational Rights and Privacy Act (FERPA). The transfer of such records is permitted under FERPA only when state statute allows or requires such record transfer to the juvenile justice system for the purpose of effectively serving the needs of the student prior to adjudication. Law enforcement authorities must verify in writing that the transferred records will not be disclosed to third parties, except as provided under state law.

The FERPA also allows the transfer of student records when a school complies with a court order or subpoena and attempts to notify the parents in advance of compliance, and when student record disclosure is made in connection with a health or safety emergency.

Unresolved Discipline Issues

From the foregoing complex details of the student discipline provisions of the IDEA, it is difficult to imagine that any issues were not covered in the 1997 Amendments. Some were not covered fully, however. The following are a few of the remaining unresolved legal issues involving the discipline of students with disabilities, and more are likely to arise owing to the complex nature of the 1997 Amendments. The implementation of virtually every IDEA provision regarding discipline will create controversy, and schools are likely to be hard pressed to defend many of their disciplinary actions in court (Mead, 1998).

Minor Discipline

The IEP requirements of the IDEA provide a proactive approach to student behavior issues so that they may be addressed through the IEP development and review process. The IEP team must give special consideration to a child whose behavior "impedes his or her learning or that of others," and identify appropriate strategies, positive behavioral interventions, and supports to address that behavior. The regular education teacher's participation on the IEP team is required, in part, to assist in the determination of appropriate positive interventions and strategies for the child, as well as the identification of supplementary aids and services, program modifications, and supports for school personnel to assist the child's successful inclusion into the regular class. Implicit in the legal requirement of supplementary aids and services is continuing support for meeting a child's behavior problem needs.

Although required "positive" behavioral interventions are not defined in the IDEA, it is likely that they refer to educational approaches to behavior concerns as opposed to purely punitive approaches. Punishment as a way of dealing with student misbehavior is apparently being replaced in the IDEA by a philosophy of bringing about changes in student behavior through educational approaches.

The IDEA does not now, nor has it ever expressly addressed issues of traditional student discipline involving minor punishments. A number of court decisions, including that of the Supreme Court in *Honig v. Doe* (1988), have stated that minor disciplinary punishments of students with disabilities, such as time-out, detention, or restriction of privileges, do not implicate the IDEA so long as they do not result in a change in placement or a change in FAPE and they are also used with children without disabilities.

In one of the few court decisions directly on point, school district officials in Indiana successfully defended disciplinary actions of a minor nature against a hyperactive elementary student with emotional disabilities, who was responsible for considerable disruption in the regular classroom and cafeteria. The traditional punitive disciplinary actions upheld included corporal punishment and isolated seating in the classroom and cafeteria. The court found that including the student in the regular classroom setting established a responsibility in the teacher to maintain a classroom environment conducive to learning for all students in the class. The court concluded that a student with a disability "is not entitled to any unique exemptions or protections from a school's normal disciplinary procedures" (*Cole v. Greenfield-Central Community School*, 1986, pp. 58–59)

In-School Suspensions

Although the U.S. Department of Education did not expressly provide for in-school suspensions in its IDEA regulations, it has consistently drawn distinctions in its interpretations of the regulations between in-school suspensions which deprive a student of an IEP program and services and those which do not.

In-school suspensions that deprive students of IEP programs and services will probably count toward the 10-day suspension limitation provisions, both consecutive and accumulated. In-school suspensions which allow access to licensed special education teachers, IEP services, and accommodations may not count toward the

10-day exclusion limit, especially when they also allow for appropriate interactions with nondisabled peers. The determinative issue is whether in-school suspension deprived the student of FAPE. If so, the time spent in in-school suspension will likely apply toward the 10-day exclusion limitations for the school year, which trigger manifestation determination, functional behavioral assessment requirements, as well as continuation of FAPE.

Dangerous Students

In *Honig v. Doe* (1988), the Supreme Court stated that when the actions of the student were hazardous to the student or to others, schools could attempt to obtain court orders which would allow schools to remove students from education placements on a temporary basis. A very heavy burden of proof was assigned to schools in their effort to obtain such court orders. The 1997 Amendments now provide that schools may request that a hearing officer direct the child be placed in an AES for behavior which presents a danger to the student or to others. It is not clear whether Congress intended to deprive schools of the right to continue to also go to court to obtain court ordered approval of their actions to temporarily remove violent students (Mead, 1998, p. 526). OSEP has taken the position that schools may do either.

What the Future Holds

Experience has shown that it pays for schools to develop clear and consistent policies based on the requirements of law. But the law is not always as straightforward as it sounds. It is not fixed; it is continually being modified by court decisions, administrative interpretations, and new legislation. The information provided in this book, because it has been simplified, is a guideline for use in many situations, but it cannot be guaranteed to predict the legal outcome of every situation. It is a good practice for edu-

cational leaders to update themselves periodically through professional publications, professional development programs, and by requesting opinions from the school district's attorney.

THE IEP PROCESS

The authors want to again remind readers that the IEP process continues to provide educators with more than adequate tools to evaluate student behavior needs, determine solutions, and marshal the resources, both inside and outside the school, necessary to provide all children with disabilities an appropriate educational program behavior plan component. The law even allows for educational programming in institutionalized and residential settings when appropriate for an individual student. Only when parents are so strongly opposed to the proposed educational solution that they will challenge the IEP team decision through due process hearings will the effective, efficient, and solution-oriented IEP process be disrupted. Compared with the near certainty of disruptions inherent in unilateral school actions, such as proposed unilateral expulsions and AES placements, and the opportunity for parent challenges to school decisions they present, the IEP process stands out as an empowering tool for educators and parents working together to resolve student behavior concerns of importance to all in the school environment.

THE CONTINUING DILEMMA

The courts have, in numerous decisions, limited the traditional unilateral discretionary authority of school officials in disciplining students with disabilities. These rulings have prevented schools from expelling students with disabilities when the misconduct was related to the disability, no matter how serious the behavioral infraction, and they have forced the readmission of some students to previous educational placements. Moreover, many court decisions have been based on what seem to be technical or procedural issues rather than on substantive ones. The result was the appearance of a dual system of discipline which required schools to discipline students with disabilities differently than students without disabilities. This resulted in a concern that the rights of violent students with disabilities took precedence over the need for a safe school environment. By creating AES placements and requiring functional behavioral assessment plans and manifestation determination in the 1997 Amendments to the IDEA, Congress attempted to strike a balance between the two interests. However, not all observers believe that the appearance of a dual system of discipline is likely to lessen under the current student discipline provisions of the IDEA (Turnbull & Turnbull, 1998, p. 60).

1997 Amendments—A New Balance, a New Approach

Zurkowski, Kelly, and Griswold (1998) agree with the Congressional assessment that the 1997 Amendments strike a balance between the rights of students with disabilities and the need for safe schools with a protected learning environment. They note that the long-term removal of students from school has had little value as a therapeutic behavioral intervention, and some students who act inappropriately actually *want* to be removed from school. They conclude that removing misbehaving students from the school environment may make schools safer for short periods, but the net effect is to make society less safe.

Zurkowski and colleagues see very positive student discipline changes in the 1997 Amendments, particularly in the shift in focus from punishment of students to one of addressing positive behavior change in students. The use of functional behavior assessment to identify the reason for the misbehavior and development of behavioral intervention plans to provide educa-

tors with the tools and resources to teach students new behaviors are viewed as the means for addressing student behavior problems in proactive, positive ways rather than from a reactive, punitive perspective. The requirement that schools continue to address behavioral problems of students, even in AES placements, is viewed favorably because it requires schools to address student behavior problems through education, rather than allowing schools to exclude students with disabilities.

When traditional disciplinary practices based on punishment are examined closely, research does not validate their continued use. Glennon (1993) has made a compelling argument that educators must create a new disciplinary paradigm which views misbehaving students as learners and behavioral education as an integral part of a general education program. According to Glennon, educators must set aside their traditional belief system that student misbehavior is the result of evil intent (justifying punishment) or illness (requiring medication) and focus on what educators do best: evaluate, diagnose, plan, and prescribe learning experiences, including those designed to improve behavior. Educators need to assume greater responsibility for focusing on the nature and causes of student misbehavior. They need to design programs and services which minimize, control, and perhaps even overcome students' previously learned inappropriate reactions to situations.

Food for Thought

What if educator and parent complaints about the unfairness of a dual system of school discipline for students with disabilities and those without disabilities are correct? What, however, if their proposed solution of allowing educators to treat students with disabilities like nondisabled students misses an important point? The question may really be about how we discipline all students, and whether we should consider using the new tools Congress requires for students with disabilities for all students. The past disciplinary approach of using punishment only has not served education or society well. Now may be the time to revisit our schools' disciplinary goals and consider better, long-lasting educational approaches to student discipline.

APPROACHES TO RESOLVING PROBLEMS

Student behavioral problems, from the most routine to the most extreme, have causes. Many of these causes—family problems and physiological, social, and economic factors—are frustratingly outside the education leader's authority and control. But there are causes that schools can address and preventive measures that educators can initiate that have been proved successful.

The first place to look is the school itself. Especially for children with disabilities, the school experience is likely to be one of frustration, which can lead to classroom failure. Resulting feelings of worthlessness, anger, and frustration may be acted out through inappropriate behavior. Students who do not find success and recognition in regular school activities often seek out negative forms of attention through inappropriate behavior. Even negative attention, such as scolding and removal from class, may be reinforcing to the student who has little other opportunity for positive recognition at home or in school.

The challenge for educators is to create an educational environment that provides all students with feelings of success and self-worth. Principals play a very important role in setting the tone for a school climate accepting of diverse students and staff. As such, they must display a sense of humor and be open to new ideas, supportive, nonjudgmental, visible, and willing to interact effectively with all students.

For students with disabilities, the IEP should be developed and placement decisions made with the school and the classroom climate in mind. An appropriate placement should be one in which the child can develop positive relationships with the school staff, with peers, and with self. If this is not happening, and if the youngster's academic record and behavior point to a lack of success in the program, then the law places the burden of responsibility for change in that program (improvement) on the school.

Frequently, changes in the school environment can have a positive effect on student behavior. The BD program mentioned at the beginning of this chapter is a good example. After the initial difficulties, the school made several changes that helped alleviate behavior problems. The program was moved from its first location in an isolated, unattractive wing of the school to a pleasant, wood-paneled classroom. The students were included in regular classes most of the day, and were viewed as regular members of the high school population. Getting to know each other in regular classes helped reduce hostility between groups and provided positive behavior models among the students' peers. Finally, staff members set high expectations for all of the students in school and stuck with them. Reasonable standards, administered fairly, are good for all students.

Preventive Measures

As the aforementioned situation suggests, preventing discipline problems begins with creating positive, receptive attitudes and relationships among special and regular students and staff. It also begins with the expectation that students with disabilities can succeed and with the understanding that appropriate behavior is, and can be, learned. There are proven techniques, adaptable for classroom use, for improving the behavior of children with disabilities. All students, including those with disabilities, benefit from sound classroom management and appropriate discipline systems.

The 1997 Amendments cleared the way for use of federal special education funds for student IEP services in the regular class and regular activities "even if one or more nondisabled children benefit from such services" [§ 1413 (a) (4) (A)]. Consequently, the IDEA will likely result in a realization that school leaders, teachers, and support staff need to anticipate problems and be equipped with the knowledge and skills to enable them to appropriately respond to behavior problems. It is very likely that the future will see more individual student IEPs expressly provide for staff-development training in behavior modification and classroom management for regular class teachers and trained teacher associates as supplementary aids and services or related services. As a result, all students in the regular school setting will benefit.

School-Wide

Nelson, Crabtree, Marchand-Martella, & Martella (1998) have written about an elementary school that implemented a school-wide comprehensive discipline plan designed to help prevent disruptive behavior from developing and then preventing it from becoming entrenched. The basis for the prevention plan was a lively, engaging curriculum and effective teaching practices. Beyond that, all students were taught the behavioral expectations of the school. Regular supervision of common school areas associated with student misbehavior was conducted primarily by trained unlicensed staff.

The teachers used a simple but effective shared system of working with student classroom problems that minimized disruptive negative classroom exchanges and power struggles, and provided a structure for change. When a student's behavior disrupted a class, the teacher sent the child with a note to a colleague's classroom. As soon as practical, the receiving teacher questioned the student privately about the situation and asked if there might have been a better way for the student to have dealt with the situation. After a brief period of reflection and

cooling down, the student was returned to the original classroom with a minimum of disruption to the learning environment of both classrooms.

Individual students exhibiting severe disruptive behavior patterns were identified and provided intensive, multi-agency positive interventions (wraparound interventions).

An important unexpected side-effect of this concerted and comprehensive effort at improving discipline from a school-wide perspective, in a school with 75% of its students qualifying for free and reduced lunch, was greatly improved academic performance (20% on standardized tests). This performance growth was attributed to teachers and students spending more time on instruction and learning and less time on disciplinary disruptions.

Efforts to build school-wide positive behavior programs are rapidly increasing through the use of new and revised social behavior curricula. Instruction on appropriate behavior school-wide is increasing in its implementation and is not used solely with students exhibiting undesirable behavior (Horner & Sugai, 2000). A study of the use of school-based prevention programs focusing on conflict resolution and peer mediation in three middle schools showed a decline in overall office referrals for disruptive and aggressive behavior (Daunic, Smith, Robinson, Miller, & Landry, 2000). It was determined that middle school students can learn and implement the skills necessary for establishing an alternative dispute resolution program, especially when committed teachers and educational leaders were involved.

Classroom Prevention

Unfortunately, some schools are experiencing greater aggressive student behavior than ever before. It is unlikely, given our current social and cultural acquiescence to portrayals of violence on television, in movies and through leisure-time activities such as video games, that schools will be able to prevent all aggressive student behavior. But staff awareness and common sense can go a long way toward preventing much of the aggressive student behavior found in schools today. Abrams and Segal (1998) have determined that student aggression in school is often directly related to teacher behaviors and great reductions in student aggression can occur when teachers modify their classroom environments. Students with emotional and behavior disorders are like typical students who benefit from positive, well-organized class environments, only more so. Abrams and Segal offer an outline of the elements of such an environment (p. 12):

- Order, structure, and consistency;
- Well-organized and predictable environment;
- Clear and realistic expectations;
- Students experience success, academically and socially;
- Teachers are able to interpret communicative intent of students;
- Students are given choices and input into classroom decisions;
- Students are encouraged to express feelings;
- Students are able to socially interact with others;
- Students' psychological needs (belonging, safety, competence, and self-esteem) are met; and
- Positive teacher-student relationships.

Smith and Rivera (1995) have studied school discipline for a number of years, and they also have concluded that prevention techniques in the classroom are the foundation for successful discipline for the entire school. Some of the Smith and Rivera suggestions are summarized as follows:

- Rules communicate the teacher's expectations of behavior and establish guidelines for predictability and a sense of security in the classroom environment;
- Rules are positive and short, e.g., "raise your hand to speak," rather than "no talking;"

- Students are involved in rule development from the perspective of creating a learning environment;
- Promotion of understanding of the rules through class discussion of examples;
- Praise for those who follow the rules;
- Provide students with reminders, especially when rules are first initiated;
- Classroom environment management promotes more engaged instructional time;
- Have student materials organized and ready in advance;
- Supervise high traffic areas where students interact;
- Have lessons planned and well-thought out;
- Plan for smooth transition times;
- Provide warning signal "In 10 minutes we will . . . ;"
- Instruct on process "line up alphabetically;"
- Reminder of expected behavior;
- Reinforcement of proper behavior;
- Use a hierarchy of discipline interventions using mild, or less intrusive, interventions as much as possible. Regular use of severe discipline establishes a climate of a punitive nature; and
- Provide specific student feedback for appropriate behavior, e.g., "I appreciate your coming to class on time and bringing all your books."

Disciplinary Alternatives

Where traditional student discipline procedures are not successful or are legally barred, a number of effective disciplinary alternatives for students with or without disabilities remain. For instance, although short-term suspensions generally are legal, emphasis should be placed on disciplinary alternatives that allow the student to remain in school. Most student difficulties in school are exacerbated by absence from the classroom.

When relevant procedures under the IDEA are followed, the student's IEP may be modified or the student can be transferred to a different educational program (see Chapter 6 on placement). Educators frequently overlook this approach, even though it is obvious. The IEP process can be used for a variety of behavior solutions, including a change to a more restrictive placement, special training for the regular class teacher, assignment of a teacher associate, and the implementation of a behavior improvement plan (Jensen, 1996).

Many educators can point to past successes and the great potential of behavior modification techniques as means of improving student behavior. A behavior modification program for an individual student begins with specific description, careful observation, and recording of the behavior to be addressed. The second step is the selection of reasonable, measurable goals. Next, an appropriate reinforcer and reinforcement schedule must be chosen and contingencies planned.

While the program is being implemented, it is important to continue to observe the behavior and how often it occurs (collect data) and also to ensure that other staff members involved with this student are using the same techniques. Consistency is very important. A program should be maintained for at least several days before considering any alterations (Rutherford & Nelson, 1995).

A reinforcer for appropriate student behavior must be something the student actually wants. For example, verbal praise may not be an effective reinforcer for a child who is shy and easily embarrassed. In fact, it may be viewed as a punishment and tend to reduce the desired behavior. Negative behavior can also be reinforced through teacher attention or peer response. This should be carefully avoided. The most desirable reinforcers are natural or social ones, such as satisfaction, praise (if appropriate), approval, and teacher time and attention. These reinforcers may not be effective with all students, however. When necessary, other types of reinforcement may be paired with social re-

inforcers and then gradually faded out. The main types of reinforcers identified by Rutherford and Nelson are:

- Tangible reinforcers: material items valued by the student, e.g., stickers, candy, toys, and pizza, are often used with younger children in conjunction with a token program;
- Activity reinforcement: the opportunity to engage in desired activities; e.g., play outside, read, play games, computer access; and
- Tokens, points, checks, or other symbols that can be accumulated and cashed in later for one of the above.

Reinforcers should be changed when they cease to produce results. If a certain action is promised as the consequence of negative behavior or positive behavior, then the teacher must follow through. Again, consistency is very important.

Punishment should never be the only means used to control behavior. It is important to work to increase appropriate behavior, even while maintaining a program to reduce problem behavior. Attempts to stop inappropriate behavior are more likely to succeed when positive behaviors are in place to replace the inappropriate behaviors.

Other Behavior Interventions

In addition to these commonly used behavior modification programs, Rutherford and Nelson also suggest other behavior interventions which have proven successful in a variety of settings:

- *Behavioral contracting.* The educator and the student negotiate and implement a formal written agreement which specifies the behavior to be increased or decreased, the student's goals regarding the behavior (remake friends), and the consequences associated with completing or not completing the content;

- *Modeling.* Students observe adults or peers demonstrating the skill steps necessary to perform appropriate social behaviors and observe their own behaviors being reinforced. The student imitates the behaviors and is reinforced. This is frequently used with complex social skills, such as responding to failure or anger, being left out, and dealing with group pressure;

- *Self-modeling using videotape.* A number of studies have confirmed the positive reinforcement value of videotaping and replaying students modeling appropriate behaviors. Buggey (1999) has established that growth in appropriate behaviors has been especially promising when coded videotapes of student behaviors are edited to remove examples of undesirable behaviors, and the student watches himself in only positive behavior reinforcing situations; and

- *Social reinforcement.* Provide consistent verbal and other feedback, attention, and approval for desired student behavior. Praise from respected adults is a powerful tool, especially when used in conjunction with other behavior enhancement efforts.

Johnson and Johnson (1999) advocate a program whereby students monitor their own behavior, compile data, and graph the results. This is especially useful when combined with classroom work involving issues of staying on task, completing assignments, appropriate behavior, and accuracy of work completed. Students are trained to perform:

- Self-observation—look at one's own behavior at a given predetermined time;
- Self-assessment—decide if the target behavior has occurred;
- Self-recording—record self-assessment results;
- Self-determination—set a goal for success and identify a reinforcer; and
- Self-administration of reinforcement—administer a reinforcer to oneself.

Self-regulation helps maintain the student's attention on the issue of concern and provides the student with ownership in the process of remediation of the target behavior.

Behavior Reduction Measures

In addition to the continuing use of behavior modification techniques and sound school-wide disciplinary policies, other measures have been used successfully by schools to reduce inappropriate behaviors. These behavior reduction procedures work most effectively when combined with behavior enhancement techniques (Rutherford & Nelson, 1995):

Response Cost

This involves the removal of reinforcers following inappropriate targeted behaviors. Two of the most common are removal of the opportunity to participate (e.g., loss of 1 minute of recess from a special recess time for each use of a vulgar term) and removal of tokens in response to inappropriate behaviors. In the latter, students are awarded a fixed number of tokens each day and tokens are retracted when targeted behaviors occur.

Time-Out

Many schools already use some form of "time-out" to remove a disruptive student from stimuli that may be reinforcing to inappropriate behavior.

Time-out is a complex intervention which may be used at different levels, from planned ignoring of the student in class to student seclusion. Some schools have carried the concept further by instituting a time-out room staffed by personnel from the guidance program. This room functions both as a means of defusing immediate problems and as a preventive measure. Students may be directed to, or may self-assign themselves to, time-out to talk out problems before they escalate into disciplinary crises.

Behaviorists caution, however, that time-out should be used primarily as a means of removing students from positive reinforcement (the attention of peers, for example). If the pupils' time-out takes them from situations they do not want to be in anyway, then what was intended as a punitive action becomes reinforcing. Time-out also should not be used over extended periods of time (30 minutes or more) as a form of punishment. The intent of the time-out strategy is not to provide respite for staff.

As a substitute for conventional suspension, some schools have experimented with:

- In-school suspension: Students are sent to a supervised room for tutoring and drills. This type of program also has been staffed by trained volunteers.
- Saturday attendance: Students are required to come in for 4 hours of school work. Many educators have reported that this alternative is especially helpful for students who experience problems with truancy or tardiness.

Some authors call for a new perspective on school discipline which substitutes a variety of prevention components for punitive approaches such as zero-tolerance rules. Skiba and Peterson (2000) suggest a comprehensive combination of preventive approaches (called an "early response model" of discipline). Included are conflict resolution, social instruction, classroom strategies to prepare teachers on how to respond to situations without escalation, parent involvement, early warning signs training, crisis planning, school-wide discipline plans, and functional assessment and behavior plans for a variety of students, not just those in special education.

CULTURAL AWARENESS

In schools experiencing changes in the cultural makeup of the student body, special attention must be given to an appreciation of and tolerance for cultural differences in the area of student discipline. Teachers and administrators who expect all students to immediately adopt the majority white culture are confronting many years of ingrained cultural practice. McIntyre (1992) has warned of the cultural differences regarding discipline, and the inherent problems of interpretation in them. As a result, culturally-based behavior that is expected in some environments may result in referral to the administration for disciplinary action. Although majority ethnic teachers expect students to be compliant, docile, and responsive to authority in a predictable manner, consistent with their own upbringing, the result is often interpreted by nonwhite students and parents as insensitive, offensive, and inappropriate and sometimes leads to counterproductive outcomes.

McIntyre has provided a number of examples of cultural misunderstandings from educational research. He noted that different cultures act differently toward authoritative methods. Although lowered eyes during disciplinary confrontations are associated by the white teachers with deceit or inattention, many Asian, African American, and Hispanic children lower their eyes as a sign of respect or submission. The direct eye contact often demanded by white educators may in some cultures actually indicate defiance, rather than respect. Some students' smiles during discipline as a result of their anxiety or an effort to appease the teacher may be misinterpreted as disrespect. The quiet, inactive, nonemotive behavior expected by white educators in some situations is often contrary to student cultures evidenced in vocal responses, physical movement, and ways of showing each other attention. As a result, many culturally ingrained behaviors are interpreted as hostile, disruptive, and evidencing an "attitude" on the part of students. Some cultures teach their young to fight so they will not be victimized in their tough neighborhoods. Some students are often under great cultural pressure to not achieve academically or be successful in school and to use misbehavior as a camouflage for their academic efforts.

Townsend (2000) has noted that many classroom activities require students to be seated and classroom arrangement is structured in ways that limit physical movement. Because African American children have a propensity for physical movement, highly structured activities and room arrangements may contribute to inappropriate behaviors. More active learning methodologies, such as cooperative learning, are recommended.

Misguided, but well-intentioned, educators may end up with counterproductive results when they do not take cultural differences into account when disciplining students. McIntyre (1992) has recommended a lessening of clear distinctions of behavior in a judgmental right or wrong mode and suggests a greater awareness of how culture impacts student and parent behavior. Better student management can often be achieved through the recognition of cultural differences and working with, rather than against, such differences. He also recommended an approach that transcends cultural differences—a positive, helpful approach to discipline, rather than a negative, confrontational one. He concluded that when educators are knowledgeable about culturally-based student behavior, they will be less likely to create much of the behavior about which they complain.

CONCLUSION

This chapter is not intended to be comprehensive in providing educational leaders with ideas for approaches to resolving problems of discipline and creating a school climate conducive to the pursuit of education. Dozens of good books, hundreds of articles in professional publications, and great staff-development opportunities are available to serve that end. The authors are truly pleased at the great variety of quality resources currently available. The key to success is to first of all get the staff and students to a point of readiness and then match to the individual school situation, probably through trial and error, the various approaches available.

One of the authors attended an IEP meeting regarding an extremely bright middle-school student with ADHD. The problem of focus for the meeting was the school's inability to maintain behavioral expectations for the boy. After about a 20-minute discussion, the boy's resource-room teacher expressed his frustration, saying, "I have run out of ideas; my bag of tricks is empty!" What would be an appropriate professional response to this situation?

The same author attended a meeting with a special education administrator from a tribal school in Mississippi. The administrator told about how her schools had previously sent its students with severe behavioral problems to private residential programs for care, treatment, and education. Then, several years earlier, the institutions told the tribal schools that they were no longer able to work with some of their students because they were too difficult. Faced with the return of students with whom school staff had not previously worked, the staff began assimilating information about alternative approaches to discipline and contacted consultants, researchers, and authors about various methodologies. After great study and discussion, the school identified a philosophy and system of discipline that met its goals for the children, the schools, and the tribe. School staff were trained in the system and the children who had been institutionalized returned home to attend school. After 4 years' time, evaluation of the program had established a marked improvement in the behavior of the returned children as well as a satisfactory assimilation back into the tribal and community environment. What would be an appropriate professional response to this situation?

View from the Court Bench

Goss v. Lopez, 1975

The well-known case, *Goss v. Lopez*, set the standard for constitutional due process in student suspensions from school. The Supreme Court ruled that the degree of due process afforded to students in the event of a suspension of 10 days or less need not be as extensive as the due process required if the suspension were to be for a longer period. In the case of a suspension of 10 days or less, the minimum due process that was required included a statement (written or oral) to the student of the charges or allegations against the student; if the student denied the charges, a statement explaining the evidence available; and, most important, an opportunity for the student to explain the student's version of what happened. (Although few, if any, courts have ruled on the issue, parents or advocates may need to be involved in situations of students unable to understand or comprehend what is occurring.) The right to a more formal hearing, the right to have counsel present, etc., may be required in situations where a more serious loss of rights is a possible outcome (i.e., long-term suspension, expulsion).

As with any student, in the event that a child with disabilities is excluded from a public school for even short periods of time, or expelled or excluded for more than 10 school days, school officials must provide appropriate constitutional procedural due process.

Honig v. Doe, 1988

In 1988, the Supreme Court reviewed a lower court ruling that held that special education students could not be unilaterally kept out of school by school officials even when the student's conduct was disruptive and potentially dangerous. The case involved students whose parents had filed appeals of their impending expulsions and argued that the "stay-put" provisions of the IDEA prohibited exclusion of the students from school while the appeal was pending. The Supreme Court agreed with the lower court. It said that in enacting the IDEA, Congress clearly meant to strip schools of their unilateral authority to exclude students with disabilities pending the outcome of appeals filed to challenge the proposed change in placement which results from expulsion. The Court concluded that schools may suspend for up to 10 days those students with disabilities who are dangerous or who severely disrupt the school environment. The 10-day period provides school officials with time to seek additional student evaluation and an alternative placement. When 10 days is not sufficient to find an alternative placement with which the parent agrees, the school must seek a court injunction to keep the student out of school for more than 10 days. In such situations, a heavy burden falls on the school to establish a safety need to keep the student out of school.

REFERENCES

Abrams, B. J., & Segal, A. (1998). How to prevent aggressive behavior. *Teaching Exceptional Children, 30* (4), 10–15.

Analysis of Comments and Changes, 1999. *Federal Register, 64* (48), 12537–12668.

Assistance to States for the Education of Children with Disabilities and the Early Intervention Program for Infants and Toddlers with Disabilities, 34 C.F.R. Part 300 (2000).

Buggey, T. (1999). "Look I'm on TV." Using videotaped self-modeling to change behavior. *Teaching Exceptional Children, 31* (4), 27–30.

Cole v. Greenfield-Central Community School, 657 F. Supp. 56 (S.D. Ind. 1986).

Daunic, A. P., Smith, S. W., Robinson, T. R., Miller, M. D., & Landry, K. L. (2000). School-wide conflict resolution and peer mediation programs: Experiences in three middle schools. *Intervention in School and Clinic, 36* (2), 94–100.

Ellingson, S. A., Miltenberger, R. G., Stricker, J., Galensky, T. L., & Garlinghouse, M. (2000). Functional assessment and interventions for challenging behaviors in the classroom by general classroom teachers. *Journal of Positive Behavior Interventions, 2* (2), 85–97.

Glennon, T. (1993). Disability ambiguities: Confronting barriers to the education of students with emotional disabilities. *Tennessee Law Review, 60,* 295–369.

Goss v. Lopez, 419 U.S. 565, 95 S.Ct. 729 (1975).

Honig v. Doe, 484 U.S. 305, 108 S.Ct. 592 (1988).

Horner, R. H., & Sugai, G. (2000). School-wide behavior support: An emerging initiative. *Journal of Positive Behavior Interventions, 2* (4), 231–232.

House Report No. 105–95 (1997). U.S.C. *Congressional and Administrative News,* West, 78–146.

Huefner D. S. (1998). The Individuals With Disabilities Education Act Amendments of 1997. *Education Law Reporter, 122,* 1103–1122.

Individuals With Disabilities Education Act, 20 U.S.C. §§ 1401–1487.

Jensen, G. (Spring 1996). Disciplining students with disabilities: Problems under the Individuals With Disabilities Education Act. B.Y.U. *Education and Law Journal,* 34–54.

Johnson, L. R., & Johnson, E. E. (1999). Teaching students to regulate their own behavior. *Teaching Exceptional Children, 31* (4), 6–10.

McConnel, M. E., Hilvitz, D. B., & Cox, C. J. (1998). Functional assessment: A systematic process for assessment and intervention in general and special education classrooms. *Intervention in School and Clinic, 34* (1), 10–20.

McIntyre, T. (1992). The culturally sensitive disciplinarian. *Severe Behavior Disorders Monograph, Vol. 15,* Reston, VA: Council for Exceptional Children, 107–115.

Mead, J. F. (1998). Expressions of congressional intent: Examining the 1997 Amendments to the IDEA. *Education Law Reporter, 126,* 511–531.

Nelson, J. R., Crabtree, M., Marchand-Martella, N., & Martella, R. (1998). Teaching good behavior in the whole school. *Teaching Exceptional Children, 30* (40), 4–9.

Osborne, A. G. (1997). Making the manifestation determination when disciplining a special education student. *Education Law Reporter, 119,* 323–330.

Rutherford, R. B., & Nelson, C. M. (1995). Management of aggression and violent behavior in schools. *Focus on Exceptional Children, 27* (6), 1–15.

Skiba, R. J., & Peterson, R. L. (2000). School discipline at a cross-roads: From zero tolerance to early response. *Exceptional Children, 66* (3), 335–347.

Smith, C. R. (2000). Behavioral and discipline provisions of IDEA '97: Implicit competencies yet to be confirmed. *Exceptional Children, 66* (3), 403–412.

Smith, D. D., & Rivera, D. P. (1995). Discipline in special education and general education settings. *Focus on Exceptional Children, 27* (5), 1–16.

Townsend, B. L. (2000). The disproportionate discipline of African-American learners. Reducing school suspensions and expulsions. *Exceptional Children 66* (33), 381–391.

Turnbull, H. R., & Turnbull, A. P. (1998). *Free appropriate public education: The law and children with disabilities* (5th ed.). Denver: Love.

Turnbull, H. R. III, Wilcox, B. L., Stowe, M., Raper, C., & Hedges, L. P. (2000). Public policy foundations for positive behavioral interventions, strategies, and supports. *Journal of Positive Behavior Interventions, 2* (4), 218–230.

Yell, M. L. (1998). *The law and special education.* Upper Saddle River, NJ: Merrill/Prentice-Hall.

Zurkowski, J. K., Kelly, P. S., & Griswold, D. E. (1998). Discipline and IDEA 1997: Instituting a new balance. *Intervention in School and Clinic, 34* (1), 3–9.

RECOMMENDED READINGS

Abrams, B. J., & Segal, A. (1998). How to prevent aggressive behavior. *Teaching Exceptional Children, 30* (4), 10–15. This excellent article reviews a great deal of the research on the causes and prevention of student aggression.

Anderson, C., & Katsiyannis, A. (1997). By what token economy? A classroom learning tool for inclusive settings. *Teaching Exceptional Children, 29* (4), 65–67. This article details a complex token economy used in an entire fifth-grade classroom.

Buggey, T. (1999). "Look I'm on TV." Using videotaped self-modeling to change behavior. *Teaching*

Exceptional Children, 31 (4), 27–30. This article reviews the research on various uses of videotaping students' behavior and provides practical uses of such videotapes to bring about changes in student behavior.

Horner R. H., & Sugai, G. (2000). School-wide behavior support: An emerging initiative. *Journal of Positive Behavior Interventions, 2* (4), 231–232. This is the introductory article to articles providing descriptions of seven different implementations of school-wide behavior support systems.

McConnel, M. E., Hilvitz, D. B., & Cox, C. (1998). Functional assessment: A systematic process for assessment and intervention in general and special education classrooms. *Intervention in School and Clinic, 34* (1), 10–20. This excellent article makes functional assessment understandable and "functional" for educators.

McIntyre, T. (1992). The culturally sensitive disciplinarian. *Severe Behavior Disorders Monograph, 15*, 107–115. Reston, VA: Council for Exceptional Children. This brief article presents an excellent summary of the issue of cultural considerations to be taken into account when disciplining students.

Nelson, J. R., Crabtree, M., Mareband-Martella, N., & Martella, R. (1998). Teaching good behavior in the whole school. *Teaching Exceptional Children, 30* (4) 4–9. This article details a school-wide discipline plan, including a classroom management strategy that has the potential for wide application.

Saren, D. (1999). The decision tree: A tool for achieving behavioral change. *Teaching Exceptional Children, 31* (4), 36–40. This article presents a

methodology to help IEP teams determine what is behaviorally important for a child and what is not.

Relevant Federal Regulations

34 C.F.R. 300.121	Free appropriate public education (including that for suspended and expelled students).
.146	Suspension and expulsion rates.
.347	IEP content.
.519	Change of placement for disciplinary removals.
.520	Authority of school personnel (discipline).
.521	Authority of hearing officer (discipline).
.522	Determination of setting.
.523	Manifestation determination.
.524	Determination that behavior was not manifestation of disability.
.525	Parent appeal.
.526	Placement during hearings (discipline).
.527	Protections for children not yet eligible for special education and related services.
.528	Expedited due process hearings (disciplinary).
.529	Referral to and action by law enforcement and judicial authorities.

PART II

ADMINISTRATIVE ISSUES

CHAPTER 10

STUDENT RELATIONSHIPS

Focus

Although the IDEA and Section 504 require that students with disabilities be educated and participate in activities "to the maximum extent appropriate" in the company of their nondisabled peers, simply placing the two groups in physical proximity may not in itself create attitudes of acceptance and, in fact, may reinforce previously learned negative stereotypes. Educational leaders are, however, responsible for providing and supporting educational programming that will serve all childrens' needs for the "long haul," not only the immediate.

Rationale

Individuals with disabilities deserve to live as typical a life as possible. To this end, the public schools have a responsibility not only to provide such children with an appropriate education but also, in support of this goal, to combat negative attitudes and to create an atmosphere of acceptance and appreciation in which disabled and nondisabled students can form a variety of positive relationships. Social factors are as important as academic ones in preparing students for an active and satisfying role in the adult community. This means that educators must develop and provide all students, those with and those without disabilities, as representative a lifestyle and personal experiences as is feasible. Because the future will be one of acceptance of and accommodation for individuality, all students should begin experiencing the future now.

Approaches

Educators must be aware that successful inclusion requires active efforts to create appropriate educational environments and receptive attitudes by regular education students. School leaders should model positive, accepting, nonjudgmental attitudes toward special education students and their teachers and provide equal opportunities for status within the school to all students. The importance of peer relationships should be stressed and principals should encourage teachers to establish structured learning experiences, such as cooperative learning, peer tutoring, and collaborative problem-solving. Students with disabilities, under reasonable expectations for their performance, can work interdependently with nondisabled peers.

PEER INTERACTIONS

It is easy for school leaders to remember that federal law, both the IDEA and Section 504, contain provisions which require that the education of children with disabilities be provided in the LRE and that consideration of educational placement must begin in the regular education classroom environment. However, many administrators without experience or background in special education programming do not fully understand the public policy behind those legal mandates. Time, experience, review of educational research, and reflection will be enough for most educational leaders to be able to better "walk in the shoes" of those children with disabilities and their parents and come to a clearer understanding of the life-long importance of inclusionary practices in schools.

Much educational theory and research in the recent past has focused on child-adult (teacher, parent) relationships. When authors referred to peer interaction at all, they were most likely to approach it as a problem of off-task behavior and classroom disruption. Parents, for their part, also were likely to take a negative tack, worrying about peer influences in such areas as drugs, disobedience, and sexuality. But those concerns, however important, are only part of the complex and vital role that peer relationships play in a child's learning. It is through interactions with their friends and classmates that children practice and learn socialized values, control of aggressive impulses, empathy for others, sex role identity, and social skills.

Because the importance of peer environment has such a significant impact on regular students, it is not surprising that the consistent separation of students with disabilities from their typically developing peer group would have some negative impact. One study reports that students with disabilities who are placed in separate classrooms for most academic subjects and in general education for only nonacademic subjects, such as art, gym, and music, do not have the same social development as do students with typical educational needs (Wenz-Gross & Siperstein, 1997). Instead, the more segregated students tend to seek social support from their peers much less than children without disabilities, and they even look less to family members for help in solving problems. As children with disabilities advance through adolescence, this lessening of both family support and peer social networking may place them at greater risk for not succeeding in life as adults.

Teachers need to make an effort to develop a favorable social as well as academic classroom environment and continue to role model acceptance of students with disabilities for the benefit of their nondisabled peers. The absence of a conscious effort by professional staff members to assist students with disabilities in their development of positive social support and intimacy in peer relationships may result in a life-long negative impact in an important area of human development.

Controversy

Many educators would argue that a greater opportunity for interaction with nondisabled students is an argument in favor of inclusion. Others, especially some parents of students with severe disabilities, would say that it is an argument against it. In a special school or classroom setting, the latter group argues, children are not judged inferior by their able-bodied classmates and are not as susceptible to teasing and exclusion as they are in an integrated class with nondisabled students. In addition to the academic advantages of smaller, more homogeneous special classes, the partisans say, there are social advantages. In a school where all children are disabled, there is widespread understanding, acceptance, and lack of prejudice. There are similar modes of communication (e.g., signing among deaf students) and similar constraints and needs—all of which foster an experience of equality and make the development of friendships less difficult. The parents and advocates of some groups of children with disabilities (e.g., aural/oral philosophy involving students with hearing impairments) argue that segregation for specialized training in the early years will allow a greater likelihood of later integration into society as adults.

Proponents of inclusion, on the other hand, emphasize the necessity not of evading situations laden with potential problems and prejudices, but of confronting them and working for change and understanding. Certainly, inclusion advocates acknowledge that stereotyping and prejudice exist. But, they argue, these never will disappear if persons with disabilities do not have an opportunity to interact with nondisabled individuals and to exchange those one-dimensional stereotypes for the richer experiences of personal contact. If the information and attitudes gleaned from such experiences are to be received clearly, then the contacts must begin in childhood.

It is unlikely that adults will ever completely eliminate teasing and ridicule among children. Educators can, however, make a conscious effort to teach students about valuing differences and showing mutual respect, but it is a full-time job. Sandra Lawrence, a former president of the National Elementary School Principals' Association once told one of the authors about how constant a job it is: "You work hard for months, thinking that you are making an important difference, then you hear one child on the playground call another 'a retard,' and you start all over again."

Villa and colleagues (1995, p. 155) have concluded that the real solution to teasing is teacher and administrator modeling. Students observe and imitate adult behaviors toward others and process adult actions in dealing with conflict. In the joint experience spanning many years, these seven educator/researchers found that less ridicule and teasing occur in inclusive schools.

Current Realities

This has been the controversy: What is the current status? Is inclusion meeting its social goals? The results, like those of racial integration programs such as magnet schools, are a resounding "yes" and "no." Which is to say:

- It is no longer a question of whether to integrate and include; the laws have clearly mandated such a change, and it is being carried out.
- On a social level there have been successes, cases in which integrated placement has resulted in greater respect and understanding among people of different groups.
- There also have been failures. Inadequately planned educational integration of the disabled, as with different racial/ethnic populations, has been known to increase existing prejudices and antagonism, rather than to dissipate them and also to contribute negatively to the self-image of students with disabilities.
- Integrated and inclusion education per se and, more specifically, the means of bringing them about, are still controversial, but are becoming much less so.
- When done properly, integration and inclusion of children with disabilities is successful for students and for staff.

In short, the need for positive social interactions in childhood is great and sometimes is difficult to meet in today's heterogeneous classrooms. Principals and other educational leaders, although they have little voice in the matter of heterogeneity, have an obligation to recognize both the benefits and the obstacles to such interactions and to work conscientiously to foster a positive educational experience for all students.

They should also recognize that students understand and accept reasonable accommodations in meeting the needs of individuals. In a synthesis of 20 studies investigating the perceptions of thousands of students in all grade levels, Klinger and Vaughn (1999) found that both students with and without learning disabilities appreciated classroom adaptations and accommodations that facilitated learning. All students liked instruction about learning strategies and a combination of text learning and activity-based learning. They valued teachers who slowed down instruction when needed, explained concepts, and taught material in different ways so that all students can learn.

THE INCLUSION MODEL

The fear of adverse consequences to the children with disabilities in inclusion settings has been of concern over the years, but has proved largely unfounded. Some educators' and parents' concerns that students with exceptionalities would become social outcasts when placed in inclusive school settings have not been supported by research findings. One study examined three inclusive elementary classrooms, and found that existing social relationships were normal for students identified as being in three categories of exceptionality: those who are academically gifted, those with learning disabilities, and those with emotional and behavioral disorders. The researchers concluded that the exceptional students in all three groups had been well-integrated into the classroom social structure (Farmer & Farmer, 1996).

A study of middle school and high school students conducted in Iowa, Illinois, and Florida has supported previous findings which indicated that students without disabilities are willing to form friendships with school peers with severe disabilities (Hendrickson, Shokoohi-Yekta, Hamre-Nietupski, & Gable, 1996). The reasons most often given by nondisabled students for their friendships were "They need friends, too," "I like to help people," "I would feel good about myself," and "It would be fun."

Interestingly, when the students in the multistate study were asked how to best arrange situations for social interactions, they advised researchers that friendships among students should be facilitated by adults. The single best method to accomplish that was identified by the nondisabled students as placement of the students with disabilities in the regular classroom setting for all or part of the school day. The youngsters theorized that students would learn better together and also learn more about disabilities.

In a study conducted in the Midwest, researchers attempted to determine whether 37 middle school students (grades six through eight) with mild disabilities attending classes with 165 nondisabled students had different feelings about themselves and their school than did their nondisabled peers. (Hansen & Boody, 1998). The school, which had a total enrollment of about 500 students, had been committed for several years to involving students with disabilities in the regular class environments. The researchers hypothesized that if the school's effort at placing students with mild disabilities in regular classes had been accomplished successfully, then the students with disabilities would express similar feelings about themselves and the school as did their nondisabled peers. The study found that the students with disabilities rated their school and positive classroom experiences slightly higher (but not statistically significant) than did the students without disabilities, and they did not express feelings of being unwelcome or being put down by the other students in the school. Some of the specific aspects evaluated by the researchers included many of those important to a good school climate:

a. feelings of being attentive and interested in, as well as participating in, class activities and doing additional work on one's own;

b. perceptions of the degree of friendship students feel for each other;

c. perceptions of the degree of help and friendship the teacher has given the students;

d. perceptions of the degree of emphasis on completing planned activities and staying on task;

e. perceptions of the degree to which students compete with each other for grades and recognition and how hard it is to achieve good grades;

f. perceptions of the degree to which students behave in an orderly and polite manner, and the overall quality of the organization of assignments and classroom activities;

g. perceptions of the degree of emphasis on establishing and following a clear set of rules;

h. perceptions of the strictness of the teacher in enforcing the rules; and

i. perceptions of the degree to which students contribute to planning classroom activities, and the extent to which the teacher uses new techniques and encourages creative thinking.

The researchers concluded that their finding of no significant differences in perceptions of school and classroom environments between students with and without disabilities had provided evidence that the school's commitment and effort to provide educational experiences to all students had been successful.

A special concern for children with severe disabilities is that, other than school, they have few social arenas in which to develop friendships. Thus, the school setting takes on a greater importance in the development of social networking for the students with disabilities, especially those with disabilities of greater severity. Some studies have established that students with severe disabilities can benefit socially from placement in preschool and elementary regular education classes, when appropriately supported in that placement. Kennedy, Shukla, and Fryxell (1997) found that students with severe disabilities who were placed and properly supported in intermediate grade classes interacted more frequently, had more social contacts outside the classroom, had reciprocity of higher levels of social support, had larger friendship networks, and had more durable relationships with peers without disabilities than did their counterparts who were educated in self-contained special education classes. Mere placement of students in the same proximity without adequate planning, coordination, and monitoring by a wide range of professionals would not likely have had as good results. Findings of substantive social benefits for students with severe disabilities who participate in inclusive educational arrangements provide additional incentive to educators and parents to consider inclusion efforts for a broader range of students with disabilities.

Educators must continue to gain awareness of the importance of favorable social interactions among all students, including those with disabilities. The lack of friendships is one of the most serious problems confronting persons with disabilities, especially in adolescence, and can have dire effects on the individuals' self-image, psychological adjustment, and even vocational skills. If individuals with disabilities (like everyone) are to lead productive and satisfying adult lives, they must have had a variety of interactive social experiences and must have found acceptance, inclusion, and bonds of friendship among the acquaintances of childhood. Obviously, this cannot occur normally when children are separated based on such artificial criteria as disabilities.

Setting the Tone

Principals and other educational leaders are in a unique position to have a great influence on the quality of student attitudes and relationships in an inclusive school. Enthusiasm and commitment on the part of building administrators will be translated through teachers to the students served. To model and communicate a positive attitude, principals should:

- Ensure that special students have the same access to status activities as other students (working in the office, carrying messages, names appearing in school newsletters and on bulletin boards, participation in assemblies);
- Get to know the students, call them by name, and model acceptance and interest;
- Encourage a variety of activities in which special students can participate and play prominent roles (provide support for students when necessary);
- Encourage awareness and efforts to foster productive social relationships among students during school and after-school activities;
- Make sure that separate special classes and resource rooms and separate special education staff members, if they exist in the building, have equal access to the same pleasant physical accommodations and desirable schedules (e.g., lunchtime) as do other classes and staff;
- Provide the fullest support possible (e.g., clerical and logistical help, materials, planning time, inservice classes) needed to make special education programs successful; and
- Remove stigmas from special programs through techniques such as renaming a resource room the activity room, stocking it with interesting resources and activities, and setting hours each day when it is open to all students and faculty members for browsing and exploring; also, invite gifted students to the room for occasional special activities.

Questions of Fairness

School leaders and teachers must be prepared for expressed student and parent concerns about students being treated unfairly as a result of some students receiving accommodations, modifications, and supplementary aids and services. They can deal with such concerns most effectively by teaching and reinforcing an under-standing of the differences between "equality," "equity," and "need" as they apply to fairness among students and staff. Fairness, from a stand-point of equality, implies that every student is treated the same; equity implies that students receive assistance proportionate to their contribution; and need implies that students receive assistance as determined by individual necessity. Differing student situations require different applications of fairness. The provision of special education, accommodations, and services are provided based on necessity and are not provided to everyone (equality) or on the basis of merit (equity) in every situation. Welch (2000) recommends that teachers be certain to respond to student expressions of concern about "fairness." Students will more likely respond favorably to individualization when they have a good understanding of basic fairness.

COOPERATIVE LEARNING ACTIVITIES

What, exactly, can educational leaders do to ensure that teachers help promote positive peer interactions? Several authors, such as Johnson and Johnson (1986, 1992) and Stevens and Slavin (1995), propose that the most effective means is through structured, cooperative activities. Johnson and Johnson in particular suggest that leadership efforts should be directed toward structuring cooperative, rather than competitive (spelling bees, grading on a curve) or individual student activities (e.g., giving the special student an alternative lesson to sit and work on alone).

Studies have demonstrated the benefits of substituting structured cooperative formats for traditional competitive or isolated individualistic approaches to learning for all students. Such benefits include greater self-esteem, higher academic achievement, increased motivation, greater liking for other students and school personnel, greater seeking and exchanging of information, and generally improved classroom climate (Gillies & Ashman, 2000). Most research results, however, involved studies of moderate length (1 to 6 months); few have looked at the long-term effect of cooperative learning. Stevens and Slavin (1995), however, have reported the results from a 2-year study of several elementary schools which used cooperative learning as a school-wide philosophy across content areas. The teachers planned cooperatively, used peer coaching (see Chapter 11), and actively sought parent involvement. Students with learning disabilities were included in cooperative learning activities, with special education teacher support on a team teaching basis.

The results at the end of the second year established that the cooperative schools had had great successes. All student grouping categories experienced significantly higher achievement in reading vocabulary, reading comprehension, language expression, and math computation; the students with learning disabilities also had significantly higher achievement results in math application. Results from gifted students showed that those with cooperative learning classes had significantly higher achievement than their peers in other schools who were provided enrichment programs without cooperative learning. It was determined that social relations were better in the cooperative learning schools and that students with disabilities were more accepted than their peers in schools with traditional pull-out programs.

The cooperative learning concept encompasses a variety of instructional strategies which encourages student-to-student interaction regarding curricular content in a supportive and cooperative environment. The students are empowered to take responsibility for both their own learning and that of their peers. Students are rewarded for fulfilling their expressed responsibility in seeing that all members of the group have learned the material. The teacher's role is transformed into that of facilitator rather than provider of information, or a combination of the two.

In contrast, according to proponents of cooperative learning, competitive or individualistic learning pits students against one another. They seek outcomes which are personally beneficial, and as such are detrimental to others in the class. Individual learning goals are unrelated to the other students and other students' goals are irrelevant. When a few students in a competitive environment win, the others lose (Johnson & Johnson, 1992).

Hundreds of studies have been conducted and reported on cooperative learning as an instructional approach, and according to Johnson and Johnson (1992), we "know more about cooperative learning than we do about lecturing, age grouping, departmentalization, starting reading, the 50-minute period, or almost any other aspect of education" (p. 175).

Antil, Jenkins, Wayne, and Vadasy (1998) have identified the factors which have contributed to the popularity of cooperative learning. It is obvious from their descriptions, why the cooperative learning concept so neatly fits the individualization desirable in inclusion settings:

a. It has great potential for accommodating individual student differences; in fact, individual differences are exploited to promote learning; and
b. It allows for the achievement of multiple educational goals; improvement of academic performance, social development, and interpersonal skills and communication development.

Goor and Schwenn (1993) have highlighted the fact that multiple learning activities and strategies exist within the cooperative learning umbrella. Some examples are:

a. *Student Teams—Achievement Divisions* which require students to complete common work in groups of four to five, but to take individualized tests. A team's score is based on individual students' improvement over previous performance.

b. *Think-Pair-Share* involves students first attempting to answer a question individually, then discussing their thoughts with a partner, and then the partners share with a small group or the class.

c. *Jigsaw* uses teams where each member is given (or researches) a piece of information and is asked to teach it to others.

d. *Team Accelerated Instruction* provides for student assignment of materials at their level (4 seventh-graders received 20 on-grade-level spelling words; one received an additional five; and 1 received 10 words from third-grade level), and peer assisted practice. Group points are awarded on improvement on individual tests.

e. *Group Investigation* is where the group decides what to investigate and what each member will contribute.

f. *Learning Together* uses teams working on one assignment to start, and stresses self-analysis of the team success in working together.

The most common example of cooperative learning—student teams—would normally involve assigning a research topic to a small, heterogeneous group. Each student could be responsible for checking a particular source or for contributing one element of the group's report. The essential characteristics of effective cooperative learning experiences that distinguish it from other student group work are as follows:

1. Students in the learning group are interdependent and must work together in order to reach a goal. Students must interact in order to promote each other's success.

2. Roles are clear and each individual is accountable for fulfilling an assigned task or for mastering the information in the lesson.

3. Work is evaluated based on the whole group's performance and each group member gets the same grade, but each member is individually accountable for the group success.

Adjustments for students with disabilities can be made in the type of role assigned, the portion of the group work for which they are held responsible, and the grading of their work. It is essential to set reasonable expectations for students so that they are challenged but not frustrated and so that other group members are not penalized for their willingness to cooperate and work with their peers with disabilities. Special educators can be consulted for assistance in making these adjustments. Special educators also can help by training all students in cooperative social skills. The role of the regular teacher in setting up these activities includes:

- Specifying, as far as possible, the instructional objectives;
- Selecting the group size most appropriate for the lesson;
- Assigning students to groups (common practice is to maximize heterogeneity);
- Setting up an appropriate physical arrangement of the classroom;
- Providing appropriate materials;
- Explaining the task and cooperative group support;
- Observing the student-student interaction;
- Intervening as a consultant, to help students solve problems and learn interpersonal skills and ensure that all members are learning; and
- Evaluating group products (Johnson & Johnson, 1992).

Depending on the activity, multiple grades may be awarded, one for achievement and one for improvement, and one for contribution.

Research indicates that some students with disabilities, especially those with behavioral disorders and mental disabilities, may require advance training or preparation in group processes, social skills, and cooperation in order to make cooperative learning successful for all participants (Goodwin, 1999; Pomplun, 1997). One group of educators has advocated the use of ongoing strategy reminders (cue cards) for use by secondary school students in group work in any setting (Goor et al., 1996).

In interdependent classroom and activity settings, students not only develop more positive attitudes about themselves and their peers, they also become more realistically aware of the nature of disabilities and their effects on the individual. The disability then takes on a dynamic, rather than a static, or stereotyped meaning and students become more able to perceive persons with disabilities as unique and worthy individuals. Whether cooperative learning activities are used for advanced training, ongoing memory joggers, or continuing training, when used as an educational methodology, cooperative learning appears to be well worth the effort.

COLLABORATIVE PROBLEM-SOLVING

Salisbury, Evans, and Palombaro (1997) have reported an interesting and successful collaborative problem-solving (CPS) process, a logical extension of the cooperative learning concept. It was undertaken over a 2-year period in an elementary school where both teachers and students were trained in CPS strategy and then used it to identify and solve problems related to the physical, social, and instructional inclusion of students with mild to profound disabilities.

CPS involves shared authority and responsibility among participants for idea generation, accountability, and the sharing of resources and rewards. Teachers modeled the process as relevant situations arose, and supported a climate of shared responsibility and shared decision-making. As a constant reminder, each classroom posted a chart of the steps in the CPS process.*

---

*From "Collaborative Problem-Solving to Promote the Inclusion of Young Children with Significant Disabilities in Primary Grades," by C. L. Salisbury, I. M. Evans, and M. M. Palombaro, 1997, *Exceptional Children, 63*(2), 199. Copyright 1997 by the Council for Exceptional Children. Adapted with permission.

- Identify the issue: "What's happening here?"
  To identify an issue, state the desired outcomes.
- Generate all possible solutions: "What can we do?"
  Brainstorm potential solutions.
- Screen solutions for feasibility: "What would really work?"
  Review for feasibility and match solutions to group value base. Predict possible benefits and detriments.
- Choose a solution to implement: "Take Action."
  Create stakeholders and thus support and commitment through the consensus process.
- Evaluate the solution: "How did we do? Did we change things?"
  Evaluate the effects of the solution and determine whether concerns remain, how the group feels about the result, and what has been learned.

In a relatively short time, CPS became the routine problem-solving mechanism for such issues as a child in a wheelchair in the cafeteria being unable to be seated with classmates, a student being excluded from playground activities owing to potential head injury, lack of participation on field trips, planning classroom game modifications, planning a Mother's Day card for a child that cannot speak or hear, planning participation in physical education activities, and involvement in class academic activities. Within 2 years, the process of CPS became intuitive among the children. In addition to being involved in successfully removing barriers to physical, social and instructional inclusion in the classroom and building, all the students achieved important personal outcomes:

- developed concern for others
- developed acceptance and value of diversity
- empowered to create change
- worked with others to solve problems

- developed meaningful ways to include everyone
- fostered understanding and friendship

Thus, the CPS process resulted not only in the resolution of many barrier problems for inclusion students, but also in growth for their typically developing peers in numerous ways. It mobilized the creativity of peers while working on participative solutions, it resulted in the promotion of positive social, cognitive and communicative outcomes, and it resulted in the use of advocacy, creative thinking, communication, and assessment skills in meaningful situations.

PEER TUTORING

Peer/cross-age tutoring is another constructive, organized student activity that not only can promote friendships and understanding among students with and without disabilities, but also can help principals and teachers meet the needs for individualizing instruction. Properly structured student tutorials have proved as effective as tutoring by adult aides, and there are added potential benefits for all those involved.

For tutors, these benefits include increased academic and social maturity as well as self-confidence and improved attitudes toward school and toward individuals who are different from themselves. Other students in the class, not directly involved, frequently benefit as a peripheral effect of the teacher's work in learning task analysis and individually designed curricular programming.

Good tutors should be dependable, responsible, caring, students—or those likely to develop those traits. Generally, they must have the required academic competence and the time to spare. It is important, however, to be cautious about possibly exacerbating existing social and racial tensions. For example, principals or teachers should not consistently choose able-bodied white boys as tutors for members of all other groups. Girls may respond better to female tutors and minority students to tutors of their same racial and ethnic group. Many students have an easier time accepting tutors who are at least somewhat older than they are. This will not be true in every case, of course; the choices demand sensitivity on the part of the staff involved. It should be possible to find appropriate tutoring roles for many students with disabilities.

Some students have participated as committed tutors for 2 or 3 years. To combat potential boredom or loss of motivation in long-term tutorial arrangements, teachers occasionally can change tutor-tutee pairs, providing reinforcing events for both members of the dyad (such as parties or celebrations), and help make tutoring a prestigious activity in the school.

Peer-Assisted Learning Strategies (PALS)

Several faculty members at Peabody College of Vanderbilt University have been working with classroom teachers and faculty of other institutions in the development of a successful instructional program for use in diverse elementary and middle school reading, spelling, and mathematics classes. Their Peer-Assisted Learning Strategies (PALS) accommodates a wide range of student diversity through the decentralization of the learning process. For only a part of the school week (two or three 30- or 40-minute sessions), students in the entire class are paired to work on loosely structured activities related to reading or mathematics. This results in 13 to 15 unique instructional experiences occurring simultaneously a classroom instead of a single incidence of teacher-directed learning. The teacher circulates about the class to provide support and individualized remediation where needed.

While tutoring pairs are selected based on needs, each session is reciprocal so that each student assumes both the "coach" and "player" role. At the end of 2 weeks, students change partners.

Learning activities are structured, planned, and use a reward system for success based on several criteria. PALS reading, spelling, and mathematics programs have repeatedly established greater academic progress among various and diverse student groupings, including inclusion students, low-performing students, average-achieving students, and high-achieving students, than that resulting in typically structured classrooms (Mathes, Fuchs, Fuchs, Henley, & Sanders, 1994; Fuchs, Fuchs, Mathes, & Simmons, 1997). Unlike some self-professed modern educational panaceas that require nearly full-time emersion of students into planned activities, PALS requires only 60 to 120 minutes per week and the rest of the class time can be used in traditional teaching methodologies.

When combined with curriculum-based measurement (CBM) strategies, PALS has become an economical and "formidable teaching tool" with built-in procedures to detect those individual students with whom the PALS procedures are not attaining the desired effect. Simply stated, CBM is a weekly or biweekly administration of short tests sampling the expected curricular skills or knowledge attained by students. Individual student performance is graphed and thus illustrates past, present, and probable future growth. Teachers can quickly identify when one student or an entire class is not making adequate progress. A remedial instructional program for a few or all may then be indicated. Teachers or associates with even limited technical skills can computerize these monitoring operations and greatly enhance teacher decision making and student learning (Mathes, Fuchs, & Fuchs, 1995).

The use of the PALS approach, sometimes referred to as Class-Wide Peer Tutoring (CWPT), with or without CBM, provides one way in which teachers can accommodate a greater range of instructional needs in their classrooms while providing critical learning strategies and increased practice time for individual students.

CWPT has proven effective across grade levels, disabilities, English as a second language classes, and in classrooms in urban, suburban, and rural settings. One group of experienced and knowledgeable educators suggested that CWPT is especially useful for teaching the subjects of health and safety (e.g., guns, drugs, fire) where peer tutors exercise a greater than usual amount of influence (Reddy et al., 1999).

A Secondary Peer Tutoring Example from Kentucky

Longwill and Kleinert (1998) have reported on a high school peer tutoring program in Kentucky. Students without disabilities enroll voluntarily in courses for which they receive grades and credit toward graduation. Part of their course requirement is to engage in self-study of beliefs and attitudes toward disabilities and the rights of persons with disabilities. Students are provided a range of opportunities, both in school and in the community setting, to engage in cooperative learning and peer tutoring activities with students with disabilities. Students meet course requirements through reflective writing assignments.

A natural project for the peer-tutoring program was an outgrowth of education reforms in Kentucky, which included the development of individual student portfolios. As nondisabled students helped their peers with disabilities prepare their portfolios, they in turn simultaneously completed materials for their own portfolios.

The Kentucky peer tutoring program has become a natural part of regular education programs, with one of the peer-tutor assignments being the identification of regular class adaptations for students with disabilities across a variety of classes. Following are a few examples of the school accommodations devised with the help of peer tutors:

- Instead of having Richard, who has severe disabilities, draw pictures in art class, he pasted pictures from magazines;

- Instead of completing research papers, Tony worked with picture symbols on the topic or theme of his choice. He used pictures arranged or copied from his communication system to make a research report;
- Instead of a large reading assignment for Karla, peers wrote summaries of each reading. This helped the students who developed the summary learn the material and helped Karla understand the basic themes or ideas;
- Instead of long assignments in typing class, Tom typed what he did in the community that day;
- Instead of writing in yearbook class, Lauren classified photographs into activity categories, such as school classes, clubs, and sports;
- Instead of an oral research presentation in biology, Derrick developed a collage of local fruits and vegetables and the best places to purchase the seeds for each of those plants.

Peer tutors in the Kentucky program have also became a natural link to the community. They introduced the students with disabilities to their own part-time jobs and co-workers, and provided support to students with disabilities in their respective job searches. Both peer tutors and students with disabilities helped each other develop job resumés. They went shopping together and practiced budgeting, banking, and nutrition skills. Some relationships continued into leisure time activities of movies, pizza, and bowling. All participants in the Kentucky program, including teachers, thought they profited by the experiences.

ATTITUDE CHANGE PROGRAMS

Should inclusion-class teachers devise and present special curriculum units on disabilities as a means of changing student attitudes? The research suggests a cautious affirmative response. Some program components that appear effective with inclusion classes include:

- Opportunities to interact with adults with disabilities
- Sufficient information to dispel fears and promote understanding
- Sanctioned opportunities for staring (either at individuals or at media representations)
- Opportunities to discuss feelings and beliefs
- Simulations (e.g., blindfolds, one hand behind back, wheelchairs) and an opportunity to explore and experiment with assistive aids and devices, such as crutches and hearing aids

Some educators suggest that school counselors are especially sensitive to the issues of peer acceptance and should make a conscious effort to provide information and understanding to the peers of students with disabilities, such as through the use of disability simulations and role playing (Bruce, Shade, & Cossairt, 1996). One study, noting that young, typically developing, kindergarten-age children have low levels of acceptance for children with disabilities, provided participants with a 6-week structured intervention consisting of stories and guided discussion about children with disabilities, structured play experiences with children with disabilities, and a home reading activity with parents. The study found that the children participating in the intervention were much more open to the integration, acceptance, and belonging of children with disabilities than children who did not participate (Favazza, Phillipsen, & Kumar, 2000).

Circle of Friends

The concept of Circle of Friends lies in a structured group project. Selected peers of a student with disabilities are first led in discussions about peoples' need for friendship and the various roles friends play. Students are then asked if they would like to befriend a student with disabilities. Those students interested are encouraged to think of ideas of what it means to be friends at school and in a variety of situations. The better alternatives are narrowed down and students volunteer to participate in "friendly" activities, in school and outside of school, with the student with a disability. Some students may drop out of the circle and others may choose to continue or even expand their relationships. Sometimes parents of the students get to know each other through the circle, and that leads naturally to joint family activities outside school.

CONCLUSION

Whether a school uses peer tutoring, cooperative learning, traditional teacher-directed learning, or a combination of these and other methodologies, the important thing to remember is that society provides schools, teachers, and staff so that all children may learn, not just a few. When students with disabilities learn in inclusion settings, so do the students without disabilities. We truly are all in this together.

REFERENCES

Antil, L. R., Jenkins, J. R., Wayne, S. K., & Vadasy, P. F. (1998). Cooperative learning: Prevalence, conceptualizations, and the relation between research and practice. *American Educational Research Journal, 35* (3), 419–454.

Bruce, M. A., Shade, R. A., & Cossairt, A. (1996). Classroom-tested guidance activities for promoting inclusion. *The School Counselor, 43,* 224–230.

Farmer, T. W., & Farmer, E. M. (1996). Social relationships of students with exceptionalities in mainstream classrooms: Social networks and homophily. *Exceptional Children, 62* (5), 431–450.

Favazza, P. C., Phillipsen, L., & Kumar, P. (2000). Measuring and promoting acceptance of young children with disabilities. *Exceptional Children, 66* (4), 491–508.

Fuchs, D., Fuchs, L. S., Mathes, P. G., & Simmons, D. C. (1997). Peer-assisted learning strategies: Making classrooms more responsive to diversity. *American Education Research Journal, 34* (1), 174–206.

Gillies, R. M., & Ashman, A. F. (2000). The effects of cooperative learning on students with learning difficulties in the lower elementary school. *The Journal of Special Education, 34* (1).

Goodwin, M. W. (1999). Cooperative learning and social skills: What skills to teach and how to teach them. *Intervention in School and Clinic, 35* (1), 29–33.

Goor, D., & Schwenn, J. O. (1993). Accommodating diversity and disability with cooperative learning. *Intervention in School and Clinic, 29* (1), 6–16.

Goor, M., Schwenn, J., Eldridge, A., Mallein, D., & Stauffer, J. (1996). Using strategy cards to enhance cooperative learning for students with learning disabilities. *Teaching Exceptional Children, 29* (1), 66–68.

Hansen, L. L., & Boody, R. M. (1998). Special education students' perceptions of their mainstreamed classes. *Education, 118* (4), 610–615.

Hendrickson, J. M., Shokoohi-Yekta, M., Hamre-Nietupski, S., & Gable, R. A. (1996). Middle and high school students' perceptions on being friends with peers with severe disabilities. *Exceptional Children, 63* (1), 19–28.

Johnson, D. W., & Johnson, R. T. (1986). Mainstreaming and cooperative learning strategies. *Exceptional Children, 52* (6), 553–561.

Johnson, D. W., & Johnson, R. T. (1992). Implementing cooperative learning. *Contemporary Education, 63* (3), 173–180.

Kennedy, C. H., Shukla, S., & Fryxell, D. (1997). Comparing the effects of educational placement on the social relationships of intermediate school students with severe disabilities. *Exceptional Children, 64* (1), 31–47.

Klinger, J. K., & Vaughn, S. (1999). Student perceptions of instruction in inclusion classrooms: Implications for students with learning disabilities. *Exceptional Children, 66* (1), 23–37.

Longwill, A. W., & Kleinert, H. L. (1998). The unexpected benefits of high school peer tutoring. *Teaching Exceptional Children, 30* (4), 60–65.

Mathes, P. G., Fuchs, D., & Fuchs, L. S. (1995). Accommodating diversity through Peabody classwide peer tutoring. *Intervention in School and Clinic, 3* (1), 46–50.

Mathes, P. G., Fuchs, D., Fuchs, L. S., Henley, A. M., & Sanders, A. (1994). Increasing strategic spending practice with Peabody class-wide peer tutoring.

Learning Disabilities Research and Practice, 9(1), 44–48.

Pomplun, M. (1997). When students with disabilities participate in cooperative groups. *Exceptional Children, 64*(1), 49–58.

Prater, M. A. (2000). Using juvenile literature with portrayals of disabilities in your classroom. *Intervention in School and Clinic, 35*(3), 167–176.

Reddy, S. S., Utley, C. A., Delquadri, J. C., Mortweet, S. L., Greenwood, C. R., & Bowman, V. (1999). Peer tutoring for health and safety. *Teaching Exceptional Children, 31*(3), 44–52.

Salisbury, C. L., Evans, I. M. & Palombaro, M. M. (1997). Collaborative problem-solving to promote the inclusion of young children with significant disabilities in primary grades. *Exceptional Children, 63*(2), 195–209.

Stevens, R. J., & Slavin, R. E. (1995). The cooperative elementary school: Effects on students' achievement, attitudes, and social relations occur in inclusive schools. *American Educational Research Journal, 32*(2), 321–351.

Villa, R. A., Vander Klift, E., Udis, J., Thousand, J. S., Nevin, A. I., Kunc, N., & Chapple, J. W. (1995). Questions, concerns, beliefs, and practical advice about inclusive education. In Villa, R. A. & Thousand, J. S. (Eds.), *Creating an inclusive school.* Alexandria, VA: Association for Supervision and Curriculum Development.

Welch, A. B. (2000). Responding to student concerns about fairness. *Teaching Exceptional Children, 32*(2), 36–40.

Wenz-Gross, M., & Siperstein, G. N. (1997). Importance of social support in the adjustment of children with learning problems. *Exceptional Children, 63*(2), 183–193.

RECOMMENDED READINGS

Goodwin, M. W. (1999). Cooperative learning and social skills: What skills to teach and how to teach them. *Intervention in School and Clinic, 35*(1), 29–33. This article highlights the teaching of social skills desirable for cooperative learning, describes several cooperative learning strategies, and provides advice for beginning cooperative learning.

Goor, M., Schwenn, J., Eldridge, A., Mallein, D., Stauffer, J. (1996). Using strategy cards to enhance cooperative learning for students with learning disabilities. *Teaching Exceptional Children, 29*(1), 66–68. This article discusses a simple "reminder" strategy that assists students in maintaining the skills and attitudes desirable in cooperative learning activities.

Longwill, A. W., Kleinert, H. L. (1998). The unexpected benefits of high school peer tutoring. *Teaching Exceptional Children, 30*(4), 60–65. This article describes a very successful high school peer tutoring program.

Mathes, P. G., Fuchs, D., & Fuchs, L. S. (1995). Accommodating diversity through Peabody classwide peer tutoring. *Intervention in School and Clinic, 31*(1), 46–50. This article presents a general overview of a highly effective and yet economical program for enhancing the learning of diverse groups of students.

Perske, R., & Perske, M. (1988). *Circles of friends: People with disabilities and their friends enrich the lives of each other.* Nashville, TN: Abingdon Press. This small book contains a great deal of inspiration about friendships. The illustrations are remarkably moving.

Prater, M. A. (2000). Using juvenile literature with portrayals of disabilities in your classroom. *Intervention in School and Clinic, 35*(3), 167–176. This article lists and describes 46 books that portray characters with disabilities and provides suggestions for classroom use. Others suggest the use of assigned children's books that include portrayals of characters with disabilities in reading, history, music, or other content areas.

Rieck, W. A., & Wordsworth, D. E. D. (1999). Foreign exchange: An inclusion strategy. *Intervention in School and Clinic, 35*(1), 22–28. This article examines a newly designed form of cooperative learning designed to maximize both cognitive and social development.

Salend, S. J. (1999). Facilitating friendships among diverse students. *Intervening in School and Clinic, 35*(1), 9–15. This article provides specific suggestions about a variety of strategies to increase the development of friendships between students with and without disabilities.

Welch, A. B. (2000). Responding to student concerns about fairness. *Teaching Exceptional Children,*

32 (2), 36–40. This excellent article explains various understandings of "fairness" and provides ideas about gaining student understanding of what is "fair" in student accommodation.

Relevant Federal Regulations

34 C.F.R. § 300.130   LRE (generally).

.344   IEP team.

.346   Development, review, and revision of IEP.

.347   Content of IEP.

.550   General LRE requirements.

.551   Continuum of alternative placements.

.552   Placements.

.553   Nonacademic settings.

.554   Children in public or private institutions.

.555   Technical assistance and training activities.

.556   Monitoring activities.

Appendix A #1, 2, 3

CHAPTER **11**

STAFF RELATIONSHIPS AND STAFFING PATTERNS

Focus

Meeting the needs of students with disabilities in inclusion classrooms and other school settings demands cooperative efforts among regular and special educators and other professionals. Such cooperation often is made difficult, however, by the traditional separation of these professional disciplines and by associated attitudes of suspicion, competition, and exclusivity. Research has proved that such barriers can be broken down through positive inclusion experiences.

Principals' Leadership Role

Educational leaders play the crucial role in the success or failure of inclusion programs. Through their role modeling of interest in and acceptance of all persons in the school community, and their support for staff in their efforts at inclusion, the principal, especially, establishes the proper school climate necessary for successful inclusion programs. Using the traditional personnel functions in the hiring, training, and supervision of staff, the principal has the opportunity to build and mold teams geared for successful inclusion programs.

Staff members will need to be provided considerable opportunity for training, planning time, and the testing and evaluation of new ideas. Collaborative roles will need to be experimented with and fine tuned, and the principal will be responsible for creating and maintaining an educational environment that allows and encourages these changes to take place.

Legal Issues

The IDEA calls for an interdisciplinary approach to the evaluation, appropriate programming, and placement of children with disabilities. Inherent in this is the necessity of proper staff training and preparation. States, through a comprehensive system of personnel development, must now ensure that the various needed staff members will be available and properly trained, and will have access to relevant research findings and best practices experiences.

Rationale

Collaborative professional arrangements, such as co-teaching and peer coaching, often are not only the most efficient means of carrying out special education requirements, but also the most child-centered. Unlike the completely separate educational environments of parallel regular and special education programs from the past, they allow students with disabilities to learn in the most typical environment appropriate. Professional commitment to pursue what is best for all children should therefore engender a commitment to collaboration.

Approaches

Educational leaders must encourage and model a positive approach toward the presence of special students in the school. School resources, physical space, and time schedules, as well as nonacademic tasks and responsibilities should be distributed equitably among regular and special education staff members. All staff should be provided adequate time for planning and coordination. Regular teachers should be encouraged to use specialists as resources and specialists should be encouraged to be flexible, tolerant of teaching differences, and nondogmatic.

The principal should consider collaboration and communication skills when hiring new staff members. When possible, the principal should expand the duties of special educators to include services to and with regular teachers and regular students (e.g., consultation on materials and curriculum modification and consultative help for all students, not just those identified as being eligible for special education).

INHERENT STAFFING ISSUES IN THE IDEA

By its very nature, implementation of the IDEA requirements for identification, appropriate programming, and placement and provision of services requires the coordination, communication, and cooperation of a number of persons. How those persons are selected, organized, supervised, and trained is an important factor in the quality of programming received by all students.

The IDEA expressly provides interdisciplinary input at several points in the special education process. The evaluation team may include the persons who will be part of the IEP team, and must include parents, and "other qualified professionals, as appropriate." Determinations of eligibility for special education, according to the IDEA, must be made by a "team of qualified professionals and the parents of the child." The team joined together for IEP development must include the parents of the child, one school representative, at least one regular education teacher, one special education teacher, an individual who can interpret evaluation results, and others as desired.

Interdisciplinary cooperation is also implicit in the requirement to provide "related services," such as physical therapy, audiological examinations, psychological services, and transportation that are necessary for the child to be able to profit from the special education programs. The list of covered services, including potential supplementary aids and services and related services, is so broad as to imply the involvement of a great number of specialists in any given school setting. Placement decisions must be "made by a group of persons, including the parents and other persons knowledgeable about the child, the meaning of the evaluation data, and the placement options," and may include other members of the IEP team.

Problems in Staffing Relationships

In schools where special and regular educators are not accustomed to working together, complaints such as the following may be all too familiar to administrators:

> "I have 28 students in my class already. Why should I have to take in *your* students, especially when you only have to deal with five or six at a time?"
>
> "If regular class teachers had better attitudes toward kids with disabilities, if they individualized their teaching in the first place instead of expecting all students to learn in the same way . . . if they just had more commitment, there wouldn't be so many special students."
>
> "I'm tired of so-called experts coming in and telling me how to run *my* class. Half the things they tell you don't work anyway."
>
> "In a regular class, *my* students don't get the acceptance and understanding they need. It's a continual experience of failure, instead of a chance to find out what they really can do."

Attitudes inherent in expressions such as these seem to make cooperation impossible, or at least difficult. Such complaints and prejudices may not actually be verbalized. They may emerge as avoidance (failure to contact a specialist for advice, for example), as subtle assertions of power (use of professional jargon that others do not understand, refusal to acknowledge the opinion of a colleague from a less statused profession), the waste of valuable meeting time on petty disputes, and so on.

Although frustrating and obstructive, such attitudes do have understandable historic origins. After all, educators' training has often been oriented toward producing autonomous experts, individuals in control of their own office, clinical setting, or classroom. There has been additional, pronounced separation between the disciplines of regular and special education—different training, different educational philosophies, different working conditions, and different populations of students. Yet, the educational philosophy embodied in the IDEA, especially the LRE, is dependent on cooperation between regular classroom teachers, special education teachers, and a variety of specialists. Therein lies an important challenge for educational leaders.

Whether a school plans to meet the legal requirements of inclusion for students where appropriate or go beyond to "full inclusion," the challenge will be present. This chapter emphasizes the issue from an "inclusion" perspective, but most of the issues discussed are also present in school efforts at full inclusion.

A study of graduate and undergraduate students in both regular and special education indicates that, although we have moved a little closer to breaking down barriers between regular and special education, much more is left to be done (Taylor, Richards, Goldstein, & Schilit, 1997). There was strong agreement among all groups surveyed with the philosophical basis of inclusion and with the position that the teaching of special education students should be a responsibility shared by both regular and special education staff members. Those surveyed also agreed that regular class structure, curriculum, and teaching methodologies would have to be re-evaluated with a view toward possible revision in order to meet the needs of a broader range of students resulting from implementing inclusion programs. However, regular educators differed from special educators in their belief that students with mental or behavioral disabilities should not be in inclusion settings. The researchers concluded that teacher preparation programs need to better reflect an understanding of an individual student's needs, which are both behind and beyond the special labels, and provide good information about modifying regular class structure, curriculum, and pedagogy.

The result of many years of special education pull-out programs where the child leaves the regular classroom in order to receive special education programs and services has been an educational environment based on a notion of "my" students versus "yours" and accompanying attitudes of suspicion, defensiveness, and intimidation. Despite the demand for cooperative efforts imposed by the IDEA, clear collaborative roles and structures have been slow to evolve. Furthermore, as a result of escalating community demands in a variety of areas, teaching has become a more stressful occupation and still commands lower salaries and less status than other professions with comparable responsibilities. Resources remain scarce and expectations have multiplied. To some extent, conflicts over special education are outlets for broader-based educator frustrations.

Some of the disparity in attitude between general and special educators over the concept of inclusion may be as much a relationship to experience and practice as anything else. In a study involving teams of regular and special educators working with children with severe disabilities in an included setting, Wood (1998) found that during the early stages of the inclusion experience, the teachers maintained traditional discrete role differences. However, those roles became less rigid and education became a more cooperative effort as the school year progressed. In addition, Phillips, Sapona, and Lubic (1995) found that for first-year inclusion teams, high anxiety levels at the beginning of the school year were typical and there was great concern expressed over lack of role clarity and constantly having other adults observe them in the work setting. Like Woods, these researchers found the teachers' anxiety had largely vanished by year's end. They intimated that all the teachers in the study had their belief systems altered, and had become supporters of and focused on inclusion settings for students.

These findings are almost universal. In a study of 19 regular education teachers having a student with a severe disability in class, similar results were identified by Giangreco, Dennis,

Cloninger, Edelman, and Schattman (1993). All the teachers shared serious apprehensions at the beginning of their inclusion experience, initially experienced minimal involvement with the students with disabilities, and had expectations that someone else would be responsible for the students' education. By the end of the first school year, 17 of 19 teachers described transforming experiences of a positive nature during the year and were able to identify many benefits of the inclusion experience to the students with disabilities, to their classmates, and to themselves as teachers. The two teachers who had not experienced this change in professional perspective had not become as involved with the students with disabilities as had their colleagues. One of the teachers who did not find the experience beneficial to herself, or the student, differed from two other teachers who had the same student included in their classes 1 or 2 years previously. Interestingly, none of the 19 teachers had any significant training to prepare them for their inclusion experience, yet almost all had successful experiences after discarding their initial apprehensions.

In another study involving almost 700 educators at 32 school sites judged as providing heterogeneous educational opportunities for all children, Villa, Thousand, Meyers, and Nevin (1996) found that experience with inclusion over time increased approval factors toward inclusion for both general and special educators. Increased support for inclusion among regular educators was found to be related to:

1. the amount of related in-service training and technical assistance that was provided;
2. the higher degree of administrative support;
3. the extent to which regular and special educators collaborated;
4. the amount of time structured for Collaboration; and
5. accompanying organizational restructuring initiatives begun within the school.

The expressed belief structure of both experienced general and special educators involved in inclusion programming in this study supported the following concepts:

1. general and special educators share a responsibility for meeting the needs of all children;
2. general and special educators are able to work together as co-equal partners;
3. the achievement level of students with disabilities does not decrease in the regular classroom;
4. team teaching enhances the feelings of competency for all teachers; and
5. inclusion practices promote participatory decision-making, collaborative practices, and mutual support.

The researchers concluded that time for staff collaboration must be a part of the school's consideration of general restructuring of school-time parameters, such as changing from traditional to block scheduling, and the concept of shared decision making must be supported by administrators.

The Principal's Role

Principals alone cannot, with a wave of the hand, be expected to work miracles to erase decades of teacher isolation, suspicion, and turf protection. They can, however, make a difference. Principals can model interest in and acceptance of all students, staff, and programs in the school; they can distribute space, schedules, and resources so as to minimize conflict; they can structure new roles and new formats in which staff members can work together supportively. One study has indicated that the most important type of support perceived as being important to both special and regular educators is the emotional support provided by principals (Littrell, Billingsley, & Cross, 1994). Because teachers generally receive so little recognition for their efforts, they are appreciative of principals who allow teachers' input into important school decisions, exhibit trust in their judgment, show concern for all students and programs, and promote a sense of importance to teachers' efforts. Even when options are severely limited by such factors as budgets, personalities, and lack of maneuvering room within district policies, the principal is in a better position to improve staff relationships than any other individual in the school.

It has never been a secret that principals must provide the leadership, role modeling, and "climate" building necessary for successful inclusion. They are the single most important factor in building interpersonal relationships and mutual support. Building staff have a need to know, that "the administrative staff notices and appreciates their efforts, and considers the time and energy spent in advancing inclusion as necessary and meaningful to the educational process" (Kochhar & West, 1996, p. 66).

Goor, Schwenn, and Boyer (1997) have identified five essential core beliefs that education leaders, particularly building principals, must have in order to establish or maintain successful school inclusion programs (pp. 134–135):

1. Believe all children can learn
2. Accept all children as part of their school community
3. Believe teachers can teach a wide range of students
4. Believe teachers are responsible for all students
5. Believe that principals are responsible for the education of all children in their building

At first glance, educators will say, "Oh yeh, that's what its like in all school buildings." Look again. Is this what really happens? Some principals tend to support programs in which they have a personal interest and ignore others. (One of the authors attended a staff development meeting for Bureau of Indian Affairs special education administrators. Attendees wanting to make a point back home wore buttons which asked: "What part of ALL don't you understand?")

Goor, Schwenn, and Boyer (1997) have also identified some of the basic skills needed by educational leaders in their efforts to build and strengthen successful inclusion programs. According to them, the effective inclusion principal:

1. Models positive attitudes toward the acceptance of all students, faculty, staff, and parents.
2. Models and expects collaboration with teachers, parents, staff, and students as equal team members.
3. Is responsive to the needs of students, staff and parents.
4. Exhibits effective listening skills, and encourages others' expressions.
5. Exhibits and expects good problem solving skills by
   a. identifying the problem;
   b. defining the problem clearly;
   c. exploring the potential solutions;
   d. implementing the best solution;
   e. evaluating the solution.
6. Is trustworthy and builds trust among others.
7. Supports and facilitates growth and learning through high-quality staff development experiences.

Even a cursory look will establish that those skills identified as being needed by principals for successful inclusion are indistinguishable from those skills exhibited by successful leaders across all educational settings.

The Educational Leader as Agent of Change

Unfortunately, educational leadership preparation programs largely ignore the special education component of many modern school settings and do not adequately provide preparation for the challenges ahead (Sirotnik &

Kimball, 1994). The desired response is at least two-fold: First, leadership preparation programs need to better integrate special education issues into their curricula, and second, individual educators need to make personal assessments of their role performance as educational leaders for all students.

Because educational leaders are the chief agents of change, new conceptions of the school administrator's role also must be developed and understood by all. In the area of improving staff relationships, a principal might, for instance, begin the process with self-evaluation along these lines:

1. Have I really accepted the special education students and teachers here?
2. Have I demonstrated that acceptance before all faculty members (in meetings, newsletters, special programs, etc.)?
3. Have I shown unfairness or favoritism in the treatment of either group of teachers (regarding room assignments, time schedules, other indications of status, etc.)?
4. Have I ensured that special students have had access to status roles and activities?
5. Have I provided the support necessary to make it possible for inclusion to succeed (planning time, in-service training, teacher associates, etc.)?
6. Are both regular and special educators convinced that I understand their problems (and their contributions) and that I am committed to the best possible use of school resources to bring needed improvements?

INTERSTATE SCHOOL LEADERS LICENSURE CONSORTIUM (ISLLC) GUIDELINES

In recognition of the fact that educational leadership in the future will require both the strengthening of existing skills and the building of new ones, a number of national groups have studied the desirable and required elements of practice exhibited by educational leaders that should be inherent in educational leadership programs. As one of these important groups, the Council of Chief State School Officers has spearheaded a consortium of state educational agencies and various professional associations to establish a proposed set of guidelines for educational leaders. The goal has been to stimulate debate about the necessary quality of educational leadership and to provide specific ideas that will enhance effective leadership of America's schools. The published report of the Interstate School Leaders Licensure Consortium (ISLLC) (Council of Chief State School Officers, 1996) provides six general, but informative, guidelines for licensure, each of which is accompanied by more specific knowledge, disposition, and performance criteria. The focus of the guidelines is the promotion of a quality education for all students. Because of space limitations, the ISLLC specific detailed criteria are not provided here, but readers are encouraged to locate and review them at their leisure. The six general guideline statements focus on matters of teaching and learning on the creation of "powerful learning environments." As you review the guidelines, think about how they parallel with the rest of the material in this chapter and the book's expressed philosophy.

A school administrator is an educational leader who promotes the success of *all* students by:

1. Facilitating the development, articulation, implementation, and stewardship of a vision of learning that is shared and supported by the school community.
2. Advocating, nurturing, and sustaining a school culture and institutional program conducive to student learning and staff professional growth.
3. Ensuring management of the organization, operations, and resources for a safe, efficient, and effective learning environment.

4. Collaborating with families and community members, responding to diverse community interests and needs, and mobilizing community resources.
5. Acting with integrity, fairness, and in an ethical manner.
6. Understanding, responding to, and influencing the larger political, social, economic, legal, and cultural context.

PERSONNEL FUNCTIONS

In the latest revision of his book on the human resources function in education, Castetter has continued his development of 11 personnel system function designations (Castetter & Young, 2000). Although all 11 designations are relevant to obtaining and maintaining a good personnel resource pool, 5 appear to stand out in importance in using the hiring and related functions in order to assure the implementation of successful inclusion programs: recruitment, selection, induction, development, and appraisal.

Whether a school is seeking regular education, special education, or support staff to fill roles involving students with disabilities, all five of these personnel functions need to be attended to, with obvious adjustments made depending on the anticipated role:

• In the area of *recruitment*, all advertisements and announcements should include expected job-related behaviors, responsibilities, and philosophies that impact an inclusion program. Therefore, it is very important to specify the school's needs, which mirror the intended results. Surprise is not something which is desired by either side when key personnel are recruited for important roles. For instance, advertisements for teaching staff might read "applicants are expected to role model behaviors that encourage acceptance of differences in others; cooperate with colleagues in problem-solving, use multimodality for instruc-

tion, evaluation, and planning learning experiences; use a variety of student assessment and information gathering techniques; maintain good professional relationships with parents; and maintain a familiarity with issues in special education and inclusion."

• In the area of *selection*, the same principles apply. Look for resumé items that provide assurance of desired experiences with inclusion or willingness to learn. During interviews, be sure that questions are asked about "how to" and perhaps engage in simulation or role playing to ensure that the person has listening, communication, collaboration, problem-solving, and the other skills required to be a successful inclusion team member.

• *Induction* to the school and to an inclusion team is a crucial component of the successful integration of staff. New staff members need to be brought up-to-date on the history and philosophy of the building's inclusion program, rules, practices, and expectations. They need to be assigned to a successful, experienced mentor and at the beginning of new employment, there should be time provided for many planned opportunities for "debriefing" and feedback (Lloyd, Wood, & Moreno, 2000). Effective mentoring is associated with educators' plans to stay in the profession (Whitaker, 2000). Mentors should be rewarded for their important work. Visitations to nearby successful school inclusion programs might also be helpful to new inductees.

• *Professional development* opportunities can be used to meet a variety of staff needs. They can reinforce good behaviors, assist in strengthening planning, communication, and problem-solving skills, bring in new knowledge, and set the tone for program assessment and changes. It is essential for a meaningful development program to include staff members in the needs assessment, planning, and delivery of their own staff development programs. Individual staff development opportunities should be developed and made available on an as-needed basis, rather than on previously scheduled dates only. Visitation to other classrooms and nearby successful programs should be available.

- *Appraisal*, or *evaluation*, must take into account whether the staff member is meeting the expectations which were made clear in the recruitment, selection, and induction processes. Staff evaluation can help to bring about or reinforce change, no matter which appraisal approach is used. There should be no surprises for either the school or staff member, however. Expectations should have been made clear all through the various personnel processes. The evaluation process merely measures individual performance against inclusion goals and school expectations in those areas. Areas of weakness, of both individuals and groups, can be identified and bolstered through professional development activities.

Although the foregoing discussion of personnel functions speaks directly to teaching and other professional staff, it also has important applications for support staff, volunteers, and others.

Celebrate Success

"Celebration" should become an inherent part of personnel functions. This is the one step in bringing about change that is frequently overlooked by many school leaders. Educators do not celebrate their successes enough. In their detailed guide for persons seeking to implement inclusion programs, Kochhar and West (1996) outline the steps to successful inclusion programs. The tenth step is to "plan for a reward system to renew the staff and celebrate success." Kochhar and West recognize that celebration and recognition of both individual staff member and program successes are important to the development and reinforcement of the spirit of collaboration and coordination.

COLLABORATIVE ROLES

The traditional approach to education of students with disabilities has often been called the "two-box" model (Reynolds & Birch, 1977); students were assigned to either regular or special education, without overlap. Staff members in one "box" had no particular reason to talk with those in the other. Today, schools are required to provide a continuum of educational placements to ensure that all students with disabilities are served in the most typical educational environment possible and in the company, to the greatest extent appropriate, of nondisabled peers (see Chapter 6). That continuum generally includes arrangements of the following types:

- Special schools for the severely disabled, with an effort to arrange some type of contact with nondisabled peers. Historically, the effort to bring nondisabled peers into segregated environments was called "reverse mainstreaming";
- Special classes in the regular schools with shared nonacademic activities—art, music, physical education, lunchtime, and assemblies, depending on the student populations involved;
- Regular class assignment with special class placement for some subjects or for parts of the day;
- Full-time regular class placement with assistance to the teacher;
- Full-time regular class placement with temporary interventions either in or outside the classroom.

With such a broad range of potential educational placements for a child and with all of the important elements of instruction and services to be provided in those settings, the collaboration among the adults that is necessary to carry out programs can appear sometimes to be daunting. Yet, the IEP development process and the placement decision process can provide an effective and meaningful opportunity for developing the collaborative process. The IEP process, like collaboration, requires shared deliberation and an interactive communication involving the exchange of individual perspectives, knowledge, and experience. Team collaboration in the IEP development process is a good model for the continuing collaboration necessary to successfully carry out the IEP. Continuing and consistent assessment of the IEP development process can help assure that collaboration skills and processes are present in the IEP process (Clark, 2000).

Although the level of services varies, each type of arrangement in the placement continuum requires some measure of cooperation among special educators and other professionals. At a minimum, there is a need to coordinate schedules. Beyond that, almost limitless opportunities exist for sharing knowledge in ways that directly benefit students with disabilities and also result in increased acceptance and understanding on the part of others. For example, through joint planning, a resource teacher can schedule remediation or skills development work to complement lessons in the regular class, and regular class teachers can learn to monitor and reinforce students' progress on these skills in the regular classroom. A special educator in a consulting role might offer help in anything from individualizing lessons or locating appropriate materials to creating an accepting social environment among classmates without disabilities.

Collaboration has no established model; it has no boundaries beyond the imagination of the persons arranging the program and organizing to meet the needs of students. For instance, Bauwens and Hourcade (1997) have described and diagrammed 17 different variations of co-teaching, which is only one form of collaboration. About the only certainty to collaborative structure is that one person does not do it alone. By definition, collaboration means joint planning, decision-making, and problem-solving di-

rected at a common, agreed upon goal. There is a great deal of room for individual initiative, experimentation, and problem-solving. Stanovich (1996) has listed six general characteristics of successful collaboration. Collaboration:

- Is voluntary
- Requires parity among participants
- Is based on mutual goals
- Depends on shared responsibility for participation
- Involves individuals who share their resources and and decision-making
- Involves individuals who share accountability for outcomes

An important key to successful collaboration efforts directed at inclusion is the volunteer regular education teacher. Many educators experienced in inclusion programs, such as Chalmers and Faliede (1996), recommend not forcing regular education teachers into inclusion efforts. Only willing teachers should be involved. Many resistant teachers will be willing to join the effort later as time passes and as success is observed. It is common for regular education teachers to at first underestimate their ability to meet the needs of a diverse student population. They must be helped to understand that successful teachers of students without disabilities have the necessary skills to teach those with disabilities (Giangreco, 1996). Small steps at the beginning of the implementation of inclusion programs will lessen frustration for the reluctant teacher and aid the inclusion effort in the long run.

Barriers to Collaboration

A number of authors have identified common barriers to successful collaboration. Principals need to pay special attention to these barriers because they, as education leaders, play a key role in their removal. Bondy and Brownell

(1997) have identified the following barriers as important inhibiters of collaboration:

Belief System

- Teachers view their roles in narrow, specialized terms, i.e., secondary mathematics, gifted, elementary education;
- Teachers view other people's students as being the responsibility of the other person, i.e., ours and theirs, the two-box model;
- Teachers have preconceived perceptions of others that may discourage approaching other teachers as partners; and
- Teachers view parents from distant and threatening perspectives.

Professional Isolation

- Limited opportunity to correct distorted perceptions

Collaboration Skills

- Weak social and communication skills
- Not used to working with other adults
- Unpracticed in problem-solving skills

The recommendations of Bondy and Brownell for resolving collaboration deficiencies include: 1) assessing honestly your own collaboration skills; 2) assessing your own interpersonal skills; 3) observing strong collaborators as role models and thinking about what makes them successful; 4) listening carefully; 5) withholding judgment; 6) respecting others' worth and opinions; 7) attempting to find common ground; and most important, 8) focusing on the needs of students. Bondy and Brownell conclude their remarks with a reminder of the underlying philosophy of collaboration, "it takes a village to raise a child" (p. 114–115).

Examples of Collaboration

Co-Teaching

One regular education teacher and one special education teacher (maybe more) teach the same class of students with diverse needs. The goal is to offer their combined expertise to all students in a coordinated fashion. Both teachers become more effective in meeting a wide range of students' needs. The specific mix of responsibilities is worked out between the partners and may change as classroom needs change. Implementation is varied:

Grazing—one teacher provides direct class instruction; the other moves among the students to assist individuals.

Teaching on purpose—one teacher provides direct class instruction. The other gives short (5 minutes or less) direct instruction to small groups of students as review, follow-up, or mini-lessons.

Tag-team teaching—teachers take turns providing direct instruction; often used early in collaboration as teachers get to know each other.

Small-group teaching—class is divided into two groups to allow for more interaction, often a follow-up or wrap-up to whole group instruction (sometimes called parallel teaching).

Flexible heterogeneous grouping by skill or need level—groups change as subject or activity changes

Multiple groups—Similar to cooperative learning or learning centers, with two teachers actively circulating to respond to student group requests for assistance, or circulating presenting mini-lessons to small groups (sometimes called station learning).

Alternative teaching at the same time—teachers teach the same lesson to the same class, only they take turns. One teacher will follow the other's lesson with examples, review, or extensions of concepts (Vaughn, Schumm, & Arguelles, 1997).

Co-teaching has many beneficial outcomes for staff and students. Cook and Friend (1995)

found that co-teaching increases instructional options, improves program intensity and continuity among staff, reduces the stigma of individual attention for many students, and increases professional support where it counts the most, in the classroom.

Cole and McLeskey (1997, p. 11) summarized their perspective of the benefits of co-teaching:

1. Administrative duties (attendance, record-keeping) often disruptive to student learning, are shared
2. Two adults in the classroom allows for problem intervention with minimal disruption
3. Students receive more individualized attention
4. Collegial feedback and evaluation enhance instructional quality
5. Regular contact enhances opportunities for quality of problem-solving and creativity
6. Renewal and reinforcement from observing each other
7. Provides students with model for collaboration and cooperation
8. Teacher strengths balance against each others' weaknesses.

In his review of 10 studies conducted on co-teaching, Reinhiller (1996) found that not only special education students benefited from greater specialized and more individualized instruction, but also the other students in inclusion classes benefited as well. As a side benefit, the school staff members involved in the ten studies reported personal and professional growth benefits resulting from their shared classroom experiences.

Peer Coaching

At least one other adult observes teacher performance and provides specific feedback. It bridges limitations in knowledge or skills. It can be used at different levels with teachers, teacher

associates or specialists, i.e., physical therapists. It facilitates early collaboration:

by experts—more of a consultation model where persons with special expertise observe teaching and provide feedback; and

reciprocal—professionals observe each other and provide feedback. Participants can be at differing experience levels for a mix of perspectives. Philosophical differences can be a problem (Vail, Tschantz, & Bevill, 1997).

Joint Planning

Groups of educators and support staff, in group sessions, discuss different ways to meet a child's needs in a variety of settings and curricular areas. Sometimes this involves only the curricular needs of students through the joint determination of curricular priorities and the joint assignment of teaching responsibilities.

ASSIST

ASSIST comprises general and special educators across content areas and often includes service and support staff. It requires a close physical proximity "cluster" of classes and staff. Direct and indirect instructional support can be planned and implemented as required by student needs, or small groups or individuals. Time for planning and communication is crucial. Sometimes parallel teaching is the goal, and sometimes review or learning strategy building is the goal. Having multiple instructional centers in a classroom at the same time leads to the alternative program nickname of "class-within-a-class" (Gable, Manning, Hendrickson, & Rogan, 1997).

Consulting

Teacher to teacher collaboration requires that special educators take a proactive role and seek out situations where regular educators are willing to develop an ongoing openness of collaboration for the benefit of all students. Ongoing communication should occur on a regular weekly basis and a journal is kept for later reference. Neither the special or regular educator should take the role of expert; both should be there to help the other. Collaboration may be begun for the benefit of a particular student, but a trusting relationship can lead to instructional practices and services which benefit all students in a classroom setting (Vargo, 1998).

Teacher-Associate Services

Because special education teachers cannot be in several regular education classrooms at once, teacher associates are trained to act as surrogates of the special education teacher in working with the regular education teacher. It is important that the special education teacher also have direct contact with the students on a regular basis.

Complementary Instruction

The regular education teacher accepts the major responsibility for content instruction and the special educator is primarily responsible for teaching strategies and skills for learning (Reinhiller, 1996).

All of the foregoing descriptions of collaborative arrangements are for the purpose of demonstrating the wide range of available options. The specific format of collaboration is dependent on student needs, available staff, and school resources. It is the principal's role to aid staff in choosing appropriate arrangements from the variety of options, facilitate the arrangement of time for planning and training, and assist in the assessment of the success of the collaborative arrangement.

Principal's Role (Again)

The importance of the building principal's role in successful inclusion has been previously discussed elsewhere in this book, but nowhere is that leadership function so closely tied to suc-

cessful programming as it is in the area of staff collaboration. Nearly every study and report published on successful inclusion collaboration programs has emphasized the necessity of administrative support through:

- Joint problem-solving
- Maintaining data
- Facilitating staff development programs
- Providing emotional support during tough times
- Modeling collaborative traits and communication
- Providing resources
- Providing advocacy
- Providing time for staff to engage in collaboration
- Assessing program efforts (Cole & McLesky, 1997; Cook & Friend, 1995; Fritz & Miller, 1995; Stanovich, 1996)

Although no one support activity of educational leaders is more important than others, the one most mentioned by researchers is the scheduling of time for collaborative planning, communication, and problem-solving. Education leaders will need to be flexible and creative in finding that crucial time. It may be through overtime pay before or after school, floating substitutes who allow several teachers to be free at the same time, use of teacher associates or volunteers, early release days for students, days set aside from instruction and devoted to consultation, combining classes temporarily, or the principal covering a classroom. At the secondary level, a well-planned block scheduling approach holds possibilities for greater staff communication and collaboration (Santos & Rettig, 1999). One of the authors has observed a successful inclusion program where the school district assured each participating staff member up to 2 full days of "floating substitute" time per year for collaboration as scheduled by group staff members. The program has been working successfully district-wide for over 10 years. With time for planning and regular communication being of great importance for successful collaboration, some authors suggest a greater use of technology to improve efficiency. Robertson, Haines, Sanche, and Biffart (1997) have described the use of specialized computer software to enhance collaborative relationships in a Canadian school district. The use of technology allows faster, more frequent communication and joint problem-solving (e.g., e-mail), better record-keeping, and immediate access to data, checklists, student assessments, forms, and notes. Principals can initiate such programs where more traditional collaboration efforts are less feasible.

Collaborative Problem-Solving

A newer type of successful collaboration is reported by Salisbury, Evans, and Palombaro (1997), who observed a group of teachers in an elementary school that modeled and taught their students a collaborative problem-solving (CPS) process that experienced great success in including children with significant disabilities in primary grade classrooms. CPS was based on an interdependent relationship among staff in the achievement of common goals. It involved a shared responsibility of idea generation, accountability for success, and the sharing of resources and rewards. This type of bottom-up approach to solving problems resulted in a commitment to the solution by those persons closest to the implementation and a continued maintenance of the process over time. It also taught students and teachers the value of consensus, tolerance of diversity of opinion, and the concept of perspective. The five steps in CPS are common steps in problem-solving approaches, and are identified in Figure 11-1.

Examples of issues dealt with in 48 sessions over a 2-year period by the school using CPS included developing ideas on how to get parents of children with special needs to interact with parents of regular education students (class picnic; T-shirt painting night); how to modify field day athletic events for a child in a wheelchair

(all activities were modified and peers took turns pushing the wheelchair through events); and how to arrange for an early-arrival child to get from the bus to the playground (peers accompany to playground and bus drivers use walkie-talkie to notify playground monitors). The modeling by staff and the teaching of the CPS process to the elementary students, along with student involvement, assisted in finding numerous solutions for other inclusion issues in the school. Not surprisingly, other research has indicated that groups of school staff members engaged in collaborative problem-solving have been able to better identify the problem, have identified more solutions, and have implemented better solutions than those staff members solving problems individually (Hobbs & Westling, 1998; Snell & Janney, 2000).

The Multidisciplinary Team

As discussed in Chapters 4 and 7, many schools have begun to use multidisciplinary teams to identify and focus on individual student educational needs before they are referred for special education evaluation. The teams may bear different names, such as Child Study Team or Student Assistance Team, and may vary in the number and professional specialty of members, but they all are similar in function: to identify alternative solutions to student learning needs other than special education. A standard arrangement is to meet weekly for set, limited time or number of cases. The first priority is to identify nonspecial education programs, services, and accommodations that may resolve the student's learning difficulties in a particular class setting. Only after it is conceded that the alternatives have not been, or will not be, successful is attention focused on the possible need for special education assessment and programming.

The potential benefits of such a team structure include increased efficiency, greater accuracy in assessment, and the fruitful and creative exchange of ideas, values, and knowledge.

FIGURE 11-1   *Steps in the collaborative problem-solving process*

1. *Identify the Issue: "What's happening here?"*
   An issue arises whenever there is a discrepancy between what is happening and what we would like to happen. To identify the issue, state the desired outcomes. Avoid referring to the issue as a problem; we want to discourage students from seeing the inclusion of their peers with disabilities as a problem.

2. *Generate All Possible Solutions: "What can we do?"*
   Brainstorm potential solutions to the issue. Creativity should not be limited, so discuss all solutions with no value judgments as to whether the solutions are viable. The intent is simply to identify any possible alternative to what is currently happening.

3. *Screen Solutions for Feasibility: "What would really work?"*
   There are two main components to this step.
   a. Once all the solutions have been proposed, review each recommendation in light of the following criteria:
      (1) *Does the solution match the value base of the group?*
      (2) *Is the solution feasible?* Can the individual or group implement the solution? Are all the materials available? Can it be accomplished in the setting where the problem arises? Is there enough time to do it?
   b. Predict the possible outcomes/success of the solution. This allows the participants to identify the potential benefits or detriments of the proposed solutions, and assists in deciding which one to implement.

4. *Choose a Solution to Implement: "Take action"*
   Reach consensus on which solution or combination of solutions to implement. By having all stakeholders involved in the process, we increase the likelihood of support and commitment to the solution agreed to by the group.

5. *Evaluate the Solution: "How did we do? Did we change things?"*
   Participants evaluate whether the proposed solution had its intended effect. Was the issue successfully resolved? Did the child or adult get what he or she needed, or are there remaining concerns? How do members of the group feel the process went? In light of what the group has learned from this experience, is further action necessary?

From "Collaborative Problem-Solving to Promote the Inclusion of Young Children With Significant Disabilities in Primary Grades," by C. L. Salisbury, I. M. Evans, and M. M. Palombaro, 1997, *Exceptional Children, 63* (2) p. 199. Copyright 1997 by the Council for Exceptional Children. Reprinted with permission.

However, the potential problems also are numerous. It is, therefore, important to use a systematic approach, such as "systematic problem-solving" and "systematic progress monitoring," combined with strong parent involvement and participation as was discussed in those earlier chapters.

NEW ROLES FOR EDUCATORS

A number of innovative ideas have been proposed for redefining the roles of both regular and special educators in inclusion schools, and the building of increased trust must be one of the primary goals. Where the history and tradition of a school have bred an environment of professional isolation, unfamiliarity, and suspicion, the first step toward cooperation and collaboration is to build that trust. Ideas for educational leaders to consider as possible roles for special educators to fill in building that trust in regular educators include:

- Team teaching combined classes where one regular and one special education teacher are jointly responsible for all students (sometimes called co-teaching);
- Providing consultation and training services for all students, including, for example, consulting with regular teachers about all pupils with learning problems, whether or not they are identified for special education; and training all students in social skills, communication skills, the nature of disabilities, and other areas of special expertise or benefit to assist in the successful integration of new students with disabilities into regular class settings;
- Consulting on the assessment and grading of special students;
- Leading in-service seminars or parent meetings
- Sharing equal responsibility for supervision of lunchrooms and playgrounds;
- Supporting regular teachers in parent meetings
- Providing occasional activities for gifted and average students (this can help remove the stigma from resource rooms and special programming);
- Sharing responsibility with regular teachers for the planning and development of school policies as well as individual programming.

Regular educators must be able to demonstrate a general understanding of disabilities in children, a sensitivity to their needs for accommodation, and the skills to adapt instruction and activities to meet needs of a diverse group of students.

TEACHER ASSOCIATES

Teacher associates are known by a number of other titles (i.e., teacher aides, paraeducators, paraprofessionals) and have a lengthy history of service to education. Their role has evolved over the years from clerical, housekeeping, and monitoring chores, to teacher support and facilitator, and to educational technicians providing instructional and support services to a variety of students (French & Pickett, 1997). As the needs of students have become more complex and shortages of some teachers, such as bilingual and special education, have not been solved, education has turned more and more to the teacher associate for support.

In collaborative situations, teacher associates often can make or break the success of an inclusion program. Specialized training for teacher associates frequently has direct benefits for students (Schepis, Ownbey, Parsons, & Reid, 2000).

One of the authors was present when a mother of six stepped forward to volunteer to provide teacher associate services to a third-grade child with autistic tendencies. Most of the school staff were concerned at the thought of attempting to work with an "impossible" child. The associate said at the time that "a mother with six children of her own isn't likely to see many completely new things in only one child." The teacher associate participated fully in the IEP meetings and communicated regularly with home, teaching staff, and consultants about concerns and successes. Four years later, working with the same associate but not in as close proximity, the boy was fully included in regular seventh-grade classes, was on the school's academic honor roll without grading accommodations, and was the recipient of awards for citizenship and writing poetry.

With the success of a great number of students' education programs dependent in part on the quality of skills and ability of a teacher associate to communicate, facilitate, and coordinate, it is surprising that more care is not demanded in the recruitment, training, and assignment of teacher associates. The Council for Exceptional Children has issued a position paper which expressly calls for improvement in several areas of the use of teacher associates. The six areas of expressed concern are: (1) clarification of teacher associate rules; (2) more systematic supervision and evaluation; (3) clarification of legal and ethical responsibilities; (4) development of job descriptions; (5) opportunities for pre-service and staff development training; (6) the training of teachers and specialists in the management of teacher associates (Hilton & Gerlach, 1997).

French and Pickett (1997) have studied related issues of teacher associates for many years and raise a number of similar issues, which are paraphrased as follows:

- Teachers supervising teacher associates have little or no preparation for their supervisory task;
- Teacher associates often have little or no training in any phase of the tasks they are assigned;
- A good deal of job role overlap results from the lack of teacher or associate preparation and a clear notion of what the role of teacher associate is to be;
- Teacher associates, as members of the community where the school is located, are often underutilized as links to the local community; and
- Teacher associates, because of interest and experience, are good sources of future teachers, but are too often overlooked as a result of their lack of formal education.

Studying some of the same issues related to teacher associates, Wadsworth and Knight (1996) have proposed six excellent suggestions for schools wishing to enhance the value of the teacher associate in collaborative inclusion team settings. Schools should:

1. Provide critical pre-service training through a centralized interdisciplinary training team. The team members can be selected from a variety of backgrounds, (i.e., intermediate agency, university) based on their expertise and experience. A great deal of practical general information about such things as laws, confidentiality, teaching methodologies, and behavior can be included.
2. Prepare teacher associates for the new roles and unique responsibilities that will be theirs in a variety of regular and special education settings.
3. Communicate and train in the skills and importance of team collaboration. As a key stakeholder, the teacher associate should feel fully involved and responsible.
4. Prepare teacher associates in a variety of instructional methodologies.
5. Enhance the teacher associate's assessment, observation, and data collection skills.
6. Train and model the use of appropriate behavior management techniques for a variety of settings.

Not all training need be completed before a teacher associate begins service. However, there should be a clear plan of providing the necessities early and the remainder soon after service begins. The sooner the teacher associate is ready to become a full-fledged member of the team, the more successful the outcome that can be reasonably expected for students. The assignment of duties by teachers should be well-thought out and planned, but the investment of time and effort frees the teacher to do those tasks which only professional educators can and should do (French, 2000). Appropriate attention must also be given to issues of training regarding confidentiality and substitute teacher associates who fill in for absent staff (Fleury, 2000).

Giangreco, Edelman, Luiselli, and MacFarland (1997) have pointed out that with nearly 500,000 teacher associates now employed in the schools, educators must play closer attention to the function and services they provide. In their study of teacher associates working with students with multiple disabilities placed in the regular classroom, researchers identified a number of major concerns related to the teacher associate's proximity to children with disabilities. When the teacher associate "hovered" near the child, even when not necessary, a number of negative results occurred, such as segregation of the student from classmates, interference with the concept of ownership by general educators, and interference with the instruction of other students. As a result of their findings, they recommend several solutions: IEP team awareness of the problem of teacher associate proximity and addressing it through training, both of associates and other team members; use of associates for the entire class and teacher, rather than individual students; and training the associates in how to decrease student dependence on them.

Teacher associates should not be used to substitute for licensed teachers and should always work under direction and supervision of licensed staff. The use of teacher associates to carry out the traditional role of a teacher (to plan, evaluate, diagnose, and prescribe, student learning) would violate the IDEA requirement that personnel assigned to work with children with disabilities be appropriately and adequately prepared for their roles.

Principals should be ready and able to take the cue from these observations and train the teacher associate to be a more meaningful team player. After all, a significant portion of students' individual contacts with adults at school are with teacher associates.

COMPREHENSIVE SYSTEM OF PERSONNEL DEVELOPMENT

The 1997 Amendments to the IDEA make it clear that Congress is aware of some of the problems associated with the lack of adequately trained and qualified staff, at all levels, to meet the educational needs of children with disabilities. Yet, it has so far shown restraint in specifying detailed training requirements and skills acquisition for staff, and continues to focus the responsibility for the systematic identification of trained staff needs and training opportunities at the state rather than the local level.

The law requires each state to develop a comprehensive system of personnel development that ensures the adequacy of the supply of trained personnel for special education, regular education, and related services. The plan must be updated at least every 5 years. It must include an analysis of state and local needs for professional development for school personnel to serve children with disabilities, including the number of personnel providing special education and related services, information on current and anticipated personnel vacancies and shortages, and ways to address and eliminate those shortages and needs. The state must develop plans for the recruitment, preparation, and retention of qualified personnel. Included must be the manner in which needs for in-service and pre-service preparation will be met in order to ensure that all personnel who work with children with disabilities have the skills and knowledge necessary. Teacher associates and other support staff must be appropriately trained and supervised in order to assist in the provision of special education and related services (34 C.F.R. § 300.381, 2000; House Report, P.L. 105-95, 1997, p. 93).

Expressly included in staff training requirements are content knowledge, collaborative skills, and the ability of staff to use behavioral interventions and strategies to address student conduct that impedes student learning, including the learning of other children. The state must acquire and disseminate to all school groups knowledge obtained from educational research and other sources, and establish a method of adoption for promising practices, materials, and technology. It must also provide for the joint training of parents and special education, related services, and regular education personnel.

Many of those involved in education view the new legal requirements as a warning to school districts, as well as states, that the adequacy of skills, training, and knowledge requirements of school staff, including teacher associates, has been insufficient and more attention must be paid to the quality of the staff assigned to work with students with disabilities. Inherent in the entire context of the current IDEA is the need for trained team members to meet the needs of a new system of integrated programs and services. Many skills, such as collaboration, problem-solving and, communication not previously exhibited on an extensive level must be considered a part of that training.

These mandates to states for improvement of personnel working with students with disabilities appear to be considerably different than what is actually occurring in many states. Both state and local school officials are now forewarned that they had better be working on the improvement of the quality of training for staff members working with students and the dissemination of research results and best practices ideas. If not, Congress may make the mandates more concrete in the future.

CONCLUSION

The organization of schools with one teacher, one class, and one classroom has served America well, but its roots are in the nineteenth century. Then, a high school education or less was considered adequate training for a teacher. Greater efforts at specialized training, dissemination of research results, and success with a variety of classroom organization models are signals that the time for change has come.

Like everything else in modern society, education has become more complex. New ways of doing things are in order. The uses of collaboration and teaming are but a small part of the overall educational reform movement that will make

schools better places to learn and better places to work. Educational leaders play the key role in bringing about the changes in practice, philosophy, and advanced training needed to best serve the needs of all students. America's educational leaders are up to the task and new delivery systems are being successfully implemented.

REFERENCES

Assistance for education of all children with disabilities. 34 Code of Federal Regulations, Part 300 (2000).

Bauwens, J., & Hourcade, J. J. (1997). Cooperative teaching: Pictures of possibilities. *Intervention in School and Clinic, 33* (2), 81–85.

Bondy, E., & Brownell, M. T. (1997). Overcoming barriers to collaboration among partners-in-teaching. *Intervention in School and Clinic, 33* (2), 112–115.

Castetter, W. B., & Young, I. P. (2000). *The human resource function in educational administration*, (7th ed.) Upper Saddle River, NJ: Merrill/Prentice Hall.

Chalmers, L., & Faliede, T. (1996). Successful inclusion of students with mild/moderate disabilities in rural school settings. *Teaching Exceptional Children, 29* (1), 22–25.

Clark, S. G. (2000). The IEP process as a tool for collaboration. *Teaching Exceptional Children, 33* (2), 56–66.

Cole, C. M., & McLeskey, J. (1997). Secondary inclusion programs for students with mild disabilities. *Focus on Exceptional Children, 29* (6), 1–15.

Cook, L., & Friend, M. (1995). Co-teaching: Guidelines for creating effective practices. *Focus on Exceptional Children, 28* (3), 1–16.

Council of Chief State School Officers (1996). Interstate school leaders licensure consortium: Standards for school leaders. Denver, CO: Author. Available at www.ccsso.org.

Fleury, M. L. (2000). Confidentiality issues with substitutes and paraeducators. *Teaching Exceptional Children, 33* (1), 44–45.

Fritz, M. F., & Miller, M. (1995). Challenges of the inclusive classroom: Roles and responsibilities. *Contemporary Education, 66* (4), 211–214.

French, N. K. (2000). Taking time to save time: Delegating to paraeducators. *Teaching Exceptional Children, 32* (3), 379–383.

French, N. K., & Pickett, A. L. (1997). Paraprofessionals in special education: Issues for teacher educators. *Teacher Education and Special Education, 20* (1), 61–73.

Gable, R. A., Manning, M. L., Hendrickson, J. M., & Rogan, J. P. (1997). A secondary student instructional support team (ASSIST): Teachers face the challenge of student diversity. *The High School Journal, 81* (1), 22–27.

Giangreco, M. F. (1996). What do I do now? A teacher's guide to including students with disabilities. *Educational Leadership, 53* (5), 56–59.

Giangreco, M. F., Dennis, R., Cloninger, C., Edelman, S., Schattman, R. (1993). I've counted joint transformational experiences of teachers educating students with disabilities. *Exceptional Children, 59* (4), 359–372.

Giangreco, M. F., Edelman, S. W., Luiselli, T. E., & MacFarland, S. Z. C. (1997). Helping or hovering? Effects of instructional assistant proximity on students with disabilities. *Exceptional Children, 64* (1), 7–18.

Goor, M. B., Schwenn, J. O., & Boyer, L. (1997). Preparing principals for leadership in special education. *Intervention in School and Clinic, 32* (3), 133–141.

Hilton, A., & Gerlach, K. (1997). Employment, preparation, and management of paraeducators' challenges to appropriate service for students with developmental disabilities. *Education and Training in Mental Retardation and Developmental Disabilities, 32* (2), 71–76.

Hobbs, T., & Westling, D. L. (1998). Promoting successful inclusion through collaborative problem solving. *Teaching Exceptional Children, 31* (1), 1–19.

House Report 105-95, P. L. 105-17 (1997). U.S.C. *Congressional and Administrative News*, 78–146.

Kochhar, A., & West, L. L. (1996). *Handbook for Successful Inclusion.* Gaithersburg, MD: Aspen.

Littrell, P. C., Billingsley, B. S., & Cross, L. H. (1994). The effects of principal support on special and general educator's stress, job satisfaction, school commitment, health, and intent to stay in teaching. *Remedial and Special Education, 15* (5), 297–309.

Lloyd, S. R., Wood, T. A., & Moreno, G. (2000). What's a mentor to do? *Teaching Exceptional Children, 33* (1), 38–42.

Phillips, L., Sapona, R. H., & Lubic, B. L. (1995). Developing partnerships in inclusive education: One school's approach. *Intervention in School and Clinic, 30* (5), 262–272.

Reinhiller, N. (1996). Co-teaching: New variations on a not-so-new practice. *Teacher Education and Special Education, 19* (1), 34–48.

Reynolds, M., & Birch, J. (1977). *Teaching exceptional children in all America's schools.* Reston, VA: The Council for Exceptional Children.

Robertson, G., Haines, L. D., Sanche, R., Biffart, W. (1997). Positive change through computer networking. *Teaching Exceptional Children, 29* (6), 22–30.

Salisbury, C. L., Evans, I. M., & Palombaro, M. M. (1997). Collaborative problem-solving to promote the inclusion of young children with significant disabilities in primary grades. *Exceptional Children, 63* (2), 195–204.

Santos, K. E., & Rettig, M. D. (1999). Going on the block: Meeting the needs of students with disabilities in high schools with block scheduling. *Teaching Exceptional Children, 31* (3), 54–59.

Schepis, M. M., Ownbey, J. B., Parsons, M. B., & Reid, D. H. (2000). Training support staff for teaching young children with disabilities in an inclusive preschool setting. *Journal of Positive Behavior Interventions, 2* (3), 170–178.

Sirotnik, K. A., & Kimball, K. (1994). The unspecial place of special education in programs that prepare school administrators. *Journal of School Leadership, 4* (6), 598–630.

Snell, M. E., & Janney, R. E. (2000). Teacher's problem-solving about children with moderate and severe disabilities in elementary classrooms. *Exceptional Children, 66* (4), 472–490.

Stanovich, P. J. (1996). Collaboration—The key to successful instruction in today's inclusive schools. *Intervention in School and Clinic, 32* (1), 39–42.

Taylor, R. L., Richards, S. B., Goldstein, P. A., & Schilit, J. (1997). Teacher perceptions of inclusive settings. *Teaching Exceptional Children, 29* (3), 50–54.

Vail, C. O., Tschantz, J. M., & Bevill, A. (1997). Dyads and data in peer coaching. *Teaching Exceptional Children, 30* (2), 11–15.

Vargo, S. (1998). Consulting: Teacher to teacher. *Teaching Exceptional Children, 30* (3), 54–55.

Vaughn, S., Schumm, J. S., & Arguelles, M. E. (1997). The ABCDEs of Co-teaching. *Teaching Exceptional Children, 30* (2), 4–10.

Villa, R. A., Thousand, J. S., Meyers, H., Nevin, A. (1996). Teacher and administrator perceptions of heterogeneous education. *Exceptional Children, 63* (1), 29–45.

Wadsworth, D. E., & Knight, D. (1996). Paraprofessionals: The bridge to successful full inclusion. *Intervention in School and Clinic, 31* (3), 166–171.

Whitaker, S. D. (2000). Mentoring beginning special education teachers and the relationship to attrition. *Exceptional Children, 66* (4), 546–566.

Wood, M. (1998). Whose job is it anyway? Educational roles in inclusion. *Exceptional Children, 64* (2), 181–195.

RECOMMENDED READINGS

Angle, B. (1996). Five steps to collaborative teaching and enrichment remediation. *Teaching Exceptional Children, 29* (1), 8–10. This article discusses co-teaching by a regular and special teacher in a class needing both remedial and enrichment work.

Bauwens, J., & Hourcade, J. J. (1997). Cooperative teaching: Pictures of possibilities. *Intervention in School and Clinic, 33* (2), 81–85, 89. This article describes, using diagrams, seventeen cooperative teaching arrangements.

Chalmers, L., & Faliede, T. (1996). Successful inclusion of students with mild/moderate disabilities in rural school settings. *Teaching Exceptional Children, 29* (1), 22–25. The authors provide specific hints for empowering rural elementary teachers for successful inclusion.

Dieker, L. A., & Barnett, C. A. (1996). Effective co-teaching. *Teaching Exceptional Children, 29* (1), 5–7. Two experienced co-teachers discuss the process in a variety of settings and emphasize the need for effective communication between teachers.

Dych, N., Sunbye, N., & Pemberton, J. (1997). A recipe for efficient co-teaching. *Teaching Exceptional Children, 30* (2), 42–45. This article discusses curriculum planning for co-teaching.

Elliott, D., & McKenny, M. (1998). Four inclusion models that work. *Teaching Exceptional Children, 30* (4), 54–58. This article discusses four collaborative and consultative models experienced by the authors.

French, N. K., & Gerlach, K. (Eds.) (1999). Paraeducator supervision notebook. *Teaching Exceptional Children, 32* (1), 65–69. This first in a proposed series of articles on paraprofessionals reviews the research on the general history and uses of paraprofessionals.

Giangreco, M. F. (1996). What do I do now? A teacher's guide to including students with disabilities. *Educational Leadership, 53* (5), 56–59. This article provides 10 specific suggestions for regular class teachers to improve their inclusion practices.

Hasbrouck, J. E., & Cristen, M. H. (1997). Providing peer coaching in inclusive classrooms: A tool for consulting teachers. *Intervention in School and Clinic, 32* (3), 172–177. This article provides a model peer coaching and assessment instrument to help in measuring feedback.

Hobbs, T., & Westling, D. L. (1998). Promoting successful inclusion through collaborative problem-solving. *Teaching Exceptional Children, 3* (1), 12–19. This article discusses the implementation and practical benefits of a collaborative problem-solving process.

Lasater, M. W., Johnson, M. M., & Fitzgerald, M. (2000). Completing the education mosaic: Paraeducator professional development options. *Teaching Exceptional Children, 33* (1), 46–51. This article provides specific suggestions for the training and development of teacher associates.

Robertson, G., Haines, L. D., Sauche, R., & Biffart, W. (1997). Positive change through computer networking. *Teaching Exceptional Children, 29* (6), 22–30. This article discusses the design and uses of computer software in the staff collaboration process.

Santos, K. E., & Rettig, M. D. (1999). Going on the block: Meeting the needs of students with disabilities in high schools with block scheduling. *Teaching Exceptional Children, 31* (3), 54–59. This article provides specific recommendations on how to design a block for greatest utility by staff.

Schumm, J. S., Vaughn, S., & Harris, J. (1997). Pyramid power for collaborative planning. *Teaching*

Exceptional Children, 29 (6), 62–66. This article discusses a curriculum planning strategy for use by regular and special education teachers.

Vail, C. O., Tschantz, J. M., & Bevill, A. (1997). Dyads and data in peer coaching. *Teaching Exceptional Children, 30* (2), 11–15. This article discusses a peer coaching model.

Vargo, S. (1998). Consulting: Teacher to teacher. *Teaching Exceptional Children, 30*(3), 54–55. This article provides practical advice for the special education teacher striving to become a consultant to regular education staff.

Vaughn, S., Schumm, J. S., Arguelles, M. E. (1997). The ABCDEs of co-teaching. *Teaching Excep-*

tional Children, 30 (2), 4–10. This article discusses a variety of co-teaching strategies.

Relevant Federal Regulations

34 C.F.R. § 300.135	Comprehensive system of personnel development.
.136	Personnel standards.
.380	General-comprehensive system of personnel development.
.381	Adequate supply of qualified personnel.
.382	Improvement strategies.

CHAPTER 12

BUDGET AND FUNDING

Focus

Understanding how school districts allocate expenditures for special education services is critical to planning, conducting, and evaluating special education programs. Funding for special education services is a partnership between local and state education agencies, with federal appropriations. As the costs of providing special education services have increased, local school districts have assumed a greater share of the funding partnership. This chapter addresses issues related to the pressure being placed on school district budgets by increases in special education spending for mandated services, as well as sources of funding to support services that are essential to students with disabilities.

Special education, by definition, is more expensive than regular education and accounts for a significant portion of school budgets. It is estimated that, on average, about twice as much is spent on special education students than on their general education counterparts (Parrish & Guarino, 1999), with national expenditures at about $35 billion per year. Because the federal government is a relatively minor player, contributing an estimated 8 percent of the total costs, most special education fiscal policy is determined at the state level. State policies vary considerably, are often complex, and are undergoing major changes. However, it is important to have a structural understanding of federal and state fiscal policies and how they impact on local services. It is also important to become knowledgeable of other sources of funding that can provide substantial support for critical services.

Legal Issues

State and federal laws, primarily IDEA, require that special education services be provided to eligible students, whether or not the government has supplied adequate funding. Most federal monies are cycled through state governments that devise their own formulas for distributing them.

Funding is available from a variety of sources at the federal, state, and local levels. Each source has specific restrictions and regulations that must be checked before funds are applied for or spent. Practices that are universally illegal include using federal funds in place of basic state allocations to all students ("supplanting") and charging more than one source for the same service ("double dipping").

A new wave of school finance legislation has led to increased involvement of the judicial branch of state government in reform of education finance systems. Recent court rulings have incorporated the concept of educational adequacy in addition to the ideal of finance equity. In essence, recent court decisions have held that excess costs related to justifiable special education services must be compensated equitably across all school districts in the state (Verstegen, 1999). These decisions, as well as the pressure of increased local share of special education funding, has led to significant policy reforms in many states.

Rationale

The federal role in education is primarily to protect the civil rights of individuals and the interests of the nation. State and local agencies, in turn, are responsible for providing the equitable public education services that the laws (and the Constitution) demand. Although state and district level administrators have ultimate responsibility for acquiring and budgeting the funds to do this, building principals with a solid understanding of special education financing often can locate additional resources, use existing ones more efficiently, implement better planning, and provide higher quality service to students.

Approaches

Principals should become familiar with funding sources and their state's funding formula. After checking with district administrators, they should take the initiative to locate and apply for new sources, such as private charity funds, state health and human development funds, and federal education programs. Moreover, they should be aware that special education students may qualify for some services that have traditionally been provided outside the schools (e.g., mental health services) or services that may not be explicitly intended for disabled populations (e.g., low income). It is important to analyze a potential funding source to be sure it is appropriate by asking:

- What types of funds are available?
- Who is eligible to receive them?
- How is application made?
- Are there any restrictions on the use of these funds? If yes, what are they?
- How are funds transferred from the funding sources (delayed payment schedule, etc.)?

It is necessary to become familiar with the five steps in budget preparation: (1) identification of educational needs, (2) analysis of service delivery options, (3) exploration of funding sources, (4) matching appropriate source to cost items, and (5) preparation and submission of budget requests.

Coping with Budgets and Funding

The intent of special education is to provide instructional and instructionally related services not available in the regular program. Therefore, the total expense of educating students with disabilities will consist of the cost of the regular program plus the special educational needs created by the disability. These special programming expenditures beyond the basic student allocation in any district are referred to as excess cost and may range from a few hundred dollars to more than $25,000 per pupil per year. They can represent a substantial portion of a school district's instructional budget. The costs of providing special education services is influenced by the type of disability, placement option selected, behavioral supports, adaptation of instructional programs, medical supports, outsourcing of services, and factors that are determined by the individual needs of the student and identified in the IEP.

Special education costs and finance policy can strongly influence delivery options. Special education funding policy has the potential to serve as an incentive to encourage "best practices" or to conflict with the provision of services essential to the welfare of special education students. It is extremely important that special education and related dollars be well-spent in support of children whose future quality of life greatly depends on the services provided while they are in school (Danielson, 1999). Administrators who are responsible for programs or schools enrolling special education students must be aware of the costs of those options and services. Administrators also must be knowledgeable about the sources of funding for special education programs, how dollars earmarked for handicapped students are distributed, alternative sources of support for their services, and the ethical and legal responsibilities in managing such finances.

This information is needed for a variety of purposes:

- To aid in planning and evaluating education programs for individual students
- To improve system-wide planning and evaluation
- To determine the levels of financing required to provide an appropriate education for all children with disabilities
- To avoid inappropriate student classification and placement that may result from a misunderstanding of special education financing.

While district directors of special education are ultimately accountable for such financing, school administrators are assuming increasing responsibility for all programs in their building, including special education. Armed with an understanding of special education finance, principals can:

- Effectively monitor the special education portion of their building's programs
- Participate as partners with special education administrators in planning for these services
- Obtain access to funds for innovation, program development, special projects, teacher inservice training, or other activities to improve the education of students with disabilities.

This chapter is designed to assist administrators in gaining the fiscal information needed for effective programming in this field.

Legal Issues

The courts have been involved in the area of special education finance as early as 1971 (*PARC v. Commonwealth*) when the practice of excluding mentally handicapped children from public school education in Pennsylvania was struck down. Requirements for the education of all students with disabilities have been derived from a number of court cases discussed in other sections of this text (e.g., *Mills v. DC Board of Education*, 348 F. Supp. 866 {D.D.C. 1972} and *Maryland Association for Retarded Children v. Maryland*, Equity No. 100/182/77676 {Cir. Ct., Baltimore Co., April 9, 1974), from legislation requiring services but providing no supportive funding (e.g., P.L. 93-112) and from laws that provide both directives for service and supporting funding (e.g., IDEA).

Although variations have occurred over time, judicial activity related to state finance systems has occurred in three waves (Thro, 1990): first, plaintiffs alleged that school finance disparities constituted violations of the equal protection clause of the U.S. Constitution; second, claims were based on equity guarantees in state constitutions, state education articles, or both; and, third, plaintiffs have generally alleged violations of the state constitution based on direct application of the education article and issues of adequacy of education services (Verstegen, 1999). Recent rulings focusing on adequacy of services have challenged provisions of school finance systems by calling for system changes that will guarantee adequate services for all children, including special education students, regardless of the school setting.

In the aforementioned sources of requirements, the public school system, even without funding, is expected to support required services and procedures. Lack of funding is not an acceptable excuse for failing to provide required services, nor should it be the major factor in determining service options. The IEP for each student is to be established without regard to cost or present availability of services in the school district. Obviously, the consequence of having requirements without funding is that state and local educational agencies must provide resources from existing, or new, dollars to meet their legal obligations.

Federal Level

Although several states had already passed legislation supporting the education of students with disabilities, the passage of the Education of All Handicapped Children Act (EAHCA) (Public Law 94-142) in 1975 committed the nation to include services for students with disabilities as part of public education. The Individuals with Disabilities Education Act (IDEA) of 1990 reaffirmed and strengthened the right to a free and appropriate public education for all students with disabilities. This law is designed to provide monetary incentives for developing nonmandatory programs, as well as monetary penalties for failure to provide required services. The IDEA is the primary source of federal aid to state and local school systems for instructional and related services for infants, toddlers, children, and youth with disabilities from birth through age 21.

The 1997 Amendments to IDEA (Public Law 105-17) continue to authorize three formula grant programs and several discretionary programs and contain four parts: Part A contains definitions, findings, and purposes; Part B includes the grants to states program and preschool program; Part C concerns the infants and toddlers program; and Part D includes discretionary grants. The most important part of IDEA is Part B, Grants to States Program, which contains over 70% of the appropriation and is the primary source of federal assistance to special education programs.

The 1997 Amendments added significant new mandates, including changes in the law's fiscal provisions. These statutes represent bold and significant changes in the implementation and development of federal special education policy and finance (Danielson, 1999). Specifically, the reauthorization provides a new federal funding formula, focuses attention on improving educational results for children with disabilities, and allows benefits from special education grants to accrue to children without disabilities under certain conditions.

Because state and federal funding provisions have provided fiscal incentives for increasing the number of students identified for special education services, the new federal policy changes are intended to eliminate these incentives as well as focus on improving educational results for students with disabilities. The new law uses a census-based formula that applies after certain levels of federal funding have been attained. Specifically, under the Part B, Grants to States Program, appropriations above $4.9 billion will trigger a new state formula that distributes a base amount to states equal to their allocations in the year before the trigger was reached. New allocations are based on the total school-age population (weighted 85%) and the total school-age population in poverty (weighted 15%). Provisions also ensure that there will be a floor and ceiling on the amount of aid states receive. As long as maintenance-of-effort provisions of the law are satisfied, districts receiving larger awards may be permitted to reduce local spending on special education (Verstegen, 1999).

The law also permits educators to use special education funding more flexibly in certain cases. Special education dollars may provide incidental benefits to nondisabled students when serving an identified student according to the student's individual education plan and allows IDEA funds to be applied to certain school-wide programs based on the number of participating students with disabilities to the total district count (Verstegen, 1999). Dollars may also be used in support of certain programs which serve students with disabilities such as Title 1 programs under section 1114 of ESEA (Parrish & Wolman, 1999).

The federal share of the total costs of special education (primarily IDEA funding) varies somewhat from state to state. For example, federal funds exceeded $9 million for the 1999–2000 school year in Montana; however, they have never paid more than 15% of the total cost of providing special education and related services in the State. According to Hartman (1980), local educational agencies often see the federal government as being in the position of dictating many rules of special education under the authority of legislative action but paying only a minor portion of the costs. From the federal perspective, laws such as the IDEA can be regarded as civil rights legislation for the disabled that reinforce the state's own statutes and need to be carried out regardless of the level of federal funding. No matter what the perspective, it is clear that federal support for special and vocational education and rehabilitation is extremely important to school districts. Moreover, recent changes in federal and, in many cases, state funding formulas are sensitive to escalating local costs for special education services and will relieve fiscal pressure on school districts created by school districts' assuming greater percentages of the overall costs of services to students with disabilities.

State Level

State educational agencies are responsible for the distribution of state (and most federal) dollars to local school districts for special education programming. This state support includes two parts: (1) the allocations for educating the students with disabilities (excess program costs); and (2) basic program allocations. The latter is made up of basic educational support for all students equally, including the disabled. It is illegal to substitute dollars provided directly or indirectly by federal allocations. For example, if state funds provide $3000 per student in basic allocations, then a federally supported allotment of $1000 for special education and related services could not be used to reduce the state commitment to $2000. This practice is known as "supplanting" and is strictly prohibited. Schools must maintain the same level of base funding for students identified for special education that is provided to other students in the district.

Each state, through its legislative authority, has established funding formulas to be used in distributing the allocations for disabled students to local educational agencies. These formulas are often complex in their consideration of staffing ratios, program costs, etc., and vary considerably from state to state. State funding formulas are divided into the following four general categories:

- Weighted—State special education funding is allocated on a per-student basis, with the amount of aid based on funding weight associated with each special education student;
- Flat Grant—Funding is based on a fixed funding amount per student, with the total state funding available for special education divided by special education count to determine the amount of state funding to be received by a district;
- Resource Based—Special education resources are allocated on the basis of dollars per unit, such as teachers or classroom units, with funding levels often derived from prescribed staff-student ratios by disability condition or type of placement; and
- Percentage Reimbursement—The amount of state funding is directly based on its expenditure for a particular program, is usually determined by allowable costs, and may be capped by the number of students served.

Several states have attempted to remove the incentives for over-identifying students for special education services that are inherent in the above funding formulas. There is also the realization that traditional formulas tend to provide disincentives for serving students with disabilities in more inclusive, integrated settings that are less expensive and generate less funding. In response to these and other issues, several states have adopted "census-based" or "population-based" funding formula wherein state aid is not based on the number of students with disabilities identified or the type of service provided. Such formulas distribute special education dollars based on total school district enrollment with the implied assumption that the number

and severity of disabilities is evenly distributed across school districts. A major consideration in these allocation processes is not only to control expenditures, but to provide maximum flexibility in the use of special education funding and eliminate the disincentives for more inclusive placements.

Although special education directors have claimed that students are receiving more inclusive education since the advent of this reform, the down side of population-based funding is the assumption of equal distribution of students with disabilities among school districts. Even though two districts of equal size may receive the same state allocation for special education, one district might identify 12 percent of their student population as needing special services while the other identifies only 6 percent. Clearly, there are both advantages and limitations to a population-based allocation process.

Local efforts also vary widely among and within states, with some providing close to 100% funding of excess costs for special education and others much smaller shares. The percentage of local funding obviously varies in relation to the percentage of costs covered by the combination of state and federal funds. Parrish and Wolman (1999) reported state expenditures per special education student ranged from $2272 in Tennessee to $18,225 in the District of Columbia. The subject of state funding formulas is extremely important and will be discussed in more detail later in this chapter.

Regional or Local Level

The greatest portion of excess cost dollars for special education comes from the federal and state levels. The remaining portion of the actual costs of providing special education and related services is the responsibility of the local school district. These funds become part of the obligation to provide adequate services to all students enrolled in the district and can be generated at the regional or local levels through some taxing scheme. Some states permit regional education units to levy taxes specifically for special education. Local school districts also may use special levies. These sources are explained in detail later in this chapter.

RELATIONSHIP BETWEEN SERVICES AND COSTS

The cost of special education is determined by the programming options selected for each student with a disability. Programs that are appropriate for students with mild disabilities obviously are less expensive than those for students with severe disabilities. However, they may vary considerably from student to student, depending on the complexity and intensity of services selected to meet unique needs. These costs also may vary within a school district from year to year, again depending on the individuals in this population.

Another factor is the extent to which the district provides its own services or contracts with other districts or cooperatives. Small districts commonly purchase or contract out services they cannot themselves supply feasibly. For example:

- Comprehensive vocational assessments may be purchased for high school students from a regional vocational assessment center. Because of the expensive equipment and highly trained staff required by this service, the per-student costs of supplying such assessments in a small district could be three or more times the expense of purchasing the service. Contracted assessments also may produce a higher quality of service.
- A residential placement may be needed for a student with unique needs, such as a deaf or blind pupil. Only very large school districts would be expected to have comprehensive services for students with such low-incidence disabilities. Although it is always preferable to keep students in their home community,

those with multiple disabilities may be served best (although not always) in a residential center. When this option is chosen, the sending district must pay for both residential care and educational services. These costs may easily exceed $25,000 per year.

- A physical or occupational therapist may be obtained by a local school district on a part-time basis from the intermediate school district or a larger neighboring district to serve a limited number of students with disabilities. In such a case, the local district would have determined in advance that because of the few students needing such therapy, it would be most economical to contract for itinerant specialists. The alternative would be to hire these specialists through the local district. Contracts may be for diagnostic services or for remedial services and can run a year or longer, depending on need.

Obviously, there is a close relationship between special education programs and their costs, suggesting that a better understanding of the basis for the costs can lead to more realistic, effective, and efficient program selections and funding decisions. The following are reasons for excess costs (beyond regular education costs) of these special programs that are noted by most authorities:

- Additional and Related Special Education Services—Most students with disabilities receive programs and services in addition to enrollment in regular education from itinerant specialists, consulting teachers, resource rooms, and other program formats described in this text.
- Special Classes—Self-contained classes for students with moderate disabilities typically have much smaller student-teacher ratios, and the additional classroom costs (teacher salaries and benefits, operation and maintenance expenses) greatly increase the per-student expenditures.
- Multiple Special Education Services—Some students require a combination of services—

for example, special classrooms plus physical therapy.

- Residential Programs—Public or private residential settings are the costliest placements because they involve such additional expenses as housing, feeding, etc.
- Identification, Assessment, and Educational Planning—The process of individualized assessment and planning required for each student with disabilities creates additional expenses, primarily in staff time.
- Additional Staff Support and Training—Support and training also are needed for teachers, principals, administrators, parents, nondisabled students, and others to make the least restrictive placement (LRE) approach effective. This involves the services of trainers, consultants, school psychologists, counselors, social workers, etc.
- Greater Age Span—The IDEA encourages education for students with disabilities under age 5 and from age 18 to 21. Such students are an additional financial burden for schools, especially because they may require large concentrations of resources for few students.

A TAXONOMY OF SPECIAL EDUCATION FINANCE

To enhance understanding of a complex system, Crowner (1985) has developed a taxonomy of special education finance. Although somewhat dated, the taxonomy appears to have advantages over other sources of finance information that lack consistent terminology and fail to cover all of the relevant elements. It is used as a basis for the following discussion of special education funding.

Crowner's taxonomy classifies financial terms into four categories:

1. Base, the element(s) upon which revenues are figured
2. Formula, the method used to compute revenues generated by the base elements

3. Source, the agency from which revenues flow
4. Type, restrictions placed on the possible use of revenue by the source (p. 504)

Bases for Computing Revenue

Different states compute the amount of funding allotted to districts according to different bases. Crowner (1985, pp. 504–505) also lists five of these upon which special education funding may be determined.*

1. *Pupil Base:* Funding is generated based on the number of students served. This base figure includes all students from the district who are eligible for special services under the guidelines of the funding source, including those in residential placement or those receiving purchased services from another agency.
2. *Resource Base:* Funding is generated based on the specific resources needed to meet student needs. The resource most typically identified is personnel, but others may include equipment, supplies, etc.
3. *Service Base:* Funding is generated on the basis of the type of service supplied—an itinerant program such as speech therapy, or placement in a resource room or a self-contained special classroom.
4. *Cost Base:* Funding is generated based on the actual cost of operating a special education program. Cost guidelines often are published for various services so that expenses claimed by districts do not exceed a percentage of the cost to be covered or level of cost per service that the funding source has established as reasonable.
5. *Unit Base:* Funding is generated based on a combination of possible funding bases. For example, a unit may include a teacher, an aide, and a fixed number of students, with

---

*From "A Taxonomy of Special Education Finance," by T. T. Crowner, 1985, *Exceptional Children, 51* (6), pp. 504–505. Copyright 1985 by The Council for Exceptional Children. Reprinted with permission.

moneys provided for the resources necessary to operate it. A school district would be reimbursed for each such unit claimed. Funding sources usually allow reimbursement for partial units (e.g., one-half a unit) because enrollment rarely matches the fixed number of students in a given unit. A special case of unit-based funding arises when reimbursed costs are limited to all or a portion of the salaries of persons who work with students with disabilities.

A sixth base described earlier is census or population, which is the funding based on the entire enrollment of students with disabilities as well as those without disabilities. This base for determining special education funding is relatively new and is becoming more popular as a method of containing costs related to the increasing number of students identified for special education services. This approach to determining funding allows financial support to follow special education students into regular educational settings. The flexibility in use of funding which is achieved through a census-based or population-based model eliminates the disincentives for inclusion that are inherent in the other methods of calculating funding for special education.

Formulas for Computing Revenue

As Hartman (1980) suggests, funding formulas for special education are simply vehicles for transferring dollars earmarked for educating students with disabilities from one governmental level to another (e.g., state department of education to local school district). The choice of formula at any level also becomes important for the incentives and disincentives it creates for school districts in providing services for students with disabilities. Although the law requires that the most appropriate education must be provided to students with disabilities, the formula used to distribute special education dollars will in effect influence the selection of services.

Crowner (1985, p. 505) lists five different (although not necessarily mutually exclusive)

types of formulas in his taxonomy of special education finance:*

Excess cost formula—This formula (a) takes the cost of a basic education program, (b) compares that figure with the cost of a given special education program, and then (c) applies funding to make up some or all of any discrepancy associated with excess costs of special education. Typically, this formula is applied to the pupil base where the per-pupil cost of a basic education is compared with the per-pupil cost of special education.

Percent of cost formula—This formula limits the revenue generated by a base to some fractional percentage of the real cost associated with that base. For example, it may be applied to the cost base by reimbursing a limit of about 70% of allowable costs.

Straight sum formula—This formula applies differential weights to base elements described above. These weights may be based on indices of actual cost or on a perceived relative need. For example, the program of a pupil with severe disabilities can be assumed to be more costly than an educational program for a mildly disabled pupil, or a resource service may be considered less costly than a self-contained class.

Mixed Formula—This formula may consist of any combination of the other four formulas. Many combinations are possible. For example, the percent of cost formula could be applied with the weighted formula, resulting in reimbursement of some percentage of the relative higher and lower cost figures associated with different services. That is, the state could

---

*From "A Taxonomy of Special Education Finance," by T. T. Crowner, 1985, *Exceptional Children, 51* (6), p. 505. Copyright 1985 by The Council for Exceptional Children. Reprinted with permission.

determine that a student in a resource room should be weighted 1.5 times a regular student in the basic education program but choose to reimburse on 75 percent of the resulting figure.

Types of Revenue

Certain restrictions are always placed on funds supplied by the various sources. These constraints may set limits to the length of the fiscal support or the population to which it is directed, or they may require a percentage of support from the recipient school district. Such controls are an attempt to ensure that the funded program reflects the goals of the financial source. For example, funding intended to stimulate program development in school districts would not be available on a continuing basis; rather, it would be provided for a fixed time to support start-up costs. Once a program is established, the school district would be expected to find other sources of support.

In his taxonomy, Crowner (1985, pp. 505–506) identifies eight types of revenue and their restrictions:*

1. *Continuing Fund*—This type can continue for several years, although the level of funding may fluctuate according to yearly appropriate levels or other factors. Continuing funds usually are stable and can be relied on to support long-term services. State funding for basic education can be considered a form of continuing funds.
2. *Noncontinuing Funds*—These are provided for a fixed period and usually are intended to remedy a short-term need (e.g., teacher inservice course), stimulate a district-supported program (e.g., establishment of an assessment center), or address other district problems of a short-term nature. Competitive grant awards offered by state or federal

agencies are examples. Although they have a definite termination date and rarely extend beyond three years, they can be excellent sources of support for program enhancement or development. However, administrators and principals must keep in mind the time limitations of this funding and not become dependent on it for essential services such as classroom teachers or aides.

3. *Targeted Funds*—This type of revenue is earmarked for specific items: program types (e.g., vocational education), classifications of students (e.g., secondary special education), or categories such as personnel and equipment. Funds not spent on targeted items are considered misused and must be returned to the funding source.
4. *Discretionary Funds*—These may be used to support whatever activities are considered relevant to the objectives of a funding source. Certain moneys coming to the states from the federal government fall in this category.
5. *Inside Formula Funds*—These are received from one funding source and must be deducted in part (or entirely) from a request for reimbursement from another source. This is simply a mechanism used internally by a school district or other agency to distribute financial support from different sources to various special education program areas.
6. *Outside Formula Funds*—This type of revenue, when received by a school district or agency, is not deducted from other primary sources of funding. However, administrators should be warned that under no circumstances may they use two sources of funding to pay for the same item. This sometimes is referred to as double dipping and is strictly illegal. An example would be requesting reimbursement from a granting source for a cost item that has been paid for by state basic education funding. Although the terms "inside" and "outside" funding are not used commonly, they do illustrate an important concept in sorting out the many

*From "A Taxonomy of Special Education Finance," by T. T. Crowner, 1985, *Exceptional Children, 51* (6), p. 505–506. Copyright 1985 by The Council for Exceptional Children. Adapted by permission.

different sources of fiscal support for special education.

7. *Matching Funds*—The restriction on this type of revenue is that the receiving agency must provide a pre-established portion of the cost of a funded program. In the true sense of the word, "matched" cost would be equal contributions from the receiving agency and the funding source. In practice, the portion contributed by each will vary depending on the funding source's guidelines. Further restrictions may exist on the source of the matching dollars contributed by, say, the school district. It often is illegal to match one batch of federal dollars with other federal dollars. This is reasonable in light of the fact that a major purpose of the matching requirement is to show commitment by the agency receiving the funding. When it is necessary to match a funding source 50-50, or at any other percentage, the matched portion may not need to be in actual dollars; "in-kind" contributions often are permissible—services, facilities, or equipment provided by the agency. Of course, these contributions must be real and must represent necessary program items.

8. *Mixed Funds*—These represent any combination of two or more of the types of funding above.

SOURCES OF REVENUE

School districts may draw on many sources of revenue to support the excess cost of special education services. Prudent administrative practice suggests that a district utilize its funding resources to the maximum extent possible. This requires knowledge of the funding possibilities, ability to match a funding source with a district need, skill in obtaining and managing funds, and a supportive school district administration that recognizes the benefits of a broad base of financial backing.

Knowledge of funding possibilities extends beyond simple awareness of the existence of a source of funds. An administrator who is effective in this area must find answers to questions such as the following:

- What are the types of items supported by the funding source?
- Who is eligible to receive funding?
- How is the application for funding made?
- What are the restrictions on the use of funds?
- What are the conditions for transferring dollars from the funding source to the recipient agency?

Government funding sources are obligated to make information available through rules and regulations that answer these and other pertinent questions. Although not required to do so, private funding sources also usually make information available to potential grantees as a means of stimulating a large pool of qualified applicants. It is preferable to request information from a funding source by means of a formal letter so that it is documented, as opposed to telephone calls that can be forgotten in the midst of a busy schedule.

Once aware of various funding possibilities, the administrator needs to determine whether a potential source can be a good match with a particular program need. Considerations in making this decision include:

- whether the intent and budgetary needs of the program to be funded are understood;
- whether any restriction on the funding would jeopardize program outcomes (e.g., necessary equipment cannot be charged to the funding source); and
- whether restrictions, either programmatic or fiscal, would be unacceptable to the school district (e.g., cost reimbursed on a delayed schedule).

Skill in obtaining and managing funds is necessary for any school district administrator, but it is especially important for those involved with special education programs. Although the same financial opportunities are available to all districts, those whose administrators have fund-seeking skills almost always will have more funds available for special education than will their counterparts. The process of writing a grant proposal, for example, is not nearly as difficult as it may seem, but it may be intimidating to the inexperienced administrator. Numerous resource materials are available to aid those seeking out-of-district funding in support of a worthwhile project. It should be made clear that the district director of special education is the person responsible for obtaining and managing continuing funding for special education programs. However, other district personnel should be encouraged to seek out special funding opportunities, too, as long as appropriate channels are followed, communication is maintained and turf infringements are avoided.

Supportive district administrators are an essential ingredient in establishing a broad base of funding for special education. Because of special accounting procedures, required reporting, or other procedural requirements that often follow such funding, a school district's central office can find it difficult to deal with requests for such moneys. The advantages and disadvantages of a source such as a federal grant award should be weighed carefully. Obviously, such consideration involves questions: (1) How badly needed is the program which requires support? (2) If it is badly needed, are other funding opportunities available?

Some of the major sources of funding in support of students with disabilities are discussed next.

Federal Sources

The role of the federal government, as noted earlier, is to protect the constitutional rights of children for equal access to educational programs and to provide the fiscal resources necessary to maintain programs of national interest.

Most federal money reaches school districts indirectly by flowing through state departments of education or intermediate school districts. Methods of dispersing federal dollars may be classified as full support, partial assistance grants, grants based on formula, and set aside moneys. A few of the many federal sources are described below.

The Individuals with Disabilities Act (IDA)

This act was described earlier in this chapter, but will be further explained here because of its prominent role in federal special education funding. It is the primary vehicle to convey federal fiscal assistance in support of local special education services and is the federal tool to promote national policy with respect to special education. The recent reauthorization of IDEA (1997 Amendments, P.L. 105-17) incorporates a census-based (or population-based) approach into the existing funding system for special education. As noted earlier in this chapter, the census-based approach is based on total district enrollments, rather than the number of students counted as eligible for special education services. However, allocation of IDEA funding is still based on a special education child count formula until appropriations for Part B (state assistance) reach approximately $4.9 billion. At this point a new formula based on total student enrollment (85%) and poverty (15%) applies to funds appropriated over the previous year's appropriations. The new formula is subject to limitations, including certain floors and caps that apply to increases and decreases. The law does allow federal funding for infants and toddlers to rise from the current appropriations of $315 million to $400 million. Allowable funding for preschoolers is up to $500 million from a level of $360 million.

The previous IDEA and regulations prohibited supplantation of state, local and other federal funds. The 1997 reauthorization of IDEA continues this requirement and establishes a state maintenance of effort provision based on state expenditures (not federal or local). However, a goal of the recent IDEA Amendments is to relieve the pressure of local school systems created by escalating costs of serving more students identified as special education.

The new law provides a more specific interpretation of responsibilities that public schools have with respect to the provision of services to private schools. Each local education agency (LEA) must consult with representatives of private school children with disabilities on how to conduct the annual count for those children to ensure that the count is conducted on established count dates and that the data are used to determine the amount of Part B funds for serving those children in the next fiscal year. Beyond this requirement, the public schools are responsible only for providing services to the extent that they have received federal funds based on children enrolled in the private school (parochial schools are considered private schools). P.L. 105-17 also contains three provisions relating to charter schools: (1) LEA charter schools may opt not to be merged into larger LEA's (unless state law specifically prevents this); (2) non-LEA charter schools must receive an appropriate share of IDEA funds; and (3) charter schools are eligible for state discretionary program grant funds.

Student eligibility criteria are specified in the implementing regulations and may be refined through state formulas for the distribution of funds. As described earlier, these formulas vary considerably from state to state. Administrators should consult their state departments of education for specific details. They are also encouraged to consult the website for the Office of Special Education and Rehabilitative Services, Department of Education, for provisions of special interest to administrators. This site, as well as the site titled "Federal Funding for Special Education," provide up-to-date information and explanations of the rather extensive provisions

of the 1997 IDEA Amendments. Information is also available to answer questions concerning provisions relating to such issues as discipline and disputes between parents and the schools.

Carl D. Perkins Vocational and Technical Education Act of 1998 (P.L. 105-332).

The Carl D. Perkins Vocational-Technical Education Act Amendments of 1998 (P.L. 105-332) restructures and reforms programs previously authorized by the Carl D. Perkins Vocational and Applied Technology Education Act. Perkins III, as it is called, supports the alignment of vocational and technical education with state and local efforts to reform secondary schools. Along with the Workforce Investment Act of 1998, Perkins III promotes the concept of integrated "one-stop" education and workforce development. The majority of funding available under Perkins III is awarded as grants to state education agencies. These State Basic Grants are allotted on a formula basis determined by the state's populations in certain age groups and their per capita income. Money is distributed by the states to local education agencies based on a complex formula that considers special populations (including students with disabilities) and the number of students enrolled in vocational education programs.

The Carl D. Perkins Amendments of 1998 also reauthorize Tech-Prep, a program that promotes the use of work-based learning and encourages partnerships with business, labor organizations, and institutions of higher education. Among the strong partnerships emerging out of Tech-Prep is the coordination of vocational and career preparation between high schools and postsecondary technical schools. These programs may be very appropriate for some students with disabilities.

Perkins III specifically identifies funding for students with disabilities who need special services in either regular programs or special needs vocational programs. Administrators are encouraged to consult their district or state director of vocational and technical education for information relating to the availability of funding from the Carl D. Perkins Vocational-Technical Education Act Amendments of 1998.

School-to-Work Opportunities Act of 1994 (P.L. 103-239)

The School-to-Work Opportunities Act is jointly administered by the Departments of Education and Labor, and provides support to states and local education agencies (and their communities) to build high school learning opportunities that prepare students for further education and careers. Many special education students can profit from involvement in programs that are initiated by School-to-Work funding.

Job Training-Partnership Act of 1983

Some sources of federal funding for schools come from outside the U.S. Department of Education. Among these is the 1983 Job Training Partnership Act (JTPA), which is administered under the U.S. Department of Labor. JTPA replaced the 1973 Comprehensive Training and Employment Act (CETA), which also had helped fund some programs for students with disabilities. The JTPA is intended to

> . . . establish programs to prepare youth and unskilled adults for entry into the labor force and to afford job training to those economically disadvantaged individuals, and other individuals facing serious barriers to employment, who are in special need of such training to obtain productive employment (sec. 2).

State and local governments, together with the private sector, have primary responsibility for development, management and administration of training programs under the JTPA. State governors have approval authority over locally developed plans and are responsible for monitoring program compliance. Although much of

the role of the JTPA is being replaced by the Work Force Investment Act of 1998, it is still important for special education.

Educational agencies may apply for funds under certain sections of the act (e.g., Title II-A and Title II-B). However, regulations governing JTPA are somewhat complicated and require a thorough understanding of the various parts of the act before an application is developed. Administrators must take the initiative in seeking out JTPA funds because school districts may not be notified of their eligibility to participate in this program.

Although individuals with disabilities are not mentioned specifically as a target population, they are eligible for services under parts of the law. Restrictions on some JTPA moneys, such as those concerning performance expectations, may prove cumbersome in working with disabled populations. Other parts of the act (Title II-B) are more flexible and offer special opportunities for students with disabilities (e.g., summer youth programs). Information about JTPA is available through the local Private Industry Council or through the governor's office. JTPA is only one example of many programs operating through the U.S. Department of Labor and other federal agencies that supply dollars which can be tapped to support services for students with disabilities.

Other Federal Funding

While it is beyond the scope of this chapter to review all possible sources of federal funding, school administrators should be aware of major sources of continuing categorical aid, including vocational education, education of children from low-income families, compensation to schools for federal tax-exempt property, school food services, and educational research and development. Although these aid programs may be intended to serve different populations, students with disabilities often qualify as a result of meeting criteria other than disability (e.g., low income).

State Sources

Although the role of the federal government in the education of the disabled has been to encourage innovation and stimulate program development, it is the responsibility of the states to provide the actual education. As noted earlier, sources of state financing for special education vary considerably across the states, but generally consist of:

- Regular state funds for each student, including special education students
- State aid for special services distributed on a formula basis
- Local tax levies

Also discussed earlier, the state formula used appears to have greater impact on the percentage of children served in any given category of disability than on the total dollar amount distributed. States using a weighted approach to funding special education report slightly higher percentages of the school-age population served as disabled, whereas states using a census-based approach indicate that this system of funding has resulted in greater placement in regular educational settings.

Education Funding

Because of the differences between states in the selection of funding formulas and the frequency with which these formulas are revised, it is not possible to discuss this area in specific terms. Administrators should obtain and become familiar with a copy of their state's regulations concerning the disbursement of such funds.

Under a one traditional formula, for example, resources (teachers, classified staff, assessment personnel, administrators, instructional materials, and equipment) are allocated to each of 13 identifiable disability categories according to assumed need. Students with more severe disabilities have greater resources than those with less severe disabilities. State guidelines assist in the reasonably objective identification of disabil-

ities; the actual program and resource provisions for each student are left for district determination. This example is very prescriptive and differs considerably from the census-based approach, which gives local districts considerable latitude in determining the best use of their combined federal, state, and local funds and serves to reinforce the choice of inclusive placements.

Funding Outside the State Education Department

As in the case with the federal government, states also provide support for school-age children from sources outside state departments of education. These may offer local school districts dollars for special projects, equipment or supplies, resource personnel, or entire programs. For example, a state department of vocational rehabilitation (DVR)—operating under federal guidelines and receiving partial federal support—often works closely with public school systems. It can enter into agreements with local districts to provide employment-related training and services to eligible secondary school students.

The IDEA requires that no later than age 14, school districts include in each student's IEP a transition plan to aid in the student's move to adult life (see Chapter 8). As part of the plan, schools must identify appropriate adult service providers and help establish links with those providers; vocational rehabilitation (VR) should be considered among those providers. To be eligible for VR services, students must show a mental, physical, or learning disability that interferes with the ability to work. Students receiving services must have an Individualized Plan for Employment (IPE), which should be coordinated with the student's IEP. States are not required to consider financial need when providing VR services.

In some states, the DVR is extremely active in the public schools, offering a variety of services to students with disabilities; in other states, it has taken a somewhat hands-off position toward involvement with potential clients who are still being served in public schools. VR agencies who are reluctant to provide services until students have completed their eligibility for special education service often cite duplication of services, or what is referred to as the comparable benefits requirement. The authors believe that the efforts of both special education and VR are enhanced when services are initiated during high school and are well-coordinated. Certainly, legitimate issues must be overcome in such collaborative arrangements, such as the ownership of assistive technology.

Administrators need to be on the lookout for other opportunities to leverage the school's resources with other state agencies to improve services for students with disabilities. A good example is the mental health services plan in the state of Montana, which opens the door for schools to be mental health centers. This arrangement allows mental health service providers to be placed in the schools. Local administrators should check such agencies as family services, mental health agencies, and VR for services that can benefit students. It is especially important to get to know the people who are responsible for agencies that can be aligned with special education students and programs.

Other Sources

Intermediate Education Agencies

These entities are geographically located to serve multiple school districts. Referred to by different names (e.g., Board of Cooperative Educational Services in Colorado), these agencies often coordinate special education regionally and provide services and materials to districts that could not provide their own services cost-effectively. The intermediate education agency can contribute funds as well as services to local districts within their jurisdiction. In some states, they may generate revenue through special regional taxing schemes. In Michigan, for example, intermediate units have authority to levy taxes for special education. However, the role of intermediate agencies usually is limited to distributing special education funds from state and federal sources for such activities as special projects, teacher inservice training, and research, or providing those services directly to local districts. They also may offer special programming options or equipment (e.g., vocational assessment, equipment for the blind) on a cooperative basis to districts. Intermediate educational agencies can be excellent sources of information about state and federal funding possibilities.

Local Sources

Local revenues for special education include funds generated by taxing mechanisms, such as property or other taxes. At the discretion of local school districts, special levies may be placed on the ballot and, if approved by voters, can support educational programs for all students, including those with disabilities. Occasionally, a levy may request bond issues to support facilities for general education, special education, or both.

Private Sources

Revenue may be given by or solicited from individuals, charities, or private businesses. This is the least-used source of funds for public school special education in part because the procedures used in obtaining private funds, as well as the specific sources, are not well-understood by school personnel. In the past, public school education has been perceived as a public obligation, rather than a cause for charitable donations. However, in recent years, school administrators have recognized the advantage of private funding to assist with special programs, to purchase equipment and supplies, to conduct research, and to improve education in other ways.

Private funding normally is obtained through some sort of application process, depending on the source and often on the level of request. Applications may range from simple to quite complex—from a simple letter requesting funds to a detailed document. Schools seeking funding for a worthwhile cause after exhausting governmental sources should explore private funding. Larger school districts will often have a grants specialist or other administrator who is responsible for assisting in soliciting extramural funding and overseeing externally funded projects. Smaller districts are encouraged to use local resources such as public libraries, which should have lists, journals, and books on funding sources.

PREPARING BUDGETS

There are five essential steps in the preparation for educational programs:

1. Identification of educational needs to be addressed
2. Analysis of services needed and cost variations between service delivery options
3. Exploration of funding sources, including restrictions and methods of disbursement of revenue
4. Matching of sources of funding to cost items or service units
5. Preparation and submission of program budget requests, along with program justifications

The regular administrators' role in budget preparation will vary, depending on the distribution of responsibilities between themselves and the special education administrators or grants specialist. At the very least, the former should provide input for the first two steps listed above. In smaller districts, or those with strong tendencies toward building level control, the regular program administrator (e.g., principal) could become involved in all five steps. Preparation and submission of a competitive grant proposal usually involves the administrator at all five steps. Therefore, four of the five are discussed next; Step 1, identification of educational needs, is addressed in other chapters.

Step 2: Analysis of Services

The cost structure of special services for students with disabilities involves the type of delivery system options available (e.g., self-contained classrooms, resource rooms), the type of students' disabilities and their severity, and the relationship between special and regular education costs (excess costs). The costs of each special program, including its activities, organizational units, or individual cost items, can be analyzed.

Step 3: Exploration of Funding Sources

This begins by looking at the continuing funds already available to the district. Funding such as state formula grants for excess costs may wholly or partially support the program under consideration. If current district funding is insufficient or cannot be matched appropriately to program activities, then the search must continue. The district's grants specialist, if there is one, should be consulted. The person in this position frequently has a broad base of information about federal, state, local, and even private funding possibilities. If there is no such individual, then the intermediate educational agency and/or the state department of education should be contacted.

Step 4: Matching of Sources of Funding

Once possible sources of funding have been identified, regulations governing the use of the moneys should be reviewed thoroughly. Special attention should be given to restrictions on the use of the funds. Among the questions that should be asked:

- Can the funds be used appropriately to support the desired activities?
- Can the funds be obtained quickly enough?
- Is there a matching requirement?
- Can the district really compete if the funds are distributed on a competitive basis?
- Does the funding agency have any expectations of the administrator or the district

that are not acceptable (e.g., reporting requirements)?

If the answers to these questions are acceptable, then a probable funding source has been found.

Step 5: Preparation and Submission of Program Budget

The annual budget request for special education is prepared along with a program justification and submitted with those from other organizational units to be reviewed by the district. These budget requests are then submitted to the school board for review and are accepted or revised.

Traditionally, in the preparation of the budget, figures are grouped by "line items" or "objects of expenditures," such as personnel, fringe benefits, supplies, equipment, travel, and so forth. These line items are called direct costs of program operation because they are related directly to the delivery of services.

Expenses of supporting activities are referred to as indirect (or overhead) costs and include administrative expenses, accounting, and other costs associated with housing the program. In budget planning for grants and contracts, these indirect charges may be fixed at a predetermined level; for example, 8 percent of the direct costs.

In addition to projecting the line item costs, it is necessary to figure costs of certain components of special and regular education. These components allow budget planners to determine excess costs of special education services and to plug necessary figures into state formulas. Components to be figured include:

- Regular program costs
- Regular program costs per pupil (regular program cost divided by the number of full-time pupils in regular education)
- Special program costs by category of exceptionality, unit, or other element upon which revenues are based

- Special program costs per pupil, unit, or other base element (cost of special education divided by the number of full-time pupils in special education, units, or other base elements)
- The cost differential or excess costs per pupil, unit, or other base element (component 4 minus component 2)
- The cost index of special to regular programs (component 4 divided by component 2)
- The cost index of special to regular programs (component 4 divided by component 2)

Once this information has been obtained, it can be applied in the state special education funding formula, and to other sources of funding, in determining the district and nondistrict share of special education financing.

A principal or administrator who has mastered these basic aspects of budget preparation and special education funding may find that the school has more resources available more easily than previously perceived.

FUNDING TRENDS

The current national interest in restructuring schools is likely to continue and focus increasingly on special education as part of regular education. Coupled with the concern for escalating costs of special education services nationally, there is strong interest in bringing together the two parallel systems of special and regular education to serve all children more effectively. Based on a 1997 survey of special education officials in the 50 states conducted by the Center for Special Education Finance, as well as contemporary literature, a reconsideration of special education policy seems to be driven by several factors, including questions about funding system incentives and the most appropriate placements for students with disabilities, the costs of special education services, and the need for increased decision-making and flexibility in how funds are used at the local level (Fruchter, Parrish, & Berne, 1999).

There is a growing realization that the dual service system that has been created in special and regular education can be better integrated to improve education for all children. Fruchter, Parrish, and Berne (1999) believe increasing the capacity of general education to address the needs of many mildly and moderately disabled students now assigned to special education programs can " . . . shift significant resources from evaluation, placement, transportation, and tracking to classroom instruction and support" (p. 178). It has already been shown that teachers who are working in more inclusive schools may see students as needing lower levels of need than do teachers working in more segregated settings (Chambers, 1999). Trends in funding policies at both the federal and state levels are beginning to reflect support for students with disabilities being served in inclusive settings. This is in contrast to previous policies that have not provided support for students in regular educational settings and, thus, discouraged placement in inclusive settings.

Coertz, McLaughlin, Roach, and Saber (1999) suggest that "special and general educators must transcend their own separateness and work together to ensure that standards-based reform does improve the outcomes for students with disabilities" (p. 52). Funding patterns for special education are beginning to reflect the same expectations for performance that are influencing general education. Regular and special educators throughout the nation must continue to strive to work more closely to eliminate the traditional lines between special and general education that have served as artificial barriers to serving all students well.

CONCLUSION

Special education costs and finance policy can strongly influence options for the delivery of services to special education students. It is the intent of special education to provide instructional and instructionally related services not available in the regular program. Therefore, the cost of serving students with disabilities is more expensive than educating nondisabled students. The federal share of the total costs of special education varies somewhat among the states, but is a minor portion of the total costs of special education. State educational agencies are responsible for the distribution of state and most federal dollars to local school districts for special education programming. Each state, through its legislative authority, has established funding formulas to be used in distributing the allocations. These formulas are often complex and vary from state to state.

The cost of providing special education services has increased considerably due to mandated services, improved technology and service to a broader range of students. States, and to a degree the federal government, are attempting to contain these costs by removing the incentives for identifying larger numbers of students for special education services. There is also a realization that traditional funding formulas tend to provide disincentives for serving students with disabilities in more inclusive, integrated settings. New formulas adopted by some states include "census-based" or "population-based" funding that distributes dollars based on total school population rather than the number of students served or type of service provided. Many of these new formulas provide more flexibility to school administrators in serving all children who require special assistance.

While the greatest portion of excess cost dollars for special education come from the federal and state levels, the remaining portion comes from local school districts as part of their obligation to provide services to all students. Local districts may generate additional funding in support of special education costs from a variety of sources, including special levies, grant funding, and funds available from other state and federal appropriations such as the Carl D.

Perkins Vocational-Technical Education Act Amendments of 1998. Students with special needs may be eligible for funding from these other sources based on qualifications unrelated to their disability (e.g., economic level). Additional funding sources can enhance services to special education students and increase their chances for enjoyable and productive lives.

The new wave of school finance legislation has led to increased involvement of the judicial branch of state government in reform of education finance systems. Recent court decisions have held that excess costs of special education must be compensated equitably across school districts. These decisions, as well as the pressure in increased local share of special education costs, have led to significant reforms in funding formulas. Administrators are advised to stay current with funding regulations that may be changing in their states.

REFERENCES

Carl D. Perkins Vocational Education Act, P.L. 98-523, 98 Stat. 2433 (1984).

Carl D. Perkins Vocational and Technical Education Act, P.L. 105-332 (1998).

Chambers, J. G. (1999). The patterns of expenditures on students with disabilities: A methodological and empirical analysis, In Parrish, T. B., Chambers, J. G., & Guarino, C. M. (Eds.), *Funding Special Education*. Thousand Oaks, CA: Corwin Press.

Coertz, M. E., McLaughlin, M. J., Roach, V., & Saber, S. M. (1999). What will it take? Including students with disabilities in standards based education reform, In Parrish, T. B., Chambers, J. G. & Guarino, C. M. (Eds.), *Funding Special Education*. Thousand Oaks, CA: Corwin Press.

Crowner, T. (1985). A taxonomy of special education finance. *Exceptional Children, 51*, 503–508.

Danielson, L. (1999). Foreword to Parrish, T. B., Chambers, J. G., & Guarino, C. M. (Eds.), *Funding Special Education*. Thousand Oaks, CA: Corwin Press.

Fruchter, N., Parrish, T. B, & Berne, R. (1999). Financing special education: Proposed reforms, In Parrish, T. B., Chambers, J. G., & Guarino, C. M. (Eds.), *Funding Special Education*. Thousand Oaks, CA: Corwin Press.

Hartman, W. T. (1980). *Policy effects of special education funding formulas*. Palo Alto, CA: Stanford University.

Individuals With Disabilities Act, P.L. 105-332 (1998).

Job Training Partnership Act, P.L. 97-300, 96 Stat. 1322 (1980).

Maryland Association for Retarded Children v. Maryland, {Equity No. 100/182/77676} Cir. Ct., Baltimore Co. April 9, 1974.

Mills v. Board of Education. 348 F Supp. 866 (D.D.C. 1972).

Parrish, T. B. & Guarino, C. M. (1999). Preface to Parrish, T. B. Chambers, J. G. & Guarino C. M. (Eds.), *Funding Special Education*. Thousand Oaks, CA: Corwin Press.

Parrish, T. B., & Wolman, J. (1999). Trends and new developments in special education funding: What the states report, In Parrish, T. B., Chambers, J. G., & Guarino, C. M. (Eds.), *Funding Special Education*. Thousand Oaks, CA: Corwin Press.

Pennsylvania Association for Retarded Citizens (PARC) v. Pennsylvania, 334 F. Supp. 1257 (E.D. Pa. 1971), 343 F. Supp. 279 (E.D. Pa. 1972).

School-to-Work Opportunity Act, P.L. 103-239 (1994).

Thro, W. F. (1990). The third wave: The impact of the Montana, Kentucky and Texas decisions of the future of public school finance reform litigation. *Journal of Law and Education, 19* (2), 243–250.

Verstegen, D. A. (1999). Trends and new developments in special education, In Parrish, T. B., Chambers, J. G., & Guarino, C. M. (Eds.), *Funding Special Education*. Thousand Oaks, CA: Corwin Press.

RECOMMENDED READINGS

Since special education funding formulas are changing very rapidly, administrators are encouraged to visit the following websites for the most current information.

United States Department of Education, Office of Special Education Programs (OSEP) *http://www.ed.gov/offices/OSERS/OSEP/index.html*

Information on all aspects of IDEA implementation including federal funding provisions are provided. A specific page to visit is Special Education Expenditure Project (completed December 2001).

Center for Special Education Finance (CSEP)

http://csef.air.org/biblio.html

Provides an up-to-date, annotated bibliography on special education finance and information related to support for special education services throughout the United States. Refer to this website for a complete listing of Center publications.

IDEA Practices

http://www.ideapractices.org/tour.htm

Provides a variety of information on the implementation of the IDEA and addresses frequently asked questions about IDEA.

Council for Exceptional Children (CEC)

http://www.cec.sped.org/

The Council for Exceptional Children is the major professional organization representing the field of special education. The organization's web pages contain numerous resources to assist school administrators to best serve students with disabilities.

Implementing IDEA, A guide for Principals was developed by the National Association of Elementary School Principals in collaboration with the IDEA local implementation by Local Administrators Partnership (ILIAD) project. This publication can be down loaded free at:

http://www.ideapractices.org/implement.pdt

Relevant Federal Regulations

38 C.F.R.	Part 21 Vocational Rehabilitation and Education
32 C.F.R.	Part 300 Assistance to States for the Education of Children with Disabilities
34 C.F.R.	Part 403 State Vocational and Applied Technology Education Program
20 C.F.R.	Part 416 Supplemental Security Income for the Aged, Blind, and Disabled
32 C.F.R.	Part 80 Provision of Early Intervention Services to Eligible Infants and Toddlers with Disabilities and their Families, and Special Education Children with Disabilities
32 C.F.R.	Part 57 Provision of Early Intervention and Special Education Services to Eligible DOD Dependents in Overseas Areas
34 C.F.R.	Part 104 Nondiscrimination on the Basis of Handicap in Programs and Activities Receiving Federal Financial Assistance
34 C.F.R.	Part 84 Nondiscrimination on the Basis of Handicap in Programs and Activities Receiving Federal Financial Assistance
34 C.F.R.	Part 106 Nondiscrimination on the Basis of Sex in Education Program and Activities Receiving or Benefiting from Federal Financial Assistance
34 C.F.R.	Part 400 Vocational and Applied Technology Education Programs—General Provisions
20 C.F.R.	Part 404, Subpart P Determining Disability and Blindness

PART III

EXCEPTIONALITY
IN CHILDREN
AND ADOLESCENTS

CHAPTER 13

AUTISM

CHAPTER PREVIEW

Autism is a life-long disability that impacts communication, social interaction, and learning. The symptoms of autism usually are apparent in the first years of life. Students with autism often receive special education and related services as infants and toddlers.

Students with autism often display behaviors characteristic of the disability, including:

- Disturbances in the rate of appearance of physical, social, and language skills
- Abnormal responses to sensations
- Abnormal speech, language, and nonverbal communication development
- Abnormal ways of relating to people, to objects, and to events in the environment

An appropriate instructional program for a student with autism would typically address communication and language skills, social skills, behavior management, vocational skills, and community living. The appropriate instructional methodology for students with autism is a controversial issue. Advocates of visual approaches (e.g., Treatment and Education of Autistic and Related Communication Handicapped Children [TEACCH]) stress the importance of structure in the physical environment, developing schedules and work systems, making expectations clear and explicit, and using visual materials. Proponents of applied behavioral analysis approaches (e.g., Lovaas) use operant conditioning and behavioral modification, described as discrete trial discrimination training. Other interactional approaches (e.g., social stories) have been used to teach language and social skills to students with autism.

The successful inclusion of students with autism requires a variety of supports, including:

- Paraprofessional availability
- Reduced class size
- Adequate teacher and staff planning time
- Access to related service
- Adequate teacher preparation

FEDERAL DEFINITION OF AUTISM

Autism is described as a developmental disability significantly affecting verbal and nonverbal communication and social interaction, generally evident before age 3, that adversely affects a child's educational performance. Other characteristics often associated with autism are engagement in repetitive activities and stereotyped movements, resistance to environmental change or change in daily routines, and unusual responses to sensory experiences. The term does not apply if a child's educational performance is adversely affected primarily because the child has an emotional disturbance. A child who manifests the characteristics of autism after age 3 could be diagnosed as having autism if the criteria are satisfied [34 C.F.R. § 300. 7(1)].

REFERRAL AND INITIAL ASSESSMENT

The unique characteristics of autism are often identified before a child's third birthday. Parents may notice that their infant does not cuddle, make eye contact, or respond to affection and touching, or has unusual responses to sensory stimulation from hearing, smelling, tasting, movement, or reaction to pain. The young child with autism may be unable to communicate appropriately, and may echo the language of others, repeat words or phrases, or use gestures in place of words. Parents may notice that their child with autism has unusual body movements, such as spinning or finger flicking, or unusual responses to objects, such as avoidance or preoccupation. The child may be unable to develop interactions with others. Because these characteristics are recognized in early development, children with autism are often referred for special education services as infants and toddlers (see Chapter 7).

The Autism Society of America (ASA, 2001) reports that there are no medical tests for diagnosing autism; thus, accurate diagnosis must be based on observation of the individual's communication, behavior, and developmental levels. Various medical tests may be included to identify other possible causes of the symptoms being exhibited. Because the characteristics of the disorder vary so widely, ideally a child should be evaluated by a multidisciplinary team which might include a neurologist, psychologist, developmental pediatrician, speech-language therapist, learning consultant, or another professional knowledgeable about autism. The U.S. Department of Education reported that 34,101 students with autism were served during the 1996–97 school year, representing 0.7 percent of the total number of students with disabilities (U.S. Dept. of Education, 1998).

CHARACTERISTICS OF AUTISM

The ASA (2001) describes autism as a severely incapacitating, lifelong developmental disability that typically becomes evident in the first 3 years of life. Autism usually manifests itself by the appearance of typical behavioral symptoms in the following areas:

1. Disturbances in the development of physical, social and language skills.
2. Abnormal responses to sensory input.
3. Disturbances in speech, language, and nonverbal communication.
4. Unusual interactions with people, objects, and to events in the environment.

Eaves (1990) researched behavior commonly ascribed to children with autism and found three factors.

Affective and Cognitive Indifference

Several dimensions and characteristics were included in this factor, including:

- Autism (e.g., avoidance of eye contact, blank expression, lack of emotion, preference for being left alone, dislike of hugging)
- Hand and body use (e.g., finger flicking, hand shaking, rocking, staring at hands)
- Sensory stimulation (e.g., spinning jar lids, plates; playing with spinning tops; fascination for rushing air and "crinkly" sounds; unusual interest in texture)
- Peculiar mannerisms (e.g., unwillingness to use hands, unusual sensitivity to smells, making peculiar sounds inside the mouth)
- Fascination for objects (e.g., saving or hoarding materials; carrying one particular object at all times; fascination for elevators, fans, lawn mowers, etc.)
- No response to pain

Affect

The dimensions and characteristics of autistic behavior included:

- Eating (e.g., picky eating)
- Aggression and conduct (e.g., biting, pulling hair, scratching others, banging head, biting own hand, whining, crying, screaming when desires are not met, noncompliance)
- Distorted affect (e.g., crying on "happy" occasions, crying without vocalizing)
- Anxiety/fear (e.g., overreacting to changes in the environment, excessive fear of loud noises, anxiety around water, fearfulness in crowds)
- Noncommunicative vocalizations (e.g., using little or no functional speech, uttering sounds for words)

Cognition

- Savant behavior (extreme skill in one area, memorization of commercials and advertisements)
- Speech (e.g., misusing pronouns, monotonal or "wooden" speech, echolalia, monotonal, loud speech)
- Skill development (e.g., uneven skill development)

Although certain characteristics are associated with autism, children with autism vary tremendously in abilities and needs. The impact of autism on a student's abilities may range from mild to severe. IEP teams need to consider this variability when planning educational programs for students with autism.

INSTRUCTION

Various approaches to instruction have addressed the "What to teach" questions for students with autism (Mirenda & Donnellan, 1987). Advocates of a development approach suggest curricular content decisions be based on activities that match the student's cognitive and conceptual abilities. Proponents of an ecological approach require selecting curricular content that will ultimately and directly enhance the ability of students to function in a variety of domestic, recreational/leisure and vocational environments. The influence of both approaches emphasizes the selection of curricular content that is developmentally appropriate and also based on an ecological assessment of potential utility to the student.

An appropriate instructional program for a student with autism would typically address communication-language skills, social skills, behavior management, vocational skills, and community living skills (ASA, 1996). The "How to teach" questions have resulted in a variety of approaches involving behavioral and interactive models. The following are examples of instructional approaches for students with autism.

Visual Approaches

TEACCH

The TEACCH approach, developed by Eric Schopler, involves the development of a program based on an autistic child's skills, interests, and needs. Structured teaching is an important component of the TEACCH model and involves organizing the physical environment, developing schedules and work systems, making expectations clear and explicit, and using visual materials. Although independent work skills are emphasized, the program also addresses communication, social, and leisure skills (Mesibov, 1996).

Students with autism have difficulty with organization and sequencing. They also have receptive language and memory deficits that cause difficulty in understanding rules and directions. Visual structures are helpful in assisting students with autism interact appropriately with their environment. Structuring the physical environment of the classroom gives these students visual cues about how and where to respond. The schedule of daily activities is also carefully structured. Visual schedules promote student organization, smooth activity transitions, and task engagement. Instructional methods are also organized and systematic. The structure within the curriculum involves "work stations" and "task organization" that provides the students with a systematic and successful way to approach each task (e.g., left-to-right sequence, matching numbers, finished work in containers). This structure also minimizes distractions, helps with personal organization and assists in personal independence.

The TEACCH model has been criticized as being not a teaching or learning system, but a behavioral management system that employs rigid routines, the need for predictability, using

objects of obsession as rewards, and a day "filled with charts and other visual aids" that become the focus of the program (Autism-PDD Resources Network, 1997).

Applied Behavioral Approaches

The UCLA Project (Lovaas, 1987)

The UCLA project, also described as the Early Intervention Project (EIP), was designed as a "special, intense and comprehensive learning environment" wherein several well-trained student therapists are assigned to work with each student in home, school, and community environment an average of 40 hours per week for 3 or more years. Parents work as part of the treatment team and are extensively trained so treatment can take place for almost all of the student's waking hours, 365 days per year.

The conceptual basis of the treatment is operant conditioning and behavioral modification using discrete trial discrimination training. Students are repeatedly presented with a stimulus (e.g., verbal direction to look at the teacher) and are reinforced for a correct response (e.g., eye contact with the teacher). Aggressive and self-stimulatory behaviors are decreased by ignoring or time-out procedures and alternative appropriate behaviors are reinforced. First year goals typically include:

1. Reduce self-stimulatory and aggressive behavior with operant techniques (e.g., differential reinforcement, time-out, verbal "No", and mild aversives such as a slap on the thigh)
2. increasing compliance to elementary verbal requests (e.g., "look at me", "sit down")
3. improve imitation
4. promoting toy play
5. extending treatment to the family setting.

Typical second year goals include: teaching expressive and early abstract language; increasing interactive play with peers; and extending treatment to the community in pre-school groups. The third year goals focus on teaching appropriate and varied expression of emotion, preacademic tasks (reading, writing, math) and observational learning from peers. Transition to regular public preschool programs is carefully planned. The number of hours of clinic treatment decreases from 40 to 10 or fewer hours per week during transition.

The Lovaas method claims to produce recovery from autism in about one-half of the cases and to greatly reduce its severity in another 42%. Many researchers have criticized the results of Lovaas' studies, citing serious methodological problems (Gresham & MacMillan, 1997), and have advised school districts to resist its adoption or endorsement as a validated treatment for children with autism because it "is at best experimental, is far from providing a cure for autism, and awaits replication before school districts are required to provide it on a wholesale basis" (p. 196). The claim of cure, the standard 40-hour week, and the "one-size-fits-all" model are possible reasons for skepticism.

In response to criticism and skepticism, Smith and Lovaas (1997) suggest that parents of children with autism are knowledgeable about the outcome research and have requested the program "to reduce their children's need for services over the course of the children's lives, not to obtain more than their fair share of help" (p. 214). Parents requesting the program have concluded their children will not benefit from other services offered to them, and have a great personal stake in the adequacy of their children's educational program.

Picture Exchange Communication System (Bondy & Frost, 1994)

This system was designed to improve the communication skills of children with autism. It features spontaneous communication in appropriate social contexts. After determining preferred objects, the child is taught to use the picture to

access the object by trainers shaping the response. It is described as an effective, efficient communication strategy.

Auditory Approaches

Auditory Integration Training (AIT)

AIT is an approach based on the conclusion that some characteristics of autism occur because of auditory dysfunction. AIT devices play processed music through headphones to reduce some of the auditory problems which may occur in individuals with autism, such as sound sensitivity and auditory processing. Currently, clinical research is not sufficient to support the effectiveness and safety of AIT devices (ASA, 1996).

Interactional Approaches

Social Stories (Gray, 1994)

Social stories are used to teach social skills to students with autism. They involve three types of sentences: descriptive, directive, and perspective. Descriptive sentences define a situation, directive sentences tell the student which response is expected, and perspective sentences describe the reactions and feelings of others in a given situation. The stories are presented to the student to guide their performance in various academic and social settings. Social stories can be used to teach routines, curriculum, and goals or to improve behavior.

RELATED SERVICES

Although students with autism may receive an array of related services (e.g., occupational and physical therapy, speech services) one interesting and controversial service is facilitated communication (FC). FC is a method in which a "facilitator" provides physical support to enable individuals with severe disabilities to use a keyboard or communication board (e.g., pictureboard, wordboard, symbolboard) to communicate. The facilitator isolates the index finger, supports the movement of the hand, minimizes extraneous actions, directs attention, and provides emotional support (Biklen & Schubert, 1991). Several attempts to validate the effectiveness of FC have shown that the communication was influenced by the facilitator (Wheeler, Jacobson, Paglicri, & Schwartz, 1993; Szempruch & Jacobson, 1993; Hudson, Melita, & Arnold, 1993; Smith & Belcher, 1993; Montee, Miltenberger, & Wittrock, 1995; and Braman, Brady, Linehan, & Williams, 1995) and thus it is not a valid or reliable communication method. Proponents contend that subjecting the FC process to empirical validation is inherently confrontational and therefore will produce conflicting and suspicious results (Biklen, 1993).

INCLUSION STRATEGIES

In planning for the successful inclusion of students with autism, Simpson (1995) identified several supports necessary to provide an appropriate program in the general education setting. These supports included:

Paraprofessional availability. The paraprofessional should be responsible for implementing instructional and management programs, collecting and charting progress, monitoring data, assisting teachers with the development and adaptations of materials, and assisting students with autism.

Reduced class size. General educators must develop and implement appropriate social and academic programs for students with autism. These significant modifications will require reasonable class loads.

Adequate teacher and staff planning time. Students with autism require development and implementation of unique instructional and management programs,

necessitating additional planning and collaboration time.

Access to related service personnel. General educators will require access to related service personnel for advice and demonstration of best practice methods. Assistance from psychologists, speech and language therapists, occupational therapists, physical therapists, social workers, special educators, and other professionals will be necessary.

Staff training and consultants. General educators will need opportunities to collaborate, consult, and engage in cooperative problem-solving with professionals who have experience and skill in working with students with autism.

Peer-mediated support strategies have been successful in assisting students with autism in general education settings. These peer-mediated strategies include cooperative learning groups in reading (Kamps, Leonard, Potucek, & Garrison-Harrell, 1995), social initiation from peers (Odom & Strain, 1986; Sasso, 1987), and peer tutoring (Blew, Schwartz, & Luce, 1985).

Self-management strategies have similarly been successful in promoting inclusion of students with autism. Self-management techniques include following visual schedules (Newman, et al., 1995) and improving social skills (Koegel, Koegel, Hurley, & Frea, 1992) by monitoring the occurrence of specific social skills.

Students with autism have unique characteristics and educational needs. IEP teams must carefully and thoughtfully plan the necessary supports to facilitate successful inclusion.

REFERENCES

Autism Society of America (2001). *How is Autism Diagnosed?* Available at: http://www.autism-society.org.

Autism-PDD Resources Network (1997). *The Realities of TEACCH.* Available at: http://www.autism-pdd. net/teach.html.

Biklen, D. (1993). *Communication unbound: How facilitated communication is challenging traditional views of autism and ability-disability.* New York: Teachers College Press.

Biklen, D., & Schubert, A. (1991). New words: The communication of students with autism. *Remedial and Special Education, 12* (6), 46–57.

Blew, P. A., Schwartz, I. S., & Luce, S. C. (1985). Teaching functional community skills to autistic children using nonhandicapped peer tutors. *Journal of Applied Behavior Analysis, 18,* 337–342.

Bondy, A., & Frost, L. (1994). The Picture Exchange Communication System. *Focus on Autistic Behavior, 9,* 1–19.

Braman, B. J., Brady, M. P., Linehan, S. L., & Williams, R. E. (1995). Facilitated communication for children with autism: An examination of face validity. *Behavioral Disorders, 21* (1), 110–119.

Cohen, D. J., & Donnellan, A. M. (1987). *Handbook of autism and pervasive developmental disorders.* New York: John Wiley & Sons.

Eaves, R. C. (1997). Autistic disorder. In P. J. McLaughlin and P. Wehman (Eds.), *Mental Retardation and Developmental Disabilities* (2nd ed.). Austin, TX: PRO-ED.

Gray, C. (1994). *The social story kit.* Jenison, MI: Jenison Public Schools.

Gresham, F. M., & MacMillan, D. L. (1997). Autistic recovery? An analysis and critique of the empirical evidence on the early intervention project. *Behavioral Disorders, 22* (4), 185–201.

Hudson, A., Melita, B., & Arnold, N. (1993). Brief report: A case study assessing the validity of facilitated communication. *Journal of Autism and Developmental Disorders, 23,* 165–173.

Kamps, D. M., Leonard, B., Potucek, J., & Garrison-Harrell, L. (1995). Cooperative learning groups in reading: An integration strategy for students with autism and general classroom peers. *Behavioral Disorders, 21* (1), 89–109.

Koegel, L. K., Koegel, R. L., Hurley, C., & Frea, W. (1992). Improving social skills and disruptive behavior in children with autism through self-management. *Journal of Applied Behavior Analysis, 25,* 341–354.

Lovaas, O. I. (1987). Behavioral treatment and normal educational and intellectual functioning in young autistic children. *Journal of Consulting and Clinical Psychology, 55* (1), 3–9.

Matson, J. L. (Ed.). *Autism in children and adults: Etiology, assessment and itervention.* Pacific Grove, CA: Brooks/Cole.

Maurice, C., Green, G., & Luce, S. G. (Eds.) (1996). *Behavioral Intervention for Young children with Autism: A Manual for parents and Professionals.* Austin, TX: PRO-ED.

Mesibov, G. B. (1996) *What is TEACH?* Available at http://www.unc.edu/depts/teacch.

Mirenda, P. L., & Donnellan, A. M. (1987). Issues in curriculum development. In D. J. Cohen, A. M. Donnellan, & R. Paul (Eds.), *Handbook of Autism and Pervasive Developmental Disorders* (pp. 211–226). New York: John Wiley & Sons.

Montee, B., Miltenberger, R., & Wittrock. D. (1995). An experimental analysis of facilitated communication. *Journal of Applied Behavior Analysis, 28,* 189–200.

Newman, B., Buffington, D. M., O'Grady, M. A., McDonald, M. E., Poulson, C. L., & Hemmes, N. S. (1995). Self-management of schedule following in three teenagers with autism. *Behavioral Disorders, 20* (3), 190–196.

Odom, S., & Strain, P. (1986). A comparison of peer-initiation and teacher-antecedent interventions for promoting reciprocal social interaction of autistic preschoolers. *Journal of Applied Behavior analysis, 19,* 59–71.

Sasso, G. M. (1987). Social interactions: Issues and procedures. *Focus on Autistic Behavior, 2* (4), 1–7.

Simpson, R. L. (1995). Children and youth with autism in an age of reform: A perspective on current issues. *Behavioral Disorders, 21* (1), 7–20.

Smith, M. D., & Belcher, R. G. (1993). Brief report: Facilitated communication with adults with autism. *Journal of Autism and Developmental Disorders, 23,* 175–183.

Smith, T., & Lovaas, O. I. (1997). The UCLA young autism project: A reply to Gresham and MacMillan. *Behavioral Disorders, 22* (4), 202–218.

Szempruch, J., & Jacobson, J. W. (1993). Evaluating facilitated communications of people with developmental disabilities. *Research in Developmental Disabilities, 14,* 253–264.

U.S. Department of Education (1998). *20th Annual Report to Congress on the Implementation of the Individuals With Disabilities Education Act.* Washington, DC: Office of Special Education Programs.

Wheeler, D. L., Jacobson, J. W., Paglieri, R. A., & Schwartz, A. A. (1993). An experimental assessment of facilitated communication. *Mental Retardation, 31* (1), 49–60.

RECOMMENDED READINGS

Aarons, M., & Gittens, T. (1992). *The handbook of autism: A guide for parents and professionals.* New York: Routledge.

Berkell, D. E. (1992). *Autism: Identification, education, and treatment.* Hillsdale, NJ: Lawrence Erlbaum Associates.

Davis, K. (1990). *Adapted physical education for students with autism.* Springfield, IL: Charles C. Thomas.

Groden, G., & Baron, G. M. (1991). *Autism: Strategies for change. A comprehensive approach to the education and treatment of children with autism and related disorders.* New York: Gardner Press.

Harris, S. L., & Handleman, J. S. (1994). *Preschool education programs for children with autism.* Austin, TX: PRO-ED.

Matson, J. L. (1994). *Autism in children and adults: Etiology, assessment, and intervention.* Pacific Grove, CA: Brooks/Cole.

Simpson, R. L., & Zionts, P. (1992). *Autism: Information and resources for parents, families, and professionals.* Austin, TX: PRO-ED.

Organizations

Autism Society of America
7910 Woodmont Ave, Ste 650
Bethesda, MD 20814
Indiana Resource Center for Autism
Indiana University
2853 E 10th St
Bloomington, IN 47408

Websites

Mesibov, G. B. (1996). *What is TEACCH?*
http://www.unc.edu/depts/teacch
Autism/PDD Resources Network (1997)
http://www.autism-pdd.net/teacch.html
Center for Study of Autism (2001)
http://www.autism.com
Autism Society of America (2001)
http://www.autism-society.org

CHAPTER 14

EMOTIONAL DISTURBANCE/ BEHAVIORAL DISORDERS (EBD)

CHAPTER PREVIEW

Students with emotional disturbance/behavioral disorders (EBD) frequently are referred for special education evaluation because of behaviors that interfere with their achievement or the achievement of other students. Students with EBD display a variety of behaviors that impact learning and achievement including:

- Physical aggression
- Verbal aggression
- Opposition and noncompliance
- Anxiety
- Depression

Students with emotional or behavioral disorders often require:

- Instructional goals and objectives dealing with social interactions and personal management
- Assistance in managing their behavior
- Related services, including counseling services by qualified social workers, psychologist, guidance counselors or other qualified personnel, or psychological counseling

Successful inclusion strategies for students with EBD are:

- Collaborative teaching
- Peer support
- Teacher assistance teams

FEDERAL DEFINITION OF EBD

The federal definition for emotional disturbance is:

I. The term means a condition exhibiting one or more of the following characteristics over a long period of time and to a marked degree that adversely affects a child's educational performance:
   A. An inability to learn that cannot be explained by intellectual, sensory, or health factors.
   B. An inability to build or maintain satisfactory interpersonal relationships with peers and teachers.
   C. Inappropriate types of behavior or feelings under normal circumstances.
   D. A general pervasive mood of unhappiness or depression.
   E. A tendency to develop physical symptoms or fears associated with personal or school problems.
II. The term includes schizophrenia. The term does not apply to children who are socially maladjusted, unless it is determined that they have an emotional disturbance (34 C.F.R. § 300.7(c) (4)).

Many professionals have criticized this definition because it lacks the precision necessary to provide objective eligibility determinations. However, defining emotional and behavioral disorders is difficult because of differences in conceptual models, problems in measuring social-interpersonal behavior, variability in normal behavior, and the transience of many childhood disorders (Kauffman, 1997).

REFERRAL AND INITIAL ASSESSMENT

Children with EBD frequently are referred for special education evaluation because of behaviors that interfere with their achievement or the achievement of other students. These behaviors might be aggressive, noncompliant, acting-out, or antisocial (often called "externalized" behavioral disorders). Or, teachers may be concerned with students who are anxious, withdrawn, or depressed (often called "internalized" behavioral disorders). Although many students exhibit "disordered" or "disturbing" behaviors at times, it is when their behaviors and emotions become significantly discrepant from those of their peers for an extended period of time that professionals choose to identify the disorder and determine an appropriate educational program (Epstein, Cullinan, Harniss, & Ryser, 1999).

Professionals trying to decide whether a child referred for assessment meets the EBD definition must examine the five defining characteristics previously mentioned. This determination involves a comprehensive evaluation of multiple factors, including the child's behavioral, cognitive, and social functioning and the influences of the family and other social systems, such as peers and school (Wicks-Nelson, & Israel, 2000). Multiple assessment methods are employed, such as structured and unstructured interviews, projective tests, observational assessment, problem checklists, and self-reports. The assessment typically includes measures of the child's intellectual or educational functioning, such as intelligence tests, developmental scales, and ability and achievement tests. Neurologic or neuropsychologic assessment is often included to measure the integrity of the central nervous system for learning, sensorimotor, perceptual, verbal, and memory tasks.

The most reasonable estimates of the prevalence of EBD is 3 to 6 percent of the student population (Kauffman, 1997). However, the identification rate is significantly less than the predicted prevalence. The U.S. Department of Education (1988) estimated that in the 1997–98 school year, schools identified and served 447,426 children with emotional disturbance, which represented 8.6 percent of the total number of students in all disability categories and 0.9 percent of the student population. Identification rates are lower for girls and young women possibly due to internalized types of EBD (e.g., anxiety, depression), which are not as frequently referred. The overrepresentation of African Americans may be owing to both teacher expectations regarding normative behavior and to culturally insensitive and linguistically inappropriate assessment instruments. Although many children with EBD exhibit problems at an early age, students with this disability are usually identified later than those with other disabilities. Students with EBD are at great risk for substance abuse disorders and involvement with the juvenile justice system.

Once identified, an assessment of the student's current performance and needs is included in the IEP. Because emotional disturbance can involve intellectual, academic, medical, motor, self-help, social, emotional, and behavioral concerns, the student's need for each area must be determined (Rosenberg, Wilson, Maheady, & Sindelar, 1997). Typically this information would fall into two categories: formal, standardized, or normative data (e.g., IQ tests, achievements tests); and informal, criterion or observational data (e.g., classroom observation, informal reading inventories, curriculum-based assessment or measures, portfolios, performance samples, checklists). Of particular importance would be formal and informal assessments of social interaction and self-control. The PLEP might include classroom observations of on-task behavior and of peer or teacher interaction. Sociometric or teacher/peer interview data might also be included.

The IDEA requires that the IEP include a statement of how the disability affects the child's involvement and progress in the general curriculum (20 U.S. C. § 1414 (d) (1) (A) (i) (I)). For students with emotional disturbance, this statement might describe how internalizing or externalizing behaviors impact the student's achievement. A summary of the student's strengths and needs will lead to the development of IEP goals and objectives.

CHARACTERISTICS OF EBD

Students with EBD display a variety of behaviors that impact learning and achievement. Characteristics of externalized behavioral disorders include:

- Physical aggression
- Verbal aggression
- Opposition and noncompliance
- Antisocial behavior

Students who are physically aggressive are often involved in hitting, fighting, or the destruction of property. They may throw objects, kick people or objects, or hurt others when they become angry or frustrated. Verbally aggressive students often swear or use profanity. They might threaten adults or other students, or attempt to intimidate others. They frequently use language or gestures in an attempt to manipulate others.

Students with EBD who are oppositional and noncompliant are often disobedient and refuse to follow rules and directions. They can be resistant and uncooperative. Their defiance might take the form of unresponsiveness (e.g., not responding in any way to adult directives) or temper tantrums. Antisocial behaviors might include inappropriate interactions with peers, such as taunting, name-calling, or embarrassing others. The student might provoke other peers into inappropriate behaviors or upset adults by their comments or actions. Antisocial behaviors might also include immature responses, such as overreacting or displaying silly or annoying behaviors.

Characteristics of internalized behavioral disorders include anxiety and depression. Students who are anxious often seem worrisome or fearful. They might exhibit such nervous behaviors as fidgeting, nail biting, or babbling. Students with anxiety disorders are also seclusive, withdrawn, or isolated, and they may be reluctant to participate in classroom activities and prefer to be by themselves. Similarly, students who are depressed seem uninvolved, apathetic, or despondent. They often appear to be uninterested in academic or social activities.

These characteristic behaviors impact and interfere with the education of students with EBD. Such students are more likely to drop courses, earn lower grade-point averages, be absent from school, be retained at grade, and fail to graduate than students with other disabilities (U.S. Department of Education, 1998). Students with EBD are unable to attend or participate in learning, particularly with cooperative or peer approaches. Their behaviors may also interrupt the learning of other students and often result in alienation or social isolation. Unprepared administrators and teachers often view these students as "bad" or "sick" and respond in punitive and punishing ways. This view "obscures their [students'] identity as learners" (Glennon, 1993), excuses teachers from addressing their needs, and exacerbates their problems by removing them from the supports that they need. Educational programs for students with EBD must provide specialized instruction in social interactions and personal management, positive behavior management, and supports for involvement in the general education curriculum and classrooms.

INSTRUCTION

Students with emotional or behavioral disorders often require instructional goals and objectives dealing with social interactions and personal management. This instruction may involve social skill instruction, self-control instruction, self-regulatory instruction (Bauer & Shea, 1999; Rutherford, Quinn, & Mathur, 1996).

Social Skill Instruction

Students with emotional or behavioral disorders typically have difficulty in three areas of social competence:

1. Building supports and friendships
2. Responding appropriately to the demands of adults and peers
3. Making adaptations to changes in the social circumstances (Kauffman, 1997).

These students may need instruction in social skills, which involves identifying and defining the target skill, modeling the skill, practicing the skill in role plays, providing feedback and reinforcement, and programming for generalization. Examples of curricula employed for students with EBD include the *Boys' Town Social Skills Curriculum* (Wells, 1990), *Skillstreaming* (McGinnis & Goldstein, 1989), and the *Walker Social Skills Curriculum* (Walker, Todis, Holmes, & Horton, 1988). Although commercial curricula are available, many authors advocate informal or incidental teaching strategies in social skill instruction (Gresham, 1998). For example, a student might role-play giving a compliment as part of a commercially available curriculum, or she might be directed by the teacher to change a comment such as "Where'd you get that jacket?" into a compliment to a peer (e.g., incidental learning). Social skill instruction has been regarded as a critical component of educational programs for students with EBD.

Self-Control Instruction

Children with deficits in self-control can be helped by instruction tailored to improve their capacity to direct and regulate their behavior. Self-control instruction may involve many approaches. Available self-control curricula include *Aggression Replacement Training: A Comprehensive Intervention for Aggressive Youth* (Goldstein, & Glick, 1987); *Anger Management for Youth* (Eggert, 1994); *Think Aloud* (Camp & Bash, 1981); and *The Self-Control Curriculum*

(Henley, 1994). Fagan, Long, & Stevens (1976) developed the *Teaching Self-Control* curriculum, which is designed to reduce disruptiveness and strengthen emotional and cognitive control (Fagan & Long, 1998). This curricular approach addresses the social and affective deficits of these students which interfere with successful school achievement and life adjustment (Edwards & O'Toole, 1998). For example, a student might be working with a teacher and small group to recognize anger arousal and develop a plan for calming down. Self-control instruction is designed to help students manage their behavior and emotions.

Self-Regulation

Students can also be taught self-regulation procedures to improve their interactions in both social and academic situations (Graham, Harris, & Reid, 1998). Goal-setting, self-monitoring, self-instruction, and self-reinforcement promote the development of self-regulated learners. As students learn to self-regulate their behaviors, they increase their level of task engagement and decrease the occurrence of disruptive or off-task behaviors. Self-regulation approaches are considered to be language-based, cognitive-behavioral strategies that assist students in selecting appropriate behaviors. An example of self-regulation instruction is Harris & Graham's *Making the Writing Process Work: Strategies for Composition and Self-Regulation* (1996).

In self-regulation, students identify target behaviors, design a step-by-step strategy to improve the behavior, and monitor their use and the success of the strategy. For example, a student might monitor her use of a "stay on task" strategy during math class. Self-regulation assists students with EBD to become more independent and successful.

Specialized instruction in self-control and social skills is a necessary ingredient in educational programs for students with EBD (Meese, 1996). The selection of an approach or a specific curriculum depends on the goals and objectives generated for an individual student. These proactive strategies teach appropriate and replacement behaviors or adaptive coping skills (Rutherford & Nelson, 1998).

BEHAVIOR MANAGEMENT

Students with EBD often need assistance in managing their behavior. These students often require intervention plans to promote appropriate behavior and reduce challenging or interfering behavior. The IDEA requires that the IEP team consider positive behavioral interventions, strategies, and supports for children with EBD to address the behavior that is impeding her learning or that of others (20 U.S.C. § (d) (3) (B) (i)). A behavior improvement plan (BIP) allows teachers and students to specifically determine the target behavior for change, design a way to promote the change, arrange documentation of change, and evaluate the rate and nature of changes (Bauer & Shea, 1999). Depending on the target behavior, the interventions may involve positive reinforcement, modeling, behavioral contracting, or token economies (Mathur, Quinn, & Rutherford, 1996; Polsgrove, 1996). For example, a student involved with a token economy system might earn points for target behaviors such as working quietly and completing assignments. The student then exchanges the points earned for a reward such as personal time (e.g., time on the computer) or school supplies (e.g., pencils, colors, notebooks). Examples of classwide token economy systems are the *Boys' Town Educational Model* (Connolly, 1995) and *Assertive Discipline* (Canter, 1976; Canter & Canter, 1993).

Supportive Strategies

Positive behavioral interventions may also include supportive strategies to assist students who are off-task or engaged in inappropriate behavior. These strategies are designed to quickly eliminate interfering behaviors and redirect the student to more productive and appropriate behavior. These strategies include:

- *Signal Interference*: any type of nonverbal behavior that communicates to the student that her behavior is inappropriate and reminds her of more appropriate behavior (e.g., finger over lips to be quiet, pointing to chair to sit down).
- *Interest Boosting*: efforts to boost the student's interest in an activity if she is losing interest or becoming bored (e.g., timing the student as she completes a task, relating the activity to her personal interests).
- *Restructuring*: changing certain aspects of the assignment to increase the student's motivation to continue (e.g., handing the student a different writing utensil, changing the location of the activity).

Alper, Schloss, Etscheidt, & Macfarlane (1995) provide a detailed description of these supportive strategies.

Crisis Management

Students with EBD are often "flooded" with intense feelings of embarrassment, frustration, self-doubt, confusion, or anger. They respond to these feeling with behaviors that are "disturbed" and "disturbing" (Zionts, 1996). The "helping teacher," addresses the emotional needs of students with EBD and continues to be a priority in educational programs.

Although the specialized instruction referenced earlier is intended to prevent emotional crises, teachers must also be prepared for crisis intervention and management. Crisis intervention is an important component of programs for students with EBD (Dice, 1993; Myles & Simpson, 1994; Meadows, 1996). The crisis or helping teacher must be available to assist students with EBD during times of crises (Wood & Long, 1991). Examples of crisis intervention models include *A Crisis Intervention Team Model* (Gra-

ham, 1994), *Crisis Intervention for Community-Based Individuals With Developmental Disabilities and Behavioral and Psychiatric Disorders* (Davidson, 1995), *The P.L.A.C.E. Crisis Intervention Model: Emotional First-Aid* (Hoggan, 1995), and *Life-Space Interviewing* (James & Long, 1992; Long & Kelley, 1994; Long & Morse, 1996). Although the approaches differ, the steps in crisis intervention typically involve a discussion of the behavior or incident, the student's perception, the central issue(s), and a plan for resolution. Crisis intervention enables students to make changes in their behavior through problem-solving with a helping professional.

Medication

Psychopharmacologic medications are often used to treat certain types of EBDs. Lithium and antidepressants such as Prozac, Tofranil, Welbutrin, and Risperdal have been used effectively as mood stabilizers for students with EBD (Forness, Kavale, Sweeney, & Crenshaw, 1999). When psychopharmacologic medications are used, administrators and teachers should carefully monitor their use, and understand their side effects.

RELATED SERVICES

In addition to their instructional program, students with EBD may require related services in order to benefit from their educational plan. Among the potentially appropriate related services for students with EBD are counseling services by qualified social workers, psychologists, guidance counselors, or other qualified personnel (34 C.F.R. § 300.24 (b) (2)). Given the types of problems and conditions experienced by students with EBD, counseling represents an important component of a comprehensive intervention program (Maag & Katsiyannis, 1996). Unfortunately, students with EBD rarely receive counseling as a related service.

Other related services might include psychological counseling for children and parents (34 C.F.R. § 300.24 (b) (9(v)). A student's educational and psychological needs may be intertwined, and psychological counseling may be necessary to assist a child with a disability to benefit from special education (20 U.S.C. § 1401 (22)). Like other related services, psychological services (e.g., psychotherapy) are provided to support the child's special education program as identified in the IEP.

INCLUSION STRATEGIES

The successful inclusion of students with EBD has been difficult to achieve. The majority of students with EBD continue to receive most of their services in environments that separate them from their peers without EBD (U.S. Department of Education, 1998). Despite specific provisions in the IDEA to address behavioral concerns, research suggests that many of these students and their teachers do not receive the supports that they need to succeed in regular class environments, particularly at a time of rising academic and behavioral standards (Lewis, Chard, & Scott, 1994). The social and behavioral difficulties of these students, the rejection and isolation by their peers, and the attitudes and expectations of general education teachers have impacted the success of inclusion efforts (Lewis, Chard & Scott, 1994). In response to these barriers, several strategies for successful inclusion have been identified.

Collaborative Teaching

Collaborative teaching is a cooperative and interactive process between two teachers which enables students with special needs to attain success in the regular education setting (Wiedmeyer & Lehman, 1991). Collaborative teaching involves using the unique expertise of several

teachers. Activities include sharing the planning, presenting and checking of assignments; adapting curriculum; and demonstrating or using special techniques and strategies. Edwards (1998) confirmed that curriculum modification was a strategy that helped students with EBD in the regular classroom. Adapting the content and format of the curriculum, combined with reinforcement for attention to task and assignment completion, is an effective strategy for students in regular classrooms.

Peer Support Systems

Enlisting the assistance of peers to facilitate inclusion for students with EBD is important for several reasons. Peer intervention can foster both academic skills and relationship skills for students with EBD (Strayhorn, Strain, & Walker, 1993). Modeling, prompting, monitoring, reinforcement, and tutoring by peers have been successful in improving the interactions of students with EBD. Peer helpers and peer mediators can assist in friendship-building and in conflict resolution. General education peers have helped students with EBD manage and express anger appropriately (Presley & Hughes, 2000), in modifying disruptive behavior (Gable, Arllen, & Hendrickson, 1994), and in improving socialization (Davis, 1995).

Teacher Assistance Models

Several models have been developed to assist general educators in successfully including students with EBD. These approaches, such as the Effective Behavioral Support model (Sugai & Horner, 1994) and the Problem Solving System (Tilly, Reschly, & Grimes, 1998) ensure that teachers receive assistance in addressing challenging behavior. The models are multidisciplinary, involving the collaboration of students, parents, teachers, support personnel, and administrators.

The key to establishing effective programs for students with EBD is understanding that the disturbed or disturbing behaviors are symptoms of a disability, similar to the inattention of the student with ADHD or the writing difficulties of the student with learning disabilities. These behaviors are also diagnostic in representing the unique needs of the child. An educational program that includes instruction in personal management and social skills, positive behavioral strategies or supports, and adjunct related services (e.g., counseling) will offer students with EBD an appropriate education in the LRE.

REFERENCES

Alper, S., Schloss, P. J., Etscheidt, S. K., & Macfarlane, C. A. (1995). *Inclusion: Are we abandoning or helping students?* Thousand Oaks, CA: Corwin Press.

Bauer, A. M., & Shea, T. M. (1999). *Learners with emotional and behavioral disorders: An introduction.* Upper Saddle River, NJ: Merrill/Prentice Hall.

Camp, B. W., & Bash, M. A. S. (1981). *Think aloud: Increasing social cognitive skills—a problem-solving program for children.* Champaign, IL: Research Press.

Canter, L. (1976). *Assertive discipline: A take-charge approach for today's educator.* Seal Beach, CA: Canter & Associates.

Canter, L., & Canter, M. (1993). *Succeeding with difficult students: New strategies for reaching your most challenging students.* Santa Monica, CA: Canter & Associates.

Coleman, M. C. (1996). *Emotional and behavioral disorders: Theory and practice* (3rd ed.). Boston: Allyn & Bacon.

Connolly, T. (1995). *The well-managed classroom: Promoting student success through social skill instruction.* Boys' Town, NE: Father Flanagan's Boys' Home.

Davidson, P. W. (1995). Crisis intervention for community-based individuals with developmental disabilities and behavioral and psychiatric disorders. *Mental Retardation, 33* (1), 21–30.

Davis, C. A. (1995). Peers as behavior change agents for preschoolers with behavioral disorders: Using high probability requests. *Preventing School Failure, 39* (4), 4–9.

Davidson, P. W. (1995). Crisis intervention for community-based individuals with developmental disabilities and behavioral and psychiatric disorders. *Mental Retardation, 33* (1), 21–30.

Dice, M. L. (1993). *Intervention strategies for children with emotional or behavioral disorders.* San Diego, CA: Singular.

Edwards, L. L., & O'Toole, B. (1998). Application of the Self-Control Curriculum with behavior-disordered students. In R. J. Wheelan (Ed.) *Emotional and behavioral disorders: A 25-year focus.* Denver: Love.

Edwards, L. L. (1998). Curriculum modification as a strategy for helping regular classroom behavior-disordered students. In R. J. Wheelan (Ed.) *Emotional and behavioral disorders: A 25-year focus.* Denver: Love.

Eggert, L. L. (1994). *Anger management for youth.* Bloomington, IN: National Educational Service.

Epstein, M. H., Cullinan, D., Harniss, M. K., & Ryser, G. (1999). The Scale for Assessing Emotional Disturbance: Test-retest and interrater reliability. *Behavioral Disorders, 24* (3), 231–245.

Fagan, S. A., Long, N. J., & Stevens, P. J. (1976). A psychoeducational curriculum for the prevention of behavioral and learning problems: Teaching self-control. In N. Long, W. Morse, & R. Newman (Eds.), *Conflict in the classroom: The education of emotionally disturbed children* (3rd ed.). Belmont, CA: Wadsworth.

Fagan, S. A., & Long, N. J. (1998). Teaching children self-control: A new responsibility for teachers. In R. J. Wheelan (Ed.) *Emotional and behavioral disorders: A 25-year focus.* Denver: Love.

Forness, S. R., Kavale, K. A., Sweeney, D. P., & Crenshaw, T. M. (1999). The future of research and practice in behavioral: Psychopharmacology and its school implications. *Behavioral Disorders, 24* (4), 305–318.

Gable, A. R., Arllen, L. N., & Hendrickson, J. (1995). Use of peer confrontation to modify disruptive behavior in inclusion classrooms. *Preventing School Failure, 40* (1), 25–28.

Glennon, T. (1993). Disabling ambiguities: Confronting barriers to the education of students with emotional disabilities. In *Tennessee Law Review*. Knoxville: The University of Tennessee.

Goldstein, A. P., & Glick, B. (1987). *Aggression Replacement Training: A comprehensive Intervention for Aggressive Youth*. Champaign, IL: Research Press.

Graham, C. S. (1994). A Crisis Intervention Team Model. In D. G. Burgess & R. M. Dedmond (Eds.) *Quality leadership and the professional school counselor*. Alexandria, VA: American Counseling Association.

Graham, S., Harris, K. R., & Reid, R. (1998). Developing self-regulated learners. In R. J. Wheelan (Ed.) *Emotional and behavioral disorders: A 25-year focus*. Denver: Love.

Gresham, F. M. Social skills training: Should we raze, remodel, or rebuild? *Behavioral Disorders, 24* (1), 19–25.

Harris, K. R., & Graham, S. (1996). *Making the writing process work: Strategies for composition and self-regulation*. Cambridge, MA: Brookline Books.

Henley, M. (1994). A self-control curriculum for troubled youngsters. *Journal of Emotional and Behavioral Problems, 3* (1), 40–46.

Hoggan, D. (1995). The P.L.A.C.E. Crisis Intervention Model: Emotional First-aid. *ERIC Digest 37955Z*.

James, M., & Long, N. J. (1992). Looking beyond behavior and seeing my needs: A red flag interview. *Journal of Emotional and Behavioral Problems, 1* (2), 35–38.

Kauffman, J. M. (1997). *Characteristics of emotional and behavioral disorders of children and youth* (6th ed.). Upper Saddle River, NJ: Merrill/Prentice Hall.

Knitzer, J., Streinberg, Z., & Fleisch, B. (1990). *At the school house door: An examination of programs and policies for children with behavioral and emotional problems*. New York: Bank Street College of Education.

Lewis, T. J., Chard, D., & Scott, T. M. (1994). Full inclusion and the education of children and youth with emotional and behavioral disorders. *Behavioral Disorders, 19* (4), 277–293.

Long, N. J., & Kelley, E. F. (1994). The double struggle: "The butler did it." *Journal of Emotional and Behavioral Problems, 3* (3), 49–55.

Long, N. J., & Morse, W. C. (1996). *Conflict in the classroom: The education of at-risk and troubled students* (5th ed.). Austin, TX: PRO-ED.

Maag, J. W., & Katsiyannis, A. (1996). Counseling as a related service for students with emotional or behavioral disorders: Issues and recommendations. *Behavioral Disorders, 21* (4), 293–305.

Mathur, S. R., Quinn, M. M., & Rutherford, R. B. (1996). *Teacher-mediated behavior management strategies for children with emotional behavioral disorders*. Reston, VA: The Council for Exceptional Children.

McGinnis, E., & Goldstein, A. P. (1989). *Skillstreaming in early childhood: Teaching prosocial skills to the preschool and kindergarten child*. Champaign, IL: Research Press.

Meadows, N. B. (1996). Behavior management as a curriculum for students with emotional and behavior disorders. *Preventing School Failure, 40* (3), 124–130.

Meese, R. L. (1996). *Strategies for teaching students with emotional and behavioral disorders*. Pacific Grove, CA: Brooks/Cole.

Myles, B. S., & Simpson, R. L. (1994). Understanding and preventing acts of aggression and violence in school-age children and youth. *Preventing School Failure, 38* (3), 40–46.

Presley, J. A., & Hughes, C. (2000). Peers as teachers of anger management to high school students with behavioral disorders. *Behavioral Disorders, 25* (2), 114–130.

Polsgrove, L. (1996). *Reducing undesirable behaviors*. Reston, VA: The Council for Exceptional Children.

Rosenberg, M. S., Wilson, R., Maheady, L., & Sindelar, P. T. (1997). *Educating students with behavior disorders* (2nd Ed.). Boston: Allyn & Bacon.

Rutherford, R. B., & Nelson, C. M. (1998). Management of aggressive and violent behavior in the schools. In R. J. Wheelan (Ed.) *Emotional and behavioral disorders: A 25-year focus*. Denver: Love.

Rutherford, R. B., Quinn, M. M., & Mathur, S. R. (1996). *Effective strategies for teaching appropriate behaviors to children with emotional behavioral disorders*. Reston, VA: The Council for Exceptional Children.

Strayhorn, J. M., Strain, P. S., & Walker, H. M. (1993). The case for interaction skills training in the context of tutoring as a preventive mental health intervention in schools. *Behavioral Disorders, 19* (1), 11–26.

Sugai, G., & Horner, R. (1994). Including students with severe behavior problems in general education settings: Assumptions, challenges, and solutions. In J. Marr, G. Sugai, & G. Tindal (Eds.), *The Oregon Conference Monograph 1994*. Eugene: University of Oregon.

Tilly, W. D., Reschly, D. J., & Grimes, J. (1998). Disability determination in problem solving systems: Conceptual foundations and critical components. In D. J. Reschly, W. D. Tilly, and J. P. Grimes (Eds.), *Functional and Noncategorical Identification and Intervention in Special Education*. Des Moines, IA: Iowa Dept. of Education.

U.S. Department of Education (1998). *20th Annual Report to Congress on the Implementation of the Individuals With Disabilities Education Act*. Washington, DC: Office of Special Education Programs.

Walker, H. M., Colvin, G., & Ramsey, E. (1995). *Antisocial behavior in school: Strategies and best practices*. Pacific Grove, CA: Brooks/Cole.

Walker, H. M., Todis, B., Holmes, D., & Horton, G. (1988). *The Walker Social Skills Curriculum: The ACCESS Program*. Austin, TX: PRO-ED.

Wells, T. (1990). *The Boys' Town Education Model*. Boys' Town, NE: Father Flanagan's Boys' Home.

Wicks-Nelson, R., & Israel, A. C. (2000) *Behavior Disorders of Childhood* (4th ed.). Upper Saddle River, NJ: Prentice-Hall.

Wiedmeyer, D. & Lehman, J. (1991). "The house plan" approach to collaborative teaching and consultation. *Teaching Exceptional Children, 23* (10), 7–10.

Wood, M. M., & Long, N. J. (1991). *Life space intervention: Talking with children and youth in crisis*. Austin, TX: PRO-ED.

Zionts, P. (1996). *Teaching disturbed and disturbing students: An integrative approach* (2nd ed.). Austin, TX: PRO-ED.

RECOMMENDED READINGS

There are several texts concerning students with EBD:

Bauer, A. M., & Shea, T. M. (1999). *Learners with emotional and behavioral disorders: An introduction*. Upper Saddle River, NJ: Merrill/Prentice Hall.

Coleman, M. C. (1996). *Emotional and behavioral disorders: Theory and practice*. Needham Heights, MA: Allyn & Bacon.

Erickson, M. T. (1998). *Behavior disorders of children and adolescents: Assessment, etiology, and intervention*. Upper Saddle River, NJ: Prentice Hall.

Rosenberg, M. S., Wilson, R., Maheady, L., & Sindelar, P. T. (1997). *Educating students with behavior disorders*. Needham Heights, MA: Allyn & Bacon.

Wicks, R. N., & Israel, A. C. (2000). *Behavior disorders of childhood*. Upper Saddle River, NJ: Prentice Hall.

There are several texts addressing behavior management strategies for students with EBD:

Cangelosi, J. S. (1997). *Classroom management strategies: Gaining and maintaining students' cooperation*. White Plains, NY: Longman.

Evans, W. H., Evans, S. & Schmid, R. E. (1989). *Behavior and instructional management*. Boston: Allyn & Bacon.

Grossman, H. (1990). *Trouble-free teaching*. Mountain View, CA: Mayfield.

Hoover, R. L., & Kindsvatter, R. (1997). *Democratic discipline: Foundation and practice*. Upper Saddle River, NJ: Merrill/Prentice Hall.

Jones, V. F., & Jones, L. S. (1995). *Comprehensive classroom management: Creating positive learning environments for all students*. Boston: Allyn & Bacon.

Kameenui, E. J., & Darch, C. B. (1995). *Instructional classroom management: A proactive approach to behavior management*. White Plains, NY: Longman.

Levin, J., & Nolan, J. F. (1996). *Principles of classroom management: A professional decision-making model*. Boston: Allyn & Bacon.

McIntyre, T. (1989). *The behavior management handbook*. Boston: Allyn & Bacon.

Queen, J. A., Blackwelder, B. B., & Mallen, L. P. (1997). *Responsible classroom management for teachers and students*. Upper Saddle River, NJ: Merrill/Prentice Hall.

Resources

There are numerous resources concerning students with EBD. The Council for Exceptional Children (CEC) has a division that specifically addresses this population of students. The Council for Children with

Behavioral Disorders (CCBD) has a website listing general information, a calendar of events, and available publications at http://www.ccbd.net. This division publishes the journal *Behavioral Disorders*, which includes articles concerning students with EBD.

The National Information Center for Children and Youth with Disabilities (NICHCY) provides a list of state and national organizations for students with EBD at http://www.nichcy.org/. Resources are also available at Special Education Resources on the Internet (SERI) at http://www.seriweb.com/.

MENTAL DISABILITIES OR RETARDATION

Students with severe mental disabilities may require extensive, intense services, whereas students with mild disabilities may benefit from intermittent, supportive services.

Students with mental disabilities are a diverse group of children with varied abilities and needs. Characteristics of students with mental disabilities include:

- *Learning characteristics*—difficulties with memory, self-regulation, generalization, and abstract concepts, and a slower learning rate
- *Adaptive skills*—difficulty coping with school demands, delayed emotional development, limited interpersonal and personal care skills
- *Physical and health characteristics*—delayed or impaired motor and sensory development affecting equilibrium, locomotion and manual dexterity, and delayed or impaired speech development

Several curricular domains are often included in educational programs for students with mental disabilities:

- Academic and functional literacy (e.g., reading, math, science, social studies, health and independent living skills (e.g., domestic, community, and employment skills)
- Personal and social adjustment may include personal care and hygiene skills (e.g., dressing, nutrition, grooming) and socialization skills (e.g., conversation, friendship, cooperation, conflict resolution).
- Contribution and citizenship (e.g., self-determination, work outcomes)
- Responsibility and independence (e.g., home and community living, meal planning, leisure activities, purchasing groceries, using a pay phone, travel and mobility training, using public transportation, traveling in and around the school building and in and outside the community, financial planning and management)

In addition to the educational program, students with mental disabilities may require related services such as assistive technology.

Several approaches have been identified to assist in integrating students with mental disabilities. These strategies include environmental modification, multilevel instruction, social interaction interventions, and paraprofessional assistance.

FEDERAL DEFINITION OF MENTAL DISABILITY OR RETARDATION

The federal definition of mental disability or retardation describes the impact on educational performance:

> Mental retardation means significantly sub-average general intellectual functioning, existing concurrently with deficits in adaptive behavior and manifested during the developmental period, that adversely affects a child's educational performance (34 C.F.R. § 300.7(c)(6).

This definition was based on the 1973 American Association on Mental Retardation (AAMR) criteria for identification. Defining mental retardation based on the degree of measured intelligence and adaptive behavior is controversial owing to the limitations and potential bias of IQ testing and to the focus on the deficiencies of individuals.

REFERRAL AND INITIAL ASSESSMENT

The question of whether individuals with mental disabilities require special education and related services depends on the severity of the disability. As with other disabilities, student needs may vary from mild to severe. Historically, individuals were classified as educable mentally retarded (EMR) or trainable mentally retarded (TMR) based on IQ scores. The AAMR (1992) has proposed a new level system that defines the intensity of support that individuals with mental disabilities require: intermittent, limited, extensive, and pervasive. Students with extensive and pervasive needs have typically been referred for special education services early as infants or toddlers, whereas students with intermittent or limited needs may have accessed services later in their educational career.

The assessment of individuals with mental disabilities frequently includes an IQ test and a test of adaptive behavior. The measurement of intellectual functioning is based on standardized IQ tests. Two widely used intelligence tests are the Stanford-Binet Intelligence Scale (Thorndike, Hagen, & Sattler, 1986) and the Wechsler Intelligence Scale for Children—Revised (WISC-R) (Wechsler, 1974). IQ scores are distributed according to a norm sample, with variance from the average described as standard deviations. The AAMR defines "significantly subaverage" as two or more standard deviations below the mean. The degree of subaverage intellectual functioning traditionally has been classified as either mild, moderate, or severe. Children with mild intellectual disabilities have IQ scores of 50 to 70, those with moderate disabilities score in the 35 to 50 range, and those classified as severely or profoundly disabled score below 35 (Heward, 2000).

Adaptive skills are related to both personal independence and social responsibility. Adaptive behavior is a developmental construct in that expected adaptive behavior varies with the age of the student. It is also important to view adaptive behaviors within cultural and environmental contexts, because expectations and demands for independence and responsibility also vary based on specific contexts (Reschley, 1990). The measurement of adaptive behavior includes assessing functional living skills. Frequently used tests of adaptive behavior include the AAMR Adaptive Behavior Scale—School (ABS-S) (Lambert, Nihira, & Leland, 1993), the Vineland Adaptive Behavior Scales (Sparrow, Balla, & Cicchetti, 1984), and the Scales of Independent Behavior (SIB) (Bruininks, Woodcock, Weatherman, & Hill, (1984).

Assessment for students with mental disabilities should include measures of performance in the general curriculum as well as measures of functional living. Ysseldyke and Olsen (1997) identified domains of essential and desirable outcomes for students with disabilities, which include:

- Academic and functional literacy
- Personal and social adjustment
- Contribution and citizenship
- Responsibility and independence
- Physical health

The assessment data can be gathered by observation (e.g., performance assessment), recollection (e.g., interview, rating scales), record reviews, and tests. The focus of the assessment must be on real-life, community-based experiences, must measure integrated skills across domains, and must be continuous (Ysseldyke & Olsen, 1997). The assessment should also document the extent to which the school system provides the needed assistive devices, people, and other supports to allow the students to function as independently as possible. The results of the assessment will provide the IEP team with information necessary to develop goals and objectives for the student and to plan instruction.

The U.S. Department of Education (1998) has estimated the prevalence of mental disabilities to be 1 percent of the school-aged population and 11 percent of all students with disabilities receiving special education.

CHARACTERISTICS OF MENTAL DISABILITIES

Students with mental disabilities are a diverse group of children with varied abilities and needs. Drew and Hardman (2000) identified several characteristics of these students:

- Difficulties with memory, self-regulation, generalization, and abstract concepts, and a slower learning rate

- Difficulty coping with school demands, delayed emotional development, limited interpersonal and personal care skills
- Delayed or impaired motor and sensory development affecting equilibrium, locomotion and manual dexterity and delayed or impaired speech development

The impact of mental disabilities on the educational performance of students depends on the severity of the disability. Some students will require extensive supports whereas others may require limited, intermittent assistance. The assessment results will guide IEP teams in developing appropriate instructional programs for students with mental disabilities.

INSTRUCTION

The curriculum for students with mental disabilities must be based on assessment results and must be individualized, person-centered, functional or practical, adaptive, and ecologically oriented (Wehman & Kregel, 1997). Several curricular domains are often included in educational programs. The domain of academic and functional literacy may include instruction in traditional academic content (e.g., reading, math, science, social studies, health) as well as instruction for independent living skills (e.g., domestic, community and employment skills) (Wolfe & Harriott, 1997). Instruction in the domain of personal and social adjustment may include personal care and hygiene skills (e.g., dressing, nutrition, grooming) and socialization skills (e.g., conversation, friendship, cooperation, conflict-resolution). Students with mental disabilities need to be taught skills that will be useful to them in the settings or contexts in which they are most likely to be living, working, and playing (Chandler & Pankaskie, 1997).

The domain of contribution and citizenship may include instruction in self-determination and work outcomes. Self-determination instruction involves skills of choice, goal-setting and self-evaluation. Students with disabilities often remain dependent on other people to make decisions, plan pursuits, and provide support. Thus, the components of self-determination must be infused into all curriculum and instruction (Sale & Martin, 1997). Work outcomes involves a curriculum to prepare students with mental disabilities for careers and employment. Although the IDEA requires specific transition planning at age 14, the entire educational careers of students with disabilities should prepare them to be productive citizens. The curriculum model teaches basic skills and processes to help students make independent and meaningful life decisions throughout the schooling process (Hanley-Maxwell & Collet-Klingenberg, 1997).

Instructional approaches for the domain of responsibility and independence may address home and community living (e.g., meal planning, leisure activities, purchasing groceries, using a pay phone). Community skills instruction is usually taught in the community (e.g., community-based instruction) or embedded into functional school-based routines (e.g., community-referenced instruction) (Dymond, 1997). Travel and mobility training (e.g., using public transportation, traveling in and around the school building) may also be included in this domain. Instruction in financial planning and management (e.g., checking account, credit cards) is also important to the development of responsibility and independence.

In addition to the instructional domains, the educational program for students with mental disabilities may include the provision of several related services. These services are required in order for individuals with mental disabilities to benefit from the educational program.

RELATED SERVICES

The provision of assistive technology is a related service for many students with mental disabilities. "Assistive technology device" means any item, piece of equipment, or product system—whether acquired commercially off the shelf, modified, or customized—that is used to increase, maintain, or improve functional capabilities of a child with a disability (20 U.S.C. 1401 (1)) and "assistive technology service" means any service that directly assists a child with a disability in the selection, acquisition, or use of an assistive technology device, including:

A. the evaluation of the needs of such child, including a functional evaluation of the child in the child's customary environments;
B. purchasing, leasing, or otherwise providing for the acquisition of assistive technology devices by such child;
C. selecting, designing, fitting, customizing, adapting, applying, maintaining, repairing, or replacing of assistive technology devices;
D. coordinating and using other therapies, interventions, or services with assistive technology devices, such as those associated with existing education and rehabilitation plans and programs;
E. training or technical assistance for such child, or, where appropriate, the family of such child; and
F. training or technical assistance for professionals (including individuals providing education and rehabilitation services), employers, or other individuals who provide services to, employ, or are otherwise substantially involved in the major life functions of such child. (20 U.S.C. 1401 (2))

The determination of whether a child with a disability requires an assistive technology device or service in order to receive FAPE must be made by the IEP team, with the focus on the child's educational needs. The appropriate devices or services must be determined on a case-by-case basis. The district may also need to screen a student to ascertain if it is necessary to conduct a formal evaluation of the student's need for assistive technology. If an IEP team determines that a student with a disability requires assistive technology services or devices in order to receive FAPE, then the specific devices and services must be identified in the child's IEP and made available at no cost to the parent.

Examples of areas in which assistive technology devices, products, or systems might be provided include mobility (e.g., standing wheelchair, wheelchair tray), computer hardware and software (e.g., expanded keyboard, voice synthesizer, cursor control, communication programs, switch operations), therapy aids (e.g., inclines, prone stander), communication (e.g., communication board, electronic augmentative communication device), vision and hearing (e.g., hearing aids, magnification systems), reading (e.g., talking dictionary, large print books), writing (e.g., wrist supports, electronic notetaker, computer), and math (e.g., calculator, talking calculator).

INCLUSION STRATEGIES

Access to and progress in the general curriculum is an important consideration for students with mental disabilities. Several approaches have been identified to assist in integrating such students, including environmental modification, multilevel instruction, social interaction interventions, and paraprofessional assistance.

Environmental Modification

Environmental modifications include flexible scheduling, flexible programming, availability of program options, appropriate space, and appropriate materials (Keenan, 1997). Scheduling involves selecting the appropriate mix of teacher and students in inclusive classrooms. The composition of classrooms is determined by the number of students, the number of regular and special education teachers, and the disabilities and needs of the students. Programming should be flexible to accommodate both group instruction and individualized instruction. Program options should encompass a continuum from general classroom instruction to one-to-one support for students with disabilities. Flexibility in scheduling, programming, and instruction requires appropriate space alloted for individualized centers, small group work, and large group instruction. The materials must be carefully considered and appropriate for both group and individualized instruction.

Multilevel Instruction

Multilevel instruction is a planning strategy that enables teachers to accommodate all students and to encourage individual participation in shared class activities. This strategy has been effective with students with mental disabilities because it focuses on developing concepts by using content as a means for teaching specific skills, rather than teaching the content as an end in itself (Perner & Porter, 1998). By including numerous methods of presentation and practice, the teacher is able to address various levels of ability within the class. Multilevel instruction improves the quality of instruction for all students.

Social Interaction Interventions

Social interaction interventions opportunities are designed to enhance the interaction between students with disabilities and their teachers and peers. Garrison-Harrell, Doelling, & Sasso (1997) describe two recent and promising social interaction interventions: cooperative learning and peer networks. Cooperative learning involves grouping students of different ability levels together to accomplish mutual goals. Cooperative learning structures require the collaboration of the general and special education teachers to prepare the lesson, prepare the students, and direct the cooperative lesson. Peer networks are groups of individuals who demonstrate an interest in and an understanding of the individual with a disability and have impact on that person's life. Peer network interventions promote a positive social environment for students with disabilities in support systems committed to the development of social competency and friends. The Circle of Friends support network is an example of this type of interaction intervention.

Paraprofessional Assistance

The availability and support of paraprofessionals is an important component in successfully including students with mental disabilities in general education programs. Simpson, Myles, & Simpson (1997) suggested that paraprofessionals may assist in a variety of tasks, including: carrying out various management programs and procedures; collecting and charting management-related data; assisting students to practice previously taught lessons; and assisting teachers with daily planning, materials development, and adaptation of curriculum.

As students with mental disabilities prepare for transition from school, their educational programs may feature community-based instruction and vocational skills. These domains should also be addressed in inclusive settings, thereby maximizing interaction with nondisabled peers and adults.

REFERENCES

Bruininks, R. H., Woodcock, R. W., Weatherman, R. F., & Hill, B. K. (1984). *Scales of independent behavior.* Chicago: Riverside.

Chandler, S. K., & Pankaskie, S. C. (1997). Socialization, peer relationships, and self-esteem. In P. Wehman & J. Kregel (Eds.). *Functional curriculum for elementary, middle, and secondary age students with special needs* (pp. 123–153). Austin, TX: PRO-ED.

Drew, C. J., & Hardman, M. L. (2000). *Mental retardation: A life cycle approach.* Upper Saddle River, NJ: Merrill/Prentice Hall.

Dymond, S. K. (1997). Community Living. In P. Wehman & J. Kregel (Eds.). *Functional curriculum for elementary, middle, and secondary age students with special needs* (pp. 197–226). Austin, TX: PRO-ED.

Garrison-Harrell, L., Doelling, J. E., & Sasso, G. M. (1997). Recent developments in social interaction interventions to enhance inclusion. In P. Zionts (Ed.) *Inclusion strategies for students with learning and behavior problems* (pp. 273–295). Austin, TX: PRO-ED.

Hanley-Maxwell, C., & Collet-Klingenberg, L. (1997). Curricular choices related to work. In P. Wehman & J. Kregel (Eds.). *Functional curriculum for elementary, middle, and secondary age students with special needs* (pp. 155–183). Austin, TX: PRO-ED.

Heward, W. L. (2000). *Exceptional children: An introduction to special education.* Upper Saddle River, NJ: Merrill/Prentice Hall.

Lambert, N., Nihira, K., & Leland, H. (1993). *Adaptive Behavior Scale—School* (2nd ed.). Austin, TX: PRO-ED.

Keenan, S. M. (1997). Program elements that support teachers and students with learning and behavior problems. In P. Zionts (Ed.). *Inclusion strategies for students with learning and behavior problems* (pp. 117–138). Austin, TX: PRO-ED.

Perner, D. E., & Porter, G. L. (1998). Creating inclusive schools: Changing roles and strategies. In A. Hilton & R. Ringlaben (Eds.). *Best and promising practices in developmental disabilities.* Austin, TX: PRO-ED, 317–330.

Reschly, D. J. (1990). Best practices in adaptive behavior. In A. Thomas & J. Grimes (Eds.). *Best Practices in School Psychology-II.* Washington, DC: National Association of School Psychologists.

Sale, P., & Martin, J. E. (1997). Self-determination. In P. Wehman & J. Kregel (Eds.). *Functional curriculum for elementary, middle, and secondary age students with special needs* (pp. 43–67). Austin, TX: PRO-ED.

Simpson, R. L., Myles, B. M., & Simpson, J. D. (1997) Inclusion of students with disabilities in general education settings: Structuring for successful management. In P. Zionts (Ed.). *Inclusion strategies for students with learning and behavior problems* (pp. 171–196). Austin, TX: PRO-ED.

Sparrow, S. S., Balla, D. A., & Cicchetti, D. V. (1984). *Vineland Adaptive Behavior Scales.* Circle Pines, MN: American Guidance Service.

Thorndike, R. I., Hagen, E. P., & Sattler, J. M. (1986). *Technical manual for the Stanford-Binet Intelligence Scale* (4th ed.). Chicago: Riverside.

U.S. Department of Education (1998). *20th Annual Report to Congress on the Implementation of the Individuals with Disabilities Education Act.* Washington, DC: Office of Special Education Programs.

Wechsler, D. (1974). *Manual for the Wechsler Intelligence Scale for Children—Revised.* New York: Psychological Corporation.

Wehman, P., & Kregel, J. (1997). *Functional curriculum for elementary, middle, and secondary age students with special needs.* Austin, TX: PRO-ED.

Wolfe, P. S., & Harriott, W. A. (1997). Functional academics. In P. Wehman & J. Kregel (Eds.). *Functional curriculum for elementary, middle, and secondary age students with special needs* (pp. 69–103). Austin, TX: PRO-ED.

Ysseldyke, J. E. & Olsen, K. (1997). *NCEO Synthesis Report 28: Putting alternate assessments into practice: What to measure and possible sources of data.* Minneapolis, MN: National Center for Educational Outcomes.

Drew, C. J., & Hardman, M. L. (2000). *Mental retardation: A life cycle approach.* Upper Saddle River, NJ: Merrill/Prentice Hall.

Hickson, L., Blackman, L. S., & Reis, E. M. (1996). *Mental retardation: Foundations of educational programming.* Needham Heights, MA: Allyn & Bacon.

Ryndak, D. L., & Alper, S. (1996). *Curriculum content for students with moderate and severe disabilities in inclusive settings.* Needham Heights, MA: Allyn & Bacon.

Thomas, G. E. (1996). *Teaching students with mental retardation: A life goal curriculum planning approach.* Upper Saddle River, NJ: Prentice Hall.

RECOMMENDED READINGS

Several books are available which address the needs of students with mental disabilities:

Beirne, M. S., Ittenbach, R., & Patton, J. R. (1998). *Mental retardation.* Upper Saddle River, NJ: Prentice Hall.

Resources

Numerous resources are available for students with mental disabilities. The Council for Exceptional Children (CEC) has a division that specifically addresses this population of students. The Division on Mental Retardation and Developmental Disabilities (MRDD) promotes the education and general welfare of individuals with mental retardation, developmental disabilities, and intellectual challenges as well as those who serve them. The Division publishes *Education and Training in Mental Retardation and Developmental Disabilities* and the *MRDD Express* newsletter. The CEC website is http://www.cec.sped.org/.

The ARC (Association for Retarded Citizens) is the national organization devoted to promoting and improving supports and services for people with mental retardation and related disabilities and their families. The association also fosters research and education regarding the prevention of mental retardation in infants and young children. Contact ARC at:

ARC National Headquarters
1010 Wayne Ave, Ste 650
Silver Spring, MD 20910
(301) 565-3842 Toll Free 1-800-433-5255
http://www.thearc.org/faqs.htm

Chapter Preview

An IEP team may determine that a child has a specific learning disability if he does not achieve commensurate with his age and ability levels and if a severe discrepancy exists between achievement and ability in one or more of the following areas:

- Oral expression
- Listening comprehension
- Written expression
- Basic reading skills
- Reading comprehension
- Mathematics calculation
- Mathematics reasoning

Although a heterogeneous group, students with learning disabilities share certain features:

- A discrepancy between a student's estimated academic ability and his actual academic performance
- Academic learning problems (e.g., reading skills and comprehension, written expression, mathematics calculations, mathematics reasoning)
- Language disorders (e.g., deficits in oral expression and listening comprehension, difficulty following oral or written directions)
- Perceptual disorders (e.g., difficulties with auditory and visual discrimination, memory, and integration)
- Metacognitive deficits (e.g., lacking awareness of the skills, strategies, and resources needed to perform a task effectively, lacking self-regulation of performance)
- Social-emotional problems (e.g., poor self-concept and self-esteem, social skill deficits, acting out and disruptive behavior)
- Memory problems (e.g., problems remembering auditory and visual stimuli such as spelling words, math facts, and directions)
- Attention problems and hyperactivity (e.g., ADHD [discussed in Chapter 19])

The instructional program for students with learning disabilities often addresses educational needs in oral and written expression, reading, and mathematics. Numerous strategies have been developed to address the needs of such students in general education classrooms, including:

- Assistive technology
- Modifying content area instruction
- Employing alternative methodology

CHAPTER 16

SPECIFIC LEARNING
DISABILITY

FEDERAL DEFINITION OF LEARNING DISABILITY

The term "specific learning disability" means a disorder in one or more of the basic psychological processes involved in understanding or using language, spoken or written, which may manifest in an imperfect ability to listen, think, speak, read, write, spell, or do mathematical calculations. The term includes such conditions as perceptual disabilities, brain injury, minimal brain dysfunction, dyslexia, and developmental aphasia. The term does not include a learning problem that is primarily the result of a visual, hearing, or motor disability, mental retardation, emotional disturbance, or environmental, cultural, or economic disadvantage (20 U.S.C. § 1401(26)).

REFERRAL AND INITIAL ASSESSMENT

The criteria for determining the existence of a specific learning disability are described at 34 C.F.R. § 300.541-300.543. An IEP team may determine that a child has a specific learning disability if he does not achieve commensurate with his age and ability levels and if a severe discrepancy exists between achievement and ability in oral or written expression, reading or listening comprehension, basic reading skills or math reasoning and calculation.

The team may not identify a child as having a specific learning disability if the severe discrepancy between ability and achievement is primarily the result of a visual, hearing, or motor impairment; mental retardation; emotional disturbance; or environmental, cultural or economic disadvantage. At least one team member other than the child's regular teacher must observe the child's academic performance in the regular classroom setting.

For a child suspected of having a specific learning disability, the documentation of the team's determination of eligibility must include a statement of:

1. Whether the child has a specific learning disability
2. The basis for making the determination
3. The relevant behavior noted during the observation of the child
4. The relationship of that behavior to the child's academic functioning
5. The educationally relevant medical findings, if any
6. Whether there is a severe discrepancy between achievement and ability that is not correctable without special education and related services
7. The determination of the team concerning the effects of environmental, cultural, or economic disadvantage. Each team member shall certify in writing whether the report reflects his or her conclusion.

The assessment of students with learning disabilities involves a variety of formal and informal tests. Formal tests include measures of intelligence (e.g., *Wechsler Intelligence Scale for Children*—III; Wechsler, 1991) and achievement or diagnostic assessments (e.g., *Kauffman Assessment Battery for Children*; Kauffman & Kauffman, 1983). Informal measures include classroom observation, criterion-referenced tests, curriculum-based measures, and alternative or portfolio assessment.

The U.S. Department of Education (1998) estimated the prevalence of learning disabilities to be 5 percent of the school-aged population. More than half of the 2.5 million students with disabilities are identified as learning disabled, a number that has increased by 37.8 percent over the past 10 years. About 70 percent of students with learning disabilities are boys.

CHARACTERISTICS OF LEARNING DISABILITIES

Mercer (1997) described several characteristics of learning disabilities. Although a heterogeneous group, students with learning disabilities share certain features, including:

- A discrepancy between a student's estimated academic ability and his actual academic performance
- Academic learning problems (e.g., reading skills and comprehension, written expression, mathematics calculations, mathematics reasoning)
- Language disorders (e.g., deficits in oral expression and listening comprehension, difficulty following oral or written directions)
- Perceptual disorders (e.g., difficulties with auditory and visual discrimination, memory, and integration)
- Metacognitive deficits (e.g., lacking awareness of the skills, strategies, and resources needed to perform a task effectively, lacking self-regulation of performance)
- Social-emotional problems (e.g., poor self-concept and self-esteem, social skill deficits, acting out and disruptive behavior)
- Memory problems (e.g., problems remembering auditory and visual stimuli such as spelling words, math facts, and directions)
- Attention problems and hyperactivity (e.g., ADHD).

Students with learning disabilities may have one or more of these characteristics, which often impact their educational achievement. The IEP team must design an instructional program to meet the specific learning disabilities of these students.

INSTRUCTION

The instructional program for students with learning disabilities often addresses educational needs in oral and written expression, reading, and mathematics.

Reading

Reading instruction for students with learning disabilities should balance decoding instruction with authentic literary experiences (Pressley & Rankin 1994). Goals and objectives for reading may include improving reading fluency and comprehension as well as increasing the diversification of reading interests and activities. Various instructional approaches in reading have been successful for students with learning disabilities, including phonics, whole language, language experience, phonological awareness, and strategy instruction. Strategy instruction, a step-by-step approach to decoding or comprehension, has been particularly effective with these students. An example of a decoding strategy is DISSECT (Lenz & Hughes, 1990):

D = *D*iscover the content of the word
I = *I*solate the prefix
S = *S*eparate the suffix
S = *S*ay the stem
E = *E*xamine the stem
C = *C*heck with someone
T = *T*ry the dictionary

Strategy instruction teaches students a step-by-step, problem-solving procedure for decoding and comprehension in reading.

Math

For mathematics, teacher modeling of explicit strategies has been found to be an effective approach for students with learning disabilities. Fact matrices, concrete teaching materials, and pictorial representations can be effective instructional tools. Students should be frequently asked to verbalize and describe math tasks.

Oral and Written Expression

Providing visual advanced organizers, presenting visual aids, and modeling processes and strategies are effective instructional strategies for oral and written expression (Vaughn, Bos, & Schumm, 1997). For example, students can be taught how to graphically organize ideas for writing through the use of a "webbing" technique. In the center of the web is the main topic or idea, and supporting details are spokes radiating from the center. Teaching alternative handwriting methods, verbalizing or dramatizing the motor sequences of letter forms, or employing multisensory techniques can all improve handwriting.

Educators have developed innovative and effective methods to address the instructional needs of students with learning disabilities. As the number of such students continues to increase, so will efforts to create, validate, and expand a methodology to meet their needs.

RELATED SERVICES

Students with learning disabilities may receive services from a speech clinician or pathologist. Classroom-based models for speech services emphasize the collaboration between the language specialist and the classroom teacher and eliminate the disadvantages of traditional "pull-out" models. The speech clinician serves as a consultant to the classroom teacher, providing direct services to both the student and the educator.

INCLUSION STRATEGIES

Although the inclusion of students with learning disabilities has been controversial and produced mixed reports of effectiveness, the number of such students educated in general education classrooms has increased significantly since 1993 (McLeskey, Henry, & Axelrod, 1999). Numerous strategies have been developed to address the needs of students with learning disabilities in general education classrooms, including using assistive technology, modifying content area instruction, and employing alternative methodology.

Assistive Technology

Recent advances in assistive technology may facilitate successful inclusion for students identified as learning disabled. Computer-assisted instruction may provide the greatest assistance. (Shea & Bauer, 1994). Students with learning disabilities have difficulty with the technical aspects of writing (e.g., handwriting, spelling, mechanics, usage). Word processor programs such as *Write: OutLoud* and *Co:Writer* help students manipulate the text to review and improve it (Lewis, 1998).

Modifying Content Area Instruction

Modifying content area instruction will also assist in the inclusion of students with learning disabilities into regular education classrooms. Modifications include changing the criteria for task performance (e.g., the amount, speed, or accuracy required) or altering the characteristics of content area tasks (e.g., the skill required). Lewis & Doorlag (1999) describe several modifications for content area instruction:

For Reading:

- Reduce the amount of reading
- Provide information through another medium (e.g., tape-recorded texts, peer tutors, audio-visual aids)
- Substitute materials from a lower reading level

For Written Assignments and Exams:

- Reduce the length of written tasks or extend the time limits
- Allow students to use a word processor
- Have students respond through a different medium (e.g., oral responses, tape-recorded responses)

For Math:

- Allow the use of calculators
- Use manipulative objects to help learn number concepts and relationships
- Provide visual and verbal prompts

Alternative Methodology

Alternative methodology may also assist in content area classes. Reciprocal teaching has been found to be an effective comprehension strategy for students with learning disabilities in inclusive settings (Lederer, 2000). Self-regulated strategy instruction for written expression improved achievement for students with learning disabilities in regular education settings (de la Paz, 1999). Etscheidt and Bartlett (1999) recommended that IEP teams discuss supplemental aids and services that can be provided to achieve goals and objectives in the regular education classroom. These questions include:

Does the student need visual aids, large print, or alternative media?

Could the student be provided process-of-reading guides, highlighted, or tape-recorded texts?

Could the student be allowed extra time for completion of assignments, have alternative assignments, or be provided a calculator or word processor?

Could the student have take-home or alternative (e.g. oral) tests?

Could the student use a study guide during a test?

Could tests be divided into parts and taken over a series of days?

Could the student be graded pass/fail or receive IEP progress grading?

Could the resource teacher and regular teacher use shared grading?

Could contracting be used?

Could portfolio evaluations be used?

Could cooperative learning or reciprocal teaching be incorporated?

Could the student be assigned a peer partner?

Does the student need an assignment notebook or home copies of texts?

Could the student be provided computer-assisted instruction, communication switches, or software?

Does the student require electronic aids or services?

Given the recent emphasis on state and national standards and outcomes, the successful inclusion of students with learning disabilities will require IEP teams to carefully examine the demands of regular classrooms and provide effective assistance to students with learning difficulties.

REFERENCES

de la Paz, S. (1999). Self-regulated strategy instruction in regular education settings: Improving outcomes for students with and without learning disabilities. *Learning Disabilities Research and Practice, 14* (2), 92–106.

Etscheidt, S. K., & Bartlett, L. (1998). The IDEA amendments: A four-step approach for determining supplemental aids and services. *Exceptional Children, 65* (2), 1–12.

Greene, G. (1999). Mnemonic multiplication fact instruction for students with learning disabilities. *Learning Disabilities Research and Practice, 14* (3), 141–148.

Heward, W. L. (2000). *Exceptional children: An introduction to special education.* Upper Saddle River, NJ: Merrill.

Kaufman A. S., & Kaufman, W. L. (1983). *Kaufman assessment battery for children.* Circle Pines, MN: American Guidance Service.

Lederer, J. M. (2000). Reciprocal teaching of social studies in inclusive elementary classrooms. *Journal of Learning Disabilities, 33* (1), 91–106.

Lenz, B. K., & Hughes, C. A. (1990). A word identification strategy for adolescents with learning disabilities. *Journal of Learning Disabilities, 33,* 149–158.

Lewis, R. B. (1998). Assistive technology and learning disabilities: Today's realities and tomorrow's promises. *Journal of Learning Disabilities, 31,* 16–25.

Lewis, R. B., & Doorlag, D. H. (1999). *Teaching Special Students in General Education Classrooms* (5th ed.). Upper Saddle River, NJ: Merrill/Prentice Hall.

McLeskey, J., Henry, D., & Axelrod, M. I. (1999). Inclusion of students with learning disabilities: An examination of data from reports to Congress. *Exceptional Children, 66,* (1), 55–66.

Mercer, C. D. (1997). Students with learning disabilities (5th ed.). Upper Saddle River, NJ: Merrill/Prentice Hall.

Pressley, M., & Rankin, J. (1994). More about whole language methods of reading instruction for students at risk for early reading failure. *Learning Disabilities Research & Practice, 9,* 157–168.

Shea, T. M., & Bauer, A. M. (1994). *Learners with disabilities: A social systems perspective of special education.* Madison, WI: Brown & Benchmark Publishers.

U.S. Department of Education (1998). *20th Annual Report to Congress on the Implementation of the Individuals With Disabilities Education Act.* Washington, DC: Office of Special Education Programs.

Vaughn, S., Bos, C. S., & Schumm, J. S. (1999). *Teaching mainstreamed, diverse, and at-risk students in the general education classroom.* Boston: Allyn & Bacon.

Wechsler, D. (1991). Wechsler intelligence scale for children (3rd ed.). San Antonio, TX: Psychological Corporation.

Mercer, C. D. (1997). *Students with learning disabilities.* Upper Saddle River, NJ: Prentice-Hall.

Myers, P. I., & Hammill, D. D. (1990). *Learning disabilities: Basic concepts, assessment, practices, and instructional strategies* (4th ed.). Austin, TX: PRO-ED.

Murphy, S. T. (1992). *On being learning disabled: Perspectives and strategies of young adults.* New York: Teachers College Press.

O'Shea, L. J., O'Shea, D. J., & Algozzine, B. (1998). *Learning disabilities: From theory towards practice.* Upper Saddle River, NJ: Prentice Hall.

Reid, D. K., Hresko, W. P., & Swanson, H. L. (1996) *Cognitive approaches to learning disabilities.* Austin, TX: PRO-ED.

Rivera, D. P. (1998). *Mathematics education for students with learning disabilities: Theory to practice.* Austin, TX: PRO-ED.

Smith, C. R. (1998). *Learning disabilities: The interaction of learner, task, and setting* (4th ed.). Needham Heights, MA: Allyn & Bacon.

Swanson, H. L. (1991). *Handbook on the assessment of learning disabilities.* Austin, TX: PRO-ED.

Vogel, S. A. (1992). *Educational alternatives for students with learning disabilities.* New York: Springer-Verlag.

RECOMMENDED READINGS

Several books are available which address the needs of students with learning disabilities:

Bender, W. N. (1998). *Learning disabilities: characteristics, identification and teaching strategies* (3rd ed.). Needham Heights, MA: Allyn & Bacon.

Hallahan, D. P., Kauffman, J. M., & Lloyd, J. W. (1999). *Introduction to learning disabilities* (2nd ed.). Needham Heights, MA: Allyn & Bacon.

Higgins, K., & Boone, R. (1997). *Technology for students with learning disabilities: Educational applications.* Austin, TX: PRO-ED.

Resources

Several resources are available for students with learning disabilities. The CEC has a division specifically addressing this population of students. The Division for Learning Disabilities (DLD) promotes improved services, research, and legislation for individuals with learning disabilities. It publishes the quarterly journal *Learning Disabilities Research and Practice.* The website is: http://www.dldcec.org/.

Several organizations address the needs of students with learning disabilities:

Learning Disabilities Association of America (LDA)
4156 Library Rd
Pittsburgh, PA 15234

The Learning Disabilities Association of America (LDA) is a national, nonprofit organization developed to advance the education and general welfare of children and adults with disabilities of a perceptual, conceptual, or coordinative nature. The website is: http://www.ldanatl.org/.

National Center for Learning Disabilities (NCLD)
381 Park Ave S, Ste 1420
New York, NY 10016

The National Center for Learning Disabilities provides national leadership in support of children and adults with learning disabilities by providing information, resources, and referral services; developing and supporting innovative educational programs, seminars, and workshops; conducting a public awareness campaign; and advocating for more effective policies and legislation to help individuals with learning disabilities. The website is: http://www.ncld.org/.

Other websites concerning learning disabilities include:

LD Online—http://www.ldonline.org.

Learning Disabilities Resources—
http://aace.virginia.edu/go/cise/ose/
categories/ld.html.

CHAPTER 17

ORTHOPEDIC IMPAIRMENTS (PHYSICAL DISABILITIES)

Orthopedic disabilities are associated with congenital anomalies, disease, or other causes. Students who are physically disabled do not demonstrate a set of common characteristics; the cognitive, academic, physical, social-emotional, and communication characteristics are specific to their impairment. Common conditions affecting students with physical disabilities include:

- Cerebral palsy
- Spina bifida
- Muscular dystrophy
- Spinal cord injury

The assessment team for students with physical disabilities will include a variety of educators and health professionals. This multidisciplinary team may include the child and the parents, general and special educators, speech clinicians, occupational and physical therapists, school psychologist, social workers, and medical professionals.

Because the medical, educational, therapeutic, vocational, and social needs of students with physical disabilities are complex and interrelated, it is important for the multidisciplinary team to work collaboratively in planning an educational program. Students with physical disabilities often require a variety of related services to support their educational program. Depending on the nature and severity of the disability, students may require:

- Occupational Therapy
- Physical Therapy
- School Health Services
- Assistive Technology

Strategies to facilitate successful inclusion for students with physical disabilities include:

- Maintaining barrier-free classrooms and schools;
- Facilitating positive peer interactions;
- Familiarizing with medically related needs and procedures; and
- Learning about adaptive equipment.

FEDERAL DEFINITION OF ORTHOPEDIC IMPAIRMENTS

Orthopedic impairment is defined as a severe impairment that adversely affects a child's educational performance. The term includes impairments caused by congenital anomaly (e.g., clubfoot, absence of some member), impairments caused by disease (e.g., poliomyelitis, bone tuberculosis), and impairments from other causes (e.g., cerebral palsy, amputation, fracture or burns that cause contractures) (34 C.F.R. § 300.7 (a) (8)).

REFERRAL AND INITIAL ASSESSMENT

Students with physical disabilities are referred for special education services when those disabilities adversely affect their educational performance. For many students, the physical disability was present at birth and services were initiated during infancy.

In addition to the student and parents, the multidisciplinary assessment team for students with physical disabilities includes a variety of educators and health professionals, such as general and special educators, speech clinicians, occupational and physical therapists, school psychologist, social workers, and medical professionals. This diversity is needed to obtain assessment information that will help the team to determine appropriate goals and objectives for the students and to select the methodology, services, adaptive technology, and adaptations necessary to meet those goals. Sirvis (1988) suggests the assessment of students with physical disabilities should focus on the following areas:

- Activities of daily living (e.g., eating, toileting, personal care, travel)
- Mobility (e.g., use of wheelchairs or supportive devices for travel)
- Physical abilities and limitations (e.g., for schooling, employment, recreation, and independent functioning)
- Psychosocial development (e.g., social and emotional development, interaction with others)
- Communication (e.g., understanding and expressing language)
- Academic potential (e.g., modified achievement tests)
- Adaptations for learning (e.g. classroom and physical adaptations to facilitate independence)
- Transition skills (e.g., factors necessary for transition from school to living and working in the community).

The multidisciplinary team should review the assessment data and plan the student's IEP. Each area affected by the disability should be addressed. The team develops goals and objectives for each area and specifies the services needed to meet those goals.

CHARACTERISTICS OF PHYSICAL DISABILITIES

Students with physical disabilities do not share common characteristics. Their cognitive, academic, physical, social-emotional, and communication characteristics are specific to their impairments (Ysseldyke & Algozzine, 1990). The nature, severity, visibility, duration, and age of onset are all variables affecting the characteristics of individuals with physical disabilities. For example, some physical disabilities are associated with mental and learning disabilities, whereas others are not. The severity of physical disabilities can also impact cognitive and affective development. The visibility of the disabling condition can influence affective development. The disability may severely impair social interactions, which will affect the development of social and emotional behaviors, communication, and self-concept. In other individuals, social or communication skills are unimpaired. The developmental process may be significantly affected if the disability has an early onset, because early motor impairment can delay development in cognitive, academic, communication, and social-behavioral areas. Advances in technology have provided individuals with physical disabilities many options for improved movement and health, which may minimize the effect of such disabilities on development delays. The following represent some common conditions affecting students with physical disabilities.

Cerebral Palsy

Cerebral palsy is the most prevalent physical disability of school-aged children. It is caused by a lesion to the brain or abnormal brain development due to injury, accident, or illness before or after birth. Children with cerebral palsy may lack control of movement, lack coordination, have involuntary movement, paralysis, or weakness of muscles, or experience sensory impairments such as loss of hearing or vision. The problems related to movement are not caused by dysfunctional muscles, but rather the brain's ineffectiveness in controlling affected muscles. The most common type of cerebral palsy is hypertonia, which is characterized by tight, contracted muscles. Students may have jerky, uncoordinated movements, exaggerated reflex reactions, and skeletal deformities. In contrast, hypotonia is a type of cerebral palsy characterized by weak, floppy muscles, particularly in the neck and trunk. Those affected may have low levels of motor movement or require postural support. Athetosis involves both tightness or rigidity of muscles as well as episodes of floppy, loose muscle tone. Children with athetosis have difficulty with mobility, language, and activities of daily living (e.g., eating, dressing).

Ataxia is the inability to make purposeful motor responses, and children with ataxic cerebral palsy have poor balance and poor motor control. Students with cerebral palsy are often stressed or fatigued, which affects learning and social-behavioral responses.

Spina Bifida

Spina bifida is a congenital physical disability affecting the vertebrae that enclose the spinal cord. The disease results from the failure of the spinal column to close completely during fetal development. There are three types of spinal bifida: spina bifida occulta, in which only a few vertebrae are malformed; meningocele, in which the casing surrounding the spinal cord protrudes from the back at birth; and myelomeningocele, the most common and serious form in which the spinal casing, spinal cord, and spinal nerve roots all protrude from the back. Myelomeningocele is often accompanied by hydrocephalus, an accumulation of spinal fluid in tissues surrounding the brain. Children with spina bifida have some degree of paralysis in the lower limbs and thus require a wheelchair, crutches, or a walker. They also have poor bladder and bowel control, often requiring the use of a catheter.

Muscular Dystrophy

Muscular dystrophy is characterized by the deterioration of tissues and muscles. By 2 to 5 years of age, children with muscular dystrophy experience muscle weakness and typically by age 12, have lost the ability to walk. The muscle weakness often leads to respiratory complications which require special attention. The progressive deterioration of muscles necessitates regular physical therapy, exercise, and mobility supports as well as emotional support for affected children and their families. Maintaining muscle function and facilitating ambulation are ongoing goals.

Spinal Cord Injury

Compression, lesions, or fracture of the vertebrae result in spinal cord injury. Car accidents, sports injuries, and violence are the most common causes of spinal cord injuries in school-aged children (Heward, 2000). Students with spinal cord injuries use wheelchairs for mobility and are involved in rehabilitation programs of physical therapy and psychological support.

Owing to advances in medical technology, there is an increasing population of students with physical disabilities. During the 1996–97 school year, 66,400 students with orthopedic impairments were served under the IDEA, which represented 1.3 percent of the total number of students with disabilities.

INSTRUCTION

Because the medical, educational, therapeutic, vocational, and social needs of students with physical disabilities are complex and interrelated, it is important for the multidisciplinary team to work collaboratively in planning an IEP (Heward, 2000). The administrator, as a member of that team, must be aware of the services provided to students with physical disabilities.

Teachers who educate students with physical and health disabilities require specialized knowledge and skills to provide an appropriate education, including:

Assessment and evaluation (e.g. modifying assessment, determining response modification, developing assistive technology plans)

Instructional content and practice (e.g., making instructional modifications, modifying reading for nonverbal students, supervising medical self-management, implementing augmentative communication, providing assistive technology, improving independent living skills, adapting lessons to minimize exertion, adapting scheduling of the school day to student's level of fatigue and endurance)

Managing learning environment (e.g., integrating health care plans in programming, supervising physical positioning and management, providing adaptive equipment, taking safety precautions)

Managing student behavior (e.g., analyzing behavior to determine the cause and intent)

Collaborative partnership (e.g., using collaboration skills, working with chronically or terminally ill students, demonstrating knowledge of resources)

Professionalism (e.g., working as member of transdisciplinary team) (Heller, Fredrick, Dykes, Best, & Cohen, 1999)

These competencies enable teachers to be effective educators, school-based consultants, and co-teachers to ensure an appropriate education for students with physical disabilities. Administrators must ensure that teachers working with students with physical disabilities are qualified and capable of providing an appropriate education program.

RELATED SERVICES

Students with physical disabilities often require a variety of related services to support their educational program. Depending on the nature and severity of the disability, students may require supplemental assistance to benefit from special education.

Occupational Therapy

Occupational therapy involves services provided by a qualified occupational therapist and includes:

1. improving, developing, or restoring functions impaired or lost through illness, injury, or deprivation;

2. improving ability to perform tasks for independent functioning if functions are impaired or lost; and

3. preventing, through early intervention, initial or further impairment or loss of function (34 C.F.R. § 300.24 (a) (5)).

The occupational therapist helps maximize the child's independence in daily activities by teaching motor skills for personal care (e.g., dressing), employment (e.g., typing on a computer), recreation (e.g., bowling), communication (e.g., head pointing to communication board), and other areas of physical development. The therapist may recommend equipment, devices, or exercises for home and school.

Physical Therapy

Physical therapy involves services by a qualified physical therapist (34 C.F.R. § 300.24 (a) (8)) and includes the development and maintenance of motor function and skills, movement, and posture. Physical therapists may prescribe certain exercises to help maintain muscle function or minimize motor restrictions, and may also recommend the use of adaptations, equipment, or assistive devices. The therapist can assist the classroom teacher with proper lifting, positioning, movement, and transportation of students with physical disabilities.

School Health Services

Students with physical disabilities often have special health care needs that require specialized procedures that are provided by a qualified school nurse or other qualified person (34 C.F.R. § 300.24 (a) (12)). Such procedures may involve administering medication, performing clean intermittent catheterization (CIC), providing gastrointestinal and tracheostomy care, assisting with respirator or ventilator support, and supervising dietary provisions.

Assistive Technology

Students with orthopedic impairments use assistive devices to enhance interpersonal relationships, sensory ability, cognitive ability, communication, motor performance, self-maintenance, leisure, and productivity. The IDEA requires IEP teams to consider whether the child requires assistive technology devices and services (34 C.F.R. § 300.346 (a) (2) (v)). Parette (1998) discusses the use of assistive technology with students with disabilities and describes the assistive technology devices in the following categories:

- Augmentative and alternative communication devices
- Adaptive toys
- Positioning equipment
- Independent living devices
- Leisure or recreation equipment
- Microcomputers and information technologies
- Environmental access devices
- Assistive listening devices
- Mobility devices
- Visual aids

The IEP team should consider several factors in selecting appropriate assistive technology for students with physical disabilities. First, the characteristics of the student must be discussed to determine future goals that can be achieved using the device or service. The device or service should be related to specific, clearly defined IEP goals. Second, the features of the assistive technology device must be addressed. The device or service should be compatible with practical constraints (e.g., available resources, training required of student or teacher) and be able to enhance performance with ease of use, comfort, and dependability. The team should discuss the transportability, longevity, durability, adaptability, safety features, and repair factors of the device. Third, the assistive technology device or service should result in the student achieving the desired goal outcome.

The administrator should be familiar with the variety of related services provided to students with physical disabilities. Although the costs and funding sources for such services are important issues, related services must be provided if they are necessary for the child to benefit from special education.

INCLUSION STRATEGIES

The provision of related services and assistive technology has facilitated the inclusion of students with orthopedic impairments in general education classrooms. In 1998, about 41 percent of students receiving services for orthopedic impairments were included in regular education classrooms, while 21 percent received resource room services and 30 percent were educated in special classes (U.S. Department of Education, 1998). The challenges facing teachers and administrators involve accessibility, social-behavioral concerns, and the complexity of physical disabilities.

Maintaining Barrier-Free Classrooms and Schools

Schools and classrooms should be evaluated for accessibility to students with physical disabilities. Evaluation should include sidewalks, ramps, doors, hallways, stairs, floors, restrooms, and water fountains. Classrooms should be arranged to facilitate mobility and provide access to chalkboards, computers, and all activity centers. Storage space for the students' aids and equipment should be provided, as well as appropriate desks and chairs (Lewis & Doorlag, 1999).

Facilitating Positive Peer Interactions

The attitudes of nondisabled peers affect successful inclusion of students with physical disabilities. Nondisabled students who have been involved with the inclusion of students with severe disabilities are supportive (York, Vander-cook, MacDonald, Heise-Neff, & Caughney, 1992). Students without disabilities benefit from inclusion experiences in several ways:

1. They learn patience, including reduced fear of others who are different
2. They feel good in helping others and successfully meeting a challenge (improved self-concept)
3. They gain future benefits in learning how to get along with others who are different
4. They develop warm and caring friendships based on common interests (Ringlaben & Dahmen-Jones, 1998)

Several strategies can promote positive interactions in inclusive classrooms. Peer networks can promote a positive social environment for students with disabilities through the creation of support systems committed to the development of social competency and friendship (Garrison-Harrell, Doelling, & Sasso, 1997). Additional strategies for promoting social acceptance include the Circle of Friends (Forest & Lusthaus, 1989), Special Friends (Cole, Vander-cook, & Rynders, 1988), peer assistance programs (Mastropieri & Scruggs, 2000), peer social initiation (Kerr & Nelson, 1998), and cooperative learning (Johnson & Johnson, 1986).

Familiarizing with Medically Related Needs and Procedures

Administrators and teachers must learn about the student's medical history and be aware of symptoms requiring attention. A teacher may provide the child's medication or dietary supplements or be involved in the management of seizures or respiratory distress. Students without disabilities should also be aware of the child's medical needs and be comfortable with medically related procedures.

Students with physical disabilities may require certain procedures to maintain their health, including clean intermittent catheterization (CIC), a process involving insertion of a clean catheter through the urethra and into the bladder as often as required; tracheostomy suctioning, a procedure in which mucus blockages in the breathing tube are removed; ventilator care, which involves checking the oxygen supply and provision); and dietary maintenance (e.g., tube feeding). Some of the procedures may be performed independently by the student (e.g., CIC), whereas others will require the services of a registered nurse (RN) or licensed practical nurse (LPN).

Learning About Adaptive Equipment

The inclusion of students with physical disabilities may be facilitated by school personnel learning about the adaptive equipment that these students may be using. Understanding how wheelchairs work, how communication boards are designed, and how switches can detect eye or muscle movement will enable administrators and teachers to be more knowledgeable and comfortable with equipment that will become a part of their schools and classrooms.

REFERENCES

Cole, D. A., Vandercook, T., & Rynders, J. (1988). Comparison of two peer interaction programs: Children with and without severe disabilities. *American Educational Research Journal, 25*, 415–439.

Forest M., & Lusthaus, E. (1989). Circles and maps. In S. Stainback, W., Stainback, & M. Forest (Eds.), *Educating all students in the mainstream of regular education.* Baltimore: Brookes.

Garrison-Harrell, L., Doelling, J. E., & Sasso, G. M. (1997). Recent developments in social interaction interventions to enhance inclusion. In P. Zionts (Ed.) *Inclusion strategies for students with learning and behavior problems.* Austin, TX: PRO-ED.

Heller, K. W., Fredrick, L. D., Dykes, M. K., Best, S., & Cohen, E. T. (1999). A national perspective of competencies for teachers of individuals with physical and health disabilities. *Exceptional Children, 65* (2), 219–234.

Heward, W. L. (2000). *Exceptional children: An introduction to special education.* Upper Saddle River, NJ: Merrill/Prentice Hall.

Johnson, D. W., & Johnson, R. T. (1986). Mainstreaming and cooperative learning strategies. *Exceptional Children, 53*, 553–561.

Kerr, M. M., & Nelson, C. M. (1998). *Strategies for managing behavior problems in the classroom* (3rd ed.). Upper Saddle River, NJ: Merrill/Prentice Hall.

Lewis, R. B., & Doorlag, D. H. (1999). *Teaching special students in general education classrooms* (5th ed.). Upper Saddle River, NJ: Merrill/Prentice Hall.

Mastropieri, M. A., & Scruggs, T. E. (2000). *The inclusive classroom: Strategies for effective instruction.* Upper Saddle River, NJ: Merrill/Prentice Hall.

Parette, H. P. (1998). Assistive technology: Effective practices for students with mental retardation and developmental disabilities. In A. Hilton & R. Ringlaben (Eds.) *Best and promising practices in developmental disabilities.* Austin, TX: PRO-ED.

Ringlaben, R., & Dahmen-Jones, D., (1998). Attitudes about individuals with developmental disabilities. In A. Hilton & R. Ringlaben (Eds.) *Best and promising practices in developmental disabilities.* Austin, TX: PRO-ED.

Sirvis, B. (1988). Physical disabilities. In E. L. Meyen & T. M.. Skrtic (Eds.). *Exceptional children and youth: An introduction.* (3rd ed.). Denver: Love.

U.S. Department of Education (1998). 20th annual report to congress on the implementation of the individuals with disabilities education act. Washington, DC: Office of Special Education Programs.

York, J., Vandercook, T., MacDonald, C., Heise-Neff, C., & Caughney, E. (1992). Feedback about integrating middle-school students with severe disabilities in general education classes. *Exceptional Children, 58*, 244–258.

Ysseldyke, J. E., & Algozzine, B. (1990). *Introduction to special education.* Boston: Houghton Mifflin.

Resources

The Council for Exceptional Children (CEC) has a division specifically addressing this population of students, the Division for Physical and Health Disabilities (DPHD) which advocates for quality education for all individuals with physical disabilities, multiple disabilities, and special health care needs who are served in schools, hospitals, or home settings. The division publishes *Physical Disabilities-Education and Related Services*. The website is: http://www.cec.sped.org/index.html.

Other resources include:

United Cerebral Palsy Association
66 E. 34th St
New York, NY 10016
http://www.ucpa.org

Spina Bifida Association of America
343 Dearborn St
Chicago, IL 60604
http://www.sbaa.org

The World Association of Persons with Physical Disabilities (WAPD)
4503 Sunnyview Dr, Ste 1121
PO Box 14111
Oklahoma City, OK 73113
http://www.wapd.org/

CHAPTER 18

SPEECH AND LANGUAGE IMPAIRMENT

CHAPTER PREVIEW

The number of students receiving speech and language services increased by 10% from 1988 to 1998 and involved 1,050,975 children or about 20% of all students with disabilities receiving services under the IDEA (U.S. Dept. of Education, 1998).

Screening procedures can detect speech and language impairments. The speech clinician may select certain articulation, voice, and fluency tests to evaluate speech impairments or specific expressive and receptive tests to assess language disorders. Students with speech and language impairments have difficulties in the expression and comprehension of language. These disorders include:

- Speech Impairments
  - Articulation disorders
  - Fluency disorders
  - Voice disorders

- Language Impairments
  - Expressive disorders
  - Receptive disorders

Speech-language pathology services are provided to students who have speech and language impairments. These services include:

- Identification of children with speech or language impairments
- Diagnosis and appraisal of specific speech or language impairments;
- Referral for medical or other professional attention necessary for the habilitation of speech or language impairments
- Provision of speech and language services for the habilitation or prevention of communicative impairments
- Counseling and guidance of parents, children, and teachers regarding speech and language impairments

Strategies to facilitate the inclusion of students with speech and language impairments include:

- The collaborative consultation model
- Instructional adjustments
- The use of augmentative and alternative communication

FEDERAL DEFINITION OF SPEECH AND LANGUAGE IMPAIRMENT

Speech or language impairment is defined as a communication disorder, such as stuttering, impaired articulation, or impairment of language or voice, that adversely affects a child's educational performance (34 C.F.R. § 300.7 (a) (11)).

REFERRAL AND INITIAL ASSESSMENT

The first step in the detection of speech and language impairment is screening. Screening may involve formal and informal measures administered by the speech and language pathologist or checklists or rating scales given by the classroom teacher. The screening procedure identifies the areas of concern and establishes a discrepancy between the student's communication abilities and developmental expectations.

Following the screening procedures, specific speech and language assessments can be administered. The speech clinician may select certain articulation, voice, and fluency tests to evaluate speech impairments or specific expressive and receptive tests to assess language disorders. The assessment may also include a hearing test and classroom observation.

CHARACTERISTICS OF SPEECH AND LANGUAGE IMPAIRMENT

Students with speech and language impairments have difficulties in the expression and comprehension of language. There are several types of speech and language disorders.

Speech Impairment

Children with speech impairments have difficulty with articulation, fluency, or voice in communication. These difficulties make it difficult for others to understand them.

Articulation Disorders

This is the most common speech impairment and involves errors in the production of speech sounds. Children with articulation disorders may substitute, distort, omit, or add sounds in their production of speech. These articulation errors can range from mild to severe and may result in difficulty understanding the child's speech.

Fluency Disorders

Fluency disorders involve the rate and rhythm of speech. Children with fluency problems usually block, repeat, or prolong the sounds, syllables, words, or phrases in speech. Stuttering is the most common impairment and involves interruption of speech production. Students who stutter may communicate with rapid repetition of sounds, particularly at the beginning of words, or experience excessive pauses and verbal blocks.

Voice Disorders

Disorders in voice involve qualities such as pitch (e.g., high or low), volume or intensity (e.g., loudness or softness), or resonance (e.g., nasality). These disorders can also affect the intelligibility of a child's speech.

Language Disorders

Children with language disorders have difficulty with the production or comprehension of language. A receptive language disorder impairs a child's ability to understand spoken language, and the child has difficulty understanding oral information. An expressive language disorder impacts verbal communication. The child may have no spoken language, and may use gestures, or incorrect words, or may have a limited vocabulary.

Vaughn, Bos, & Schumm (1997) describe the characteristics of children with language disorders. The child with a receptive language impairment frequently asks for information to be repeated or clarified and has difficulty with:

- following directions
- understanding the meaning of concepts (particularly technical or abstract concepts)
- seeing relationships among concepts (e.g., temporal, causal, conditional relationships)
- understanding humor and figurative language
- understanding multiple meanings
- understanding less common and irregular verb tenses
- understanding compound and complex sentences
- detecting breakdowns in comprehension

Children with expressive language impairments often communicate less frequently than their peers and have difficulty with:

- using correct grammar
- using compound and complex sentences
- thinking of the right word to convey the concept (word retrieval or word finding)
- discussing abstract concepts
- changing communication style to fit different social contexts
- providing enough information to the listener
- maintaining the topic during a conversation
- repairing communication when the listener does not understand

The number of students receiving speech and language services increased by 10 percent from 1988 to 1998 and involved 1,050,975 children or about 20 percent of all students with disabilities receiving services under the IDEA (U.S. Dept. of Education, 1998).

INSTRUCTION AND RELATED SERVICES

Speech-language pathology services are provided to students who have speech and language impairments. As with special education, these related services are provided according to the individual child's needs. These services include:

- Identification of children with speech or language impairments
- Diagnosis and appraisal of specific speech or language impairments
- Referral for medical or other professional attention necessary for the habilitation of speech or language impairments
- Provision of speech and language services for the habilitation or prevention of communicative impairments
- Counseling and guidance for parents, children, and teachers regarding speech and language impairments (34 C.F.R. § 300.24 (b) (14))

Speech and language services are based on the assessment data and are provided in conjunction with goals and objectives determined by the student's IEP team. The speech and language clinician guides the development of language programs and services. For articulation impairment, there are several factors which influence the selection of education approaches: the child's auditory discrimination skills, the nature of the articulation errors, and the child's ability to imitate. Heward (2000) reported that four models are widely used for articulation disorders:

1. The discrimination model (e.g., developing the child's ability to listen and detect differences in sounds and match his speech to a model using auditory, visual, and tactual feedback)
2. The phonologic model (e.g., identifying and modifying the pattern of sound production)
3. The sensorimotor model (e.g., emphasizing the repetitive production of sounds)

4. The operant model (e.g., shaping articulatory responses).

The speech clinician selects the approach most suited for the individual child's needs.

Fluency disorders, including stuttering, have been addressed with various methods. Behavioral and cognitive (e.g., self-monitoring of fluent speech) are typical approaches. Voice disorders, however, often require medical intervention. The clinician works in conjunction with the child's pediatrician to address instructional approaches.

Educational approaches for language disorders are diverse. Classroom-based language models (e.g., team teaching involving language specialists and general or special classroom teachers or consultation by clinician to teachers) have employed cognitive strategies, imitation and modeling strategies, and commercial language programs. Mercer (1997) advised that the language intervention curriculum be relevant to the general curriculum, respond to setting demands, reflect areas of academic concern, integrate spoken and written language systems, and focus on generalization.

INCLUSION STRATEGIES

A variety of strategies can be used in general education classrooms to address the needs of students with speech and language impairments. These strategies include the collaborative consultation model, instructional adjustments, and the use of augmentative and alternative communication.

The collaborative consultation model is an effective tool for the inclusion of students with speech and language impairments. In this model, the speech clinician provides consultation to the general education teacher and guides the student's language program. The model is a classroom-based, naturalistic approach to addressing speech and language impairments.

Adjustments in the instructional environment can positively influence speech and language skills. Smith, Polloway, Patton, & Dowdy (1995) have suggested that teachers

- Increase receptive language in the classroom (e.g., give students practice following directions, have students pair up and practice describing objects, work on categorizing words, teach specific listening skills and strategies)
- Elicit language from students (e.g., present numerous opportunities for children to ask for objects, assistance, or clarification)
- Use naturalistic techniques to increase language use (e.g., problem-solving, questioning)
- Simulate real-life activities to increase language use (e.g., newscasts or commercials, charades, telephones)
- Use music to improve language (e.g., singing, rhythm sticks)
- Play games that require receptive or expressive language (e.g., Simon Says, Musical Chairs, 20 Questions)
- Arrange the classroom for effective interactions (e.g., give instructions when distractions are minimized, use attention-getting devices, use a chalkboard, flipchart, or overhead projector to support verbal information, add gestures and facial expression to verbal communication, pair students with peers, allow for conversation time so students can share information and ideas)
- Use storytelling and process writing (e.g., retelling stories, whole-language approaches)

Additional strategies include:

1. encouraging alternative oral responses (e.g., choral responding, pair responding, singing, whispering)
2. pre-recording responses (e.g., videotape or audiotape response to be played for class)
3. augmenting responses (e.g., illustrating, dramatizing)

For students with more severe disorders, the use of augmentative and alternative communication (AAC) may be appropriate. AAC techniques can be aided by an external device (e.g., communication board, computer-assisted program) or unaided (e.g., the use of the student's own body).

REFERENCES

Adler, S., & King, D. A. (Eds.). (1994). *Oral communication problems in children and adolescents.* Boston: Allyn & Bacon.

Bernstein, D. K., & Tiegerman, E. (1993). *Language and communication disorders in children* (3rd ed.). New York: Macmillan.

Heward, W. L. (2000). *Exceptional children: An introduction to special education.* Upper Saddle River, NJ: Merrill.

Mercer, C. M. (1997). *Students with learning disabilities.* (5th ed.). Upper Saddle River, NJ: Merrill/ Prentice Hall.

Reed, V. A. (1998). *An introduction to children with language disorders* (3rd ed.). Boston: Allyn & Bacon.

Smith, T. E. C., Polloway, E. A., Patton, J. R., & Dowdy, C. A. (1995). *Teaching children with special needs in inclusive settings.* Boston: Allyn & Bacon.

U. S. Department of Education (1998). *20th Annual Report to Congress on the Implementation of the Individuals with Disabilities Education Act.* Washington, DC: Office of Special Education Programs.

Vaughn, S., Bos, C. S., & Schumm, J. S. (1997). *Teaching mainstreamed, diverse, and at-risk Students in the general education classroom.* Needham Heights, MA: Allyn & Bacon.

RECOMMENDED READINGS

Several texts address the needs of students with speech and language disorders:

Bernstein, D. K., & Tiegerman-Farber, E. (1997). *Language and communication disorders in chil-*
dren (4th ed.). Needham Heights, MA: Allyn & Bacon.

Coleman, T. J. (2000). *Clinical management of communication disorders in culturally diverse children.* Needham Heights, MA: Allyn & Bacon.

Kuder, S. J. (1997). *Teaching students with language and communication disabilities.* Needham Heights, MA: Allyn & Bacon.

Love, R. J. (2000). *Childhood motor speech disability* (2nd ed.). Needham Heights, MA: Allyn & Bacon.

McCormick, L., Loeg, D. F., & Schiefelbusch, R. L. (1997). *Supporting children with communication difficulties in inclusive settings.* Needham Heights, MA: Allyn & Bacon.

Nelson, N. W. (1998). *Childhood language disorders in context: Infancy through adolescence* (2nd ed.). Needham Heights, MA: Allyn & Bacon.

Owens, R. E. (1999). *Language disorders: A functional approach to assessment and intervention* (3rd ed.). Needham Heights, MA: Allyn & Bacon.

Resources

Several organizations serve as resources for information concerning students with speech and language impairments. The Council for Exceptional Children (CEC) has a division specifically addressing this population of students, the Division for Children's Communication Development (DCCD), which is dedicated to improving the education of children with communication delays and disorders and hearing loss. The division publishes the *Communication Disorders Quarterly.* The DCCD has four constituent committees: Communication Delays and Disorders in Infants, Toddlers, and Preschool Children; Speech and Language Learning Disabilities in Children; Communication Delays and Disabilities in Children With Severe Multiple Handicaps; and Communication Delays and Disabilities in Persons Who Are Hard of Hearing. The website is: http://www.cec.sped.org/.

An additional resource is:

The American Speech-Language-Hearing Association
   10801 Rockville Pike
   Rockville, MD 20852
   http://www.asha.org/

CHAPTER 19

OTHER HEALTH IMPAIRMENTS (OHI)

Chapter Preview

Other health impairments (OHI) may impact the educational performance of students in many ways. Students with such impairments may miss a significant amount of school due to illness or hospitalization. They may experience difficulty in adjusting to their health condition. Their learning time also may be restricted owing to limited alertness, fatigue, or pain. OHI may include allergies or asthma, diabetes, HIV/AIDS, and seizure disorders (including epilepsy).

Students with ADHD may qualify for special education and related services as OHI. The core characteristics of ADHD are inattention, impulsivity, hyperactivity, and social problems. The instructional program for students with ADHD requires carefully planned educational interventions which address the physical environment, the classroom schedule, and the curriculum.

The use of medication for ADHD is controversial. Research now suggests that giving the correct dosage of the appropriate carefully monitored drug results in remarkable improvement in behavior and facilities learning in about 90 percent of students with ADHD.

Classroom characteristics which promote successful inclusion for many children who have ADHD include:

- predictability
- structure
- shorter work periods
- small teacher to pupil ratio
- more individualized instruction
- interesting curriculum
- positive behavior management (e.g., positive reinforcers, cueing, self-monitoring)

The desirability and feasibility of accommodations should be discussed with the regular education teacher prior to inclusion.

FEDERAL DEFINITION OF OHI

OHI is defined as limited strength, vitality, or alertness, including a heightened alertness to environmental stimuli, that results in limited alertness with respect to the educational environment, that 1) is due to chronic or acute health problems such as asthma, ADHD, or attention deficit hyperactivity disorder, diabetes, epilepsy, a heart condition, hemophilia, lead poisoning, leukemia, nephritis, rheumatic fever, and sickle cell anemia; and 2) adversely affects a child's educational performance (34 C.F.R. § 300.7 (c) (9)).

REFERRAL AND INITIAL ASSESSMENT

The U.S. Department of Education (1998) reported that the largest percentage of increases in the number of students with disabilities served under the IDEA occurred in OHI. The states' most common explanation for the greater numbers was increased identification of and service to children with attention deficit disorder (ADD) and attention deficit hyperactivity disorder (ADHD). This increase in the number of students with OHI since 1992–93 may in part be a response to a 1991 Department of Education, Office of Special Education and Rehabilitative Services' (OSERS) memorandum which explained that students with ADD (and inclusively, ADHD) should be included in the OHI category when ADD is a chronic or acute health problem resulting in limited alertness that adversely affects educational performance. The growth in the OHI category may be a combined result of increased identification of students with ADD and the reporting of such students in the OHI category. Previously, students with ADD had been reported in other disability categories. During the 1997–98 school year, 160,824 students were served in the OHI category, representing 3.1 percent of the total number of students with disabilities served.

CHARACTERISTICS OF OHI

OHI may impact the educational performance of students in many ways. Students with OHI may miss a significant amount of school owing to illness or hospitalization while others may experience difficulty in adjusting to their health condition. Their learning time may be restricted because of limited alertness, fatigue, or pain. Teachers need to be aware that OHI adversely affects educational performance.

OHI may include a variety of conditions, including: allergies or asthma, diabetes, HIV/AIDS, and seizure disorders (including epilepsy). The IEP team must determine how the health condition affects educational performance and must develop an educational program to provide the student special education and related services or supplementary aids and services to meet his unique learning needs.

ADHD

Students with ADHD may qualify for special education and related services as other health impaired. It is conservatively estimated that 3 percent to 5 percent of America's school-aged population is affected by ADHD (American Psychiatric Association [APA], 1994). Students are often diagnosed with ADHD according to criteria for inattention, hyperactivity, and impulsivity found in the *Diagnostic and Statistical Manual of Mental Disorders* (DSM-IV) (APA, 1994) or according to criteria from a model developed by

Russell Barkley (1990) involving interviews, behavior checklists, questionnaires, and observation. Most educational definitions suggest that ADHD is a developmental disorder involving attention and activity that is evident relatively early in life (before the age 7 or 8), persists throughout the life span, involves both academic and social skills, and is frequently accompanied by other disorders. The difficulties in focusing and sustaining attention, controlling impulsive action, and inhibiting hyperactivity, irritability, destructiveness, and unpredictability impact the educational performance of students with ADHD (Kauffman, 1997). Although the characteristics of ADHD may be noticed by parents or others before the child enters school, the seriousness of the problem may not be obvious until the child is confronted by the demands of the classroom. The core characteristics of ADHD are inattention, impulsivity, hyperactivity, and social problems.

Attention Deficits

A child with ADHD is usually described as having a short attention span and frequent attention shifts. The child is easily distracted and has difficulty concentrating, listening, beginning or completing tasks, and following directions. The child attends to only certain parts of auditory or visual information (e.g., listens to only part of the teacher's directions, looks at only part of the numbers in a math problem) or attends to irrelevant information that interferes with work completion (e.g., listens to noises from outside, looks around the room and not at task materials). The child fails to give close attention to details or makes careless mistakes, has difficulty sustaining attention, does not seem to listen or follow through on instructions, has difficulty organizing tasks, and is forgetful in daily activities (APA, 1994). These characteristics impact the educational performance of the student with ADHD.

Impulsivity

Impulsivity is a deficiency in inhibiting behavior or "acting without thinking." The child may blurt out answers before a question is complete, interrupt others, rush through tasks, or ask irrelevant questions. The child seems unable to wait, take turns, or hold back behaviors. The child may exhibit inappropriate or immature behaviors, such as silliness, uncontrolled laughing, or temper tantrums.

Hyperactivity

Hyperactive children fidget with their hands or feet, run about or climb excessively, talk excessively, or act as if they are "driven by a motor" (APA, 1994). These children are often "on the go" and engaged in physical activity not related to schoolwork (e.g., moving about the classroom, handling materials inside the desk, squirming). The movement is disorganized and unpredictable. Some children may talk rapidly, loudly, or incessantly. They have difficulty controlling movement, particularly in settings requiring sitting or with limited opportunity for activity. The intensity and inappropriateness of the movement impact their classroom performance.

Social Problems

Social difficulties are commonly reported for students with ADHD. They are described as having high social impact: they are often talkative, socially busy, annoying, or bothersome (Wicks-Nelson & Israel, 2000). In social situations, these children may be overly sensitive, easily frustrated, or inconsiderate. Although children with ADHD often exhibit socially inappropriate behavior, teachers' concerns about their pupils' academic performance most often lead them to refer pupils for special education (Lloyd, Kauffman, Landrum, & Roe, 1991).

INSTRUCTION

The instructional program for students with ADHD requires carefully planned educational interventions, which address the physical environment, the classroom schedule, and the curriculum.

Physical Environment

Carefully arranging the physical environment of the classroom can assist the child with ADHD (NICHCY, 1999). Some effective strategies include:

- Help the student channel his physical activity (e.g., let the student do some work standing up or at the board).
- Provide regularly scheduled breaks.
- Post rules, schedules, and assignments. Clearly stated rules and routines will help a student with ADHD. Appoint set times for specific tasks.
- Call attention to changes in the schedule.
- Minimize distractions in the environment. Have an isolated area in the classroom for work.

Classroom Schedule

Organizing the classroom schedule can be an effective educational intervention (Bender & Mathes, 1995). Suggestions include:

- Arrange the student's schedule in short units of work followed by regularly scheduled activity breaks.
- Break assignments into short, sequential steps.
- Set specific times for specific tasks.
- Alternate activities to eliminate desk fatigue.
- Plan for the most difficult work to be done in the morning, with peer or teacher assistance.
- Prepare the student for transitions or changes.
- Show the student how to use an assignment book and a daily schedule.

- Help the student set up an organizational system using color coding by subject area
- Provide the student with a regular program in study skills, test-taking skills, organizational skills, and time management skills

Curriculum Modification

Fowler (1994) suggests that modifying the curriculum is a necessary educational intervention for students with ADHD. Some suggestions include:

- mixing high- and low-interest activities;
- providing computerized learning materials;
- simplifying and increasing visual presentations;
- teaching organization and study skills;
- using learning strategies, such as mnemonic devices and links; and
- using visual references for auditory instruction.

Additionally, the curriculum can be modified by changing standards (e.g., reduced or different standards such as fewer assignments, shorter assignments, more time alloted for assignments), increasing the child's involvement (e.g., providing choices to the child), and by enlisting outside support (e.g., notes to parents about homework) (Zentall, 1993).

Students with ADHD selectively attend to novelty, such as color and changes in size and movement (Fiore, Becker, & Nero, 1993). A variety of novel curriculum modifications can be effective with students with ADHD.

Listening

Encourage visual imagery (mental blackboard) of main points.

Plan teacher movement and gestures when speaking or lecturing.

Maintain eye contact between teacher and student.

Provide visual displays (charts, pictures).

Teach students to use keyword note-taking.

Use storytelling to give directions/instructions and for concept development.

Provide attention alerts (e.g., lights off, teacher moves to a certain location).

Arrange advanced listening organizers (e.g., worksheet with blanks for main ideas to be presented).

Plan cues to direct students to listen (e.g., listening flags).

Have students actively self-monitor listening (e.g., record on a notecard when they listen to directions).

Mathematics

Highlight difficult parts of algorithms with colored pens, highlight markers.

Employ Touch Math for basic facts.

Offer calculators, talking calculators, and microcomputers.

Use graph paper or graph boxed paper.

Provide wallet-sized math reference sheets (e.g., fact charts, conversion tables).

Plan manipulative and concrete teaching aids (e.g., pattern blocks, base 10 blocks, interlocking cubes).

Reading Comprehension

Highlight important information by underlining, highlighting, or using bold print.

Use story frames, story boards, or story maps.

Employ choral and echo reading.

Provide character webs (e.g., character's name in center of web with traits/descriptors radiating out).

Have student retell information as newscast, or dramatize or illustrate.

Design a word or picture collage of events.

Have student create a book jacket or perform an original song related to the story.

Use tape recordings of information.

Spelling

Use visualization strategies.

Present configuration cues (e.g., shapes of words).

Offer spell checkers.

Employ multisensory techniques (e.g., visual, auditory, kinesthetic, tactile).

Medication

The use of medication for treatment of ADHD is controversial. Medication has proved effective for many children with ADHD. Most experts agree, however, that medication should never be the *only* treatment used. The parents' decision to place a child on medication is a personal one and should be made after a thorough evaluation of the child has taken place and after careful consideration by both the parents and the physician (Fowler, 1994). Psychostimulants are the medication most widely prescribed for ADHD. These drugs include Ritalin (methylphenidate), Dexedrine (dextroamphetamine), or Cylert (pemoline). Research now suggests that administering the correct dosage of the appropriate drug, carefully monitored, can result in remarkable improvement in behavior and facilitates learning in about 90 percent of students with ADHD (Kauffman, 1997).

INCLUSION STRATEGIES

According to CHADD (1999), approximately 50 percent of children with ADHD can be taught in the regular classroom. The other 50 percent will require some degree of special education and related services. Of the latter 50 percent, about 35 percent to 40 percent will primarily be served in the regular classroom with additional support personnel or "pull-out" programs that provide special services outside of the classroom. The most severely affected students (10 percent to 15 percent) may require a self-contained classroom.

Classroom characteristics which promote success for many children with ADHD include:

- predictability
- structure
- shorter work periods
- small teacher-to-pupil ratio
- more individualized instruction
- interesting curriculum
- positive behavior management (e.g., positive reinforcers, cueing, self-monitoring)

A number of teacher characteristics that will be helpful in teaching children with ADD include:

- positive academic expectations
- frequent monitoring and checking of work
- clarity in giving directions
- warmth, patience, and humor
- consistency and firmness
- knowledge of different behavioral interventions
- willingness to work with a special education teacher

Students with ADHD need assistance and support in regular classroom environments. Booth (1998) lists several considerations to support inclusion:

- Provide consistent coaching from all teachers to support organizational skills, time management skills training, study skills training, and test-taking skills.
- Designate one teacher as the advisor/supervisor/coordinator/liaison for the student and the implementation of this plan who will periodically review the student's organizational system and whom other staff may consult when they have concerns about the student; and to act as the link between home and school.
- Permit the student to check in with this advisor first thing each week (Monday mornings) to plan and organize the week, and last thing each week (Friday afternoons) to review the week and to plan and organize homework for the weekend.
- Support the formation of study groups and the student seeking assistance from peers; encourage collaboration among students.
- Match the student's needs and learning style with teachers who have the appropriate attributes to provide the student with the best education and support possible and who know how to create ("engineer") opportunities for academic and social success; can increase the frequency of positive, constructive, supportive feedback; and can identify, recognize, reinforce, and build the student's strengths and interests.
- Create a nonthreatening learning environment where it is safe to ask questions, seek extra help, make mistakes, and feel comfortable in doing so.
- Provide the student with an environment where it is safe to learn academically, emotionally, and socially; give any needed reprimands privately and, whenever possible, provide public recognition for student accomplishments; encourage empathy and understanding from faculty, staff, and the peer group, and do not permit humiliation, teasing, or scape-goating.

Although a variety of accommodation strategies have been identified in the literature, Zentall & Stormont-Spurgin (1993) found that regular educators had not and would not implement accommodations that substantively changed the curriculum (e.g., modifying tests, restructuring assignments, allowing such alternative response modes as computers). Similarly, Schumm & Vaughn (1991) found that general education teachers were willing to provide reinforcement and encouragement, but viewed substantive instructional adaptations as undesirable. The researchers suggested that the desirability and feasibility of accommodations be discussed with the regular education teacher prior to implementing inclusion.

REFERENCES

American Psychiatric Association (1994). *Diagnostic and statistical manual of mental disorders* (4th ed.). Washington, DC: APA.

Barkley, R. A. (1990). *Attention-deficit hyperactivity disorder: A handbook for diagnosis and treatment.* New York: Guilford Press.

Bender, W. N. & Mathes, M. Y. (1995). Students with ADHD in the inclusive classroom: A hierarchial approach to strategy selection. *Intervention in School & Clinic, 30* (4) 226–234.

Booth, R. C. (1998). *List of appropriate school-based accommodations and interventions for a 504 Plan or for adaptations and modifications section of an IEP.* Highland Park, IL: National Attention Deficit Disorder Association.

Fiore, T. A., Becker, E. A., & Nero, R. C. (1993). Educational interventions for students with attention deficit disorder. *Exceptional Children, 60* (2), 163–173.

Fowler, M. (1994). *Briefing paper: Attention-deficit/ hyperactivity disorder.* Washington, DC: NICHCY.

Kauffman, J. M. (1997). *Characteristics of emotional and behavioral disorders of children and youth* (6th ed.). Upper Saddle River, NJ: Merrill/Prentice Hall.

Lloyd, J. W., Kauffman, J. M., Landrum, T. J., & Roe, D. L. (1991). Why do teachers refer pupils for special education? An analysis of referral records. *Exceptionality, 2,* 115–126.

National Information Center for Children and Youth with Disabilities (1999). *Attention-deficit/Hyperactivity disorder (AD-HD).* Washington, DC: NICHCY.

Schumm, J. S., & Vaughn, S. (1991). Making adaptations for mainstreamed students: General classroom teacher's perspectives. *Remedial and Special Education, 12* (4), 18–27.

U.S. Department of Education (1998). *20th Annual Report to Congress on the Implementation of the Individuals With Disabilities Education Act.* Washington, DC: Office of Special Education Programs.

Wicks-Nelson, R., & Israel, A. C. (2000). *Behavior disorders of childhood* (4th ed.). Upper Saddle River, NJ: Prentice Hall.

Zentall, S. S., & Stormont-Spurgin, M. (1993). Research on the educational implications of attention deficit hyperactivity disorders. *Exceptional Children, 60,* 143–153.

RECOMMENDED READINGS

There are several texts addressing OHI, including ADHD:

Bowe, F. G. (2000). *Physical, sensory, and health disabilities: An introduction.* Upper Saddle River, NJ: Merrill/Prentice Hall.

DuPaul, G. J., & Stoner, G. (1994). *ADHD in the schools: Assessment and intervention strategies.* New York: Guilford.

Fiore, T. A., Becker, E. A., & Nero, R. C. (1993). Educational interventions for students with attention deficit disorder. *Exceptional Children, 60* (2), 163–173.

Friedman, R. J., & Doyal, G. T. (1992). *Management of children and adolescents with attention deficit-hyperactivity disorder* (3rd ed.). Austin, TX: PRO-ED.

Gordon, S. B., & Asher, M. J. (1994). *Meeting the ADD challenge: A practical guide for teachers.* Champaign, IL: Research Press.

Guyer, B. P. (2000). *ADHD: Achieving success in school and in life.* Needham Heights, MA: Allyn & Bacon.

Hill, J. L. (1999). *Meeting the needs of students with special physical and health care needs.* Upper Saddle River, NJ: Merrill/Prentice Hall.

Lerner, J. W. (1995). *Attention deficit disorders: Assessment and teaching.* Pacific Grove, CA: Brooks/ Cole.

Rief, S. F. (1993). *How to reach and teach ADD/ ADHD children: Practical techniques, strategies, and interventions for helping children with attention problems and hyperactivity.* West Nyack, NY: The Center for Applied Research in Education.

Weaver, C. (1994). *Success at last! Helping students with AD (H) D achieve their potential.* Portsmouth, NH: Heinemann.

Wodrich, D. L. (1994). *Attention deficit hyperactivity disorder (ADHD).* Baltimore: Paul H. Brookes.

Resources

Organizations that address the needs of individuals with ADHD include:

Attention Deficit Disorder Association (ADDA)
 PO Box 972
 Mentor, OH 44061
Children and Adults with Attention Deficit Disorder
 (CHADD)
 8181 Professional Pl, Ste 201
 Landover, MD 20785
 www.chadd.org

National Attention Deficit Disorder Association
 PO Box 1303
 Northbrook, IL 60065-1303
 E-mail: mail@add.org; website: www.add.org
National Information Center for Children and Youth
 with Disabilities (NICHCY)
 PO Box 1492
 Washington, DC 20013

CHAPTER 20

LOW-INCIDENCE DISABILITIES

CHAPTER PREVIEW

Low-incidence disabilities include traumatic brain injury (TBI), visual impairments (including blindness), deafness and hearing impairments, multiple handicaps and deafness/blindness.

TBI

The first step in developing an educational program for a student with TBI is to carefully plan for the student's reentry to school. After planning for reentry, the IEP team needs to develop educational strategies to meet the specialized needs of the students with TBI. Students with TBI may require rehabilitation counseling as a related service. These services focus specifically on:

- Career development
- Employment preparation
- Achieving independence

Schools must be prepared to deal with the increasing number of students with TBI. The number of such students served during the 1997–98 school year was 10,378 or 0.2 percent of the total number of students with disabilities (U.S. Department of Education, 1998).

Visual Impairment

The degree to which students with visual impairment can use visual materials is the basis for educational definitions.

- *Totally Blind.* A student who is totally blind receives no visual information and uses tactile and auditory modalities for learning.
- *Visually Impaired.* A student who is visually impaired (i.e., functionally blind) has impaired visual acuity, but can supplement auditory and tactile modalities with limited visual input.
- *Low Vision.* A student with low vision has a visual impairment requiring accommodations and modifications, but uses vision as the primary means of learning.

Students with low vision represent the majority of students receiving services in this category in public schools, yet the total number of students with visual impairments is 0.04 percent of the school-aged population (U.S. Dept. of Education, 1998). The degree to which visual impairment affects development depends on the age of onset, the nature and severity of the loss, and the student's cognitive and developmental level. The lack of vision or reduced vision may result in delays or deficits in motor, linguistic, cognitive, and social-behavioral development.

Advances in technology and a variety of related services have facilitated the inclusion of students with visual impairments in general education classrooms. The U.S. Department of Education (1998) estimated that 48 percent of school-aged students with visual impairments are in regular classes, 21 percent receive services in resource rooms, and 17 percent are educated in separate classes.

Hearing Impairment

The communication, academic, intellectual, medical, and audiologic characteristics of a child who is deaf or hearing impaired are included in the assessment of learning needs. The assessment should guide the IEP team in the development of appropriate goals and objectives for the student.

The effects of hearing loss on academic achievement and social competence depends on several factors, including:

- type and degree of hearing loss;
- age of onset;
- attitudes of the child's parents, siblings, and peers;
- opportunities available for the child to acquire a first language; and
- presence or absence of other disabilities.

The U.S. Department of Education (1998) reported that 36 percent of students who are deaf or hearing impaired receive services in regular education classrooms, 19 percent are served in resource rooms, and 27 percent are educated in separate classrooms.

Deafness-Blindness

Deafness-blindness is concomitant hearing and visual impairment, the combination of which causes severe communication and other developmental and educational needs that cannot be accommodated in special education programs designed solely for children with deafness or children with blindness. Most individuals identified as deaf-blind have some useful vision, hearing or both. They often receive incomplete or indistinct visual or auditory information, but can learn to interpret with training and assistive devices.

TBI

Federal Definition of TBI

TBI is an acquired injury to the brain caused by an external physical force, resulting in total or partial functional disability, psychosocial impairment, or both, which adversely affects a child's educational performance. The term applies to open or closed head injury resulting in impairments in one or more areas, such as cognition; language; memory; attention; reasoning; abstract thinking; judgment; problem-solving; sensory, perceptual, and motor abilities; psychosocial behavior; physical functions; information processing; and speech. The term does not apply to congenital or degenerative brain injuries, or to brain injuries induced by birth trauma (34 C.F.R. § 300.7 (c) (12)). Public Law 94–142 did not include TBI as a disability category, but when amended in 1990, the IDEA specified TBI as a new area of eligibility.

Characteristics of TBI

Common symptoms of TBI include seizures, loss of balance or coordination, difficulty with speech, limited concentration, memory loss, and loss of organizational and reasoning skills. Hill (1999) identified several signs and effects of TBI, including physical and sensory changes, cognitive changes and academic problems, and social, emotional and behavioral problems. Other characteristics include reduced stamina, irregular growth, memory problems, helplessness, apathy (Mira, Tucker, & Tyler, 1992), flat affect and depression (Tucker & Colson, 1992). The number of students with TBI served during the 1997–98 school year was 10,378 or 0.2 percent of the total number of students with disabilities (U.S. Dept. of Education, 1998).

Instruction

The first step in developing an educational program for a students with TBI is carefully planning for the student's reentry to school (Tyler & Mira, 1999). The IEP team must arrange for the student's safety and for necessary adaptive equipment. The school staff should be informed about the returning child and about TBI as a disability. Regional or state specialists in TBI should be contacted and invited to participate in IEP planning. The child's daily schedule and yearly calendar should be carefully reviewed. Classmates should be prepared for the student's reentry and assigned certain responsibilities to make the transition go smoothly.

After planning for reentry, the IEP team needs to develop educational strategies to meet the specialized needs of the student with TBI. Cognitive retraining, also called cognitive rehabilitation or remediation, refers to the treatment of cognitively based deficits associated with TBI. The goal of cognitive rehabilitation is to enhance residual cognitive skills so the child can function as effectively as possible. The educators' role in cognitive retraining is to incorporate the academic curricula and daily activities to redevelop or enhance attention, memory, and organization skills. Using rapid retrieval activities, planning trips with maps, or employing computer games can facilitate the memory and problem-solving skills of students with TBI. Skills such as developing judgement, reasoning, and analysis can also be addressed in the daily curriculum. Direct instruction (Glang, Singer, Cooley, & Tish, 1992), and strategy instruction (see Chapter 19) have proved to be effective instructional techniques for students with TBI. Such students often have behavioral problems associated with neurologic and psychosocial variables. Strategies for addressing behavioral concerns include:

1. Helping the child to understand TBI
2. Teaching the child appropriate behavior
3. Providing direct social skill training and arranging for positive interaction with peers
4. Providing rest breaks and adequate supervision
5. Establishing a behavior management system (Tyler & Mira, 1999)

D'Amato & Rothlisberg (1997) suggest that teachers modify their teaching methods in terms of an "SOS" for students with TBI: structure, organization, and strategies. TBI leads to a sense of disorientation and low tolerance for environmental change, particularly during the initial months of recovery. As the child struggles, much structure and stability must be provided. Minimal distractions, clear expectations and a basic routine will assist the child with TBI. Organization involves providing the student the necessary environmental cues and aids to foster acquisition of new learning and retrieval of previous knowledge. Students need to learn "how to learn." Providing advanced organizers, guidelines for completing assignments and multiple cues (e.g., visual, auditory) can be helpful. In addition, instruction in the development of learning strategies will help the student with TBI select problem-solving methods and tactics to make learning more effective and efficient.

Related Services

Students with TBI may require rehabilitation counseling as a related service. This service is provided by qualified personnel in individual or group sessions that focus specifically on career development, employment preparation, achieving independence, and integration in the workplace and community of a student with a disability (34 C.F.R. § 300.24 (b) (11)).

Inclusion Strategies

The student with TBI will require modifications in the physical, instructional, and social dimensions of the school and classroom. In the phys-

ical dimension, the student with TBI may benefit from minimized visual and auditory distractions, special seating, and specialized equipment (Smith, Polloway, Patton, & Dowdy, 1995). In the instructional dimension, the student with TBI may require a shortened school day, reduced class load, resource personnel (e.g., peers, counselors, therapists), modified materials, adjusted testing procedures, and frequent review of goals and objectives (Tyler & Mira, 1993). In the social-behavioral dimension, the teacher should modify language interactions (e.g., limit amount of information presented at one time, use concrete language, tell the student to look for cues from listeners), reduce impulsiveness (e.g., teach the student to mentally rehearse steps before beginning an activity, frequently restate and reinforce rules), and maintain attention (e.g., check for understanding, model, teach student to use self-regulating techniques) (Mira, Tucker, & Tyler, 1992).

For the student with TBI, successful inclusion will require both student-centered and environment-centered strategies, which may include direct training of social skills, training parents to encourage skill generalization, inservice and peer training about TBI, "peer liaisons," and pairing community volunteers with TBI students (Glang, Cooley, Todis, Stevens, & Voss, 1995). The integration of the medical, rehabilitation, and educational perspectives is necessary for the student with TBI to be successfully included in general education classrooms.

Schools must be prepared to deal with the increasing number of students with TBI. Silver and Oakland (1997) outlined a six-step process to enable school districts to become better prepared to meet the needs of students with TBI:

1. Survey existing special education and related service provider staff to determine their expertise and interests in this area.
2. Form a TBI committee consisting of those with expertise and interest in TBI who

are responsible for providing district-wide leadership.

3. Develop district-wide policies and procedures relevant to TBI services (e.g., referral evaluations, consultation).

4. Develop district-wide in-service for administrators, teachers, parents, support staff, and others in the community.

5. Create an advisory board consisting of the district TBI committee and other professionals within the community or region.

6. Employ one or more professionals with expertise in TBI as a part-time consultant to the district.

The district should also use existing resource personnel, such as the school psychologist, speech and language pathologist, occupational therapist, school counselor, and school nurse, on the committee. The six steps outlined above should enable the school to more effectively meet the needs of students with TBI.

VISUAL IMPAIRMENTS INCLUDING BLINDNESS

Federal Definition of Visual Impairment

Visual impairment including blindness is defined as an impairment in vision that, even with correction, adversely affects a child's educational performance. The term includes both partial sight and blindness (34 C.F.R. § 300.7(a) (13)).

Characteristics of Visual Impairment

The degree to which visual impairment affects development depends on the age of onset, the nature and severity of the loss, and the student's cognitive and developmental level. The lack of vision or reduced vision may result in delays or deficits in motor, linguistic, cognitive, and social-behavioral development. These delays are often most evident in the early years of development owing to restricted environmental experiences. The delays impact the student's orientation and mobility.

Instruction

The curriculum for students with visual impairment or blindness includes reading and writing through the use of braille, listening skills, personal-social and daily living skills, orientation and mobility, career education, instruction in the use of special aids and equipment, and instruction in the efficient use of vision and in the use of optical aids and alternative learning materials (ERIC, 1992). The IDEA requires the IEP team to "provide for instruction in braille and the use of braille unless the IEP team determines, after an evaluation of the child's reading and writing skills, needs, and appropriate reading and writing media (including an evaluation of the child's future needs for instruction in braille or the use of braille), that instruction in braille or the use of braille is not appropriate for the child" (34 C.F.R. § (300.346(a)2) (iii)).

The IEP goals for reading and writing may focus on increasing reading fluency with braille text or improving keyboarding skills. Listening objectives may include following two- or three-step verbal directions. Using telephone and developing money skills may be included as goals in the personal and daily living skills domain. Orientation and mobility objectives may focus on independent travel around the school building. Transition planning will be an important component of career education, and includes planning courses of study and post-school assistance.

Educators must be familiar with media and materials designed to teach skills and concepts that are normally acquired through vision. Specifically trained personnel facilitate the development of goals, objects, and methodology for students with visual impairments.

Related Services

Students with visual impairments may benefit from several related services, including orientation and mobility services and assistive technology. The need for these services is determined by the student's IEP team.

Orientation and Mobility Related Services

Students with visual impairments often will require orientation- and mobility-related services. These services are provided to blind or visually impaired students by qualified personnel to enable these students to attain systematic orientation to and safe movement within their school, home, and community environments. These services include teaching the students:

- Spatial and environmental concepts and use of information received by the senses (e.g., sound, temperature, vibrations) to establish, maintain, or regain orientation and line of travel (e.g., using sound at a traffic light to cross the street);
- To use the long cane to supplement visual travel skills or as a tool for safely negotiating the environment for students with no available travel vision;
- To understand and use remaining vision and distance low vision aids; and
- Other concepts, techniques, and tools (34 C.F.R. § 300.24 (b) (6)).

Assistive Technology

Assistive technology is also important in educational programs for students with visual impairments. This technology may include the braille system of literacy (e.g., braille personal note-takers, Braille Lite, Braille 'N Speak), talking devices (e.g., clocks, spelling aids, speech calculators), computers (e.g., speech recognition, magnification, scan and read synthesizers), optical to tactile converters, and optical devices (e.g., magnifiers, mini-telescopes). Heward (2000) reported that various curricular materials have been developed for students with visual impairments, including MAVIS (Materials Adaptation for Students with Visual Impairments in the Social Studies) and SAVI (Science Activities for the Visually Impaired). Large-print materials, braille materials, and tape-recorded materials are also available.

Inclusion Strategies

Historically, students with visual impairments were educated in segregated residential facilities. Currently, with the aid of supports and strategies, these students are educated in general classroom settings. Strategies that provide support and assistance are classroom adaptations, an instructional assistant, and collaboration with support personnel.

Classroom Adaptations

Often the physical environment of the classroom must be modified for students with visual impairments. Clear traffic patterns must be established, and the student should be provided with an orientation to the physical arrangement of the classroom and the school. A classmate can assist with classroom orientation by serving as a guide and describing changes in the classroom layout. Seating is important for students who are able to use residual vision.

Glare can reduce the use of residual vision in students with visual impairments. Thus, special consideration must be given to lighting, windows, floor and ceiling materials, and presentation media (e.g., blackboards, overhead projectors) to reduce glare.

A variety of curriculum strategies have been developed for students with visual impairments, including the use of activity boxes (Dunnett, 1999) to enhance cognitive and motor development in young children with visual impairments and the use of descriptive video (Cronin & King, 1990). Although excellent materials are available for students with visual impairments, teachers may need to adapt or develop supplemental materials.

Teachers or peers may want to provide auditory supplements to visual information (e.g., reading information presented on overheads or chalkboards, describing pictures that accompany text) or enhance visual information (e.g., providing large and dark print, using dry-erase boards). Manipulatives, concrete representations, real-life materials, or three-dimensional models will also assist students with visual impairments.

Collaboration with Support Personnel

Collaboration with an itinerant visual specialist or vision teacher is also an important component of the educational program for students with visual impairments. The vision specialist may provide direct, supplemental instruction, such as using visual aids and mobility training. She may also translate material into braille. The specialist will also serve as a consultant to the general education teacher. Services of a physical therapist, occupational therapist, or school nurse may be necessary if physical disabilities accompany the student's visual impairment.

Advances in technology and a variety of related services have facilitated the inclusion of students with visual impairments in general education classrooms. The U.S. Department of Education (1998) estimated that 48 percent of school-aged students with visual impairments are in regular classes, 21 percent receive services in resource rooms, and 17 percent are educated in separate classes.

DEAFNESS AND HEARING IMPAIRMENT

Federal Definition of Deafness and Hearing Impairment

Federal regulations distinguish children who are deaf and children who have hearing impairment in their definitions. Deafness means a hearing impairment that is so severe that the child is impaired in processing linguistic information through hearing, with or without amplification, which adversely affects the child's educational performance (34 C.F.R. § 300.7 (a) (3)). Hearing impairment means an impairment in hearing, whether permanent or fluctuating, which adversely affects a child's educational performance but which is not included under the definition of deafness (34 C.F.R. § 300.7 (a) (5)). A child who is deaf cannot respond to speech or auditory stimuli and cannot use hearing to understand speech, even with the assistance of a hearing aid or device. This child must rely on vision for language reception and learning. The child with hearing impairment can respond to speech and auditory stimuli and can use hearing to understand speech, often with the assistance of a hearing aid. The latter's language reception and expression are primarily auditory, although speech skills are often delayed.

Characteristics of Hearing Impairment

The effects of hearing loss on the academic achievement and social competence depend on several factors, including the type and degree of hearing loss; the age of onset; the attitudes of the child's parents, siblings, and peers; the opportunities available for the child to acquire a first language; and the presence or absence of other disabilities (Heward, 2000). Although most children who are deaf have normal intellectual capacity, academic achievement, as measured by standard tests, is significantly lower than that of their hearing peers. Lower achievement levels and smaller achievement gains are attributed to the "bad fit" between the student's perceptual abilities and the demands of spoken and written English. Because reading and writing involve graphic representation of a phonologically based language, the child who is deaf or hearing impaired must decode and produce text based on a language to which she has had limited access.

Instruction

The most appropriate approach to instruction for children who are deaf or hearing impaired has been hotly debated for years. Drasgow (1998) suggests that this disagreement over the best approach is not simply a discussion over which language or code is best to use, but rather represents "profound, and often polarized, differences in educational philosophy" (p. 329). Methods are grounded either in a clinical-pathological model or a cultural model. The former views deafness as a disability stemming from a biological deficit and focuses educational goals on overcoming or compensating for hearing loss so that students can learn to speak, read, and write English.

One approach of the clinical model is the oral-aural method, which views speech as essential and incorporates producing and understanding speech and language into all aspects of the child's education. Educational methods associated with the clinical oral approach to develop speech and maximize hearing include:

Amplification—hearing aids and classroom amplification systems (e.g., FM devices)

Auditory training and oral language development—discriminating sounds in listening and producing speech

Speech reading—understanding spoken language by observing production in the speaker's face

Cued speech—visual representation of spoken language by eight handshapes representing groups of consonants which are placed in four positions around the face that indicate groups of vowel sounds. Combined with the natural lip movements of speech, the cues assist the child who is deaf or hearing impaired to identify sounds that are difficult to distinguish through speech reading.

Another approach of the clinical model is the total communication method, which emphasizes the use of both manual communication (e.g., signs and finger spelling) and speech (e.g., speech reading, amplification). Sign systems such as Seeing Essential English, Signing Exact English, and Signed English are called Manually Coded English and are based on English usage. Finger spelling uses different hand positions to represent the letters of the alphabet. The total communication approach, also called simultaneous communication, enables teachers to use the communication methods most appropriate for a particular child at a particular stage of development. Hawkins & Brawner (1997) found that although individualization was at the heart of total communication and it can open several avenues of communication for children who are deaf or hearing impaired, many students are immersed in a form of total communication that does not match their level of linguistic readiness or ability. Further, combining the visual and spoken mode may cause signers and speakers to alter their messages to accommodate one or the other mode, causing a compromise between the two methods. Teachers are limited to the number of modes they can simultaneously use.

The cultural model views deafness as a difference, not a disability. This model acknowledges that deaf people have a unique identity with their own language, history, and social organization. This bilingual-bicultural educational approach recognizes American Sign Language (ASL) as the child's natural language and the language of instruction. Thus, the child becomes proficient in two languages: ASL and English.

The IDEA requires the IEP team to "consider the communication needs of the child, and in the case of a child who is deaf or hard of hearing, consider the child's language and communication needs, opportunities for direct communications with peers and professional personnel in the child's language and communication mode, academic level, and full range of needs, including opportunities for direct instruction in the child's language and communication mode" (34 C.F.R. § 300.346 (a) (2) (iv)). The IEP team should discuss the options for instruction and select an approach based on the child's unique strengths and needs.

Related Services

Students who are deaf or hearing impaired often require audiology as a related service. Audiology includes:

- Identification of children with hearing loss;
- Determination of the range, nature, and degree of hearing loss, including referral for medical or other professional attention for the habilitation of hearing;
- Provision of habilitative activities, such as language habilitation, auditory training, speech reading (lip-reading), hearing evaluation, and speech conservation;
- Creation and administration of programs for prevention of hearing loss;
- Counseling and guidance of children, parents, and teachers regarding hearing loss; and
- Determination of children's needs for group and individual amplification, selecting and fitting an appropriate hearing aid, and evaluating the effectiveness of amplification. (34 C.F.R. § 300.24 (b) (1))

Additional related services may include the use of interpreters and television captioning. Jones, Clark, & Soltz (1997) examined the characteristics and practices of sign language interpreters in inclusive education programs. The duties performed by the interpreters included expected activities, such as interpreting in the mainstream academic classroom and vocational classes, as well as noninterpreting activities, such as tutoring, teaching sign language to hearing students, correcting assignments, and other teacher assistance tasks. The researchers suggested that state departments of education should coordinate the development and implementation of guidelines related to the roles and responsibilities of educational sign language interpreters, because using them as teachers aides was questionable practice. They found that 63% of the interpreters had no certification for sign language interpreting of any kind and suggested an upgrading of training and skills for interpreters if ready access to general education is to be achieved.

Inclusion Strategies

The inclusion of students who are deaf or hearing impaired has been controversial. The merits of an inclusion setting compared with the benefits of membership in the deaf culture has been an ongoing debate. Nowell and Innes (1997) described the benefits and limitations of inclusion for students who are deaf or hard of hearing. Benefits included:

1. Opportunity for the student who is deaf to live at home
2. Opportunity for communication with the hearing world
3. Opportunity for learning the standards of the hearing world
4. Availability of academic or vocational programs

The possible limitations of inclusion included:

1. Potential isolation from teachers, peers, and other members of the school community who are not adept at communicating in deaf individuals' preferred language and mode of communication
2. Limited opportunities for direct instruction as translators or interpreters intervened
3. Limited opportunities for direct and independent interaction and communication with peers and professional support staff

Students who are deaf or hearing impaired may constantly require an interpreter to communicate effectively with peers and professionals. School counselors, medical personnel, and administrators often are not able to communicate directly with a student who is deaf, which limits these students' access to support services that are readily available to other students. There may not be an adequate supply of qualified interpreters or other support staff in the local school district to provide a desirable level of communication access to the educational process.

Despite the potential limitations, the U.S. Department of Education (1998) reported that 36 percent of students who are deaf or hearing impaired receive services in regular education classrooms, 19 percent are served in resource rooms, and 27 percent are educated in separate classrooms. Vaughn, Bos, and Schumm (1997) recommended the following accommodations for students who are deaf or hearing impaired:

- Provide preferential seating (e.g., place student close to teacher, within view of interpreter, and away from classroom noise and glare from windows or lights)
- Minimize nonmeaningful environmental noise (e.g., use carpets and curtains to absorb noise, avoid unnecessary background noise)
- Use visual clues and demonstration (e.g., use overhead projectors, gestures, modeling, pictures, diagrams, graphs, experiential learning)
- Maximize use of visual media (e.g., use closed-captioned televisions and computers)
- Monitor students' understanding (e.g., ask students to repeat, rephrase)
- Promote cooperation and collaboration (e.g., use peers, classroom tutors, and note takers).

Additional strategies that have been successful in facilitating the inclusion of students who are deaf or hearing impaired in general education classrooms include:

- Interactive writing between teacher and student on instant computer access (Holcomb & Peyton, 1992)
- Computer-assisted notetaking (Youdelman & Messerly, 1996)

- Pretutoring (English, 1999)
- Lecture guides (Rees, 1992)
- Writing rubrics (Schirmer, Bailey & Fitzgerald, 1999)

Students who are deaf or hearing impaired should be encouraged to develop self-advocacy and self-determination skills to facilitate the success of their educational programs. Marttila and Mills (1995) have developed curricula for enhancing self-advocacy skills.

MULTIPLE HANDICAPS AND DEAFNESS-BLINDNESS

Federal Definitions of Multiple Handicaps

Many students have dual or multiple disabilities. Federal regulations define multiple disabilities as concomitant impairments (e.g., mental retardation-blindness, mental retardation-orthopedic impairment), the combination of which causes such severe educational needs that students cannot be accommodated in special education programs designed solely for children with only one of the impairments (34 C.F.R. § 300.7(c) (7)). Types of multiple disabilities include mental retardation with physical disabilities (e.g., cerebral palsy, spina bifida, traumatic brain injury), or mental retardation with visual or hearing impairments. The reader is referred to chapters dealing with specific disabilities for assistance in working with students with multiple handicaps. This chapter focuses on students with deafness-blindness, or dual sensory impairments.

The regulations define deafness-blindness as concomitant hearing and visual impairments, the combination of which causes such severe communication and other developmental and educational needs that students cannot be accommodated in special education programs designed solely for children with deafness *or* blindness (34 C.F.R. § 300. 7 (c) (2)). Although federal regulations use the deafness-blindness reference, most professionals view these students as having dual sensory impairments or multiple sensory impairments.

In 1996–97 a total of 99,638 students with multiple disabilities were served, representing about 2 percent of the total number of students with disabilities served under the IDEA, whereas the 1286 students with dual sensory impairments represented less than 0.1 percent of the total (U.S. Dept. of Education, 1998).

Instruction

The curriculum for students with dual sensory impairments should include components that have been shown to assist students with visual impairments, hearing impairments, or severe mental disabilities. Skills that are taught should be those that the students need to function in all the different environments of their daily life. An ecological assessment will determine the skill needed to function in home, school, and community environments and should involve teachers, therapists, parents, and other individuals who work with the students. Marchant (1996) identified the steps to be included in an ecological curriculum development process:

Step 1. Delineate curriculum domains (vocational, domestic, community, recreation/leisure)

Step 2. Delineate the variety of current and subsequent natural environments in each domain in which students function or might function.

Step 3. Inventory and delineate the subenvironments within each environment.

Step 4. Inventory and delineate the activities performed by nondisabled persons in those subenvironments.

Step 5. Prioritize activities to delineate goals of the IEP.

Step 6. Delineate the skills needed to perform the activities.

Step 7. Conduct a discrepancy analysis to determine required skills not currently in the student's repertoire.

Step 8. Determine necessary adaptations.

Step 9. Develop an instructional program.

The instructional program typically includes orientation and mobility training, a functional vision and hearing program, communication methods, and daily living skills.

Inclusion Strategies

Environmental accommodations for students with dual sensory impairments include the use of kinesthetic and tactile materials for instructional presentation and schedules and use of objects for marking pathways and for communication (Rikhye, Gotheif, & Appell, 1989). Communication partners can also assist students with deafness-blindness (Heller, Ware, Allgood, & Castelle, 1994), while tactile teaching techniques can supplement information obtained through auditory and visual modalities.

REFERENCES

Barraga, N. C., & Erin, J. N. (1992). *Visual handicaps and learning* (3rd ed.). Austin, TX: PRO-ED.

Bishop, V. E. (1996). *Teaching visually impaired children* (2nd ed.). Springfield, IL: Thomas.

Cronin, B. J., & King, S. R. (1990). The development of the Descriptive Video Service. *Journal of Visual Impairment and Blindness, 86* (12), 503–506.

D'Amato, R. C., & Rothlisberg, B. (1997). How education should respond to students with TBI. In E. D. Bigler, E. Clark, & J. E. Farmer (Eds). *Childhood traumatic brain injury: Diagnosis, assessment and intervention*. Austin, TX: PRO-ED.

Downing, J., & Eichinger, J. (1990). Instructional strategies for learners with dual sensory impairments in integrated settings. *Journal of the Association for Persons with Severe Handicaps, 15*, 98–105.

Drasgow, E. (1998). American Sign Language as a pathway to linguistic competence. *Exceptional Children, 64*(3), 329–342.

Dunnett, J. (1999). Use of activity boxes with young children who are blind, deaf-blind, or have severe learning disabilities and visual impairments. *Journal of Visual Impairment and Blindness, 93* (4), 225–232.

Easterbrooks, S., & Baker-Hawkins, S. (Eds.) (1994). *Deaf and hard of hearing students: Educational service guidelines.* Alexandria, VA: National Association of State Directors of Special Education.

Eccarius, M. (1997). *Educating children who are deaf or hard of hearing: Assessment.* Reston, VA: ERIC Clearinghouse on Disabilities and Gifted Education.

English, K. (1999). Inclusion tips for the teacher: Students who are hard of hearing. In R. B. Lewis & D. H. Doorlag (Eds.) *Teaching special students in general education classrooms* (5th ed.). Upper Saddle River, NJ: Merrill/Prentice Hall.

ERIC (1992). *Visual impairments.* ERIC Digest #E511. Reston, VA: ERIC Clearinghouse on Disabilities and Gifted Education.

Glang, A., Singer, G., Cooley, E., & Tish, N. (1992). Tailing Direct Instruction techniques for use with elementary students with brain injury. *Journal of Head Trauma Remediation, 7* (4), 93–108.

Glang, A., Cooley, E., Todis, B., Stevens, T., & Voss, J. (1995). *Enhancing social support and integration for students with traumatic brain injury. Final report.* Eugene, OR: Teaching Research.

Hawkins, L., & Brawner, J. (1997). *Educating children who are deaf or hard of hearing: Total communication.* ERIC Digest #559. Reston, VA: ERIC Clearinghouse on Disabilities and Gifted Education.

Heller, K. W., Ware, S., Allgood, M. H., & Castelle, M. (1994). Use of dual communication boards with students who are deaf-blind. *Journal of Visual Impairment and Blindness,* (July/August), 368–376.

Heward, W. L. (2000). *Exceptional children: An introduction to special education.* Upper Saddle River, NJ: Merrill/Prentice Hall.

Hill, J. L. (1999). *Meeting the needs of students with special physical and health care needs.* Upper Saddle River, NJ: Merrill/Prentice Hall.

Holcomb, T., & Peyton, J. K. (1992). *Literacy for a linguistic minority: The deaf experience.* ERIC Digest #353861. Reston, VA: ERIC Clearinghouse on Disabilities and Gifted Education.

Jones, B. E., Clark, G. M., & Soltz, D. F. (1997). Characteristics and practices of sign language interpreters in inclusive education program. *Exceptional Children, 63* (2), 257–268.

Luetke-Stahlman, B., & Luckner, J. (1991). *Effectively educating students with hearing loss.* New York: Longman.

Mahshie, S. N. (1995). *Educating deaf children bilingually.* Washington, DC: Gallaudet University.

Marchant, J. M. (1996). Deaf-Blind. In P. J. McLaughlin & P. Wehman (Eds.). *Mental retardation and developmental disabilities* (2nd ed.). Austin, TX: PRO-ED.

Marschark, M. (1997). *Raising and educating a deaf child.* New York: Oxford University Press.

Marttila, J., & Mills, M. (1995). *Knowledge is power.* Bettendorf, IA: Mississippi Bend Area Education Agency.

McAnally, P. L., Rose, S., & Quigley, S. P. (1994). *Language learning practices with children who are deaf* (3rd ed.). Austin, TX: PRO-ED.

Mira, M. P., Tucker, B. F., & Tyler, J. S. (1992). *Traumatic brain injury in children and adolescents: A sourcebook for teachers and other school personnel.* Austin, TX: PRO-ED.

Moores, D. F. (1996). *Educating the deaf* (4th ed.). Boston: Houghton Mifflin.

Nowell, R., & Innes, J. (1997). *Educating children who are deaf or hard of hearing: inclusion.* ERIC Digest #E557. Reston, VA: ERIC Clearinghouse on Disabilities and Gifted Education.

Orelove, F. P., & Sobsey, D. (1996). *Education of children with multiple disabilities: A transdisciplinary approach.* Baltimore: Brookes.

Paplinger, D., & Sikora, D. (1990). Diagnosing a learning disability in a hearing impaired child. *American Annals of the Deaf, 118*, 480–487.

Paul, P. V., & Jackson, D. W. (1993). *Toward a psychology of deafness: Theoretical and empirical perspectives.* Needham Heights, MA: Allyn & Bacon.

Pollack, B. J. (1997). *Educating children who are deaf or hard of hearing: Additional learning problems.* ERIC Digest #E548. Reston, VA: ERIC Clearinghouse on Disabilities and Gifted Education.

Rees, T. (1992). Students with hearing impairments. In L. G. Cohen (Eds.), *Children with exceptional needs in regular classrooms.* Washington, DC: National Education Association.

Rikhye, C. H., Gotheif, C. R., & Appell, M. W. (1989). A classroom environment checklist for students with dual sensory impairments. *Teaching Exceptional Children, 22* (1), 44–46.

Ross, M. (Ed). *Hearing-impaired children in the mainstream.* Monkton, MD: York.

Roth, V. (1991). Students with learning disabilities and hearing impairment: Issues for the secondary and post-secondary teachers. *Journal of Learning Disabilities, 24* (7), 391–397.

Ryndak, D. L., & Alper, S. (1996). *Curriculum content for students with moderate and severe disabilities in inclusive settings.* Boston: Allyn & Bacon.

Schirmer, B. R. (2000). *Language and literacy development in children who are deaf.* Needham Heights, MA: Allyn & Bacon.

Schirmer, B. R., Bailey, J., & Fitzgerald, S. M. (1999). Using a writing assessment rubric for writing development of children who are deaf. *Exceptional Children, 65* (3), 383–397.

Silver, C. H., & Oakland, T. D. (1997). Helping students with mild traumatic brain injury: Collaborative roles within schools. In E. D. Bigler, E. Clark, & J. E. Farmer (Eds). *Childhood traumatic brain injury: Diagnosis, assessment and intervention.* Austin, TX: PRO-ED.

Smith, T. E. C., Polloway, E. A., Patton, J. R., & Dowdy, C. A. (1995). *Teaching children with special needs in inclusive settings.* Boston: Allyn & Bacon.

Snell, M. E. (2000). *Instruction of students with severe disabilities* (5th ed.). Upper Saddle River, NJ: Merrill/Prentice Hall.

Terzieff, A. S. (1988). Visual impairments. In. E. W. Lynch & R. B. Lewis (Eds.). *Exceptional children and adults: An introduction to special education.* Glenview, IL: Scott, Foresman.

Tucker, B. F., & Colson, S. E. (1992). Traumatic brain injury: An overview of school re-entry. *Intervention in School and Clinic, 27,* 198–206.

Tyler, J. S., & Mira, M. P. (1993). Educational modifications for students with head injuries. *Teaching Exceptional Children, 25* (3), 24–27.

Tyler, J. S., & Mira, M. P. (1999). *Traumatic brain injury in children and adolescents: A sourcebook for teachers and other school personnel* (2nd ed.). Austin TX: PRO-ED.

U.S. Department of Education (1998). *20th Annual Report to Congress on the Implementation of the Individuals with Disabilities Education Act.* Washington, DC: Office of Special Education Programs.

U.S. Department of Education (1999). *21st Annual Report to Congress on the Implementation of the Individuals with Disabilities Education Act.* Washington, DC: Office of Special Education Programs.

Vaughn, S., Bos, C. S., & Schumm, J. S. (1997). *Teaching mainstreamed, diverse, and at-risk students in the general education classroom.* Needham Heights, MA: Allyn & Bacon.

Vernon, M., & Andrews, J. (1990). *Psychology of deafness.* New York: Longman.

Wilcox, S. (1989). *American deaf culture.* Silver Spring, MD: Linstok Press.

Youdelman, K., & Messerly, C. (1996). Computer-assisted notetaking for mainstreamed hearing-impaired students. *Volta Review, 98* (4), 191–199.

RECOMMENDED READINGS

Beukelman, D. R., & Yorkston, K. M. (1991). *Communication disorders following traumatic brain injury: Management of cognitive, language, and motor impairments.* Austin, TX: PRO-ED.

Bigler, E. D., Clark, E., & Farmer, J. E. (1997). *Childhood traumatic brain injury: diagnosis, assessment, and intervention.* Austin, TX: PRO-ED.

Bishop, V. E. (1996). *Teaching visually impaired children.* Springfield, IL: Charles C. Thomas.

Bornstein, H. (1990). *Manual communication: Implications for education.* Washington, DC: Gallaudet University Press.

Bradley-Johnson, S. (1994). *Psychoeducational assessment of students who are visually impaired or blind: Infancy through high school.* Austin, TX: PRO-ED.

Chen, D. (1999). *Essential elements in early intervention.* New York: American Foundation for the Blind Press.

Cummings, L. (1992). *Signs of success: A progressive sign language manual for the deaf-blind and multihandicapped.* Glen Ellyn, IL: Philip J. Rock Center.

DeBoskey, D. S. (1996). *An educational challenge: Meeting the needs of students with brain injury.* Alexandria, VA: Brain Injury Association.

Dominguez, B., & Dominguez, J. (1991). *Building blocks: Foundations for learning for young blind and visually impaired children.* New York: American Foundation for the Blind.

English, K. M. (1997). *Self-advocacy for students who are deaf or hard of hearing.* Austin, TX: PRO-ED.

Goldberg, A. L. (1996). *Acquired brain injury in childhood and adolescence: A team and family guide to educational program development and implementation.* Springfield, IL: Chares C. Thomas.

Goodrich, J., & Kinney, P. (1985). *ADAPTIPS: Adapting curricula for students who are deaf-blind and who function in the sensorimotor developmental stage.* Lexington, KY: Kentucky University.

Hagood, L. (1997). *Communication: A guide for teaching students with visual and multiple impairments.* Austin, TX: TSBVI

Harley, R. K., Truan, M. B., & Sanford, L. D. (1997). *Communication skills for visually impaired learners: Braille, print and listening skills for students who are visually impaired* (2nd ed.). Springfield, IL: Charles C. Thomas.

Harrison, F., & Crow, M. (1993). *Living and learning with blind children: A guide for parents and teachers of visually impaired children.* Toronto: University of Toronto Press.

Hazekamp, J., & Huebner, K. M. (Eds.) (1989). *Program planning and evaluation for blind and visually impaired students: National guidelines for educational excellence.* New York: American Foundation for the Blind.

Kluwin, T. M., Moores, D. F., & Gaustad, M. G. (1992). *Toward effective public school programs for deaf students: Context, process, and outcomes.* New York: Teachers College.

Livingston, S. (1997). *Rethinking the education of deaf students: Theory and practice from a teacher's perspective.* Portsmouth, NH: Heinemann.

Leatherby, J., & Wasson, T. (1991). *Curriculum modules for teaching students with dualsensory impairments.* Lexington, KY: Kentucky University.

Luetke-Stahlman, B., & Luckner, J. (1991). *Effectively educating students with hearing impairments.* New York: Longman.

McAnally, P. L., Rose, S., & Quigley, S. P. (1994). *Language learning practices of deaf children* (2nd ed.). Austin, TX: PRO-ED.

McAnally, P. L., Rose, S., & Quigley, S. P. (1999). *Reading practices with deaf learners.* Austin, TX: PRO-ED.

Pogrund, R. L., Fazzi, D. L., & Lampert, J. S. (Eds.). (1992). *Early focus: Working with young blind and visually impaired children and their families.* New York: American Foundation for the Blind.

Ponchillia, P. E., & Ponchillia, S. V. (1996). *Foundations of rehabilitation teaching with persons who are blind or visually impaired.* New York: AFB Press.

Rogow, S. M. (1988). *Helping the visually impaired child with developmental problems: Effective practice in home, school, and community.* New York: Teachers College Press.

Sall, N., & Mar, H. (1992). *Technological resources for students with deaf-blindness and severe disabilities.* New York: NY Center for Adaptive Technology.

Savage, R. C., & Wolcott, G. F. (1994). *Educational dimensions of acquired brain injury.* Austin, TX: PRO-ED.

Savage, R. C., & Wolcott, G. F. (1995). *An educator's manual: What educators need to know about students with brain injury.* Alexandria, VA: Brain Injury Association.

Schloss, P. J., & Smith, M. A. (1990). *Teaching social skills to hearing-impaired students.* Washington, DC: Alexander Graham Bell Association for the Deaf.

Scott, E. P., Jan, J. E., & Freeman, R. D. (1995). *Can't your child see? A guide for parents and professionals about young children who are visually impaired* (3rd ed.). Austin, TX: PRO-ED.

Specht, K. Q. (1996). *Physical management of students who have sustained a traumatic brain injury: Guidelines and strategies for school personnel.* Alexandria, VA: Brain Injury Association.

Trief, E. (1992). *Working with visually impaired young students: A curriculum guide for birth–3-year-olds.* Springfield, IL: Charles Thomas.

Tyler, J. S., & Mira, M. P. (1999). *Traumatic brain injury in children and adolescents: A sourcebook for teachers and other school personnel* (2nd ed.). Austin TX: PRO-ED

Wilson, J. J. (1996). *The classroom notetaker: How to organize a program serving students with hearing impairments.* Washington, DC: Alexander Graham Bell Association for the Deaf.

Wolcott, G., Lash, M., & Pearson, S. (1995). *Sign and strategies for educating students with brain injuries: A practical guide for teachers and schools.* Alexandria, VA: Brain Injury Association.

Resources

Several websites address low-incidence disabilities, including:

American Association of the Deaf-Blind (AADB)
814 Thayer Ave, Ste 302
Silver Spring, MD 20910
http://www.tr.wou.edu/dblink/aadb.htm

The American Foundation for the Blind
15 W 16th St
New York, NY 10011
http://www.afb.org/

Brain Injury Association USA Home Page
http://www.biausa.org/

DB-Link: National Information Clearinghouse on Children Who Are Deaf-Blind
Teaching Research
Western Oregon University

345 N Monmouth Ave
Monmouth, OR 97361
http://www.tr.wou.edu/dblink

Helen Keller National Center for Deaf-Blind Youths and Adults (HKNC)
111 Middle Neck Rd
Sands Point, NY 11050-1299
http://www.helenkeller.org/national/

National Association of the Deaf
814 Thayer Ave
Silver Spring, MD 20910
http://www.nad.org

National Federation of the Blind
1800 Johnson St
Baltimore, MD 21230
http://www.nfb.org/

National Information Center on Deafness
Gallaudet University
800 Florida Ave, NE
Washington, DO 20002
http://www.gallaudet.edu/

Traumatic Brain Injury Resource Guide
http://www.neuroskills.com/index/html

Traumatic Brain Injury
http://www.tbiguide.com/

Traumatic Brain Injury Resources
http://acce.virginia.edu/go/cise/ose/categories/tbi.html

There are several organizations for the blind and visually impaired:

Association for Education and Rehabilitation of the Blind and Visually Impaired
206 N Washington St
Alexandria, VA 22314

National Association for the Visually Impaired
22 W 21st St
New York, NY 10010

APPENDIXES

A EXAMPLES OF EXCERPTS FROM PLEP STATEMENTS

1. In the general education curriculum, students are expected to complete all assignments. John turns in an average of 60% of his math assignments, 50% of his reading and language assignments (on average per week). Of assignments turned in, fewer than 75% are complete. Accuracy of turned-in work fluctuates markedly from less than 10% to 100%.

2. Christine is working on the district's standard to be able to read, understand, and respond to a variety of materials for various purposes. Our focus will be on functional vocabulary. Christine is able to say the sounds of 15 to 26 letters of the alphabet independently (missed *v, d, l, r*). With a gestural prompt she was able to say the sounds of *w, x, y, z, g, l, n*. Christine is able to read 19 survival words.

3. Charlie is having difficulties in math. He is unable to meet the general education standards in the area of understanding and applying a variety of problem-solving strategies. He can compute addition problems when using touch math. He has difficulty processing story problems when they are read to him in a one-to-one situation. He does not understand the relationship of the language in the problems and the computation. He needs to learn to set up and solve story problems. He was not able to complete any of the addition or subtraction story problems on the second grade math assessment.

B EXAMPLES OF GOALS

A. *Presence and Participation*
In 32 weeks, when in a 10-minute or longer teacher-directed question-and-answer activity, Jan will raise her hand and volunteer an answer at least 2 times across 3 consecutive opportunities.

B. *Accommodation and Adaptation*
In 32 weeks, prior to beginning each new class or activity, Renee will meet with the teacher, ask questions about the activities and content, and identify for herself and for the teacher the visual accommodations (e.g., enlarged type, books on tape) that will be needed for her to succeed in the course or activity for 100% of her classes.

C. *Physical Health*
In 32 weeks, during snacks and meals at school, Gigi will independently eat using a spoon and independently drink from a tippy cup with more than ½ of the food and liquid going into her mouth, across all meals on 3 consecutive days.

In 10 weeks, when feeding from a bottle, Marion will consume at least 5 ounces of formula per feeding for at least 5 feedings per day across all days.

In 32 weeks, across all settings, Ian will identify 20 major warning words and symbols (e.g., Stop, Poison, Danger, Hazard) with 95% accuracy and will identify appropriate actions to take when these words are seen with 100% accuracy.

D. *Responsibility and Independence*
In 30 weeks, while at school, Peter will appropriately and independently use the toilet when necessary for a period of at least 3 weeks.

In 31 weeks, while at school, Kendra will appropriately use her walker to get to all of her classes within 4 minutes of the tardy bell for three consecutive weeks.

In 32 weeks, before snack time, Jacob will prepare a simple snack of his choice and eat it, at school, for 3 consecutive weeks.

In 32 weeks, when a grocery item or items are needed, Marlo will go shopping at the grocery store, pay for her purchases using the nearest dollar strategy and count change (± $1.00), on 3 consecutive trips to the store.

E. *Contribution and Citizenship*

In 30 weeks, across all classroom activities that require taking turns, Joe will wait his turn on 80% of turn-taking opportunities for 3 consecutive data days.

In 32 weeks, when engaged in a cooperative learning activity, Jessie will participate with the rest of the group throughout the entire activity across 5 cooperative learning activities.

F. *Academic and Functional Literacy*

In 31 weeks, when conversing with the Speech Language Pathologist using multiple word phrases, Mandy will use T, D, P, B, and M sounds with 90% accuracy.

In 32 weeks, during 30-minute play sessions, Jerry will independently solve problems in order to play with toys in 4 out of 5 situations presented on 3 consecutive school days.

In 29 weeks, when asked descriptive questions about classroom activities by an adult, Glenn will correctly answer 80% of these questions using appropriate multiple word phrases.

In 32 weeks, when presented with 20 randomly chosen pictures (from a pool of 300 representing basic vocabulary word/concepts), Martin will correctly label 18 of the 20 pictures for 5 consecutive sessions.

In 25 weeks, when presented with serially presented phonemes, Carol will imitate the sounds in order to form words on 9 of 10 presentations across 3 consecutive days.

In 26 weeks, after silently reading a previously unread story from third grade trade books, Bob will orally retell the story and identify all of the major characters and events for 5 consecutive stories.

In 26 weeks, when presented with a randomly selected passage from third grade trade 3 books, Felicia will read aloud 120 words correctly in 1 minute with 4 or fewer errors.

G. *Personal and Social Adjustment*

In 30 weeks, when on the playground, Spencer will appropriately play beside other children in all situations for 2 consecutive weeks.

In 30 weeks, when given a direct verbal direction by an adult, Joe will begin to comply with the direction within 10 seconds on 80% of opportunities for 3 consecutive data days.

In 18 weeks, when confronted with teasing by peers, Rambo will physically remove himself from the situation across all occurrences, times, and settings in school.

In 32 weeks, during teacher-led instruction in all of his classes, Arnold will raise his hand prior to asking a question or offering an opinion 90% of the time for 2 consecutive weeks.

In 32 weeks, in free play situations, Maryann will use appropriate phrases to request object or activities 70% of the time across 5 consecutive free play situations.

C EXAMPLES OF OBJECTIVES

David will write answers to simple addition facts with sums 0 to 20 (e.g., 4 + 5) in 5 minutes on a worksheet at a rate of 40 digits correct per minute with no errors by October 1999.

Given different board games and 2 to 3 peers, Mary will play cooperatively for 15 consecutive minutes for 10 turn-taking exchanges.

D Examples of Integrated PLEPs, Goals, Benchmarks (Major Milestones)/ Short-term Objectives

1. *PLEP*

   At 36 months, Abigail is working on developmental skills of early object use and functional play with toys/objects. Abigail is able to perform exploratory schemes (banging, shaking, throwing) as she plays with toys/objects. She applies the same schemes to all objects, and she does not demonstrate an understanding of the functions of toys/objects. Abigail has learned to imitate her parents' and other adults actions when provided with a model of combining two schemes to manipulate a toy in a functional play activity. Abigail's parents want her to play with her toys without her requiring their constant attention and modeling of actions.

   When given toys/objects, Abigail will perform 5 schemes with them (shake, role, bang, throw, push). She does not combine schemes into a functional play sequence with the toys/objects. Children between 18 to 24 months of age typically play with toys/objects by combining schemes to see a cause-and-effect relationship and to use objects according to their functions. By 36 months, children are beginning to engage in symbolic or pretend play.

   Annual Goal

   In 36 weeks, when given the opportunity to play with 6 to 8 different toys/objects, Abigail will spontaneously link 4 discrete schemes according to the toys/objects intended functions 3 times per observation period across 5 consecutive play times.

   Benchmarks
   Link 2 discrete schemes
   Link 3 discrete schemes

2. *PLEP*

   John displays difficulties writing his thoughts on paper. He has very creative ideas but does not understand sentence construction or how to develop paragraphs. He needs to use punctuation and capitalization consistently. John received 12 out of 50 points on the district's assessment for expressive writing. He needs to learn to write the four different sentence types (simple, compound, complex, and compound-complex) correctly and integrate them into a paragraph.

   Annual Goal

   In 36 weeks John will write at least a 6-sentence paragraph using at least three different sentence types scoring 45 out of 50 on the writing rubric.

   Benchmarks
   Write simple sentences
   Write compound sentences
   Write complex sentences
   Write compound-complex sentences

3. *PLEP*

   Michelle is working on the standard of the general education curriculum to enhance reading fluency. Michelle has difficulty identifying words in isolation. When reading a text, she uses context clues and picture clues to identify words unfamiliar to her. When reading words in isolation, she attempts to dissect the word phonetically, but has difficulty drawing closure to the word and pronouncing the word as a whole. Michelle studied the DISSECT word identification strategy in seventh grade. It appears she still uses this strategy with some limited success.

   When asked to read passages from her government textbook, Michelle read at an average rate of 82 words per minute with 96% accuracy in word identification. This compares to a norm of 150 to 200 words per minute with 98% to 99% accuracy for high school juniors. During this reading probe,

Michelle stated that she can read faster when she reads aloud. It seems that her literal comprehension also improves when she is able to read aloud. She used a ruler as a guide to enable her to read line by line.

Annual Goal

Given sample passages of at least 200 words from high-school level textbooks, Michelle will read grade level materials at an average rate of 100 words per minute with 98% accuracy or better in word identification.

Objectives

Michelle will read 200-word passage 90 wpm/98% accuracy.

Michelle will read 200-word passage 95 wpm/98% accuracy.

E IEP MODEL FORM COMPLETED

CENTER LAKE AREA EDUCATION AGENCY	**Meeting Type**
Individualized Education Program [IEP]	[ ] Initial
	[ ] Review
Date of Meeting: ___1_/_17_/_98___	[ ] Revision
(Month/Day/Year)	[•] Reevaluation

Student _____Flannery_____Patrick_____
          Last (legal)   First (no nicknames)   M.I.

Birthdate: __5_/_23_/_84__   Current Grade: __9__   Soc. Sec. #: __505_-_99_-_3765__
          (Month/Day/Year)

Resident District: __Loveland__   Attending District: __Loveland__

[√] if: [ ] Tuitioned   or   [ ] Open Enrollment   Attending Building: __High School__

[•] Parent   Name: __Colon / Kate Flannery__   Home Phone: __552-3571__
[ ] Foster Parent
[ ] Guardian   Address: __962 Monarch Road__   Work Phone: __552-9657__
[ ] Surrogate   __Loveland, IA   50632__

          Student Address: _____   Phone: _____

          (if different from above) _____

          _____

Date this IEP will be implemented: __1_/_18_/_98__   Duration of this IEP: __One Academic year__

Annual IEP Review is due before: __1_/_18_/_99__   Reevaluation is due before: _1_/_17_/_01_

Parent Notification of IEP Meeting: Method: __Phone and notice__ by: __Myrna Fenster, SE Teacher__

Describe attempts to involve parents (if not in attendance): _____

_____

Parental Due Process Rights were reviewed by: __Myrna Fenster, teacher and Basil Markham, Psychologist__

Persons Present at Meeting* and Position or Relationship to Student

Colon Flannery	Parent	Patrick Flannery	Student
Kate Flannery	Parent	Basil Markham	School Psychologist
Myron Bailey	LEA Rep	Martha Graham	DVRS Counselor
Sarah Wilson, English	Reg Ed Tchr	Kay Thomas	SLP
Myrna Fenster	Sp Ed Tchr		

Additional, Outside Agency Sources of Written Input: Name/Agency & Date of Report

_____ _____ _____ _____

*   Signature or listing only indicates presence at meeting, not approval or acceptance of the IEP

Designation:	Model/Level:	Weighting:	Roster:

Name: P. Flannery _____   Date: __1/17/98__   Page   2 of 14

Student and Family Vision

Patrick would like to participate in sports and drama while in high school.   After high
school he wants to work in the entertainment field, without additional post secondary
training.

In developing the IEP, the team must consider: the strengths of the student, the concerns of the parents
for enhancing the education of their child, and relevant results of the most recent evaluation or
reevaluation.   Additionally, the team must consider:

- the need for positive behavior interventions, strategies, and
  supports for any student whose behavior interferes with his
  or her learning or the learning of others
- communication needs, particularly if the student is deaf or
  hard of hearing

- Braille instruction needs of students with visual impairments
- needs related to English language proficiency
- the need for assistive technology services or devices
- health needs

Present Levels of Educational Performance: This statement must include a description of:

- the effect of the disability on the student's involvement and progress in the general curriculum , or
- the effect of the disability on the participation of a preschool child in appropriate activities, and
- transition needs (required to be addressed at age 14 and older).

Patrick is currently a freshman at Balmora High School receiving content instruction through the general
education curriculum in science, math, health, P.E., Art and English at the 9-12 benchmark level.
Special education instructional services are provided in social studies, support for general education
classes, and accommodations for taking tests. Patrick is working on the Level III (grades 4-5)
benchmarks in the general education standards for reading (demonstrates competence in reading) and
writing (demonstrates competence in writing) and on the Level IV (grades 6-8) in listening (demonstrates
competence in speaking, listening, and viewing). Patrick's performance in the general education classes,
based on 1st semester grades has been average or better (given accommodations and support): English
9-B, Basic Algebra-A, Health/PE-Pass, Life Science-C, Choir-A- and Art C+. Government has been
within the special education program, with a B.   Patrick's reading and writing difficulties result in
missing assignments, late projects, and difficulty with note taking. He will ask for help, primarily with
reading the assignment, at school. He accurately records what assignment is due when, but chooses not to
work on assignments at home about 50% of the time.

On academic testing, Patrick demonstrated difficulty in reading decoding skills and putting words
together after breaking them into syllables. He scored at the 3.8 grade level. Passage comprehension is
significantly better, he understands about 4 grade levels above his decoding skill level (7.7 grade level)
because he uses context clues to decode and understands unfamiliar structures. Patrick uses capitals and
ending punctuation correctly.

Math skills show strengths in applied mathematical, understanding and applying basic operations in short
story problems (9.4 grade, consistent with his grades in basic algebra).

Patrick participates in extra-curricular activities including choir, football and swimming. He would like
to participate in drama and school plays. He reports he has not tried-out for the plays because his

Name: <u>P. Flannery</u>   Date: <u>1/17/98</u>   Page   3 of 14

reading problems cause extreme difficulty with sight reading.   He performs frequently with a blue-grass band.

Transition Needs:

Instruction: Patrick needs to improve reading and math skills. He may need oral testing for his Driver's License Exam, and additional tutoring while studying for the exam and the class.

Employment and Post School Adult Living Goals: Patrick would like to move to Florida and be an entertainer at Disney World. He will need to investigate the specific requirements of this career and look at related careers.

Related Services: Patrick needs to consider the use of talking books to keep up with reading demands in the general education classes. He needs the services of a proof reader for long reports.

Community Experiences: Patrick is interested in a summer job. He needs to contact JTPA and the local Workforce Development office. He will eventually need to contact Vocational Rehabilitation to help with career planning.

Patrick is working on daily living skills at home and does not need services in this area. He has skills for his career goal and does not need a functional vocational evaluation at this time.

Patrick was diagnosed as having vocal nodules by Dr. Evans, an Ear, Nose, and Throat Specialist. Dr. Evans recommended Patrick should receive therapy regarding appropriate use of his voice to post-pone possible surgical removal of the vocal nodules. Patrick has been imitating various voice personalities and cartoon characters with his interest in being an entertainer. He needs to work on limiting the amount and type of vocal abusive practices. Patrick's voice difficulty limits his participation in his speech and drama class; he cannot participate in giving speeches or acting in the class drama play.

Name: P. Flannery   Date: 1/17/98   Page 4 of 14

Annual Goal and Progress Indicators   I-SEE Goal Code:

Baseline (What is the student doing now?): ___ Patrick is able to verbalize 2 career/occupational choices, but not the training or skills required for these occupations ___

Goal: include **conditions** (when and how the student will perform); **behavior** (what the student will do); and **criterion** (acceptable level of performance)

In 16 weeks, given 2 career interest areas or occupation, Patrick will develop a course plan and activities list through two years of PS training to develop the necessary occupational skills

Evaluation procedures (how progress will be measured): ___ Weekly review of job log and portfolio review ___

Position(s) responsible for services: ___ Counselor and Special Education Teacher ___

Major milestones/Short term objectives	Comments/Progress Notes/Dates Achieved
1. Patrick will complete a career search using Choices career software to identify needed training/classes for his career choices.	
2. Patrick will complete an interest survey to determine if his interests match his career choices.	
3. Patrick will develop a 5 year plan to cover 10th grade through 2 years of post high training in his chosen career fields.	
4. Patrick will identify extra curricular activities which will support his career choices.	

Update and provide to parents with report cards

1 = This goal has been met.
2 = Progress has been made towards the goal. It appears that he goal will be met by the time the IEP is reviewed.
3 = Progress has been made towards the goal but the goal may not be met by the time the IEP is reviewed.
4 = Progress is not sufficient to meet this goal by the time the IEP is reviewed. Instructional strategies will be changed.
5 = Your child did not work on this goal during this reporting period (provide an explanation to the parents).

___/___/___	1 2 3 4 5	___/___/___	1 2 3 4 5	___/___/___	1 2 3 4 5
___/___/___	1 2 3 4 5	___/___/___	1 2 3 4 5	___/___/___	1 2 3 4 5
___/___/___	1 2 3 4 5	___/___/___	1 2 3 4 5	___/___/___	1 2 3 4 5

At the end of the IEP goal period, answer the following questions

Progress: Is the child making progress expected by the IEP team? (√ one)	**Independence:** Is the child more independent in the goal area? (√ one)
[ ] Goal met [ ] Goal not met; but performance improved [ ] No change or poorer performance [ ] Insufficient data for decision making	[ ] Greater independence [ ] Unchanged independence [ ] Less independence [ ] Insufficient data for decision making

Comparison to peers or standard: How does the child's performance compare with general education peers or standards? (√ one)	**Goal Status:** Will work in the goal be discontinued or continued? (√ one)	
[ ] Comparison to age or grade level peers or standards not appropriate [ ] Less discrepancy from peers or standard [ ] Same discrepancy from peers or standard [ ] More discrepancy from peers or standard [ ] Insufficient data for decision making	**Discontinue goal area** [ ] Success, no further special education needs in goal area [ ] Goal area is not a priority for the next year [ ] Limited progress, plateau	**Continue goal area** [ ] More advanced work in goal area [ ] Continue as written

Name: P. Flannery _____   Date: __1/17/98__   Page 5 of 14

Annual Goal and Progress Indicators	I-SEE Goal Code:

Baseline (What is the student doing now?): _____ Currently does not take notes _____

Goal: include **conditions** (when and how the student will perform); **behavior** (what the student will do); and **criterion** (acceptable level of performance)

    In 36 weeks Patrick will write a 2 paragraph synopsis to include comparisons and contrast with his own experiences or the current reading selection with a thesis statement, evidence from the film, personal experience and/or reading selection and a conclusion at Level 3 of the district writing rubric.

Evaluation procedures (how progress will be measured): __Every two weeks Patrick will view film/video to a social studies topic and write a paper__

Position(s) responsible for services: _____ Special Education Teacher _____

Major milestones/Short term objectives	Comments/Progress Notes/Dates Achieved
1. Patrick will write down the key points from a film/video presentation using a pre-prepared outline with 95% accuracy.	
2. Patrick will write down the key points from a film/video presentation based on class discussion before the viewing with 90% accuracy.	
3. Patrick will write a one paragraph summary of the key ideas to include main topic, supporting statement, conclusion sentence.	

Update and provide to parents with report cards

1 = This goal has been met.
2 = Progress has been made towards the goal. It appears that he goal will be met by the time the IEP is reviewed.
3 = Progress has been made towards the goal but the goal may not be met by the time the IEP is reviewed.
4 = Progress is not sufficient to meet this goal by the time the IEP is reviewed. Instructional strategies will be changed.
5 = Your child did not work on this goal during this reporting period (provide an explanation to the parents).

___/___/___	1	2	3	4	5	___/___/___	1	2	3	4	5	___/___/___	1	2	3	4	5
___/___/___	1	2	3	4	5	___/___/___	1	2	3	4	5	___/___/___	1	2	3	4	5
___/___/___	1	2	3	4	5	___/___/___	1	2	3	4	5	___/___/___	1	2	3	4	5

At the end of the IEP goal period, answer the following questions

Progress: Is the child making progress expected by the IEP team? (√ one)	**Independence:** Is the child more independent in the goal area? (√ one)
[ ] Goal met	[ ] Greater independence
[ ] Goal not met; but performance improved	[ ] Unchanged independence
[ ] No change or poorer performance	[ ] Less independence
[ ] Insufficient data for decision making	[ ] Insufficient data for decision making

Comparison to peers or standard: How does the child's performance compare with general education peers or standards? (√ one)	**Goal Status:** Will work in the goal be discontinued or continued? (√ one)	
	Discontinue goal area	**Continue goal area**
[ ] Comparison to age or grade level peers or standards not appropriate	[ ] Success, no further special education needs in goal area	[ ] More advanced work in goal area
[ ] Less discrepancy from peers or standard	[ ] Goal area is not a priority for the next year	[ ] Continue as written
[ ] Same discrepancy from peers or standard		
[ ] More discrepancy from peers or standard	[ ] Limited progress, plateau	
[ ] Insufficient data for decision making		

Name: P. Flannery _____   Date: 1/17/98   Page 6 of 14

Annual Goal and Progress Indicators	I-SEE Goal Code:

Baseline (What is the student doing now?): ___ 20 word/phrase errors of pitch, loudness and quality during speech ___

Goal: include **conditions** (when and how the student will perform); **behavior** (what the student will do); and **criterion** (acceptable level of performance)

Patrick will increase appropriate voice characteristics(pitch, loudness, and quality) when presenting a speech in drama class with no more than 2 word/phrase errors of pitch loudness and quality.

Evaluation procedures (how progress will be measured): _____ Weekly speech in drama class using rubric _____

Position(s) responsible for services: ___ Classroom teacher and speech and language pathologist

Major milestones/Short term objectives	Comments/Progress Notes/Dates Achieved
15 word/phrase errors	
10 word/phrase errors	
5 word/phrase errors	

Update and provide to parents with report cards
1 = This goal has been met.
2 = Progress has been made towards the goal. It appears that he goal will be met by the time the IEP is reviewed.
3 = Progress has been made towards the goal but the goal may not be met by the time the IEP is reviewed.
4 = Progress is not sufficient to meet this goal by the time the IEP is reviewed. Instructional strategies will be changed.
5 = Your child did not work on this goal during this reporting period (provide an explanation to the parents).

___/___/___	1	2	3	4	5	___/___/___	1	2	3	4	5	___/___/___	1	2	3	4	5
___/___/___	1	2	3	4	5	___/___/___	1	2	3	4	5	___/___/___	1	2	3	4	5
___/___/___	1	2	3	4	5	___/___/___	1	2	3	4	5	___/___/___	1	2	3	4	5

At the end of the IEP goal period, answer the following questions

Progress: Is the child making progress expected by the IEP team? (√ one)	**Independence:** Is the child more independent in the goal area? (√ one)
[ ] Goal met	[ ] Greater independence
[ ] Goal not met; but performance improved	[ ] Unchanged independence
[ ] No change or poorer performance	[ ] Less independence
[ ] Insufficient data for decision making	[ ] Insufficient data for decision making

Comparison to peers or standard: How does the child's performance compare with general education peers or standards? (√ one)	**Goal Status:** Will work in the goal be discontinued or continued? (√ one)
[ ] Comparison to age or grade level peers or standards not appropriate	**Discontinue goal area** **Continue goal area**
[ ] Less discrepancy from peers or standard	[ ] Success, no further special [ ] More advanced work
[ ] Same discrepancy from peers or standard	education needs in goal area in goal area
[ ] More discrepancy from peers or standard	[ ] Goal area is not a priority [ ] Continue as written
[ ] Insufficient data for decision making	for the next year
	[ ] Limited progress, plateau

Name: P. Flannery _____   Date: __1/17/98__   Page 7 of 14

Annual Goal and Progress Indicators	I-SEE Goal Code:

Baseline (What is the student doing now?): ___Patrick currently writes simple and compound sentences with 60% on structure and 30% accuracy for spelling, capitalization and punctuations.___

Goal: include **conditions** (when and how the student will perform); **behavior** (what the student will do); and **criterion** (acceptable level of performance)

In 36 weeks when given a classroom writing assignment Patrick will write simple and compound sentences, with 100% correct structure, 90% correct mechanics, capitalization, punctuation, and spelling.

Evaluation procedures (how progress will be measured): __Weekly evaluation of classroom writing assignments__

Position(s) responsible for services: _____ English teacher and special class teacher_____

Major milestones/Short term objectives	Comments/Progress Notes/Dates Achieved
Write simple sentences with correct structure, capitalization, mechanics, punctuation	
Write compound sentences with correct structure, capitalization, mechanics, punctuation	
Combine simple and compound sentences into a paragraph	

At the end of the IEP goal period, answer the following questions	
Progress: Is the child making progress expected by the IEP team? (√ one) [ ] Goal met [ ] Goal not met; but performance improved [ ] No change or poorer performance [ ] Insufficient data for decision making	**Independence:** Is the child more independent in the goal area? (√ one) [ ] Greater independence [ ] Unchanged independence [ ] Less independence [ ] Insufficient data for decision making

Comparison to peers or standard: How does the child's performance compare with general education peers or standards? (√ one)
[ ] Comparison to age or grade level peers or standards not appropriate
[ ] Less discrepancy from peers or standard
[ ] Same discrepancy from peers or standard
[ ] More discrepancy from peers or standard
[ ] Insufficient data for decision making
	Goal Status: Will work in the goal be discontinued or continued? (√ one)
	Discontinue goal area **Continue goal area**
	[ ] Success, no further special | [ ] More advanced work
	    education needs in goal area | in goal area
	[ ] Goal area is not a priority | [ ] Continue as written
	    for the next year |
	[ ] Limited progress, plateau |

Name: __P. Flannery__   Date: __1/17/98__   Page 8 of 14

Annual Goal and Progress Indicators	I-SEE Goal Code:

Baseline (What is the student doing now?): ___9th grade passage 80% decoding and 60% correct paraphrases___

Goal: include **conditions** (when and how the student will perform); **behavior** (what the student will do); and **criterion** (acceptable level of performance)

___In 36 weeks Patrick will read a grade level text with 95% accuracy on decoding and 80% correct paraphrases.___

Evaluation procedures (how progress will be measured): ___Weekly evaluation probes reading a 400 word passage from grade level texts, administered by the special education teacher___

Position(s) responsible for services: ___Special Education teacher___

Major milestones: 1: __80% decoding/65% correct paraphrases__   2: __85% decoding/70% correct paraphrases__
   3: __90% decoding/75% correct paraphrases__   4: __95% decoding/80% correct paraphrases__

Update and provide to parents with report cards

1 = This goal has been met.
2 = Progress has been made towards the goal. It appears that he goal will be met by the time the IEP is reviewed.
3 = Progress has been made towards the goal but the goal may not be met by the time the IEP is reviewed.
4 = Progress is not sufficient to meet this goal by the time the IEP is reviewed. Instructional strategies will be changed.
5 = Your child did not work on this goal during this reporting period (provide an explanation to the parents).

_10/__/_98	1 2 3 4 5	_6/__/_99	1 2 3 4 5	__/__/__	1 2 3 4 5
1/__/_99	1 2 3 4 5	__/__/__	1 2 3 4 5	__/__/__	1 2 3 4 5
4 /__/_99_	1 2 3 4 5	__/__/__	1 2 3 4 5	__/__/__	1 2 3 4 5

At the end of the IEP goal period, answer the following questions

Progress: Is the child making progress expected by the IEP team? (√ one)
[ ] Goal met
[ ] Goal not met; but performance improved
[ ] No change or poorer performance
[ ] Insufficient data for decision making

Independence: Is the child more independent in the goal area? (√ one)
[ ] Greater independence
[ ] Unchanged independence
[ ] Less independence
[ ] Insufficient data for decision making

Comparison to peers or standard: How does the child's performance compare with general education peers or standards? (√ one)
[ ] Comparison to age or grade level peers or standards not appropriate
[ ] Less discrepancy from peers or standard
[ ] Same discrepancy from peers or standard
[ ] More discrepancy from peers or standard
[ ] Insufficient data for decision making

Goal Status: Will work in the goal be discontinued or continued? (√ one)

Discontinue goal area
[ ] Success, no further special education needs in goal area
[ ] Goal area is not a priority for the next year
[ ] Limited progress, plateau

Continue goal area
[ ] More advanced work in goal area
[ ] Continue as written

Name: P. Flannery _____   Date: 1/17/98   Page   9 of 14

> **Transition Planning:** Age 14 and older address course of study; age 16 and older, address all transition items. Consider the student's post-high school outcomes and the goals of this IEP, based on the needs, interests, and preferences of the student.

Focus of student's courses of study (e.g., vocational education program, advanced placement classes, etc.)

_____

   Patrick will take the general core curriculum with elective classes in the Arts and Humanities

career pathway to include art and drama classes._____

_____

_____

Transition services & activities	Agency/position responsible
Will instruction be provided to this student? [x] Yes (explain) [ ] No (provide justification) **Special education services will be provided to develop strategies in reading & writing**	Loveland High School
Will support or related services be provided to this student? [x] Yes (explain) [ ] No (provide justification) **Assistance in accessing talking books through various sources.**	Family JTPA Workforce Development
Will community experiences be provided to this student? [ ] Yes (explain) [x] No (provide justification) **Skills are progressing satisfactorily.** **Patrick will look for summer work opportunities.**	
Will activities and services to develop employment and other post-high school adult living objectives be provided? [x] Yes (explain) [ ] No (provide justification) **Patrick will identify the specific requirements of his career interest and take drama classes for more experience.**	Loveland High School
[x] Yes [ ] No Will activities and services to develop daily living skills be provided?	Loveland High School
[ ] Yes [x] No Is a functional vocational evaluation required? **Skills & experiences are currently appropriate for vocational goals.**	

Vocational Education: [x] Regular   [ ] Modified — describe below   [ ] Specially designed — requires goal(s)

   Patrick will need accommodations for reading any printed material and written exams.

Anticipated graduation date (must be provided at least 18 months prior to potential graduation: 6/3/01

Graduation criteria: The minimum ITED level in reading, 9.06E will be waived for Patrick's grade requirement. He will take the test and the required core classes with accommodations.

Notice of transfer of rights provided: 5/23/00 **Transfer of rights will occur at age 18: (5/23/01)**

Name: P. Flannery   Date: 1/17/98   Page   10 of 14

Linkages to community service providers (consider for all students)			
Linkage with:	Contacted by:	Timeline:	Outcome:
Vocational Rehab	Special Class teacher and Patrick	March	Development of career plans
JTPA	Patrick and Counselor	January	Completion of summer youth application
Workforce Development	Patrick and Family	February	Completion of Workforce applications and job search techniques

Appropriate education in the least restrictive environment. Consider accommodations, modifications, adaptations, assistive technology, and supplementary aids and services. What does the student require to be successful and to be educated to the maximum extent appropriate with nondisabled peers? What supports are needed by teachers or other personnel?

Patrick will have a reader for general education class tests, usually taken in the resource room with the special education teacher. When participating in the performing arts program, the drama/music teachers will provide the special education teacher with the audition materials so he may pre-read the materials. Patrick will obtain and use a calculator in math for daily work and exams.   He will have the opportunity to use talking books upon his request for any of his classes, the counselor will assist with registration for this service. He will be provided assistance in obtaining a full set of notes in all classes through peer notetakers or the teacher providing a copy of their instructional notes.   Patrick and the classroom teacher will receive support from the special education teacher for accommodations for testing and proofreading written assignments. They will receive assistance in monitoring assignment completion from the special education teacher and Patrick's parents.

_____ SPED Services

_____ Instructional Services:

_____ Learning Strategies

_____ Social Studies

LRE% is 43% as he is pulled out three class periods.

[ ] Yes   [x] No Are **assistive technology** services or devices required? If yes, describe in appropriate section(s).

[ ] Yes   [x] No Does this student require a **functional behavioral assessment and a behavioral intervention plan**? If yes, include all necessary information in this IEP.

Will this student participate in all district-wide assessments?

[ ] Yes   [x] Yes, with modifications (complete documentation form) [ ] No (alternate assessment, complete documentation form)

_____

_____

Physical Education: [ ] Regular   [ ] Modified — describe below   [ ] Specially designed — requires goal(s)

_____

Name: P. Flannery _____   Date: 1/17/98   Page 11 of 14

| Description of Special Education Services: instructional, support and related services |

Service	Time & Frequency	Setting for Special Education Services
Learning Strategies	100 minute daily	[ ] General ed. [x] Special ed. [ ] _____
Social Studies	50 minutes daily	[ ] General ed. [x] Special ed. [ ] _____
Speech	80 minutes monthly	[x] General ed. [x] Special ed. [ ] _____
_____	_____	[ ] General ed. [ ] Special ed. [ ] _____
_____	_____	[ ] General ed. [ ] Special ed. [ ] _____
_____	_____	[ ] General ed. [ ] Special ed. [ ] _____
_____	_____	[ ] General ed. [ ] Special ed. [ ] _____
_____	_____	[ ] General ed. [ ] Special ed. [ ] _____
_____	_____	[ ] General ed. [ ] Special ed. [ ] _____
_____	_____	[ ] General ed. [ ] Special ed. [ ] _____

Description of special education service delivery: Patrick will receive direct instruction in social studies. following an abbreviated general curriculum at a slower pace. He will receive help with reading comprehension and proof reading of reports for general classes. He will also develop time management skills by planning projects with the aid of his teacher. He will learn and practice reading and writing strategies to use in all classes. Patrick will receive speech and language services in the speech room with follow up in the classroom.

[ ] Yes   [x] No   Are **specialized transportation services** required? If yes, describe. _____

| Setting consideration: Consider any potential harmful effects of the selected setting(s) on the student or on the quality of services received. |

Options considered for the setting of special education services: general classroom, resource room _____
_____
_____

Removal from general education: 33 % If greater than 0%, answer the following questions:

1. How would providing special education services and activities in the general education environment impact this student?

Needs direct instruction on learning strategies and a slower pace than possible in general education. He would not progress

because of the limited time to teach learning strategies _____

2. How would providing special education services and activities in the general education environment impact other students?

_____Pace would be to slow and time taken from instruction _____
_____

| Extended School Year Services |

[ ] Yes   [x] No   Are extended school year services (ESYS) required? If yes, the IEP must describe ESYS services.

| Progress reports |

Parents: You will be informed of your child's IEP progress   4   times per year. You will receive:

[x]   An IEP report with report cards and progress reports   [x] Updated copies of the IEP goal pages

[ ] _____

Name: P. Flannery   Date: 1/17/98   Page 12 of 14

?? Community Schools Individualized Education Plan Report Card

1st report ___/___/___	2nd report ___/___/___	3rd report ___/___/___	4th report ___/___/___
5th report ___/___/___	6th report ___/___/___	7th report ___/___/___	8th report ___/___/___

Goal Area:

1st report _____	2nd report _____	3rd report _____	4th report _____
5th report _____	6th report _____	7th report _____	8th report _____

Comments:

Goal Area:

1st report _____	2nd report _____	3rd report _____	4th report _____
5th report _____	6th report _____	7th report _____	8th report _____

Comments:

Goal Area:

1st report _____	2nd report _____	3rd report _____	4th report _____
5th report _____	6th report _____	7th report _____	8th report _____

Comments:

Goal Area:

1st report _____	2nd report _____	3rd report _____	4th report _____
5th report _____	6th report _____	7th report _____	8th report _____

Comments:

Progress Codes	1 = This goal has been met.
	2 = Progress has been made towards the goal. It appears that he goal will be met by the time the IEP is reviewed.
	3 = Progress has been made towards the goal but the goal may not be me by the time the IEP is reviewed.
	4 = Progress is not sufficient to meet this goal by the time the IEP is reviewed. Instructional strategies will be changed.
	5 = Your child did not work on this goal during this reporting period (provide an explanation to the parents).

Name: P. Flannery _____   Date: 1/17/98   Page 13 of 14

?? Community Schools Individualized Education Plan Report Card

1st report ___/___/___	2nd report ___/___/___	3rd report ___/___/___	4th report ___/___/___

Goal Area:

1st report _____	2nd report _____	3rd report _____	4th report _____

Comments:

Goal Area:

1st report _____	2nd report _____	3rd report _____	4th report _____

Comments:

Goal Area:

1st report _____	2nd report _____	3rd report _____	4th report _____

Comments:

Goal Area:

1st report _____	2nd report _____	3rd report _____	4th report _____

Comments:

Progress Codes	1 = This goal has been met. 2 = Progress has been made towards the goal. It appears that he goal will be met by the time the IEP is reviewed. 3 = Progress has been made towards the goal but the goal may not be me by the time the IEP is reviewed. 4 = Progress is not sufficient to meet this goal by the time the IEP is reviewed. Instructional strategies will be changed. 5 = Your child did not work on this goal during this reporting period (provide an explanation to the parents).

Name: P. Flannery _____   Date: 1/17/98   Page   14 of 14

Documentation for Determining Participation in District Wide Assessment

The Individuals with Disabilities Education Act presupposes that all special education students will fully participate in all district wide assessments in the same manner as their non-disabled peers <u>unless</u> a staffing team determines that: (1) such participation is not appropriate without reasonable accommodations or (2) such assessment is not appropriate and identifies an alternate form of assessment.

I. Determine which of the following statements best describes the student's *curriculum* and then determine the appropriate assessment approach.

		District Wide Assessment		Alternate Assessment
	General Description of **Curriculum** Presented	No Accom. Needed	Accom. Needed	Alternate Assessment
A.	Student participates with no or only slight modification in general academic **curriculum**.			████████
B.	Student participates with significant modification to the general academic **curriculum**.	████████		
C.	Student does not participate in general academic **curriculum**. Student receives an alternative **curriculum**.	████████	████████	

II. Accommodations: List accommodations necessary for student to participate in district wide assessment.

III. Alternate Assessment

1. Describe why district wide assessment is not appropriate.

2. Describe how student will be assessed.

F SAMPLES OF DIFFERENT IEP ANNUAL GOALS AND SHORT-TERM OBJECTIVES AS PART OF TRANSITION IEPs

Instruction

Situation: Student has indicated an interest in pursuing post-high school training in either a 2-year or 4-year college. After discussion of PLEP, student indicated she believes she needs to improve her written and oral communication skills in order to be successful.

Sample Goals and Objectives

Student will develop keyboarding/word processing skills.

- Student will be able to type/keystroke at 35 words per minute.
- Student will use the spell check and the grammar check for each document with 100% accuracy of spelling and grammar.
- Student will use learning strategies to assist in improving spelling and writing accuracy.
- Student will request proofreading assistance from teacher/tutor. Student will communicate needs for accommodation in the classroom to others, including strangers.
- Student will articulate her personal learning and working style to document understanding.
- Student will identify accommodations which make her more successful.
- Student will communicate her needs for accommodation to her teacher and to strangers 80% of available opportunity.

Student will demonstrate oral communication skills.

- Students will develop a plan for oral communication situations (e.g., interviews, expressing opinion, requesting assistance).
- Student will demonstrate use of the plan for teacher at least twice a week in varied settings (school, home, community).
- Student will communicate her needs, opinions, etc. orally to her teachers, peers and to strangers in varied settings (school, home, community).

Community Experiences

Situation: Student plans to work in a city some distance from the small community near which he lives. He believes he needs to learn how to manage an apartment and how to become integrated into a new community.

Sample Goals and Objectives

Students will learn to live independently

- Student will complete home management class and demonstrate budgeting for living expenses and minor home maintenance with 80% accuracy.
- Student will complete consumer math class and demonstrate completion of insurance, banking, and tax forms.
- Student will complete driver's education class and obtain driver's license.
- Student will open and manage a personal checking account with 100% accuracy of balancing monthly statement.
- Student will assume responsibility for family food shopping 50% of the time.

Student will develop community integration skills

- Student will register to vote on his 18th birthday
- Student will evaluate personal recreation/leisure interests and communicate preferences to teacher and family.
- Student will explore recreation/leisure activities available in the city and explore how to access those activities.
- Student will develop skills in preferred recreation activity through enrollment in high school physical education class, adult education class, attending school or community functions, etc.

- Student will develop and demonstrate use of map reading skills.
- Student will learn to use information section of telephone book and will demonstrate obtaining information in this section of the telephone book with 80% accuracy.

Employment

Situation: Student states she does not know what an appropriate job might be for her after high school. She states a need to determine some employment objectives.

Sample Goal and Objectives

Student will identify potential long-term career goals and identify a career major area to pursue during final year of secondary school.

- Student will complete an interest inventory and identify three possible career majors to pursue.
- Student will participate in a functional community-based vocational evaluation to match aptitudes and interests.
- Student will job shadow at least three businesses to identify how her career interest fits within the business.
- Student will interview a worker in each business to identify worker activities and responsibilities.

- Student will attend Career Day at the area community college to identify training needs of occupations and compare it to her aptitudes and learning style.

Postschool Adult Living Objectives

Situation: Student's postschool goal is to live in an apartment with a friend. He believes he needs to improve his ability to manage his clothing. Discussion of PLEP supports the need for development of specific skills to assist in meeting this postschool goal.

Sample Goal and Objectives

Student will care for his clothing.

- Student will complete home economics and home management class.
- Student will make appropriate clothing purchases (style, quality, appropriateness for use) 80% of the time.
- Student will maintain clothing in wearable condition (clean, pressed, mended, etc.) 100% of the time.
- Student will develop an adequate clothing budget and will maintain wardrobe within that budget.

G BEHAVIOR OBSERVATION FORM

Baseline _____

Student Tom Clark

Behavior Destroys assignments

Intervention _____

Observer Sue Best

Date	Time	Length of Behavior	What occurred Prior to the Behavior	Describe Behavior	Outcome of Behavior
9/17/97	1:20–1:30 p.m.	20–30 seconds	The students were assigned independent seat work. The teacher gave individual help to students as she walked around the classroom. The teacher stands at Tom's desk.	Tom wads up his paper, then tears it up and wipes the pieces to the floor.	Other students turn to look. The teacher says to Tom, "Get out another sheet of paper and start over." She waits at his desk another 45 seconds.
9/22/97	1:15 p.m.	15 seconds	Verbal instructions were given on how to complete a pre-lab worksheet.	Tom wads up his paper and clenches it in his fist.	Several students turn to look at Tom. The teacher tells him the work must be completed by the end of class or he will have to stay after school.
9/23/97	1:00–1:10 p.m.	25 seconds	The class completed watching a film.	Tom picks up his paper in one hand, then puts his head on his desk and wads up his paper.	The teacher tells him to sit up, straighten out his worksheet, and get to work.
9/24/97	1:15–1:25 p.m.	20 seconds	Students were assigned to answer questions from their book after viewing a teacher demonstration.	Tom takes out a sheet of paper. He starts to write, then wads up his paper and slams his book shut.	A few students giggle. Some turn to look. The teacher says, "Tom you are wasting time."
9/25/97	1:05–1:15 p.m.	25 seconds	Students completed oral review questions and were given directions to complete a review study guide for a test.	Tom receives his study guide, looks at it, then separates the pages. He then wads up each page, one at a time, loudly.	The teacher tells Tom to take his things and go to the office.

B FUNCTIONAL ASSESSMENT INTERVIEW FORM

Student: Tom Clark   Teacher: Jennifer Braun

Team Member's Name   Team Member's Position

Ms. Jones   English Teacher
Mr. Smith   Principal
Ms. Clark   Mother
Ms. Johnson   Case Manager

A. Describe the Behavior

1. What is the behavior?

   Tom destroys his written assignments.

2. How is the behavior performed?

   When given written assignments to be completed independently, Tom wads up and/or tears up his paper. When he is reminded to get to work, he says he does not want to do the work.

3. How often does the behavior occur?

   The behavior occurs on days when written work is to be completed, 3–4 days a week.

4. How long does the behavior last when it occurs?

   15–30 seconds

5. What is the intensity of the behavior when it occurs?

   The behavior results in destruction of paper and detracts from peer work time.

B. Define Setting Events and Environmental Factors That Predict the Behavior (describe the following variables):

1. Classroom structure (physical).

   Science 7 is a classroom with work tables and storage cabinets for lab equipment/materials.

2. Class rules and procedural expectations.

   Students are responsible for the care of all materials, including their work. Written work must be completed before lab work can begin.

3. Instructional delivery (lecture, cooperative learning, labs, etc.).

   Lecture, cooperative group work, discussion, lab activities, and independent seatwork.

4. Instructional materials (textbooks, worksheets, hands-on activities).

   Textbook and/or worksheets.

5. How are directions presented?

   Verbal directions are given by the teacher. Some directions are read independently by the students.

6. Assessment techniques (multiple-choice tests, essay tests, rubrics, authentic assessment).

   A multiple choice test is given weekly. One essay question is included in each test. Each test covers a combination of labwork and writtenwork.

C. Define Specific Immediate Antecedent Events That Predict When the Behaviors Are Most Likely to Occur:

1. When are the behaviors most likely to occur?

   The behaviors generally occur after the lecture and prior to independent seatwork.

2. When are the behaviors least likely to occur?

   The behaviors occur least often when Tom is interacting with his peers and feels a part of the group.

3. Where are the behaviors most likely to occur?

   The behaviors occur frequently in his science class.

4. Where are the behaviors least likely to occur?

   The behaviors are least likely to occur in social settings and in classrooms where tom is not the only one asked to sit alone.

5. During what activities are the behaviors most likely to occur?

   Behaviors occur most often during independent seatwork time when he is asked to work alone.

6. During what activities least likely to occur?

   The behaviors occur least often during group activities.

D. Identify Specific Consequences That Follow the Behavior:

1. What specific consequence is most likely to immediately follow the behavior?

   Teacher/peer attention. The student receives a "0" for the assignment.

2. What seems to be the effect of the consequence on the student's behavior?

   The effect seems to be somewhat reinforcing in that Tom continues the problem behavior.

3. Does the consequence remove the student from an uncomfortable situation?

   Yes, temporarily. It delays work time and provides attention.

4. Is there consistency between the consequences given by the classroom teacher and the consequences given by the administrators?

   Yes.

5. Is there consistent follow-through with all consequences both in the classroom and in the school office?

   Yes.

C BEHAVIORAL INTERVENTION PLAN

Student: Tom Clark   School: Middle School

Date Developed: 9/30/97   Date Implemented: 10/3/97

Grade: 7

Baseline Data Results:

Tom destroyed assignments 5 out of 5 observation days

Hypothesis Statement:

Tom's behavior is related to frustration brought on by a discrepancy between his skill level and the skill level necessary to complete the assignments. Much of Tom's destructive behavior is related to his isolated seating from his peers in the classroom. Tom feels singled out because he sits at a table by himself.

Type of Interview Plan: Educational × Behavioral _____

Person(s) Responsible for Implementing plan: Science teacher

Description of the Behavior:

Behavior	Behavior Defined
Tom destroys his written assignments	Tom wads up and tears up his assignment papers

Intervention Goal:

To decrease the number of occurrences that Tom destroys his assignments to 0 per week.

Intervention Plan:

1. Seat Tom with a peer that has good on-task behavior. The peer will review directions with Tom and assist him in getting started with assignments.
2. Provide Tom a daily monitoring assignment check list to improve the following areas of difficulty.

Assignment Checklist

___ I understood teacher directions

___ I asked for help when I needed it

___ I answered all questions

___ I understood the assignment

___ I need more time

___ I turned in my assignment

3. Provide Tom with academic modifications, including:
   1. Extended time to complete and turn in assignments if needed.
   2. Provide Tom with a word/definition list to use when completing work-sheet assignments.
   3. Provide Tom with a word definition list to use when completing work-sheet assignments.
   4. Provide peer assistance with some assignments.
   5. Provide additional instructional modifications as needed.
4. Provide directions to Tom in a variety of ways (verbal, written, direction instructions, and peer assistance.
5. Reinforce Tom's academic productivity and assignment completion.

Sample Behavioral Intervention Plan.

When and Where the Plan Will Be Implemented:

The plan will be implemented in Tom's science class for three consecutive weeks beginning 10/3/97

Intervention Data Collection Summary:

Week 1	Decrease in behavior to three occurrences.
Week 2	Decrease in behavior to two occurrences.
Week 3	Decrease in behavior to one occurrence.

Follow-up and Review Date(s):

Follow-up and review meeting 10/24/97

Comments:

The intervention plan is successful with Tom.

The team agreed to write the interventions outlined in this plan in Tom's IEP.

The team will meet in three weeks for another review.

Team Meeting Participants:

Name: _____   Position: _____

D DISCIPLINARY ACTION FORM

Disciplinary Action

Student Name: _____ Date: _____

Code of Conduct Violation:
_____
_____

Description of Incident:
_____
_____
_____

Short term suspension for _____ day(s) at: _____ home, _____ in-school, _____ other _____

Total number of days for year: _____
Parent(s) notified by: _____ phone, _____ letter, _____ other _____

Exclusion being considered for more than 10 days.

Interim action:
_____

Manifestation determination review date: _____
Parent(s) notified by: _____ phone _____ letter _____ other _____
_____ Regarding interim action
_____ Regarding manifestation determination review date
_____ Regarding rights

Persons present:
_____ Parent(s)
_____ Special education teacher
_____ General education teacher
_____ LEA representative
_____ Student
_____ Other

Information sources:
_____ Evaluation & diagnostic results
_____ IEP*
_____ BIP
_____ Observations (Dates:)
_____ Interviews:
   _____ student
   _____ parent(s)
   _____ general education teacher
   _____ special education teacher
   _____ others
_____ Environmental assessment

1. Were the student's IEP, including BIP, and placement appropriate in respect to the behavior under consideration? (Provide evidence in support of answer.)
_____

2. Were special education services and supplementary aids and services provided in compliance with IEP and placement? (Provide evidence in support of answer.)
_____

3. Did the student's disability impair the student's ability to understand the impact and consequences of the behavior? (Provide evidence in support of answer.)
_____

4. Did the student's disability impair the student's ability to control the behavior? (Provide evidence in support of the answer.)
_____

If yes to questions 1 & 2, and no to questions 3 & 4, team may determine that behavior was not manifestation of disability. Discipline procedures used with students without disabilities may be imposed. Action taken:
_____

If no to questions 1 or 2, or yes to questions 3 or 4, manifestation is shown. Action taken:
_____

*IEP = Individualized Education Program, BIP = Behavioral Intervention Plan; FBA = Functional behavioral assessment.

381

NAME INDEX

SUBJECT INDEX